Principles and Practices for Teaching English as an International Language

What general principles should inform a socioculturally sensitive pedagogy for teaching English as an International Language and what practices would be consistent with these principles? Designed for pre-service and in-service teachers of English around the world, this text

- highlights the importance of socially sensitive pedagogy in contexts outside of inner circle English-speaking countries, in light of the geographical spread of English, its multicultural basis, its pervasiveness in high-stakes decisions, and a widespread belief in the benefits of learning the language
- provides comprehensive coverage of topics traditionally included in second language methodology courses (such as the teaching of oral skills and grammar), as well as newer fields (such as corpora in language teaching and multimodality)
- features a balanced treatment of theory and practice
- offers 'Exploring the Ideas' and 'Applying the Ideas' activities in each chapter to encourage teachers to apply the pedagogical practices to their own classrooms and to reflect on the effects of such practices.

Principles and Practices for Teaching English as an International Language fills a critical need in the field.

Lubna Alsagoff is Associate Professor and Head of English Language and Literature at the National Institute of Education, Nanyang Technological University, Singapore.

Sandra Lee McKay is Professor Emeritus of English at San Francisco State University.

Guangwei Hu is Associate Professor in the English Language and Literature department of the National Institute of Education, Nanyang Technological University, Singapore.

Willy A. Renandya is Senior Lecturer in the English Language and Literature department of the National Institute of Education, Nanyang Technological University, Singapore.

ESL & Applied Linguistics Professional Series
Eli Hinkel, Series Editor

Visit www.routledge.com/education for additional information on titles in the ESL & Applied Linguistics Professional Series

Principles and Practices for Teaching English as an International Language

Edited by
Lubna Alsagoff
Sandra Lee McKay
Guangwei Hu
Willy A. Renandya

Routledge
Taylor & Francis Group
NEW YORK AND LONDON

First published 2012
by Routledge
711 Third Avenue, New York, NY 10017

Simultaneously published in the UK
by Routledge
2 Park Square, Milton Park, Abingdon, Oxon OX14 4RN

Routledge is an imprint of the Taylor & Francis Group, an informa business

Library of Congress Cataloging in Publication Data
Principles and practices for teaching English as an international
language / edited by Lubna Alsagoff ... [et al.].
    p. cm. — (ESL & applied linguistics professional series)
Includes bibliographical references and index.
1. English language—Study and teaching—Foreign speakers.
2. Lingua francas. I. Lubna Alsagoff.
PE1128.A2P725 2012
428.0071—dc23   2011039473

ISBN: 978-0-415-89166-0 (hbk)
ISBN: 978-0-415-89167-7 (pbk)
ISBN: 978-0-203-81915-9 (ebk)

Typeset in Sabon
by HWA Text and Data Management, London

SFI Certified Sourcing
www.sfiprogram.org
SFI-00453

Printed and bound in the United States of America
by Edwards Brothers, Inc.

Contents

Preface

In an era of globalization where English enjoys the status of an international, global, and world language, learnt and spoken by millions around the world, across linguistic and cultural boundaries, there is, inevitably, a critical need for new perspectives, principles, and practices in the teaching of English to multilingual and multicultural societies. This book addresses such a need. Comprised of chapters from internationally renowned scholars in their respective fields, the book presents insights into the ways in which traditional "methods" of teaching English must be re-examined and transformed to serve the needs of teachers and learners in the dynamic, multilingual, and multicultural contexts where English is used as an international language.

The two main sections in the book offer readers two different ways of exploring the issues. In the first, "Calling for Change," the chapters examine issues at a more theoretical level, while the chapters in the second section, "Implementing Change," present new pedagogical approaches and practices for EIL teaching.

This book represents contemporary ideas and thinking on language education, and addresses fundamental issues related to the teaching and learning of EIL. We believe that it will be a useful text for scholars, teachers, and students, especially those enrolled in graduate programs in teacher education or applied linguistics, who are interested in exploring new perspectives on teaching English, especially in multilingual and multicultural contexts. We hope that the book will be a critical resource in EIL teacher education programs across the world, and perhaps a catalyst for future research in the field of EIL research by teacher practitioners of EIL classrooms.

Lubna Alsagoff
Sandra Lee McKay
Guangwei Hu
Willy A. Renandya

Acknowledgments

We are grateful to our authors for taking this journey with us, for making this book possible.

We would also like to thank Christine Xavier, for her hard work in helping us prepare the manuscript for press.

Why Another Book on EIL

Chapter 1

Another Book on EIL?

Heralding the Need for New Ways of Thinking, Doing, and Being

Lubna Alsagoff

The English Language and Literature department in Singapore where I (and two of my co-editors) work is not unusual in having to balance its responsibilities in teaching and research. Straddled between the needs of the Ministry of Education, where we are to serve as gatekeepers and professors of standards of "internationally acceptable English" (Ministry of Education, 2010, p. 10)—especially given the fact that we are the only teacher education institute serving all of Singapore—and those of our parent university for which we attend to international standards of research, we strive to manage and negotiate a fine balance in how we represent English in our teaching and research in ways that are contextually and culturally appropriate, but which also keep faith to our knowledge of the field. We negotiate this with some apprehension given our fledgling research on teaching and learning in the Singaporean context, but with great passion and conviction, given our call to serve the nation, and our desires for our voices to be heard in the international academic arena.

In the past seven years, with the increasing concerns about Singapore's "standards of English," our department has grown. But this growth, happily, has not just been in size, but also in diversity—our faculty members come from all reaches of the globe. Apart from our US, Australian, British, and Canadian faculty, we are also proud to call as colleagues, past and present, Chinese, Congolese, German, Hungarian, Indian, Indonesian, Korean, Malaysian, Myanmarese, Filipino, Taiwanese, Tunisian, and Vietnamese teachers, researchers, and scholars.[1] This inclusivity of faculty representing the different and diverse global communities where English is spoken has been deliberate—an embracing in practice of what we know in theory to be the status of "English as an international language" (EIL) through the purposeful statement of the pluricentric ownership of English, thereby demonstrating what "internationally acceptable English" is.

It is this desire to explore the possible enactments and realizations in practice, of what we know from current theoretical research and discussions on English language teaching and about EIL, that has been the primary impetus for this project. It is a response to the need for new practices in the teaching and learning of English in the many communities it calls home, and for the many multilingual speakers who use it as an additional language to expand their linguistic repertoires. While there have been many recent books about EIL as well as the role of English as a global language written from a wide variety of perspectives, e.g., Block and Cameron (2002), Brutt-Griffler (2002), Canagarajah (2005), Jenkins (2003), McKay (2002), Pennycook (2007), Rubdy and Saraceni (2006), Saxena and Omoniyi (2010), and Sharifian (2009), to name a few, we feel that there remains a need to sound this clarion call for reflection on the way English, in its worldwide spread, is taught to, and learnt by, multilingual speakers and learners across the globe.

This book is celebratory in the sense that it includes a range of perspectives and understandings of EIL, and what it means to teach English as a language that bridges nations and cultures; and which while diverse, agree on the need to herald change, signaling the necessity for new ways of thinking and seeing, and more essentially, of new ways of doing and being, as teachers, students, and scholars. The authors have addressed this call for change in a variety of ways, but again with a confluence of sentiment that privileges the learner and teacher as active participants, that fosters respect for the diversity of speakers who call English their tongue, and that furthers new understandings of classroom and teaching practices that acknowledge the local alongside the global.

Our authors, in each of the chapters, explore innovative pedagogical understandings and practices to properly acknowledge and address the complexity of classrooms, learners, and teachers in EIL contexts. They discuss topics traditionally included in second language methodology courses, e.g., curriculum development, assessment, the teaching of reading, writing, oral skills, and grammar; as well as newer areas, e.g., corpora in language teaching and the use of new media, multimodal texts in language classrooms, with fresh perspectives that explicate and clarify concepts and principles that they believe should inform the practice of the teaching and learning of EIL, and which address the needs of EIL classrooms.

That such a call for change in the way we teach English was necessary, for the editors, was clearly evident. We are all familiar with the seminal and internationally well-established published collections on teaching methods and approaches (e.g. Harmer, 2007; Richards & Renandya, 2002; Carter & Nunan, 2001) which form the staple reading of many beginning teacher-scholars of the field. However, these textbooks on teaching methodology are often premised on contexts of practice, primarily of ESL classrooms in English-speaking communities, that are far removed from the realities of the majority of the global English classrooms of today. In our teacher-education programs, for example, our

Singaporean, Malaysian, Chinese, and ASEAN graduate students struggle to understand, extrapolate, and shape this knowledge for enactment in the contexts where they teach, where English is generally learnt, not for integration into an L1 English-speaking community, but for meaning making in local and global conversations; and where English is practiced, not in largely monolingual contexts, but in diversely multilingual and multicultural contexts.

It must, however, be made clear that our intention is not to write an EIL methodology book to replace these other volumes. There can be no one method or teaching approach that can embrace the diversity of contexts and needs that EIL engenders, and that can be locally-meaningful the way such books need to be in order to be useful to teachers and learners. Rather, our goal is for the authors, respected scholars in their fields, to share ideas and principles to guide critical and informed practice and reflection in teaching; and more importantly, to raise questions whose answers can only be discovered by teachers and learners of EIL in each of their unique contexts.

Given these intended perspectives and outcomes, the concept for this book is necessarily founded on a view that EIL is not a hapless consequence of the insidious hand of Western imperialism, but rather as an expected outcome of the inevitable acceleration of globalization that brings with it opportunities (as well as challenges) for change. EIL compels new ways of thinking about language because it is about the transformations of language, culture, and identity into hybrid third spaces (Bhabha, 1994). It is in these hybridized liminal spaces that EIL teaching and learning take place, in which speakers appropriate and shape English, as individuals, and as members of global communities, intra-nationally as well as internationally, in developing their own voices.

The chapters are organized into two sections, with the first, entitled "Calling for Change." Here the authors question established notions, and present new ideas and ways of conceptualizing what we accept as "taken-for-granteds" in the field. Kumaravadivelu and McKay open the book by setting a general direction and tone for the volume. In the second section, "Implementing Change," the authors share new approaches to pedagogical practices that are appropriate for EIL teaching and learning contexts. The volume ends with McKay's fitting conclusion, "Forging Ahead," in which she draws on her experience and knowledge of the field, and offers a reading of the chapters in the book, and suggests how we move ahead to enact and realize EIL pedagogies.

Note

1 We of course include many Singaporeans as part of our faculty.

References

Bhabha, H. K. (1994). *The location of culture*. New York: Routledge.

Block, D., & Cameron, D. (2002). *Globalization and language teaching*. London: Routledge.

Brutt-Griffler, J. (2002). *World Englishes: A study of its development*. Clevedon, UK: Multilingual Matters.

Canagarajah, A. S. (2005). *Reclaiming the local in language policy and practice*. Mahwah, NJ: Lawrence Erlbaum.

Carter, R., & Nunan, D. (Eds.). (2001). *The Cambridge guide to teaching English to speakers of other languages*. Cambridge: Cambridge University Press.

Harmer, J. (2007). *The practice of English language teaching with DVD (4th ed.)*. Harlow: Longman Pearson.

Jenkins, J. (2003). *World Englishes*. New York: Routledge.

McKay, S. L. (2002). *Teaching English as an international language: Rethinking goals and approaches*. Oxford: Oxford University Press.

Ministry of Education. (2010). English Language Syllabus: Normal and Express. Singapore: Curriculum Planning Division, Ministry of Education.

Pennycook, A. (2007). *Global Englishes and transcultural flows*. London: Routledge.

Richards, J. C., & Renandya, W. A. (Eds.). (2002). *Methodology in language teaching: An anthology of current practice*. New York: Cambridge University Press.

Rubdy, R., & Saraceni, M. (2006). *English in the world: Global rules, global roles*. London: Continuum.

Saxena, M., & Omoniyi, T. (2010). *Contending with globalization in World Englishes*. Bristol: Multilingual Matters.

Sharifian, F. (Ed.). (2009). *English as an international language: Perspectives and pedagogical issues*. Bristol, UK: Multilingual Matters.

Part II

Calling for Change

Individual Identity, Cultural Globalization, and Teaching English as an International Language

The Case for an Epistemic Break

B. Kumaravadivelu

Introduction

This chapter is based on two inter-related propositions. First, the on-going process of cultural globalization with its incessant and increased flow of peoples, goods, and ideas across the world is creating a novel "web of interlocution" that is effectively challenging the traditional notions of identity formation of an individual or of a nation. Second, the teaching of English as an international language (EIL) cannot remain insulated and isolated from globalization's impact on the formation of individual identities of English language learners, teachers, and teacher educators around the world.

In this chapter, I present critical perspectives on some of the broad issues concerning the above propositions (for specific principles of teaching, see McKay, this volume). In the first part of the chapter, I briefly outline two familiar narratives of identity formation—modernism and postmodernism—and argue that a third—globalism—is fast emerging as a crucial factor in the construction of identity. I try to highlight how globalism presents challenges as well as opportunities for individuals to exercise their agency in order to construct their identities. In the second part, I assert that, in order to successfully meet the challenges of globalism, the teaching of EIL requires no less than an epistemic break from its dependency on Western-oriented or, more specifically, Center-based (aka Inner Circle-based) knowledge systems. I conclude the chapter by pointing out some of the impediments facing any genuine epistemic break in EIL.

Narratives of Identity Formation

Etymologically speaking, the term identity means *sameness*. It entails membership in one or more categories such as nation, ethnicity, race, religion, class, profession, or gender. Being a white American

Christian woman, for instance, connects one with aspects of whiteness, Americanness, Christianness, and womanhood—whichever way they are defined. Although sameness is a salient feature of identity, it is *difference* that most often stands out in marking one's identity. Each of us can justifiably say "I am who I am because I am not you" or, in the words of Amin Maalouf (2000, p. 10), "my identity is what prevents me from being identical to anybody else."

We can best understand the concept of identity by understanding the concept of Self. An individual's sense of Self is broadly defined by the relationship between the individual and the community, and how the individual navigates the complex terrain of Self and society. Although there is no single, overriding concept of identity, there are two sociological narratives that have well-articulated positions on it—modernism and postmodernism (for a detailed discussion on self and identity, see Ferguson, 2009).

Identity and Modernism

To put it in a nutshell, during the days of modernity (a period ranging from mid-17th to mid-20th century), the individual was largely expected to constitute his/her identity in tune with pre-existent and relatively unchanging societal norms. More than anything else, the individual's identity was tied almost inextricably to affiliation to family and community. Everybody had a neatly designated, hierarchically-coded place under the sun. And, they were expected to remain there. While some maneuvering was indeed possible, individuals encountered an essentialized and totalized concept of identity within which they had to find personal meaning. With socially accepted boundaries of an objectified external world imposed on them, individuals had very little meaningful choice outside of clearly delineated characteristics of birth and ethnic origin. In other words, the "modern" Self was more externally imposed than self-constructed.

Identity and Postmodernism

Unlike modernism, the currently prevailing narrative of postmodernism (a period ranging from the mid-20th century onwards) treats individual identity as something that is actively constructed on an on-going basis. It sees identity as fragmented, not unified; multiple, not singular; expansive, not bounded. It bestows a modicum of agency on the individual in determining a sense of Self. In this view, identity formation is conditioned not merely by inherited traditions such as culture, or by external exigencies such as history, or by ideological constructs such as power, but also on the individual's ability and willingness to exercise agency.

The catchword for postmodern identity is *fragmentation*. It captures the epitome of postmodern life. The fragment, according to sociologist Harvie Ferguson,

> is not like a splinter of wood or a shard of glass; a piece broken off from an intact and uniform whole. The fragment is a detached portion that takes on a life of its own and may even gain the appearance of self-sufficiency as something *unlike* its parent body.
>
> (2009, p. 154, emphasis as in original)

The fragmented identity takes on a life of its own through a process of becoming—a process that is continuous, non-linear, and unstable. It is less preoccupied with the formation of a durable identity. Instead, it embraces the idea that identity is fluid and amorphous, one that is constantly and endlessly invented and reinvented. It is because of this dynamic and incomplete nature of identity formation that Ferguson characterizes it as "the continuous creation of the fragment; a *bricolage* of the disjointed" (Ferguson, 2009, p. 184, emphasis as in original).

Identity and Globalism

As my brief account of the two narratives suggests, postmodernism has a much greater explanatory power than modernism in helping us understand and analyze the problematic nature of the concept of Self. However, it is my contention that we need even a broader perspective in order to fully understand the construction of self-identity in this globalized and globalizing world. I believe yet another narrative, globalism, is fast emerging as a crucial factor in identity formation. This is necessitated by fast-evolving global, national, social, and individual realities of the 21st century. A brief discussion follows; for details, see Kumaravadivelu (2008).

Globally, our world is marked by a near-collapsing of space, time, and borders, resulting in a run away flow of peoples, goods, and ideas across the world. This phenomenon is aided and accelerated by information revolution, or Internetization. Cultural images from far off lands are flashed across small screens in our living rooms in real time, enabling closer cultural contact than ever before. People now have a greater chance of knowing about others' cultural way of life—the good, the bad, and the ugly.

The impact of globalization on the national psyche is telling. While people around the world see unparalleled opportunities for cultural growth, they also see unparalleled threats to their national and cultural identity. Islamic terrorism can in part be seen as one, extreme, response to the threat to local identity. In fact, globalization has only accentuated tribalization. As a result, people are simultaneously coming together and pulling apart. Giddens (2000) was right when he asserted that globalization is indeed the reason for the revival of local cultural identities in different parts of the world.

With the revival of local cultural identities, social life has come under severe stress. Ethnic, religious, or linguistic affiliations and affinities within a nation get played up. Each community strives to protect and preserve its own identity. Whenever there is a real or perceived threat to this identity, social unrest erupts. This undeniable social reality has a huge effect on the formation of individual identity, so much so that Richard Jenkins (2004, p. 4) claims that "all human identities are by definition *social* identities" (emphasis as in original).

In spite of the pulls and pressures from global, national, and social realities, the individual still retains a considerable degree of agency in determining a sense of Self. After all, self-identity is "a matter of choosing, producing, expressing, and forming identities adequate to reflect the self that chooses and forms them" (Ferguson, 2009, p. 65). In choosing and forming identities in this complex world, individuals require critical knowledge that can help them tell the difference between information and disinformation, between ideas and ideologies, between the trivial and the consequential. The Internetization of information systems makes such critical knowledge available to those individuals who seek it. Using the easily accessible knowledge-base and engaging in critical self-reflection, individuals now have the opportunity to evaluate their and others' cultural value systems and develop a global cultural consciousness that has the potential to enrich their lives.

Identity and the Teaching of EIL

So, what has all the above to do with language learners and language teachers? Simply put, learners and teachers are individuals too. They too are engaged in the task of forming and reforming their identities in this globalized world. Because of the intricate connection between language and culture, language classes offer a unique opportunity for them to try to wrestle with, and articulate their anxieties about, the complexities of identity formation. EIL learners and teachers, in particular, have an added burden thrust upon them because of the globality and coloniality of the language they are dealing with. The interconnectedness between cultural globalization, identity formation, and English language education has started getting the attention it truly deserves from EIL educators (for recent book-length works, see Higgins, 2009; Kubota & Lin, 2009; Kumaravadivelu, 2008; Lin, 2008).

Recent explorations in EIL learning, teaching, and teacher education have brought to the surface certain creative tensions that characterize the formation of individual identities, compelling us to rethink some of the taken-for-granted theoretical and pedagogical assumptions about EIL. For instance, the role of integrative motivation for EIL learning has come under serious scrutiny in the context of contemporary realities of self and identity. Finding the notion of integrative motivation antithetical to identity formation, Coetzee-Van Rooy (2006) declares it untenable for EIL learners. Following her, Ushioda and Dörnyei (2009, pp. 2–3) convincingly ask: "Does it make sense to talk about integrative attitudes when ownership of English does not necessarily rest with a specific community of speakers, whether native speakers of British, or American English varieties or speakers of World English varieties?"

In a similar vein, language teachers have started critically analyzing and questioning their own readiness to deal with learner/teacher identities in their cross-cultural classrooms. In one such study, Connelly (2008) investigates how she, with her dominant constructed subject position as an Australian white woman, can address all the subjectivities that she encounters in her class full of students from various indigenous communities. She concludes:

> Mindful of the knowledge created through this narrative analysis, an educational implication is to ask what now must be done, and how can this knowledge about performance tensions inside subjectivities generate different pedagogical understandings and possibilities for the education of Australian indigenous students?
>
> (p. 100)

Consequent to still unfolding learner/teacher demands and expectations in this globalized environment, language teacher educators are faced with the task of helping student-teachers become aware of how they are positioned in various historical and institutional contexts, and also become aware of the possibilities and strategies for transgression and transformation. Several expatriate teachers teaching EIL around the world as well as teachers who hail from local cultural communities are slowly realizing that the kind of personal and professional identities they bring with them to the classroom are becoming increasingly inadequate (Clarke, 2008; Widin, 2010). They are faced with the challenge of moving beyond well-entrenched discourses found in the professional literature that they have heavily relied upon. How participants' subjectivities shape classroom climate, and how might potential tensions be negotiated have become an important issue in EIL teacher education.

In light of the global and local developments both in the society at large and in our professional community, it is only legitimate to ask whether the teaching of EIL as a profession has been sensitive to these developments and has come out with a sensible response that is commensurate with the challenges and opportunities. My reading of the prevailing situation leads me to answer the question with a resounding "no." What I see is a profession that continues to get entangled in terminological knots and one that easily gets distracted by superficial solutions instead of confronting the underlying causes that call for a radical re-conceptualization. It seems to me that, in order for our profession to meet the challenges of globalism in a deeply meaningful way, what is required is no less than an epistemic break from its dependency on the current West-oriented, Center-based knowledge systems that carry an indelible colonial coloration.

Epistemic Break

Although the concept of epistemic break has been around for quite some time, it came to prominence during the 1970s when the French sociologist Michel Foucault presented his sociological interpretations beginning with two of his seminal works: *The Order of Things: An Archeology of the Human Sciences* (1970) and *The Archeology of Knowledge* (1972). Later, scholars in the field of postcolonial studies have employed the concept gainfully to interpret and shape postcolonial epistemologies (for a recent treatment, see Mignolo & Escobar, 2010).

To paraphrase Foucault's thoughts in simple terms, an *episteme* is a set of relations that unite, at a given period, the discursive practices that give rise to formalized knowledge systems. Regardless of their inherent constraints and limitations, such knowledge systems are gradually imposed on disciplinary discourses. Practitioners of an academic discipline work within the epistemic discourse to understand, express, and predict patterns of meaning within their discipline. Foucault used the break from the knowledge systems governing the classical age and those of the modern age as illustrative examples of epistemic break. The break from the "modern" concept of self-identity to its "postmodern" concept may also be considered as another example.

An epistemic break, then, represents a thorough re-conceptualization and a thorough re-organization of knowledge systems. As mentioned earlier, Foucault argues that the great epistemological discontinuities that mark the characteristics of the classical age and the modern age constitute an epistemic break from the past. In other words, an epistemic break is deemed to have occurred if and when new epistemological orientations appear with a considerable degree of regularity (for a detailed discussion on what constitutes an epistemic break, see Reed, 2008).

It is instructive to contrast Thomas Kuhn's *paradigm shift* (Kuhn, 1962) and Foucault's *epistemic break*. The Kuhnian concept is confined to scientific world views and practices whereas the Foucauldian concept covers a wider range of discourses. More importantly, a paradigm is invariant; and, therefore, a paradigm shift represents a near total replacement of one paradigm with another. The new paradigm becomes an all-pervading knowledge system that informs scientific research activity almost universally. An epistemic break, on the other hand, may not enjoy such a universal understanding and application. An epistemic discourse, therefore, is normally employed descriptively and contextually by its users. That is why Foucault readily accepts the possibility of many epistemes within a particular discourse.

Epistemic Break and EIL

A good example of an enduring episteme in the field of teaching EIL, in spite of its conceptual and definitional ambiguities, is that of the *native speaker* and its benevolent twin, *native-speaker competence*. We may have only an unreal (or, to use a more familiar terminology, idealized) version of who a native speaker is or what constitutes native-speaker competence. But, that has not prevented us from letting the episteme take an all-encompassing hold on the knowledge systems governing almost all aspects of English language learning and teaching. The episteme symbolizes West-oriented, Center-based knowledge systems that EIL practitioners in the periphery countries almost totally depend on. It is analogous to a tap root from which all primary and secondary roots and rootlets sprout laterally. It spreads itself largely in terms of the importance given to matters such as native-speaker accent, native-speaker teachers, native-like target competence, teaching methods emanating from Western universities, textbooks published by Western publishing houses, research agenda set by Center-based scholars, professional journals edited and published from Center countries ... The list is long.

It is true that much has been written highlighting the firm grip this particular episteme has on our discipline. For over two decades, we have been hearing critical voices helping us become acutely aware of linguistic imperialism, discourses of colonialism, native speakerism, the political economy of English language teaching, reclamation of local knowledge ... The list here too is long. But, for all practical purposes, the native-speaker episteme has not loosened its grip over theoretical principles, classroom practices, the publication industry, or the job market. What is surely and sorely needed is a meaningful break from this epistemic dependency if we are serious about sanitizing our discipline from its corrosive effect and sensitizing the field to the demands of globalism and its impact on identity formation. How and where do we start?

Breaking the Dependency on Terminologies

To start with, we must recognize, and act on the recognition, that we have for long been unnecessarily and unwisely entangling ourselves in terminological knots that have mainly contributed to the preservation of the native-speaker episteme. The field of English language learning, teaching, and research seems to have developed a fascination for labels which appear on the scene with some clock-work regularity. And, they all come neatly abbreviated—ESL, EFL, EAL, WE, ELF, EIL. Predictably, there is no consensus in the field about any of these labels and what they stand for. On the contrary, there have been severe criticisms, particularly about the hidden political and ideological agenda behind them (Holliday, 2009; Pennycook, 2007). Besides, some of these labels and what they stand for have been described as unreliable, untenable, and unworkable (Maley, 2009). In fact, this fascination with terminologies is largely confined to scholars and researchers. Practicing teachers are "sublimely unaware" (Maley, 2009, p. 196) of the debate and even for those who are aware, it remains "something of a side issue" (Young & Walsh, 2010, p. 136).

To what extent our fascination with the name game has contributed to the central mission of improving English language learning and teaching is far from clear. Nevertheless, the editor of a recently published volume on EIL enthusiastically characterizes it as something that "marks a *paradigm shift* in TESOL, SLA and the applied linguistics of English ..." (Sharifian, 2009, p. 2, emphasis added). A doubtful claim indeed, considering that there are scholars who argue that EIL is no more than a myth (Pennycook, 2007), is no more than an alternative terminology (Holliday, 2009), and that it overlaps with other labels (Modiano, 2009). It is worthwhile to remember that a paradigm shift in the Kuhnian sense does not happen through pious proclamations, however well-intentioned.

What does not seem to have been adequately recognized is that name games can dupe us into distraction and lull us into a false sense of liberation. We can easily become prisoners of a label, with our thoughts and actions dictated by it. More than half a century ago, Wittgenstein warned us about such a terminological imprisonment. "A picture held us captive," he said. "And we could not get outside it, for it lay in our language and language seemed to repeat it to us inexorably" (1958, p. 132). Getting outside it, in the context of EIL, means not just changing the terms of the conversation but changing the terms of the conduct of knowledge production.

Breaking the Dependency on Western Knowledge Production

In order to break the current epistemic dependency on the production, application, and dissemination of EIL knowledge systems, we have to critically examine the very ways in which we conduct applied linguistic inquiry. An epistemic break here warrants more than moving away from positivistic and towards ethnographic approaches to research. Rather, it requires a fundamental re-conceptualization of research itself. As the Australian indigenous scholar Linda Tuhiwai Smith (1999) asserts in her classic book *Decolonizing Methodologies*, "research is not an innocent or distant academic exercise but an activity that has something at stake and that occurs in a set of political and social conditions" (p. 5). She correctly points out that "most of the 'traditional' disciplines are grounded in cultural world views which are either antagonistic to other belief systems or have no methodology for dealing with other knowledge systems" (p. 65).

The world view that characterizes most part of the studies in second language acquisition (SLA), for instance, has for long been premised upon notions such as interlanguage, fossilization, acculturation, communicative competence, intercultural competence—all of which are heavily tilted towards the episteme of the native speaker. Conditioned by a strong monolingual bias, theory construction in SLA has by and large stayed away from comprehensive, longitudinal, empirical studies grounded in multilingual and multicultural environments particularly on issues such as acquisitional pathways, classroom input and interaction, and, tellingly, the role and use of learners' first language. Belatedly and haltingly, the field of SLA has started paying attention to the concept of multicompetence and the second language user (Cook, 2002).

Entrapped within such a biased mode of knowledge production and unable to break from their dependency on them, scholars in periphery countries have been doing mostly reactive, not proactive, research. That is, with all sincerity and seriousness, they acquaint themselves with the method and content of Western research and use them for their own investigative purposes, rarely questioning the premises governing it. For instance, studies by periphery-based researchers on pragmatic (in)competence, that is, how EIL learners fail to perform certain speech acts in a way that is acceptable to the native-speaking community, are indeed numerous (see, for instance, Rose & Kasper, 2001, and the references therein). Not surprisingly, even when questions are raised about the wisdom of relying on a native-speaker model of pragmatic competence, they usually come from Center-based scholars (for a recent example, see McKay, 2009).

What is partly needed to break the epistemic dependency on Center-based knowledge production is proactive research on the part of scholars from the periphery. Proactive research involves paying attention to the particularities of learning/teaching in periphery countries, identifying researchable questions, investigating them using appropriate research methods, producing original knowledge and applying them in classroom contexts. Such a research agenda may shed useful light leading to a better understanding of second language development in a bi-/multilingual environment and eventually lead to an alternative model of SLA that is not constrained by Western-oriented epistemes. Breaking the dependency on Western knowledge production will open up avenues for breaking other lateral dependencies pertaining to teaching methods, the teaching of culture, and instructional materials—three of the pedagogic domains where the native-speaker episteme has a direct bearing on what shapes classroom climate and classroom discourse.

Breaking the Dependency on Center-based Methods

As I have stated elsewhere, since the 1940s, our profession

> has seen one method after another roll out of Western universities and through Western publishing houses to spread out all over the world. On each occasion, teachers in other countries and other cultures have been assured that this one is the correct one, and that their role is to adapt it to their learners, or their learners to it.
>
> (Kumaravadivelu, 2006a, p. 20)

These Center-based methods (such as audiolingual, communicative) have been aptly characterized as products of "interested knowledge" (Pennycook, 1989) which is clearly linked to the native-speaker episteme. That is, these methods highlighted and promoted the native speaker's language competence, learning styles, communication patterns, conversational maxims, cultural beliefs, and even accent as the norm. The native speaker is deemed to possess these norms autogenetically and L2 learners have been accultured to accept them as markers of native-like competence they should aspire to achieve. These assumptions have since come under severe strain leading to calls for an alternative to the concept of method.

I have written extensively on method and postmethod (see Kumaravadivelu, 2006b, for a consolidated presentation). I shall not, therefore, go into details. Briefly, Center-produced methods are based on idealized concepts geared towards idealized contexts. Since language learning and teaching needs, wants, and situations are unpredictably numerous, no idealized method can visualize all the variables in advance in order to provide situation-specific suggestions that practicing teachers need to tackle the challenges they confront in the practice of their everyday teaching. As a predominantly top-down exercise, the conception and construction of methods have been largely guided by a one-size-fits-all-cookie-cutter approach that assumes a common clientele with common goals. The construction of any meaningful alternative to the Center-produced concept of method, therefore, is premised upon breaking this epistemic dependency and striving to design context-specific, locally-generated instructional strategies that take into account the particular, the practical, and the possible.

Breaking the Dependency on Center-based Cultural Competence

Yet another aspect of epistemic dependency relates to the concept of cultural competence. For a long time, developing L2 linguistic competence has also meant developing L2 cultural competence. Cultural assimilation has been the desired destination, with integrative motivation as the preferred path to get there. This belief was based on the notion that languages and cultures are inextricably linked. This notion, though flawed, is still prevalent and popular in certain quarters. In the recently published book, *Globish: How the English Language Became the World's Language*, Robert McCrum (2010) declares that the world has an "appetite for English language and culture" (p. 9), and that "English plus Microsoft equals a new cultural revolution" (p. 14). He triumphantly, and simplistically, links English not only with cultural identity but also with fundamental human values such as freedom. He proclaims:

> (C)ulture is about identity. For as long as the peoples of the world wish to express themselves in terms of ideas like "freedom", "individuality" and "originality", and for as long as there are generations of the world's school children versed in Shakespeare, The Simpsons, the Declaration of Independence, and the Bible, Globish will remain the means by which an educated minority of the planet communicates.
>
> (p. 285)

McCrum miserably fails to distinguish between the world's appetite for English language and its appetite for English culture. That the non-English speaking world learns and uses English language for communicational purposes and not for cultural identity formation has been apparent for quite some time. From India, we learn that Indians learn English to meet their educational and institutional needs and they keep it separate from their cultural beliefs and practices (Krishnaswamy & Burde, 1998). For Pakistanis, English reflects Islamic values, and embodies South Asian Islamic sensitivities (Mahboob, 2009). Turks have no difficulty whatsoever in privileging "their Turkish and Muslim identities over the Western way of existence presented during English-language courses" (Atay & Ece, 2009, p. 31). The volumes edited by Kubota and Lin (2009), and Lin

(2008) confirm how, although the English language has been appropriated by the Center as an instrument for spreading Western cultural beliefs and practices, people across the world see it and use it as a communicational tool.

Awareness of identity formation dictated by emerging globalism has intensified the desire of EIL learners and teachers to preserve and protect their own linguistic and cultural identities. In response to such a development, there have been attempts to move from biculturalism to interculturalism (Byram, 1997; McKay, 2002), and from interculturalism to cultural realism (Kumaravadivelu, 2008). Biculturalism in the teaching of EIL requires the learners to acquire and use the pragmatic rules of the L2 community. Interculturalism, on the other hand, requires them to be merely aware of those rules. This is certainly a necessary, but not a sufficient, shift. Claiming that interculturalism is good for a multicultural society of the 20th century but not good enough for a global society of the 21st century, cultural realism seeks the development of global cultural consciousness that results not just in cultural literacy but also in cultural liberty (see the United Nations' *Human Development Report 2004* for more on cultural liberty). It requires a willingness and ability "to learn *from* other cultures, not just *about* them. Learning *about* other cultures may lead to cultural literacy; it is learning *from* other cultures that will lead to cultural liberty" (Kumaravadivelu, 2008, p. 237).

It is rather evident that in order for the teaching of EIL to be sensitive to the emerging processes of identity formation in this global society, breaking its dependency on the Center-based concept of cultural competence is a must. But, this cannot be achieved unless and until yet another dependency is broken.

Breaking the Dependency on the Center-based Textbook Industry

Produced and promoted by the Center-based publishing industry, textbooks used for learning and teaching EIL in large parts of the world represent the most visible Center dominance that has developed a subtle and stubborn character. Textbooks have a direct bearing on teaching methods because it is through them a particular method is propagated and preserved. Notice how the textbooks that are currently used promote Communicative Language Teaching. They also have direct bearing on the teaching of culture, because it is through them a particular cultural knowledge is imposed on teachers and students. Although it is widely known that Center-based textbooks embody Western cultural values, beliefs, and attitudes often presenting stereotypical pictures that valorize Western societies, they continue to be adopted and used in classrooms across the world. They have a magical hold on both teachers and learners most of whom just can not do without them.

Center-based textbooks seem to be impervious to the challenges posed by heightened cultural consciousness and identity formation that globalism has created—a testimony to the dominating agency exercised by the Western publishing industry. However, sensing a possible threat to its hegemony, and recognizing the need to appear to be sensitive to the on-going processes of globalism, the publishing industry has started producing global textbooks with a local flavor. A chief strategy they seem to follow is to produce core texts with a variety of add-ons to meet the demand for a local fit. Creative strategies and innovative marketing techniques cleverly mask the fact that global textbooks remain centrally-controlled and continue to cater to the preservation of the native-speaker episteme.

The importance of breaking the epistemic dependency on Center-based textbooks can hardly be overstated. Clearly, textbooks should reflect the lived experiences teachers and students bring to the classroom because, after all, their experiences are shaped by a broader social, cultural, economic, and political environment in which they grow up. It is not impertinent to suggest that textbooks should be written and produced by local practitioners. Nor is it an impractical suggestion. Because global textbooks are methodologically—and culturally—loaded, many teachers find it necessary to design context-sensitive supplementary materials anyway. What they may need is systematic training so that they can do the job professionally satisfactorily. A core course on materials production for pre-service teachers, and hands-on workshops for in-service teachers can easily facilitate the development of the knowledge, skill, and disposition necessary for them to produce instructional materials. The information revolution that has spawned online newspapers, blogs, tweets, YouTube, Facebook, and other forms of social networking are valuable sources that can be exploited for designing instructional materials. It is true that the prevailing practice in several countries compels teachers to use Center-produced, Ministry-approved textbooks. This surely makes it difficult for teachers to switch to teacher-generated textbooks. But, if we are deterred by difficulties, we can never make the changes that we deem desirable. A beginning can be made if teachers design, and use in their classes, more and more systematically produced "supplementary" materials which, eventually, can pave the way for teacher-generated textbook production and, eventually, for breaking the epistemic dependency on Center-produced textbooks. If the World Wide Web can accommodate user-generated content, there is no reason why the profession of teaching EIL can not get accustomed to teacher-generated textbooks.

Impediments for Progress

The magnitude of the epistemic dependency that enslaves the teaching of EIL is enormous. Above, I discussed five of its manifestations. None of them is a totally new revelation. But all of them continue to sway the direction the profession takes. All the critical voices that are raised against them from time to time have not in any significant way shaken their firm grip. The reasons are not far to seek: the epistemic dependency stands solidly on the twin rocks of the process of marginalization and the practice of self-marginalization (Kumaravadivelu, 2006a). The former pertains to the ways in which the coloniality of the English language is exploited to maintain the authority of the center over the periphery. The latter refers to the ways in which the periphery surrenders its voice and vision to the center.

The results of meticulously researched case studies offer the latest authentication of how marginalization and self-marginalization play out. Jacqueline Widin (2010) investigated what she calls "illegitimate practices" that plague global English language education. Focusing on Australia-sponsored International English Language Education Projects (IELEPs) aimed at assisting English language learning and teaching in Japan and Laos, she explored the role of Australian universities and their liaison with host-country Ministry of Education officials and local non-native scholars. What she found was "increasing commodification and corporatisation of English" (p. 1) made possible by marginalization and self-marginalization.

The process of marginalization is tellingly revealed by a key stakeholder from the Australian Government Agency sponsoring the projects. Referring to his agency's work in Japan, the official frankly admits (Widin, 2010):

> The purpose of this particular project is not to deliver great, you know, English language teaching methodology into this country's teaching system. Actually by doing that we put many Australians out of a job...I mean...in fifteen years time if great English is being taught here then we're, you know, Australians out of business. ...
>
> So I couldn't care less whether this country wants it, or needs it, or likes it, at the end of the day it's not the judgment of teachers, it is decision we've made against the background of what would enhance Australia's interest.
>
> (p. 2)

Widin goes on to demonstrate how the projects "exerted symbolic violence" (p. 191) by imposing Communicative Language Teaching on exam-oriented educational systems that require competence only in reading and writing skills, by prescribing teaching materials with trivial and biased cultural content, by ignoring the importance of learners' first language, and above all, by marginalizing the commendable expertise and experience that host-country teachers bring to the projects.

Widin also makes it clear that marginalization is sustained only because the host-country officials and teachers "are buying into what was offered by the dominant stakeholders, dismissing their own expertise and indigenous knowledge, engaging in the practice of self-marginalisation" (p. 60). They self-marginalize themselves in spite of the fact that they are highly skilled professionals holding prominent positions in their country. Pointing out how they hold native speakers' linguistic and cultural capital in high esteem, and referring specifically to a Lao scholar, Widin says:

> He revealed significant positionings of participants in the field and even with the absence of foreigners, the field would still be dominated by those players who have more valuable capital: "I don't know why, may be it is this country's style … we don't work completely 100%, just only 80 or 90 per cent if we work with our Lao colleagues. If we work with the expatriate staff we work well. I don't know why it happens like this." He made a further point that his country's participants would not take the project seriously if it was run by Lao teacher trainers.
>
> (p. 105)

Widin convincingly shows that "the notion of 'native speaker' legitimacy in knowledge and work practices is deeply embedded in ELT projects" (p. 119).

If EIL as a profession is serious about breaking its native-speaker epistemic dependency, both marginalization and self-marginalization have to be tackled in an effective way. In fact, of the two, tackling self-marginalization may turn out to be more challenging because it requires a concerted effort that has to do with "changing the consciousness of the oppressed, not the situation that oppresses them" (Freire, 1972, p. 47).

In Closing

In this chapter, I have portrayed the notion of the native speaker as an overarching episteme that envelopes Center-based knowledge systems EIL professionals in periphery countries heavily depend on for carrying out their scholarly tasks and pedagogic duties. Comparing the native-speaker episteme with a tap root, I have described five interlinked epistemes as primary and secondary roots that get their sustenance from it. I have maintained that the five epistemic dependencies come into conflict with

EIL teachers' and learners' desire to preserve and protect their linguistic and cultural identity in this era of globalization. I have argued that nothing less than an epistemic break is required in order to help EIL professionals meet the challenges of teaching English which is marked by globality as well as coloniality. Finally, I have pointed out external (marginalization) and internal (self-marginalization) challenges that might impede any progress towards breaking the epistemic dependency.

If the teaching of EIL as a profession is serious about helping its professionals generate sustainable knowledge systems that are sensitive to local historical, political, cultural, and educational exigencies, then it must get away from an epistemic operation that continues to institutionalize the coloniality of English language education. The case for epistemic break goes way beyond the pressing problems of principles and practices of teaching EIL, though admittedly they are crucial. Merely tinkering with the existing knowledge systems will only reinforce them rather than reinvent them. What a real epistemic break will eventually ensure are new ways of constructing knowledge systems and new ways of applying them in classroom contexts. What is needed, in the words of postcolonial critic Walter Mignolo (2010, p. 306), is "a delinking that leads to de-colonial epistemic shift and brings to the foreground other epistemologies, other principles of knowledge and understanding …"

Exploring the Ideas

1 As a practicing (or, prospective) language teacher, what specific professional development strategies will you follow in order to prepare yourself (a) to recognize multiple identities that your learners may bring with them that are different from yours, and (b) to deal with any potential classroom tensions that may arise out of those differences?

2 If you wish to move away from the dependency on the current West-oriented, Center-based knowledge systems that are closely linked to (a) teaching methods, (b) the teaching of culture, and (c) textbooks, what do you think you can do as an individual?

3 Given the imposition of institutionally-designed syllabi, and Ministry-approved textbooks, what opportunities and limitations do you anticipate if you wish to design and use instructional materials that you think would be more appropriate for your learners?

Applying the Ideas

1 The Internet provides many possibilities for producing teaching materials. Select a class you are familiar with and describe one activity

that makes use of resources on the Internet to further students' English proficiency and address issues of individual identity. Be certain to describe how the activity furthers their language learning.

2 One useful strategy you might want to follow to produce teaching materials that are contextually-relevant and culturally-sensitive is to form a small group of interested colleagues in your institution, design materials, use them in your classes, get feedback from teachers and learners, revise them, and circulate them digitally for wider use. Undertake a small pilot study that does this.

3 Most probably, your learners are young adults who are well-versed in using the Internet and various forms of social networks. Describe how you might involve them in selecting raw materials for you to use in designing instructional materials that appeal to them.

References

Atay, D., & Ece, A. (2009). Multiple identities as reflected in English language education: The Turkish perspective. *Journal of Language, Identity, and Education, 8*(1), 21–34.

Byram, M. (1997). *Teaching and assessing intercultural communicative competence*. Clevedon: Multilingual Matters.

Clarke, M. (2008). *Language teacher identities: Co-constructing discourse and community*. Clevedon: Multilingual Matters.

Coetzee-Van Rooy, S. (2006). Integrativeness: Untenable for world Englishes learners. *World Englishes, 25*, 437–450.

Connelly, J. (2008). White women teachers in indigenous classrooms: Ruptures and discords of Self. In A. Lin (Ed.), *Problematizing Identity* (pp. 85–100). New York: Lawrence Erlbaum.

Cook, V. (Ed.). (2002). *Portraits of the L2 user*. Clevedon: Multilingual Matters.

Ferguson, H. (2009). *Self-identity and everyday life*. London: Routledge.

Foucault, M. (1970). *The order of things: An archeology of human sciences* (Trans. Les Mots et les choses.). New York: Vintage Books.

Foucault, M. (1972). The *archeology of knowledge and the discourse on language* (Trans. Sheridan Smith.). New York: Pantheon Books.

Freire, P. (1972). *Pedagogy of the oppressed*. New York: Seabury Press.

Giddens, A. (2000). *Runaway world*. London: Routledge.

Higgins, C. (2009). *English as a local language: Post-colonial identities and multilingual practices*. Bristol: Multilingual Matters.

Holliday, A. (2009). English as a lingua franca, "Non-native speakers" and cosmopolitan realities. In F. Sharifian (Ed.), *English as an international language: Perspectives and pedagogical issues* (pp. 21–33). Bristol, UK; Buffalo, NY: Multilingual Matters.

Human Development Report 2004. (2004). *Cultural liberty in today's world*. United Nations Development Programme and Oxford University Press.

Jenkins, R. (2004). *Social Identity* (2nd ed.). London: Routledge.

Krishnaswamy, N., & Burde, A. (1998). *The politics of Indians' English: linguistic colonialism and the expanding English empire*. Delhi: Oxford University Press.

Kubota, R., & Lin, A. (Eds.). (2009). *Race, culture, and identities in second language education*. New York: Routledge.

Kuhn, T. (1962). *The structure of scientific revolution*. Chicago, IL: The University of Chicago Press.

Kumaravadivelu, B. (2006a). Dangerous liaison: Globalization, empire and TESOL. In J. Edge (Ed.), *(Re)Locating TESOL in an age of empire* (pp. 1–26). London: Palgrave/Macmillan.

Kumaravadivelu, B. (2006b). *Understanding language teaching: From method to postmethod*. Mahwah, NJ: Lawrence Erlbaum.

Kumaravadivelu, B. (2008). *Cultural globalization and language education*. New Haven, CT: Yale University Press.

Lin, A. (Ed.). (2008). *Problematizing identity*. New York: Lawrence Erlbaum.

Maalouf, A. (2000). *On identity*. London: The Harvill Press.

Mahboob, A. (2009). English as an Islamic language: A case study of Pakistani English. *World Englishes, 28*(2), 175–189.

Maley, A. (2009). ELF: a teacher's perspective. *Language and Intercultural Communication, 9*(3), 187–200.

McCrum, R. (2010). *Globish: How the English language became the world's language*. London: W.W. Norton & Company.

McKay, S. L. (2002). *Teaching English as an international language*. Oxford: Oxford University Press.

McKay, S. L. (2009). Pragmatics and EIL pedagogy. In F. Sharifian (Ed.), *English as an international language: Perspectives and pedagogical issues* (pp. 227–241). Bristol, UK, Buffalo, NY: Multilingual Matters.

Mignolo, W. D. (2010). Delinking: The rhetoric of modernity, the logic of coloniality and the grammar of de-coloniality. In W. D. Mignolo & A. Escobar (Eds.), *Globalization and the decolonial option* (pp. 303–368). London: Routledge.

Mignolo, W. D., & Escobar, A. (Eds.). (2010). *Globalization and the decolonial option*. London: Routledge.

Modiano, M. (2009). EIL, native-speakerism and the failure of European ELT. In F. Sharifian (Ed.), *English as an international language: Perspectives and pedagogical issues* (pp. 58–77). Bristol, UK, Buffalo, NY: Multilingual Matters.

Pennycook, A. (1989). The concept of method, interested knowledge, and the politics of language. *TESOL Quarterly, 23*(4), 589–618.

Pennycook, A. (2007). The myth of English as an international language. In S. Makoni & A. Pennycook (Eds.), *Disinventing and reconstituting languages* (pp. 90–115). Clevedon: Multilingual Matters.

Reed, I. (2008). Justifying sociological knowledge: From realism to interpretation. *Sociological Theory, 26*(2), 101–129.

Rose, K. R., & Kasper, G. (2001). *Pragmatics in language teaching*. Cambridge: Cambridge University Press.

Sharifian, F. (2009). English as an international language: An overview. In F. Sharifian (Ed.), *English as an international language: Perspectives and pedagogical issues* (pp. 1–18). Bristol, UK, Buffalo, NY: Multilingual Matters.

Smith, L. T. (1999). *Decolonizing methodologies: Research and indigenous people.* London: Zed Books.

Ushioda, E., & Dörnyei, Z. (2009). Motivation, language identities and the L2 self: A theoretical overview. In Z. Dörnyei & E. Ushioda (Eds.), *Motivation, language identity and the L2 self* (pp. 1–9). Buffalo: Multilingual Matters.

Widin, J. (2010). *Illegitimate practices: Global English language education.* Bristol: Multilingual Matters.

Wittgenstein, L. (1958). *Philosophical investigations* (G. E. M Anscombe, Trans.). Oxford: Blackwell.

Young, T. J., & Walsh, S. (2010). Which English? Whose English? An investigation of "non-native" teachers' beliefs about target varieties. *Language, Culture and Curriculum, 23*(2), 123–137.

Chapter 3

Principles of Teaching English as an International Language

Sandra Lee McKay

Literature on the spread of English has grown tremendously in the last 20 years. Scholarly discussions on the global use of English have produced such terms as *World Englishes* (e.g., Brutt-Griffler, 2002; Jenkins, 2003; Kachru, Kachru & Nelson, 2006; Kirkpatrick, 2007), *English as an international language* (e.g., McKay, 2002; 2008), and *English as a lingua franca* (e.g., House, this volume; Jenkins, 2000; Seidlhofer, 2004). Issues surrounding the global spread of English have been discussed from various perspectives. These discussions are often framed from a macro-perspective, focusing on the social, political, and economic value of English as a global language (e.g., Crystal, 1997), inequalities between English and other languages as symbolized by linguistic imperialism (e.g., Phillipson, 1992, 2003), and the ultimate loss of minority languages described as language death or linguistic genocide (e.g., Nettle & Romaine, 2000; Skutnabb-Kangas, 2000).

However, there is far less discussion on the pedagogical implications of these perspectives or comprehensive reviews of what has been learned about English pedagogy in the current era of globalization. The goal of this chapter, and indeed of this book, is to carefully explore the role of English today and reflect on what this means for English pedagogy. The chapter begins by examining the current users and uses of English and what this suggests for the teaching of English as an international language (EIL). The chapter closes with principles that should inform a socially sensitive English pedagogy.

Users of English

Bilingual Speakers

It is widely agreed that today there are more bilingual speakers of English than there are first language speakers of English. Currently it is estimated that over 1 billion people are learning English world wide and according to the British Council, 750 million of these learners are what are traditionally called English as a foreign language (EFL) speakers while approximately 375 million are English as a second language (ESL) speakers (Beare, 2010). Hence, most learners of English today are adding English to their linguistic repertoire, not replacing their first language with English, as is often the case with ESL immigrant learners. Instead, they are using English alongside their first language, often for limited purposes. At the same time, it is important to recognize that over 5 billion people globally do not speak English as either their first or second language (Graddol, 2006). This means that over three-quarters of the world population are non-English-speaking. Thus, contrary to the common belief about English, not all contexts for cross-cultural communication rely on English to serve as the mutually shared language. Such contexts often exist within Expanding-Circle countries with an increasing migrant population in which migrants rely on the language of the host country, not English, for cross-cultural communication.

Traditionally L2 pedagogy and research have been dominated by the assumption that the goal of bilingual users of English is to achieve native-like competence in English. However, for those individuals who use English essentially as a language of wider communication alongside one or more other languages they speak, achieving native-like competence is often not necessary or desired. Nevertheless, as Cook (1999) notes,

> SLA [second language acquisition] research has often fallen into the comparative fallacy (Bley-Vroman, 1983) of relating the L2 learner to the native speaker. This tendency is reflected in the frequency with which the words succeed and fail are associated with the phrase native speaker, for example, the view that fossilisation and errors in L2 users' speech add up to "failure to achieve native-speaker competence."
>
> (p. 189)

Rather than relying any longer on the native-speaker model it is time for L2 professionals to investigate the language use patterns of speech communities that use English alongside other languages. Graddol (1997) aptly summarizes the issue in the following manner.

> But a full understanding of the role of English in a world where the majority of its speakers are not first-language speakers requires an understanding of how English relates to the other languages which are used alongside it. The European concept of bilingualism reflects an idea that each language has a natural geographical "home" and that a bilingual speaker is therefore someone who can converse with monolingual speakers from more than one country. The ideal bilingual speaker is thus imagined to be someone who is like a monolingual in two languages at once. But many of the world's bilingual or

multilingual speakers interact with other multilinguals and use each of their languages for different purposes: English is not used simply as a "default" language because it is the only language shared with another speaker; it is often used because it is culturally regarded as the appropriate language for a particular communicative context.

(p. 12)

What is needed then is a much more robust picture of how bilinguals in various communities around the world use English for specific communicative purposes. In many instances, particularly in what are traditionally called Outer-Circle countries, their use of English occurs in the context of code-switching and code-mixing. This has important implications for EIL pedagogy that we will address later in the chapter.

Economic Elite

In addition to most speakers of English today being bilingual, many language learners come from privileged economic backgrounds. Currently language policies enacted by the Chinese Ministry of Education, for example, have tended to promote English language learning for the elite in China. In 1978, the Ministry of Education issued the first unified primary and secondary curriculum for the era of modernization. The directive mandated that efforts in promoting English language proficiency were to be aimed at strengthening English language teaching in elite schools, which were expected to produce the English-proficient personnel needed to successfully undertake national modernization. In fact, in 1985 the Ministry of Education exempted poorly resourced schools from providing English instruction (Hu, 2005).

The same situation is presently occurring in Hong Kong where in 1997, the Department of Education in Hong Kong announced a sweeping change in the medium of instruction so that most schools were asked to adopt Chinese as the medium of instruction. At the same time, the government made an exemption for a minority of schools which had been operating successfully in English to continue using English as the medium of instruction. According to Choi (2003), the policy,

which provided for the selection of the best primary school graduates for monolingual education, was designed to be a cost-effective way of training in English skills for those who had the economic and cultural capital to benefit from it. Meanwhile, the majority of students were barred from sufficient exposure to English, the language of power and wealth.

(p. 673)

Choi contends that the policy was basically engineered by business interests right before the change over in 1997 and that its ultimate effect was to "perpetuate a form of linguistic imperialism" (p. 673).

An economic divide in the teaching of English is also evident in South Korea where Park and Abelman (2004) argue that

> English has long been a class marker in South Korea: namely knowledge of and comfort with English has been a sign of educational opportunity, and for some, of the experience of travel or study abroad and contact with foreigners in South Korea.
>
> (p. 646)

Park and Abelman contend that today in South Korea "there is a veritable English language mania" (p. 646). In fact, the size of the English language market in South Korea is estimated to be about $3,300 million dollars a year with another $830 million spent on study abroad programs. The private after-school education market is also booming particularly after it was announced in 1995 that English would become an elementary school subject. However, participation in this English-education market is not within the reach of those with fewer economic assets.

What do these economic and educational inequalities suggest for EIL practices? To begin, it is important for local educators to grapple with the difficult question of whether or not English learning should be promoted for all young people in a country. Second, English language educators and Ministries need to consider who should be involved in making decisions regarding the promotion of English language learning—Ministries of Education, local school administrators, teachers, students, or a combination of such individuals and institutions. We will return to this very difficult issue later in the chapter.

Uses of English

As Coulmas (2005) points out, there are many reasons why someone today might choose to study English. These develop from the fact that English is:

- the dominant language of the world's greatest military power;
- allocated (co-)official status in a third of the world's countries;
- used across a wide range of ethnicities and nationalities;
- employed for every conceivable literary genre;
- the basis of the world's biggest language industry;
- the most common second language;
- more widely taught as a foreign language than any other;

- the most valuable linguistic component of human capital;
- the foremost language of international scholarship;
- the language most connected with others by means of bilingual dictionaries;
- involved in more language-contact situations than any other language.

(p. 225)

Access to Jobs

A very prevalent belief is that being proficient in English allows one better and more job opportunities. Whereas English proficiency alone is not sufficient for a good job, for a growing number of professional jobs, English does appear to be a great asset. For example, JobsinHubs is a new website based in Europe that focuses exclusively on jobs requiring English proficiency. On their home page they note that their rationale for starting the job portal was their conviction that more and more companies are requiring English as their working language (JobsinHubs, 2010).

Phillipson (2003) notes that the trend in transnational corporations throughout Europe is to shift to English as the in-house corporate language. A 2001 Danish survey, for example, reported that one-third of Danish companies are planning on a shift to the use of English in the work context in the next ten years. In addition, Chrysler workers in Germany are required to learn English, though there is no comparable requirement for English speakers to learn German (Phillipson, 2003). To the extent that this trend continues, English will be an important language to know in order to be employed in transnational corporations.

Outsourcing is another facet of the world market that is largely undertaken in English. Friedman (2005), for example, argues that even though India has few natural resources, its present economy is growing rapidly, largely because it is good at doing one thing—"mining the brains of its own people by educating a relatively large slice of its elites in the sciences, engineering and medicine" (p. 104). This mining of brains, however, is only economically rewarding in a global context if the educated work force speaks English. Since India is one of the few places where one can find a surplus of English-speaking engineers, companies that need technical expertise can now get this help cheaply over the Internet.

The centrality of English in transnational corporations and outsourcing is an indication of changing work categories. Reich (1991, as cited in Warschauer, 2000) categorizes the present work force into three categories:

1 *Routine-production service workers* include factory workers but also routine information workers, such as data processors and payroll clerks.

2 *In-person service workers* include workers such as janitors, hospital attendants, and taxi drivers.

3 *Symbolic analysts* spend much of their time analyzing symbol-based (numerical and textual) information. These workers include software engineers, management consultants, strategic planners, lawyers, real estate developers, and research scientists.

(pp. 517–518)

It is the last category of employees that is increasing in a globalized economy. It is such workers who frequently use English in the work context and are experiencing a rise in income, status, and career opportunities.

What do these changing trends in the work force suggest for the teaching of EIL? As Warschauer (2000) notes,

First ... they underscore the role of English as an international language for global communication. Secondly, they signal a change in the types of communication required in English. A large and increasing number of people, even if they never set foot in an English-speaking country, will be required to use English in highly sophisticated communication and collaboration with people around the world. They will need to be able to write persuasively, critically interpret and analyze information, and carry out complex negotiations and collaboration in English.

(p. 518)

While routine-production workers and in-person service workers may need to use some English on the job, the type of English they will need is far more restricted than that required of the symbolic analysts. The fact that a high level of English proficiency is often required for symbolic analysts and that such individuals typically reap higher economic benefits than other workers indicate the manner in which English can contribute to an economic divide in which those who can afford to develop their English proficiency are those that may be able to reap the economic benefits that it brings.

Communication

Central to the spread of English is its role in providing a means of communication for a variety of purposes—scientific advancements, advertising, education, diplomacy, entertainment, and so on. We will consider some of these roles as a way of illustrating the centrality of English today in accessing and sharing information.

Research and Publishing

In many fields, but particularly in scientific fields, there is pressure for scholars to publish in English. Phillipson (2003) points out the negative effects of such a policy:

> ... the pressures to publish "internationally" rather than locally are intense, and are seen as applicable to all scholars. This can lead to a neglect of local or national topics. It can also lead to a false sense of priorities when posts are filled, if writing for an "international" journal is assumed to imply better quality than in a national one.
>
> (p. 81)

Schrock (2009), for example, summarizes the situation of Chinese scholars publishing in English. Not long ago, China adopted the American university system of professional ranks in which publication in the highest ranking international journals, most of them published in English, has become essential. Because of the pressure to publish in English a new industry has developed in which foreign companies from English-speaking countries offer Chinese academics proofreading services. One important question is whether or not the pressure for Chinese scholars to learn English might impede advances in research since much time is demanded for English language learning. Kirkpatrick (2009) laments the fact that writers and scientists for whom English is not a first language are often forced to work with "an empirical-scientific knowledge paradigm and 'Anglo' rhetorical styles" that puts them at a disadvantage (p. 254).

Diplomacy

International diplomacy is another area in which English is becoming essential. Many foreign diplomats are under pressure to learn English to keep their job. For example, an article in the *Jakarta Post*, entitled, "No English, no diplomacy," argues that foreign diplomats in Indonesia and other countries must increase their skills in English or they will risk "humiliating the country" and decrease the chances of the country winning more foreign investments (Khalik, 2010).

In fact many international organizations whether for diplomacy or other purposes rely on English. In 1996 there were about 12,500 international organizations in the world with about a third of these listing the language they use for official purposes. Of these 85% made official use of English. In Asia and the Pacific about 90% of the international bodies carry on their work entirely in English. In Europe, too, organizations which use English are quite common, especially in science (Crystal, 1997, p. 87).

Information Sharing on the Internet

Information sharing on the Internet is still dominated by English websites though Chinese websites are close behind. According to the Internet World Stats, the number of English websites is currently 27.3% while the number of Chinese is 22.6%. Each of the following languages have less than 8% of websites today in decreasing percentages—Spanish, Japanese, Portuguese, German, Arabic, French, Russian, and Korean (Internet World Stats, 2010). Such percentages, however, may mask the predominance of English on the web. Crystal (2003), for example, points out that many websites in other languages provide an English translation of their site.

Some contend that English proficiency is essential to take full advantage of the information on the Internet. Specter (as cited in Crystal, 2003) claims that "if you want to take full advantage of the Internet there is only one way to do it: learn English." As he puts it,

> To study molecular genetics, all you need to get into the Harvard University Library or medical library at Sweden's Karoinska Institute is a phone line and a computer.
>
> And, it turns out, a solid command of the English language. Because whether you are a French intellectual pursuing the cutting edge of international film theory, a Japanese paleobotanist curious about a newly discovered set of primordial fossils or an American teen-ager concerned about Magic Johnson's jump shot, the Internet and the World Wide Web really only work as great unifiers if you speak English.
>
> (p. 117)

Pedagogical Implications

What does the above discussion on the present-day users and uses of English suggest for the teaching of English? The intention of the following discussion is to highlight some of the major ramifications of these features of English on EIL pedagogy and to set forth principles that we believe should inform a socially-sensitive EIL pedagogy.

A Respect for and Promotion of Multilingualism

The majority of English users today use English alongside one or more of the other languages they speak. The various languages they speak frequently serve different purposes, with one language often used for family and social interaction and another, in some instances English, used for more public and professional purposes. All of the languages in an individual's repertoire serve as a source of personal and social identity. It is important that we, as language educators, recognize this fact and work to preserve and promote all languages that an individual has access to.

With colonialism and more recently with vast immigration to English-speaking countries, the ELT profession has frequently operated within an English-only framework in which any language other than English is discouraged in the English classroom. Phillipson (1992), in his widely circulated book, *Linguistic Imperialism*, documents past and present colonial policies enacted by Britain and the United States. He sets forth five tenets that he argues developed from colonial history and presently inform the English teaching profession.

- Tenet one: English is best taught monolingually.
- Tenet two: the ideal teacher of English is a native-speaker.
- Tenet three: the earlier English is taught, the better the results.
- Tenet four: the more English is taught, the better the results.
- Tenet five: if other languages are used much, standards of English will drop.

The idea of an English-only classroom is one tenet that has been espoused as part of communicative language teaching (CLT) and is being adhered to in many EFL countries. Korea, for example, supports a Teaching English through English (TETE) policy that encourages English teachers to use only English in their classroom (Kim, 2002, 2008).

What problems arise from an English-only policy? First, such a policy fails to recognize the linguistic resources learners have and how these resources can be used to promote the acquisition of English. Second, the policy is often unenforceable, particularly in the use of group work, where it is much more natural for learners in EFL contexts to communicate with one another in their first language. Finally, by ignoring the learners' multilingual competency, teachers lose an opportunity to promote learners' awareness of both the relationship between languages and the manner in which learners make use of their mutilingualism.

A recognition of the role of English as an additional language suggests that teachers need to examine how they can judiciously use learners' other languages to promote the learning of English as well as to encourage a better understanding of the role all of the learners' languages play in their personal and social identity. An EIL classroom that supports a multilingual policy will use code-switching as a learning strategy when it is warranted. In some cases, code-switching can be used to make the meaning of lexical items clear, to allow group planning of English learning tasks, and to make comparisons between syntactic and lexical features of the various languages learners use.

A Pedagogy That Resonates With the Local Linguistic Landscape

As our earlier discussion of the users and uses of English illustrates, English is used by many kinds of speakers with many different purposes. In some cases, English is being taught as a required subject in a context in which learners, seeing no apparent reasons for learning English, have little motivation to learn the language. In other contexts, learners are convinced that the acquisition of English will bring them significant rewards in terms of higher education opportunities, job possibilities, job promotions, acquisition of scholarly knowledge, entertainment and enjoyment, and so on. Under such circumstances, it is clearly not possible to suggest a pedagogical approach that can serve all these needs. (See Brown, this volume, for a similar conclusion in relation to curriculum planning.)

Rather teachers need to consider factors such as the following in making pedagogical decisions.

- What languages are used in the local linguistic landscape and how are they used?
- What are the learners' attitudes toward these languages?
- What standards are adhered to in the local linguistic landscape?
- What are the major purposes the learners have for acquiring English?
- What is the proficiency level and age of the learner?
- What are features of the local culture of learning?

The following examples illustrate how a consideration of the local landscape can influence both the choice of which language to teach and which variety of English to promote.

Japan, like many countries, is witnessing an influx of workers from other ethnic and linguistic backgrounds to support the country's local and global economy. Brazilian workers are being recruited to work in Japanese communities, often for industrial work. In these communities, young people, both Japanese and Brazilian, are in English language classrooms because the Ministry believes that English is critical for the country's international trade and status. Yet on the local level, it is Japanese and Portuguese that are needed to promote cross-cultural communication and understanding. (See Kubota & McKay, 2009, for a full description of this situation.) Under such circumstances, the critical question for Ministries of Education and local administrators and teachers is what the best policy is for foreign language learning given the local linguistic resources and needs. In short, attention to the local linguistic landscape suggests that one central concern for EIL pedagogy is whether or not compulsory English learning is beneficial for all.

Attention to the local linguistic landscape also has ramifications for the choice of which varieties of English to permit in the classroom. Singapore is a case in point. Here a debated question is whether or not Singapore colloquial English (SCE) should be allowed in the classrooms. Currently, its use is highly discouraged. However, it is commonly agreed that this variety of English serves particular purposes in indicating camaraderie and informality. Clearly it is important that Singaporeans acquire standard Singapore English both because of the status it enjoys within Singapore and in the international community. At the same time, an opportunity is missed by not using the English classroom to explore the uses of SCE in the local linguistic landscape and to permit the natural use of this variety for informal purposes within the school context.

Language Awareness Courses for All Students

The fact that English is currently being used in such a diverse array of bilingual and multilingual contexts suggests the importance of integrating language awareness activities in all EIL courses. Discussing the teaching of English as a lingua franca, Seidlhofer (2004) offers a bold proposal to replace English as a school subject with language awareness which would focus on the awareness of English as a lingua franca, including communication strategies and accommodation skills through a multilingual approach. The course could include strategies such as "drawing on extralinguistic cues, identifying and building on shared knowledge, gauging and adjusting to interlocutors' linguistic repertoires, supportive listening, signaling noncomprehension in a face-saving way, asking for repetition, paraphrasing, and the like" (Seidlhofer, 2004, p. 227).

In addition, teachers and students can undertake what Peirce (1995) terms *classroom-based social research (CBSR)*. Such research involves collaborative projects carried out by language learners in their local community under the guidance and support of the teacher. In such projects, students are asked to gather examples of when they see individuals in their local community using English with other L2 speakers. They can also gather examples of their own use of electronic written English with other L2 writers. The point of such assignments is to encourage students to become aware of how they use English for communication across international borders, often with other L2 speakers. Teachers can also contribute to the project by gathering and audio-taping examples of L2–L2 interactions. The reason for stressing L2–L2 interactions in such projects is that in general language learners have been exposed, through classroom materials, to many examples of L1–L2 interactions. What they now need is an awareness that English is an international language that can be used not only with native speakers but also with L2 speakers in a wide variety of cultural and social contexts.

Beyond this practical level, it is also essential for teachers and students to develop *critical language awareness* in order to understand and challenge unequal relations of power that are manifested not only in language and culture but also in race, gender, class, and other social categories. Such awareness would scrutinize the dominant discourses on language and examine the interrelationship between identities, ideologies, and hierarchical relations of power between groups (Alim, 2005).

An Examination of the Discourse Promoting the Learning of English

One factor that has fueled the spread of English is a prevalent belief in the power of English. While in some instances, the learning of English can result in actual economic, educational, and social advantages, in other cases, the discourse surrounding the use of English promises learners unrealistic accounts of what a knowledge of English may bring to their lives. This belief in the power of English has resulted in many language learners imagining the various benefits that can develop if they learn English. Often these "imagined communities" (Anderson, 1983) are depicted in the narratives of language learners. Such narratives reinforce the belief of many English learners that if they only invest in English learning, they will reap the benefits of social and intellectual mobility.

The concept of an imagined community is one that has not gone unnoticed by ELT private schools. Evidence of this is the establishment of theme villages that depict an imagined environment. Seargeant (2005), for example, describes British Hills in Japan, a leisure language-learning complex that seeks to simulate an "authentic" English-speaking environment. In fact, the sales slogan "boasts that the complex is 'More English than England itself'" (p. 327). The village is staffed by native speakers recruited from Britain, Canada, Australia, and New Zealand.

By hiring only native speakers and promoting native-speaker competency, the village promotes a reality that is far different from the multilingual/ multicultural Britain of today. In doing so,

The overall effect is to create an environment which is not necessarily truthful to the original upon which it is purportedly based but is instead an imagined idea with its own logic and reality. The authenticity upon which British Hills prides itself is not a representation of Britishness as it is currently constructed and enacted in mainstream British society. Instead, it is an image drawn from aspects of the popular imagination in Japan, from a tourist industry template ... and also from local protocol for foreign language education.

(Seargeant, 2005, p. 341)

In this context, authenticity becomes not the genuine item but an imagined representation of a different reality. As Seargeant (2005) puts it,

A place like British Hills is not merely representing Britishness but reconstructing it, thus presenting itself as a detailed realistic image of something that actually exists only within its own depiction. The use of the concept of authenticity is almost an irony of the process ...

(p. 341)

These imagined communities can be a powerful force in commercial aspects of language learning. Given such discourses, it is imperative that English educators present a realistic view of the benefits that the acquisition of English may reap. While in some instances English proficiency may be one factor that affects an individual's educational, economic, and social standing, in most cases English proficiency is only one of a myriad of factors that affects the personal, social, and professional status a person has.

Curricula That Promote Cross-cultural Awareness

The fact that English is frequently used for cross-cultural communication suggests that curricula should be culturally sensitive, encouraging students to learn about other cultures as a way of reflecting on their own values and beliefs. The goal then is not to learn primarily about the culture of English-speaking countries but rather to learn about many cultures and about differing cultural values as a way of increasing the learners' sensitivity to cross-cultural differences. In Kramsch's (1993) words, language classrooms need to establish a "sphere of interculturality" in which students learn about the culture of other countries as a way of gaining greater understanding of their own culture.

To take a simple example, the primary purpose of reading about American garage sales or holidays in an English language class should not be merely to present information about aspects of American culture, but rather to provide an opportunity for cross-cultural comparisons. Thus the discussion and activities following a reading on American garage sales should not be on researching American garage sales but rather on researching what the host culture traditionally and presently does with used items. Are used items sold? If so, where? If they aren't sold, what is done with them? How does this differ from what Americans often do with used items? What might be the reason for such differences? In this way students reflect on their own culture in the process of learning about other cultures.

Equality of Access for All Learners

Frequently, English learning is far more accessible to those with economic resources, often young people living in urban areas. These children often have opportunities for private tutoring and for traveling and studying in English-speaking environments. Meanwhile, young people in rural areas and those from less privileged backgrounds are denied such access. For those who desire English proficiency either for themselves or for their children, equal access to English classes should be available.

For that to happen Ministries of Education and local administrators and educators need to advocate for English classes for all those who desire the opportunity to study English. This suggests that Ministry of Education directives need to be more localized and flexible so that these policies can respond to local and individual needs and desires. The benefit of having such a policy is that those who are motivated to learn English will have an opportunity to do so. Meanwhile those who see no need for acquiring English and immigrants who would benefit far more from acquiring the language of their host country will not need to be in classrooms in which there appears to be no apparent reason for learning English.

A Re-examination of the Concept of Qualified Teachers of English

It goes without saying that none of the changes listed above will occur unless teachers of English, in all of the varied learning contexts that exist today, work to implement these changes. Clearly, what is needed for this to happen are informed and qualified teachers of English. From an institutional perspective, this suggests that Ministries of Education and educational administrators need to provide teachers with opportunities for professional development and with needed resources.

On a subtle but perhaps more significant level, changes also need to occur on a discourse level. For too long, bilingual teachers of English, particularly in so-called Expanding-Circle countries, have been labeled and marginalized as non-native English-speaking teachers (NNESTs). Unfortunately, such labeling typically elevates the so-called native English-speaking teacher (NEST) and suggests that in some ways NNESTs lack the native-speaker intuition necessary to be ideal teachers of English (Braine, 2010). Fortunately, several terms to capture new and more progressive perspectives of teachers of English have been proposed, focusing on the skills and knowledge relevant to teaching, as for example, "proficient user" (Paikeday, 1985), "language expertise" (Rampton, 1990), "English-using speech fellowship" (Kachru, 1992), and "multi-competent speaker"(Cook, 1999). More essentially, discussions in the literature have acknowledged the value of the bilingual speaker and teacher and emphasized the fact that proficient speakers of English have equal ownership of English, regardless of their "nativeness" (Widdowson, 1994).

Despite theoretical agreement in the field of the problems of the NEST/NNEST dichotomy, the TESOL industry, in general has been slow in adopting these new perspectives. Advertisements on TESOL websites recruiting English teachers in Japan, Korea, and other countries where English is valued for its economic capital, continue to demand the American, British Caucasian native speaker as English teachers. The only way this will change is through the promotion of a counter-discourse that recognizes and legitimizes the value of proficient and qualified bilingual teachers of English, no matter what their first language may be. This is especially important today when globalization has encouraged peoples across a wide range of countries to call English their language, appropriating it in a multitude of ways to fulfill their needs. Thus, a label that divides people as native or non-native is a poor theoretical construct for expanding understandings of what it means today to be a competent teacher of English.

Conclusion

It is clear that today the majority of English speakers are bilingual and often from economically and educationally more privileged backgrounds. In addition, they tend to use English primarily for job access and for accessing and sharing information. Given this situation, we have argued that an EIL pedagogy that is socially sensitive and responsible needs to adhere to the following principles:

- the promotion of multilingualism and multiculturalism;
- localized L2 language planning and policies;
- the development of an awareness of language variation and use for all students;

- a critical approach to the discourse surrounding the acquisition and use of English;
- equal access to English learning for all who desire it; and
- a re-examination of the concept of qualified teachers of English.

The remaining chapters will illustrate specific classroom practices that can promote these principles.

Exploring the Ideas

1 In your opinion do you believe Ministries of Education and local educational leaders should strive to make English learning available for all young people in your country? Why or why not? If you believe all young people should have the opportunity to learn English, what policies should be established in your country to see that this is done? If you don't believe English access is necessary for everyone, who do you believe should make the decision as to who has access to English?

2 In your opinion should an English teacher strive to promote an English-only classroom? Why or why not? Do you think the policy should be the same for all ages and all levels of learners? If you would allow the use of a student's first language in an English classroom, list contexts in which you think the first language could be productively used.

3 If you were to design a language awareness course such as the one suggested in this chapter, what would be your goals and what are some activities you would include in such a course?

4 What are the advantages and disadvantages of using information about a foreign culture as content for an English classroom? What are advantages and disadvantages of using information about the local culture as content for an English class? Whether you use foreign or local culture as content, what are some ways you might seek to promote cross-cultural comparisons?

Applying the Ideas

1 If you yourself are a bilingual speaker of English, keep a log for one day in which you document in what situations you use some English, who you speak English with, and for what purposes. Be certain to record both your oral and written uses of English. To the extent that your use of English may be typical of other English speakers in your local context, what does your use of English suggest for the teaching

of EIL? If you are not a bilingual speaker of English, ask a bilingual English speaker you know to keep a record for you.

2   Research various employment websites in your country to determine what percentages of jobs include a requirement for English proficiency. Then characterize the type of jobs that require English proficiency and what English skills appear to be needed. Are they primarily written or oral skills? What does this suggest for the teaching of EIL?

3   Examine at least three websites or brochures that are designed to advertise local English language institutions. List the types of claims that are made regarding the advantages of acquiring English and the types of life style associated with the acquisition of English. How might you use such examples to help your students become aware of the imagined benefits of learning English as opposed to the real benefits?

References

Alim, S. (2005). Critical language awareness in the United States: Revisiting issues and revising pedagogies in a resegregated society. *Educational Researcher, 34*(7), 24–31.

Anderson, B. (1983). *Imagined communities*. New York: Verso.

Beare, K. (2010). *How many people learn English globally?* Retrieved July 6, 2010 from http://esl.about.com/od/englishlearnngresources/f/f_eslmarket .htm

Braine, G. (2010). *Nonnative speaker English teachers: Research, pedagogy, and professional growth*. New York: Routledge.

Brutt-Griffler, J. (2002). *World Englishes: A study of its development*. Clevedon: Multilingual Matters.

Choi, P. K. (2003). "The best students will learn English": Ultra-utilitarianism and linguistic imperialism in post-1997 Hong Kong. *Journal of Education Policy, 28*(6), 673–694.

Cook, V. (1999). Going beyond the native speaker in language teaching. *TESOL Quarterly, 33*(2), 185–209.

Coulmas, F. (2005). *Sociolinguistics: The study of speakers' choices*. Cambridge: Cambridge University Press.

Crystal, D. (1997). *English as a global language*. Cambridge: Cambridge University Press.

Crystal, D. (2003). *English as a global language*. Cambridge: Cambridge University Press.

Davies, A. (1991). *The native speaker in applied linguistics*. Edinburgh: Edinburgh University Press.

Friedman, T. (2005). *The world is flat*. New York: Farrar, Straus and Giroux.

Graddol, D. (1997). *The future of English?* London: The British Council.

Graddol, D. (2006). *English next: Why global English may mean the end of "English as a Foreign Language"*. London: British Council.

Hu, G. (2005). English language education in China: Policies, progress, and problems. *Language Policy, 4*, 5–24.

Internet World Stats (2010). Retrieved August 6, 2010 from http://www.internetworldstats.com/stats7.htm

Jenkins, J. (2000). *The phonology of English as an international language.* Oxford: Oxford University Press.

Jenkins, J. (2003). *World Englishes: A resource book for students.* London: Routledge.

JobsinHubs (2010). Retrieved August 6, 2010 from http://www.jobsinhubs.com / jobsinhubs/about-us.aspx

Kachru, B. (1992). *The other tongue: English across cultures.* Urbana, IL: University of Illinois Press.

Kachru, B. B., Kachru, Y., & Nelson, C. L. (Eds.). (2006). *The handbook of world Englishes.* Malden, MA: Blackwell.

Khalik, A. (2010, July 7). No English, no diplomacy, experts tell RI attachés. *The Jakarta Post.* Retrieved July 7, 2010 from www.thejakartapost.com/news/2010/02/24/no-english-no-diplomacy-experts-tell-ri-attaches.html

Kim, S. Y. (2002). Teachers' perceptions about teaching English through English. *English Teaching, 57*(1), 131–148.

Kim, S. Y. (2008) Five years of teaching English through English: Responses from teachers and prospects for learners. *English Teaching, 63*(1) 51–70.

Kirkpatrick, A. (2007). *World Englishes: Implications for international communication and English language teaching.* Cambridge: Cambridge University Press.

Kirkpatrick, A. (2009). English as an international language of scholarship: Implications for the dissemination of "local" knowledge. In F. Sharifian (Ed.), *English as an international language: Perspectives and pedagogical issues* (pp. 254–270). Bristol: Multilingual Matters.

Kramsch, C. (1993). *Context and culture in language teaching.* Oxford: Oxford University Press.

Kubota, R., & McKay, S. L. (2009). Globalization and language learning in rural Japan: The role of English in the local linguistic ecology. *TESOL Quarterly, 43*(4), 593–619.

Llurda, E. (2009). Attitudes towards English as an international language: The pervasiveness of native models among L2 users and teachers. In F. Sharifian (Ed.), *English as an international language: Perspectives and pedagogical issues* (pp. 119–134). Bristol: Multilingual Matters.

McArthur, T. (1998). *The English languages.* Cambridge: Cambridge University Press.

McKay, S. L. (2002). *Teaching English as an international language: Rethinking goals and approaches.* Oxford: Oxford University Press.

McKay, S. L., & Bokhorst-Heng, W. (2008). *International English in its sociolinguistic contexts: Towards a socially sensitive pedagogy.* New York: Routledge.

Nettle, D., & Romaine, S. (2000). *Vanishing voices: The extinction of the world's languages.* Oxford: Oxford University Press.

Paikeday, T. (1985). *The native speaker is dead!* Toronto, Canada: Paikeday Publishing Inc.

Park, S. J., & Abelman, N. (2004). Class and cosmopolitan striving: Mothers' management of English education in South Korea. *Anthropological Quarterly,* 77(4), 645–672.

Peirce, B. (1995). Social identity, investment, and language learning. *TESOL Quarterly, 29*(1), 9–31.

Phillipson, R. (1992). *Linguistic imperialism.* Oxford: Oxford University Press.

Phillipson, R. (2003). *English only Europe? Challenging language policy.* London: Routledge.

Rampton, M. B. H. (1990). Displacing the native speaker: Expertise, affiliation, and inheritance. *ELT Journal, 44*(2), 97–101.

Seargeant, P. (2005). "More English than England itself": The simulation of authenticity in foreign language practice in Japan. *International Journal of Applied Linguistics, 15*(3), 326–345.

Schrock, J. (2009). China: Publishing in English creates western industry. Retrieved July 14, 2010 from http://www.univeristyworldnews.com /article.php?story=20090611224150392

Seidlhofer, B. (2004). Research perspectives on teaching English as a lingua franca. *Annual Review of Applied Linguistics, 24,* 209–239.

Shin, H. (2006). Rethinking TESOL from a SOL's perspective: Indigenous epistemology and decolonizing praxis in TESOL. *Critical Inquiry in Language Studies, 3,* 147–167.

Skutnabb-Kangas, T. (2000). *Linguistic genocide in education—Or worldwide diversity and human rights?* Mahwah, NJ: Lawrence Erlbaum Associates.

Warschauer, M. (2000). The changing global economy and the future of English teaching. *TESOL Quarterly, 34*(3), 511–535.

Widdowson, H. G. (1994). "The ownership of English." *TESOL Quarterly 28*(2): 377–389.

Chapter 4

Language Teaching and Learning in the *Postlinguistic Condition?*

Mark Evan Nelson and Richard Kern

Introduction

Teaching English as an international language (EIL) raises important questions about the kinds of pedagogical methods that might be appropriate in different cultural settings and even about the nature of what is to be taught, since the particular dimensions of English that are relevant or appropriate to one group in one place and time may not be so to another in a different place and time. In this chapter we extend the idea that we are now in a "postmethod" era to propose that we may also be in a "postlinguistic" era in two senses. First, because phonetic, morphological, syntactic, semantic, and pragmatic dimensions of "the English language" are not absolute, but relative, there is no monolithic, fixed set of core material that all EIL teachers will teach everywhere. Second, because new technologies have introduced new platforms for multimodal expression and communication that rely crucially on nonlinguistic modes of meaning-making (video, music, sound, graphics, etc.), language must now be taught as only part of a larger constellation of semiotic resources.

First, the postmethod argument. Addressing a perceived disconnection between theoretical and practical aspects of language pedagogy, Kumaravadivelu (1994, 2001, 2003) advances a radical methodological— or *anti-methodological*—perspective that he labels "postmethod." The "postmethod condition," for Kumaravadivelu (1994), is about reconfiguring the relationship between theorizers and practitioners:

> theorizers have traditionally occupied the power center of language pedagogy while the practitioners of classroom teaching have been relegated to the disempowered periphery. If the conventional concept of method entitles theorizers to construct knowledge-oriented theories of pedagogy, the postmethod condition empowers practitioners to construct classroom-oriented theories of practice. If the concept of method authorizes theorizers to centralize pedagogic

decision-making, the postmethod condition enables practitioners to generate location-specific, classroom-oriented innovative practices.

(pp. 28–29)

What Kumaravadivelu advocates is an informed and adaptive pedagogical disposition, as opposed to a prescriptive methodology as such. He grounds his case in the belief that teachers' intuitions, experience, and intimate knowledge of their respective contexts, students, and educational aims enable them to construct valid, practicable approaches of their own. Prescribing generic language teaching methods is not helpful because it disregards "the fact that the success and failure of classroom instruction ... depends on the unstated and unstable interaction of multiple factors" which include "teacher cognition, learner perception, societal needs, cultural contexts, political exigencies, economic imperatives, and institutional constraints, all of which are inextricably interwoven" (Kumaravadivelu, 2003, p. 29).

Kumaravadivelu's ostensibly "ecological" language pedagogical project (cf. Kramsch, 2002, 2008; van Lier, 2004) can be taken a step further, to envisage an approach to language teaching and learning that we will describe as "postlinguistic"—perhaps a bit facetiously, but not entirely so. Kumaravadivelu's project shares more than a nominal similarity to our own. Just as he aims to bridge the gap between what researchers and theorists prescribe and what teachers know and do, we seek to reconcile language pedagogy with the increasing importance of extra-linguistic resources for communication made available via multimedia technologies. However different these problems seem, their solutions may be surprisingly similar; they both require awareness and evaluation of (and adaptation to) the unique purposes, participants, and contexts involved in every instance of communication and learning.

What this perspective requires, however, is a foundational assumption that will strike many language educators as controversial or even nonsensical: that language learning and teaching cannot be understood as wholly concerned with language per se. This is perhaps clearest if one limits "language per se" to the structural and semantic aspects of a specific language to be taught and learned. But even if one includes the pragmatics of language use— "how speakers organize what they want to say in accordance with who they are talking to, where, when and under what circumstances" (Yule, 1996, p. 3)—a focus on "language" alone cannot adequately account for how language interacts with non-linguistic modes of expression, including still and moving images, sounds, music, and spatial arrangements (Kress, 2003, 2010; Kress & van Leeuwen, 1996/2006; van Leeuwen, 1999). This commingling of language with elements of other semiotic modes is now commonly discussed in terms of "multimodality." And as Kress (2003) explains, "language alone cannot give us access to the meaning of the multimodally constituted message" (p. 35). Kress (2010) urges us to look at meaning-making from a "satellite view," in which we see language, like our Earth when viewed from space, as "only one small part of a much bigger whole" (p. 15).

We would also point out that while the predominance of multimodal texts does not necessarily imply that language occupies less semiotic space within the landscape of contemporary communication, it does imply that some of the roles conventionally ascribed to language have changed qualitatively. In Kress and van Leeuwen's (1996/2006) words,

> Language is moving from its former, unchallenged role as *the* medium of communication, to a role as *one* medium of communication, and perhaps to the role of the medium of comment, albeit more so in some domains than in others, and more rapidly in some areas than in others.

> (p. 34, italics in original)

Just as language alone cannot offer a full explanation of meaning-making, neither would an "autonomous" (Street, 1995), or context- and ideology-free, approach to understanding multimodal texts be acceptable. No semiotic resource, be it a road sign, a hand gesture, or a spoken word, contains some fixed, a priori meaning in and of itself. Rather, it constitutes a basis for constructing meaning in its relations with the particular context and conditions in which an act of meaning-making occurs and the particular purposes and interests of the meaning-makers involved (Harris, 1995, 1998, 2001, 2009a; Jewitt, 2009; Kress, 2003, 2010; van Leeuwen, 2005). So, a multimodal text, and the language integrated within it, may *mean differently*, and often radically so, to the respective individuals interacting with it. Acknowledging the complex cultural flows of people, language(s), and multimodal texts around the globe (Appadurai, 1996), we become that much more aware of how vastly complicated communication is and how technologically mediated it has become. We thus shift from a conception of language as a fixed, autonomous system to a conception of language as a dynamic semiotic resource that individuals combine with other semiotic resources to act in the world.

The crucial question then becomes: how are we, as language educators, to theoretically and practically reconcile our understandings of the increasingly multimodal and supra-linguistic texture of everyday communication with the persistent, diverse needs of global language learners? Although there is no simple way to address such a complex question, we advance the notion that the goals of language learning and teaching in an era of globalized, digitally mediated communication will most effectively, efficiently, and ethically be served by an approach that is principally focused on processes of meaning-making writ large, and the roles that language plays in such broader semiotic processes (cf. Kern, 2000). To underpin such an approach we will revisit Kumaravadivelu's postmethod stance in the light of two additional theoretical perspectives: *integrational linguistics* (Harris, 1995, 1998, 2009a, 2009b, 2001, 2010), and *multiliteracies* (New London Group, 1996).

"Language Making" and the Priority of Signs and Meaning Design

The content of this second section differs somewhat from that of other chapters in this volume: we will not specifically describe a shift in thinking and practice from the "traditional" toward the "international." Instead, we will discuss two distinct but inextricably linked processes we consider to be fundamentally important to any language pedagogy, including EIL: *globalization* and *mediation*. Globalization may be understood as the "intensification of worldwide social relations which link distant localities in such a way that local happenings are shaped by events occurring many miles away and vice versa" (Giddens, 1990, p. 64). Mediation, in the sense we intend, is "the fundamentally, but unevenly, dialectical process in which institutionalised media of communication (the press, broadcast radio and television, and increasingly the World Wide Web), are involved in the general circulation of symbols in social life" (Silverstone, 2002, p. 762; cited in Couldry, 2008).

Globalization and mediation are intimately connected complexes of processes. The global interconnectedness of people has very much to do with the proliferation of digital media, which in turn are integrated, supported, and promoted through global networks of human relationships. It is also important to note that "mediated language" increasingly comprises just one part of a multimodal textual whole. One look at a profile page on *Facebook* amply demonstrates the tendency within digital texts to combine language, image, and other modes to various semiotic effects.

At the moment, the most globally mediated language is English, and its influence is undeniably vast and complex. Returning to Facebook, this influence is exemplified by the fact that in Indonesia (currently the country with the second highest number of Facebook users), over 21% of the tens of millions of active users opted for English over the country's official language, Bahasa Indonesia, when they used the site in 2010.[1]

This synergy of globalization and mediation compels us to reconsider the nature of language itself. If linguistic communication is inextricably multimodal, where does meaning reside? And if people in different places and social circumstances can now "meet" and communicate in ways heretofore unseen, applying different experiential frames and knowledge sets to their interpretations of these new multimodal texts, how do we anticipate the requirements for successful, productive interchange and also prepare our students to understand and meet these requirements? These questions have yet to be satisfactorily answered, but we suggest that the most fruitful perspectives will be those that do not regard language as the default access point from which to derive meaning, but rather look at how people combine linguistic elements with other resources (e.g., images, spatial arrangement, sounds, color, typeface, animation, and video) when they interpret texts. Here we will present two such perspectives, elements of which we feel may be usefully adapted within an EIL framework. The first is "integrational linguistics," developed by Roy Harris and colleagues.

Harris (2010) explains that the term "integrational" "alludes to the recognition that the linguistic sign alone cannot function as the basis of an independent, self-sufficient form of communication, but depends on its integration with non-verbal activities of many different kinds" (3a). He goes on to assert that

> Every episode of communication, however trivial, necessarily involves creative activity by the participants, including their own interpretation of the situation in which it occurs ... Words are not temporal invariants (as dictionaries like to present them) ... The lexicographer's view of language is a case of trying to impose a normative straitjacket on an open-ended flux of relations between linguistic acts and the world.
>
> (8b)

Harris's "integrationist" approach is founded on a number of contentious, yet compelling claims. Harris (1998, 2010) rejects conceptions of linguistic study and language use that have been traditionally treated as self-evident truths. For example, he declares the notions of grammatical rules and the "standard languages" underwritten by these rules to be "pedagogical fictions" (2010, 6c), explaining that rule creation and standardization are "mythological" artifacts of simplifying the teaching and learning of languages and that these rules have been wrongheadedly adopted by "segregationist" linguists as natural features of linguistic description and analysis (1998, pp. 46–47). Harris draws an analogy between language and the Highway Code:

> The Highway Code does not describe how motorists actually behave on the road, but prescribes how they have to behave in order to keep

within the law. To imagine that rules are just descriptive generalizations of some kind (e.g. of linguistic usage, or of postulated brain processes, or of a corpus of texts) is to confuse rules with regularities.

(2010, 6e)

To an integrationist way of thinking, the key to all signification is "contextualization": in Harris's concise phrase, "no contextualization, no sign" (Harris, 2010, 4b). This is not merely an acknowledgement of the meaning-shaping role that context plays in linguistic interaction, but a recognition that contextualization is what allows signs, linguistic or otherwise, to exist at all. Moreover, context is not "shared" by interactants, like the water that surrounds two swimmers in the same pool. Rather, context is constructed, by and for each person in a given instance of communication according to her or his priorities, objectives, values, and prior experiences and knowledge. To an integrationist, meaning in any sign, including a word, is "radically indeterminate," precisely because "alternative contextualizations are always possible" (Harris, 2009a, p. 81). This principle is of key importance to EIL teachers who work with students from varying backgrounds, since students' interpretations of signs and texts will always be influenced by their experiences, knowledge, and attitudes.

Integrational linguists have only recently begun to explore how languages might best be learned or taught (see Toolan, 2009), suggesting, for example, the importance of reflexive understandings of meaning and appropriateness in language as it is learned formally in the classroom and as it is used in real-world contexts of communication (e.g., Davis, 2009; Hutton, 2009) and asserting the priority of learning "language" (qua communication) over "languages," or particular linguistic systems: "communication is the core, and languages are the variable extra" (Harris, 2009b, p. 44).

In our own broadly integrationist interpretation, language proficiency certainly involves linguistic knowledge, but it is developed and directed through a strategic sensitivity to how language is always enmeshed within a broader fabric of signification and action and an awareness of how we and others creatively use a panoply of semiotic resources—the spoken word, written text, visual impressions and images, social conventions, memories, feelings, and more—to "make language" (Harris, 2010), and continually remake it, as befits our purposes and interests. The integrational perspective thus seems to accord well with many features of EIL communication, such as the fundamental role of contextualization, the importance of being sensitive to the need to negotiate meaning, and having the creative wherewithal to do so in varied circumstances.

The abovementioned phrase "semiotic resources" signals our second focal construct, "multiliteracies." Here, "resource" refers to the raw material, the "stuff" of meaning-making. The notion of multiliteracies arose out of a meeting in 1994 in New London, New Hampshire of ten prominent scholars representing various disciplines, but with a common concern for language and literacy education. Known as the New London Group, these scholars published an article-length manifesto entitled "A Pedagogy of Multiliteracies: Designing Social Futures" in which they assert that the essential purpose of education "is to ensure that all students benefit from learning in ways that allow them to participate fully in public, community, and economic life" and that "[l]iteracy pedagogy is expected to play a particularly important role in fulfilling this mission" (New London Group, 1996, p. 60). They go on to argue that a literacy pedagogy appropriate for the achievement of "full and equitable social participation" needs to accommodate the new literacy needs that arise from increased plurality and diversity in the global community:

> First, we want to extend the idea and scope of literacy pedagogy to account for the context of our culturally and linguistically diverse and increasingly globalized societies, for the multifarious cultures that interrelate and the plurality of texts that circulate. Second, we argue that literacy pedagogy now must account for the burgeoning variety of text forms associated with information and multimedia technologies. This includes understanding and competent control of representational forms that are becoming increasingly significant in the overall communications environment, such as visual images and their relationship to the written word—for instance, visual design in desktop publishing or the interface of visual and linguistic meaning in multimedia.
>
> (New London Group, 1996, p. 61)

This second point speaks to the importance of multimodality in contemporary texts and literacy practices. But again, these aspects of multiplicity in the forms of texts and in the sociocultural contexts of literacy are fundamentally and inextricably interrelated, since "the proliferation of communications channels and media supports and extends cultural and subcultural diversity" (New London Group, 1996, p. 61). "Multiliteracies" is the pedagogy the New London Group devised to address the interaction of these trends (which we have discussed to this point in terms of "globalization" and "mediation") and their implications.

The operative principle and central practical process of multiliteracies is "design," which describes a kind of adaptive meaning-making capacity. According to Kress (2003), design "asks what is needed now, in this one situation, with this configuration of purposes, aims, audience, *and with these resources*, and given *my* interests in this situation" (p. 49, italics in original). Design is expressly meaning-oriented, not language-oriented, involving selection and coordination of elements from the whole range of semiotic modes as befits specific communication needs. The notion of "designing meaning," then, refocuses conceptions of literacy and learning in fundamental ways; and multimodality is deeply implicated in these changes.

A core presupposition of multimodal meaning design, within the broader framework of multiliteracies and the associated field of social semiotics (e.g., Halliday, 1978; Hodge & Kress, 1988; Kress, 2010; van Leeuwen, 2005), is that meaning is constructed both in and in between different semiotic modes. In traditional conceptions of literacy, there is a tendency to regard meaning as residing within texts. A literacy that mobilizes a diversity of resources toward building meaning "in the moment," however, is an essentially relational one. This is to say that the "meaning potential" (possible interpretations not yet "actualized") resides as much *between* the pictures, elements of language, spatial arrangements of features, etc. as *within* them. When we view a website on the Internet, we attend not only to titles, banners, and other written-language texts, but also to color choices, graphics, photos, spatial arrangements, sounds, etc. Analysis of these multimodal juxtapositions can help us to see the meaning potentials of the component resources as they interact with other resources.

Though these frameworks exhibit significant compatibility, there is scant literature that puts them into conversation or synthesizes them.[2] This is our next aim. Rather than draw these perspectives together "in the abstract," we will elaborate, compare, and coordinate these positions with an eye to the priorities of language pedagogy and an EIL framework, adapting Kumaravadivelu's (2001, 2003) pedagogic parameters of *particularity, practicality*, and *possibility*.

Toward a Meaning-based Language-pedagogical Framework

Perhaps most primary among the recognizable affinities between the integrationist and multiliteracies approaches is the will to complicate understandings of language as the principal, self-contained means of encoding and conveying meaning. Such a mistaken assumption, proponents of both integrationism and multiliteracies aver, is predicated on a belief in false universals (e.g., grammar rules, semantic invariance) and an incomplete, superficial accounting of the dynamically assembled constellation of resources, signs, and processes involved in every act of meaning-making. If we were to substitute "language teaching" for "meaning-making" in the sentence above, this same criticism would also generally capture Kumaravadivelu's appraisal of methods-based language pedagogy. In his book *Beyond Methods: Macrostrategies for Language Teaching*, Kumaravadivelu (2003) discusses the limitations of the concept of method:

> Methods are based on idealized concepts geared toward idealized contexts. Since language learning and teaching needs, wants, and situations are unpredictably numerous, no idealized method can visualize all of the variables in advance in order to provide situation-specific suggestions that practicing teachers sorely need to tackle the challenges they confront every day of their professional lives.
>
> (p. 28)

If "method" were cognate with "fixed linguistic rule" or "determinate meaning" (which in an important sense it is), the likes of Harris, Kress, and the New London Group would, we suspect, heartily agree. Noticing these resonances, we were drawn to Kumaravadivelu's notion of postmethod pedagogy as a potentially useful scaffold within which to imagine a meaning-based, contextually responsive, global, multimodal language pedagogy. As a starting point, we test the applicability of the three foundational constructs of the postmethod perspective, "particularity," "practicality," and "possibility."

Particularity

"The parameter of particularity," Kumaravadivelu (2003) explains,

> requires that any language pedagogy, to be relevant, must be sensitive to a particular group of teachers teaching a particular group of learners pursuing a particular set of goals within a particular institutional context embedded in a particular sociocultural milieu.
>
> (p. 34)

Operationally, this involves "a continual cycle of observation, reflection, and action" (p. 35), that is, teachers continually evaluating the relevance and effectiveness of their teaching practices in terms of student responses and learning outcomes and then redesigning their practices in accordance with what they learn from this evaluation.

Actually, the cycle above describes what reflective practitioners (Schön, 1983) have always done; however, most often it seems that assumptions about relevance are made retrospectively on the basis of "tangible" summative measures of effectiveness, like test scores. Kumaravadivelu's crucial contribution here is in regarding particularity as both "a process and a goal" (2003, p. 35), meaning that relevance is not simply a means of achieving desired pedagogic outcomes, it *is* a desired pedagogic outcome. Relevance, or particularity, is identified as a core criterion for defining effectiveness itself. Again, this is entirely consonant with both the integrationist and multiliteracies frameworks, and these perspectives may offer potential augmentations to the parameter of particularity that could be helpful in extending Kumaravadivelu's ideas toward integrating language learning and multimodal meaning-making.

What Harris (1998, 2010) calls "contextualization," for example, is directly relevant to Kumaravadivelu's notion of particularity. Contextualization, we recall, has to do with making connections among words, texts, situations, culture, mentalities, and knowledge. Context is therefore not a static, pre-established surround into which signs can be inserted, but a personal, dynamic amalgamation of meaningful elements (both abstract and material) produced or modified through actions and interactions.

Obviously, this notion of contextualization shares with particularity an acknowledgment of the vital connection between meaning, relevance, and subjectivity. Attempting to combine these constructs, we see that contextualization adds importantly to particularity by getting us to think and talk about the integral role that non-linguistic representations and actions play alongside language in processes of meaning-making. Contextualization impels language educators to consider more deeply and seriously the question of why particularity is so important. Is it because the values, needs, aspirations, and lived experiences of different learners are formative factors in explaining why, how, and how well they learn language? Yes, but there is more. Integrationism suggests that these factors also continually shape what language is to different learners, i.e., what different words and expressions can and cannot mean, when silence does what language cannot or should not do (cf. Stein, 2007), the qualities of meaning-making that different modes of communication "afford" in view of different actions, circumstances, and perceived consequences.

In short, integrationism points to a pedagogical approach in which "language presupposes communication" (Harris, 1998, p. 5) rather than the other way around. It is an approach that addresses the needs of particularity by investigating the processes, contexts, and multiple modalities through which language learners make meaning and then reflecting on the nature of these processes and practices.

The terms "afford" and "affordance" index a related central principle of multiliteracies. Adapted from work in the fields of ecology and the psychology of perception (Gibson, 1977, 1979), *affordance* denotes the relation between the needs of an organism, the capacities of features of a given environment to serve these needs, and the organism's recognition of how these capacities might be activated. Within multiliteracies, affordance refers to "the question of potentials and limitations of a mode" (Kress, 2010, p. 84). Affordance, in this latter sense, is the means for gauging particularity. It asks questions such as "What, actually, is language like?", "What other means for meaning-making are there?", and "What are they like; what can they be used for; what can they do?" (Kress, 2010, p. 84). The answers to these questions speak directly to how and to what extent the English language fits within the overall meaning-making ecology of the EIL classroom.

Following on the above, it might seem that the needs of EIL (and language education generally) might be met through highlighting and teaching different characteristics and regularities of English*es* in different contexts; however, this too would be inadequate. Such an approach to EIL would only reproduce, in a finer-grained, fragmented form, the same hegemonies represented by a unitary English pedagogy. For Singaporeans, Koreans, and Latinos, for example, features of "Singlish," "Konglish," and "Spanglish" actually do not go much farther toward capturing what is meant and understood in "this instance using this constellation of resources for these purposes" than Standard British or American English would. A language pedagogical approach can and should be situated within larger meaning-design activities, and series of such activities, examining the meaning-making affordances of all forms of design— spoken-linguistic, written-linguistic, visual, audio, gestural, spatial, and multimodal (New London Group, 1996). In so doing, the often assumed equation of language with meaning itself can be dispelled, via meaning design work and engagement of semiotic awareness (Nelson, 2006, 2008) and a reflexive meta-perspective on language, situated within a larger frame of meaning-making and communication, can develop.

Recalling globalization and mediation, particularity becomes an increasingly vexed subject from an EIL perspective. How do we ensure particularity in situations where the learning and use of English and other languages is characterized by "global connection" and "local fragmentation"[3] (New London Group, 1996), where students may have had radically diverse experiences of language learning and use, and may be in far-flung locations even as we teach them (as in the case of distance learning)? A partial solution, perhaps, lies in seeing the utterances that we and our students produce not as more or less correct instantiations of a language code we commonly understand to be "English," for example, but rather as elements within larger multimodal designs for meaning-making. In this way, we are more apt to apprehend and appreciate the individual contextualizations of others, and thereby gain a fuller, more nuanced grasp of the needs of particularity.

Practicality

Kumaravadivelu's (2003) second parameter, interwoven with the first, is *practicality*, "which entails a teacher-generated theory of practice" and "recognizes that no theory of practice can be fully useful and usable unless it is generated through practice" (p. 35). In view of the above, we might ask what a practice-based theory-generating mechanism might look like.

Drawing upon van Manen's phenomenological take on teaching practice, Kumaravadivelu proposes that practicality is realized through "pedagogical thoughtfulness" (van Manen, 1991), practical theorizing developed reflexively through "action in thought and thought in action" (Kumaravadivelu, 2001, p. 541). As well, Kumaravadivelu advances the complementary notion of "sense-making," also adapted from van Manen (1977), which accounts for how teachers' intuitions and judgments become refined over time through synthesizing classroom experience with their own beliefs and values, their perceptions about institutional and societal constraints and learner expectations, and other factors that influence how teachers understand their work (p. 542). These processes are assumed to facilitate the validation of teacher-generated, practice-based theory.

What we find especially helpful and intriguing about Kumaravadivelu's prescription for generating theory through praxis is the crucial link between thought and action in teaching. We may take for granted that thought and action are inherently linked, but the question of *how* begs a semiotic answer. As signifying creatures, we understand the elements of our life-worlds not in terms of what they *are* in an objective sense, but what they *mean*, i.e., the implications and associations (e.g., causal, symbolic, metaphorical, indexical, intertextual) between them. Practical theories, essentially, are articulated explanations of experience-based, relational meanings.

So, as with particularity, the parameter of practicality is fundamentally semiotic; but practicality is distinguished from particularity by its emphasis not only on a teacher's valuation and awareness of learners' contextualized meaning-making, but on how this valuation and awareness can theoretically frame a personal pedagogy. "Pedagogical thoughtfulness," and the accrued intuition (i.e., "sense-making") that emerges out of it, is achieved by bringing to conscious attention the semiotic links between concrete experience and action and one's relational understandings of these links. Moreover, reflection upon the ways in which thought and action are mediated by texts, artifacts, spatial arrangements, etc. in the classroom and in the wider world is vital to unlocking the theoretical in the practical and the practical in the theoretical.

As a practical means of teasing out complex linkages between thought, action, text, and context, "A Pedagogy of Multiliteracies" advances the core pedagogical process of "critical framing." Critical framing is one component of a four-part program for literacy learning, also comprising "Situated Practice," "Overt Instruction," and "Transformed Practice" (New London Group, 1996, pp. 75–79).[4] Essentially, these four curricular components were conceived to guide learners through meaningful involvement in authentic tasks within a community of learners (Situated Practice), explicit introduction to new concepts and metalanguage (Overt Instruction), critical attention to the symbolic meanings, social positionings, and ideologies in discourse (Critical Framing), and recontextualizing and redesigning texts for contexts of communication other than those for which they were originally intended (Transformed Practice). Besides creative and effective communication, one goal of these curricular components is to foster explicit awareness of both the communicative and larger sociocultural contexts in all forms of meaning-making.

Of course, this brief sketch cannot do justice to the complexity of the "How" of multiliteracies. But for present purposes, we would draw special attention to the Critical Framing component, the linchpin of the entire process, whose aim is "to help learners to denaturalize and make strange again what they have learned and mastered" (New London Group, 1996, p. 78). Critical Framing involves mining the often unseen and taken-for-granted meaning potential in seemingly normal, obvious, and innocuous texts, actions, and interactions. The process of creating distance from the familiar, making it "strange again," is as useful for teachers themselves as it is for their charges.

We are put in mind of a learner of English in a Japanese university, Hazuki, who, in a course on multimedia narrative composing, authored a "digital story," incorporating English language, that described how busy and tired she felt given the responsibilities of school, a part-time job, maintaining her apartment, etc. (Nelson, 2007). In conjunction with the phrase "I have been busy these days because of ...," she deployed in her story a photo of then Japanese Prime Minister Junichiro Koizumi, who she deemed the person "busiest in Japan," and a suitable "visual definition" of "busyness" itself. Revisiting her piece even a few months after creating it, Hazuki would have seen that Koizumi, no longer Prime Minister, would no longer have expressed her semiotic intent as well; after finishing his term, he famously led a comparatively leisurely life. So we might see that the difference between analogy and irony in linguistic meaning can be just a matter of time. And scaffolding learners into making such critical realizations can help them to make the conceptual move from superficial, conventional understandings of meaning in language to nuanced, contextualized understandings (e.g., the situational, temporal specificity in the word "busy"). The teacher can also re-theorize her teaching approach on the basis of critically framing the meaning-making that the students do and her participation in it.

Critically examining the representational, ideological character of workaday routines and communication—treating these as meaning designs to be semiotically unpacked and subsequently redesigned and creatively transformed—is the means to fostering practicality in any pedagogical condition. But within an EIL framework, this kind of critical semiotic reflection is doubly important, for both teachers and students, in that the considerable diversity of varieties of English, life circumstances of users, and contexts of use imply an even greater degree of indeterminacy to the meanings of representations we might otherwise take for granted. EIL requires that we critically anticipate and semiotically construct the meaning designs of others, just as we become aware of our own.

Possibility

"Metamorphosing" out of the parameter of practicality is what Kumaravadivelu (2003) terms "possibility," which "is derived mainly from the works of critical pedagogists of Freirean persuasion" (p. 36), referencing, of course, the "problem-posing," liberation-oriented pedagogy of Paulo Freire (1970). "Possibility" attends to relations of power and control in language pedagogical situations and processes, recognizes "learners' and teachers' subject positions, that is, their class, race, gender and ethnicity" and calls for "sensitivity toward [these factors'] impact on education" (Kumaravadivelu, 2003, p. 36). On this score, Kumaravadivelu (2001) exhorts,

> language teachers can ill afford to ignore the sociocultural reality that influences identity formation in the classroom, nor can they afford to separate the linguistic needs of learners from their social needs. In other words, language teachers cannot hope to fully satisfy their pedagogic obligations without at the same time satisfying their social obligations.
>
> (p. 544)

Possibility, then, urges English teachers to ask, with and on behalf of their students, the uncomfortable, consequential question of "What is the point?" From a multiliteracies perspective, we might also ask "how are learning English, and being someone who knows English, related to designing a productive, fulfilling 'social future'?" For proponents of multiliteracies, learners' life-long satisfaction and full social participation are the point. The potential roles of languages and language learning in these processes of personal and social becoming remain to be considered.

Kumaravadivelu (2003) rightly points out that language and language learning are sites of contestation for individual subjectivity and social belonging (p. 37), the locus of identity work, and processes of self-authoring (Holland, Lachicotte, Skinner, & Cain, 1998). Still, to ascribe excessive credit to language for the discursive construction of selves would be a mistake, even though we are involved in language pedagogy; this would be to disregard the semiotic power of other modes of communication. Obviously, the semiotic currency of identity work is not merely linguistic; more and more, reflecting the abovementioned globalization and mediation, we see people around the world defining themselves and affiliating with one another through the mediation of photographic images, video, music, and other modes and media. But they do make use of language(s) too, in creative and multimodally combinative ways. The parameter of possibility, then, could usefully be rephrased to state that students' sociocultural needs cannot be separated from their *semiotic* needs, which account for how language, image, and all other modes of representation and communication position learners within relations of power and symbolically afford and constrain future possibilities and possible selves.

All of the above puts into question certain traditional goals of language teaching such as accuracy, fluency, and appropriateness. But the value of postmethod, postlinguistic teaching may be found elsewhere. We are not looking at language learning in the traditional sense of acquisition of morphosyntax or vocabulary, or even of academic writing. Rather, we are looking at learners' acquisition of a meta-communicative ability— the ability to reflect generally on signifying practices, and specifically on textualization and contextualization, considering language as one important dimension of semiosis among others.

What we are proposing is a relational pedagogy (Kern, forthcoming) whose central focus is on understanding relationships between forms, contexts, and meanings. A pedagogy whose aim is not just the learning of conventions and competencies but above all focused on the creative (and transformational) use of symbolic resources. A pedagogy not as much about "things" or "acquired knowledge" as about relations *between* things—between contexts, between people, between English and other languages, and between cultures.

Conclusion

In this chapter we have aimed to do several things. First, we have attempted to demonstrate that language educators have good reason to consider broadening their purview to include extra-linguistic forms of meaning-making as part of what they teach. Second, we set out to reconcile two frameworks that seek meaning both within and beyond language—integrationism and multiliteracies—with Kumaravadivelu's postmethod perspective to yield a pedagogical approach to EIL that highlights critical framing of situated practice. We have found that these perspectives are highly compatible in spirit, not because they share the same specific objectives and concerns, but because they each are founded on the understanding that knowledge, whether pedagogical, social, or semiotic, is constructed and transformed from the ground up. And in a world where that ground is constantly shifting—a globalized, mediated world such as that in which English and other languages are now taught and learned—brave re-conceptions of language must be formed that are compatible with the dynamic fluidity, contextual contingency, and fundamental multimodality of meaning-making.

The Postlinguistic Condition, then, is not a rejection of language, or of the importance of learning and teaching language. What it problematizes is a narrow traditional definition of what counts as the matter to be taught and learned. The field of English as an International Language has long acknowledged the rich diversity of forms, contexts, cultures, and ideologies associated with the label "English." What the Postlinguistic Condition calls for now is greater acknowledgment of how learning and using language—English or any other language—must be understood as embedded within broader processes of communication and action. We hope that this chapter offers one small step in that direction.

Exploring the Ideas

1 When we communicate linguistically, it is not just the dictionary meanings of words that count. If the communication is spoken, the sounds, the rhythms, the pacing of speech play an important role in constructing meaning. If it is written, the layout of the text, the typeface, the physical surface on which the writing is inscribed, and the means used to make the inscription all contribute to the construction of meaning. As we think about other modes, such as film, music, theater, dance, visual art ... what are some of the semiotic resources that contribute to the construction of meaning in EIL?

2 Harris (2009a) describes meanings as "values conferred upon signs by their role in articulating the integration of activities" (p. 76) and offers an example involving a driver and a tree. The tree has no meaning per se, but because it marks the point where the driver typically turns left on his way home, it is assigned a "semiological value"—it is made a sign that means "turn left here." But this tree-sign only has this meaning insofar as it is integrated within a particular activity sequence performed by a particular driver. Choose a routine that you regularly carry out, and think about the objects, locations, etc. to which you

assign semiological value. Would the values of these signs be different if the routine were changed in some way? In this case, how might you think and speak differently about these objects and places?

3   The parameter of possibility fosters the imagining and semiotic construction of possible worlds and selves. For your EIL students, what aspects of identity do you think are easiest and/or best expressed in written language with pen and paper? How about in a photograph? Under what circumstances might these assumptions not be true?

Applying the Ideas

1   Record a face-to-face conversation, and compare it with a chat or IM or online videoconferencing interaction, looking at the role of mediation. In the face-to-face interaction consider language, timing, gesture, body posture and movement, clothing, hairstyle, surrounding people, and surrounding happenings. In the online interactions, consider language, timing, spatial arrangement, emoticons, abbreviations (and gesture, body language, clothing, etc. in the videoconferencing). How does language interact with nonverbal resources? Which of these things are you normally most conscious of? Which are you normally least conscious of? See if your analysis of the normally unconscious features makes you more aware of these things in your future online and offline interactions.

2   Think about ways that point of view can be expressed in language versus in film. Pick a scene of a novel that has been made into a film, and compare it feature by feature with the corresponding scene in the film. Whose point of view is expressed? How is it expressed? Does it change during the scene? If so, how is the shift marked? How might a director express in film what an author expresses in an interior monologue written in free indirect discourse?

3   Compare essay writing versus blogging versus creating a website. In each activity, what balance of the total communicative load gets handled via language compared to other modes? How do modes interact in helping you create meaning? How does the communicative load get handled differently across different languages or language varieties that you are familiar with?

Notes

1   These statistics were generated by Inside Network (http://gold.insidenetwork.com/ facebook/), but reported in the technology blog *Inside Social Games* (Morrison, 2010).

2   For one example, see Malinowski and Nelson (2011)

3 These terms take account of the presently observable condition in which people around the world are connected via technology to other people and in ways they would otherwise likely not be, while concomitantly being less directly or deeply involved with their more immediate (physical) neighbors.
4 These four curricular components were renamed by Cope and Kalantzis (2009) as Experiencing, Conceptualizing, Analyzing, and Applying—terms which we find overly general and less useful in guiding pedagogical practices than the original terms.

References

Appadurai, A. (1996). *Modernity at large: Cultural dimensions of globalization.* Minneapolis, MN: University of Minnesota Press.

Cope, B., & Kalantzis, M. (2009). "Multiliteracies": New literacies, new learning. *Pedagogies, 4*(3), 164–195.

Couldry, N. (2008). Digital storytelling, media research and democracy: Conceptual choices and alternative futures. In K. Lundby (Ed.), *Digital storytelling, mediatized stories: Self-representations in new media* (pp.123–141). New York: Peter Lang.

Davis, D. R. (2009). Language learning, grammar and integrationism. In M. Toolan (Ed.), *Language teaching: Integrational linguistic approaches* (pp. 73–87). New York and Oxford: Routledge.

Freire, P. (1970). *Pedagogy of the oppressed.* New York: Continuum.

Gibson, J. J. (1977). The theory of affordances. In R. E. Shaw & J. Brandsford (Eds.), *Perceiving, acting, and knowing* (pp. 67–82). Hillsdale, NJ: Lawrence Erlbaum.

Gibson, J. J. (1979). *The ecological approach to visual perception.* Boston, MA: Houghton Mifflin.

Giddens, A. (1990). *The consequences of modernity.* Stanford, CA: Stanford University Press.

Halliday, M. A. K. (1978). *Language as social semiotic: The social interpretation of language and meaning.* London: Edward Arnold.

Harris, R. (1995). *Signs of writing.* London: Routledge.

Harris, R. (1998). *Introduction to integrational linguistics.* Oxford, UK: Elsevier Science.

Harris, R. (2001). *Rethinking writing.* London: Continuum.

Harris, R. (2009a). The integrational concept of the sign. In R. Harris (Ed.), *Integrationist notes and papers: 2006–2008* (pp. 61–81). Bedfordshire, UK: Authors Online Ltd.

Harris, R. (2009b). Implicit and explicit language teaching. In M. Toolan (Ed.), *Language Teaching: Integrational linguistic approaches* (pp. 24–46). New York: Routledge.

Harris, R. (2010). *Integrationism: A brief introduction.* Retrieved from http://www. royharrisonline.com/integrational_linguistics/integrationism_introduction. html#aims_integrational_linguistics

Hodge, R., & Kress, G. (1988). *Social semiotics.* Ithaca, NY: Cornell University Press.

Holland, D., Lachicotte, W. J., Skinner, D., & Cain, C. (1998). *Identity and agency in cultural worlds.* Cambridge, MA: Harvard University Press.

Hutton, C. (2009). Grammaticality and the English teacher in Hong Kong: And integrational analysis. In M. Toolan (Ed.), *Language teaching: Integrational linguistic approaches* (pp. 88–103). New York and Oxford: Routledge.

Jewitt, C. (2009). An introduction to multimodality. In C. Jewitt (Ed.), *The Routledge handbook of multimodal analysis* (pp. 14–27). London: Routledge.

Kern, R. (2000). *Literacy and language teaching.* Oxford, UK: Oxford University Press.

Kern, R. (in preparation). *Language, technology, and literacy.*

Kramsch, C. (2002). Introduction: "How can we tell the dancer from the dance?" In C. Kramsch (Ed.), *Language acquisition and language socialization: Ecological perspectives* (pp. 1–29). London: Continuum.

Kramsch, C. (2008). Ecological perspectives on foreign language education. *Language Teaching, 41*(3), 389–408.

Kress, G. (2003). *Literacy in the new media age.* London: Routledge.

Kress, G. (2010). *Multimodality: A social semiotic approach to contemporary communication.* London: Routledge.

Kress, G., & van Leeuwen, T. (1996/2006). *Reading images: The grammar of visual design.* London: Routledge.

Kumaravadivelu, B. (1994). The postmethod condition: (E)merging strategies for second/foreign language teaching. *TESOL Quarterly, 28*(1), 27–50.

Kumaravadivelu, B. (2001). Toward a postmethod pedagogy. *TESOL Quarterly, 35*(4), 537–560.

Kumaravadivelu, B. (2003). *Beyond methods: Macrostrategies for language teaching.* New Haven, CT: Yale University Press.

Malinowski, D., & Nelson, M. E. (2011). What now for language in a multimedial world? In C. Ho, A. Anderson, & A. Leong (Eds.), *Transforming literacies and language: Multimodality and literacy in the new media age* (pp. 51–68). London: Continuum.

Morrison, C. (June 25, 2010). *Inside English use in Indonesia, Facebook's third largest country.* Retrieved from http://www.insidesocialgames.com/2010/06/25/inside-english-use-in-indonesia-facebooks-third-largest-country/

Nelson, M. E. (2006). Mode, meaning, and synaesthesia in multimedia L2 writing. *Language Learning and Technology, 10*(2), 56–76.

Nelson, M. E. (2007). *Designing synthesis in image and word: Multimodal composing in a Japanese university context.* Unpublished doctoral dissertation, University of California, Berkeley.

Nelson, M. E. (2008). Multimodal synthesis and the "voice" of the multimedia author in a Japanese EFL context. *Innovation in Language Learning and Teaching, 2*(1), 65–82.

New London Group. (1996). A pedagogy of multiliteracies: Designing social futures. *Harvard Educational Review 66*(1), 60–92.

Schön, D. (1983). *The reflective practitioner: How professionals think in action.* New York: Basic Books.

Silverstone, R. (2002). Complicity and collusion in the mediation of everyday life. *New Literary History, 33*(4), 745–764.

Stein, P. (2007). *Multimodal pedagogies in diverse classrooms: Representation, rights and resources.* London: Routledge.

Street, B. (1995). *Social literacies: Critical approaches to literacy in development, ethnography, and education.* London: Longman.

Toolan, M. (Ed.). (2009). *Language teaching: Integrational linguistic approaches.* New York: Routledge.

van Leeuwen, T. (1999). *Speech, music, sound.* New York: St. Martin's Press.

van Leeuwen, T. (2005). *Introducing social semiotics.* London: Routledge.

van Lier, L. (2004). *The ecology and semiotics of language learning: A sociocultural perspective.* Norwell, MA: Kluwer Academic Publishers.

van Manen, M. (1977). Linking ways of knowing with ways of being practical. *Curriculum Inquiry, 6*(3), 205–228.

van Manen, M. (1991). *The tact of teaching: The meaning of pedagogical thoughtfulness.* Albany: State University of New York Press.

Yule, G. (1996). *Pragmatics.* Oxford: Oxford University Press.

Chapter 5

The Use of Digital Media in Teaching English as an International Language

Paige Ware, Meei-Ling Liaw, and Mark Warschauer

The use of digital media in language learning has its roots in individualized computer-based drill and practice activities to assist learners in mastering grammar, vocabulary, and pronunciation (for a historical overview, see Warschauer, 1996). Later, computer-based activities were designed to stimulate authentic communication, but the computer was still viewed as an occasional tool to promote learning rather than as an integral medium of language and literacy. In this chapter, we discuss a newer approach to technology in teaching English as an international language (EIL), in which digital media become essential tools of global interaction and global literacy. In this approach, mastery of language, mastery of new technologies, and the ability to combine language and technology to read and write the world become inseparable goals of the international English language classroom. Students deploy a variety of autonomous learning tools, such as concordancers and automated scoring engines, and an even greater variety of communication tools, from Skype and podcasts to blogging and microblogging, to hone their language and literacy skills as they use English to interact with others, publish their work, and leave their mark on society. Traditional goals of accuracy and fluency get expanded to include global agency, that is, the power to make meaningful choices and see the results of those choices both near and far. These forms of global communication and agency match well with the context of international English, in which the ability to meaningfully interact in diverse media with speakers of many varieties of English from around the world takes precedence over mastery of a more narrowly defined set of skills, such as achievement of native-like pronunciation.

We view practices of global literacy, interaction, and agency as situated within new technological developments, changing social norms, evolving modes of production and consumption, and competing social, economic, and political forces. We thus consider literacy within a *power* framework (Warschauer & Ware, 2008), which emphasizes that the goal of literacy instruction should be to enable individuals and communities to participate in the creation and exchange of meaning for greater "civic, economic, and personal participation in a world community" (Coiro, Knobel, Lankshear, & Leu, 2008, p. 14). We explore the various resources and challenges of incorporating digital media within the context of teaching EIL so that students develop the multiple and multimodal literacies necessary for this participation. We suggest that teachers consider how digital media might be incorporated into their local contexts so as to foster not just the skills associated with language proficiency, but also the knowledge and attitudes needed to participate fully in an interconnected, global society.

Digital Media and the EIL Classroom: Traditional Principles and Practices

In this section, we explore digital media in EIL classrooms that are organized around more traditional principles and practices in a skills-based approach to instruction. In some contexts, for example, pedagogical decisions might be made with an eye on efficiently preparing students for gate-keeping exams or on assisting them within a pre-determined curricular scope and sequence. Even within these scenarios, however, instructors can use digital media to help learners develop language skills in tandem with fostering their autonomy and creativity and with preparing them to engage in and communicate with others outside of the classroom.

One key question related to digital media in the EIL classroom concerns the development of appropriate materials. Too often, English curricular materials rely on importing resources that flow uni-directionally and uncritically from Western countries (Canagarajah, 1999). In discussing the need for materials designers to develop resources that more flexibly incorporate local cultures and intercultural mindsets, McKay (2002) forwarded a vision of the EIL classroom as "an international community *par excellence*" (p. 99, italics in original). Such an international community need not be grounded in Western, English-speaking countries, nor would it necessarily prioritize local cultures; rather, it should provide space for multiple converging and contested voices in English from around the world to interact. For teachers, then, the design of such materials, even within a skills-based approach, involves emphasizing opportunities for critical engagement with content, while also avoiding the primacy of predominantly English-speaking countries' cultural materials.

Digital media offer a number of ways to enhance materials development and learner feedback across the traditional skills (for an extended discussion, see Levy, 2009). In reading, for example, Chun (2006) reviewed a number of technologies available to support reading in a second language, some of which are available non-commercially such as electronic and online dictionaries, hyperlinks to vocabulary words that are embedded within many online texts, or the use of the Internet to obtain a wider range of sources. She also points to software that can provide annotations through multimedia and promote word recognition. A few examples of such support at the secondary education level include e-Lective (Cummins, 2008) and Text Adaptor from Educational Testing Services (2010), both of which allow teachers to quickly translate grade-level texts into language appropriate for their English language learners. Visual-syntactic text formatting via Live Ink software also can make authentic English language materials more comprehensible to learners (Walker, Schloss, Fletcher, Vogel, & Walker, 2005). While these commercial products are unlikely to be currently available for many EIL teachers, they suggest a possible trend in the near future and also point to other types of textual supports that teachers can create themselves with the Internet. Simple English Wikipedia (http://simple.wikipedia.org), for example, provides texts with less complex syntax and reduced vocabulary and can be used as a supplemental resource for reading materials on a wide range of topics.

For fostering writing, digital media provide numerous options to support writing when the focus is primarily on formal features of written language in traditional classrooms. For grammar instruction, teachers can access any number of websites that provide individualized practice of grammar (cf., Purdue Online Writing Lab, http://owl.english.purdue. edu), or they can create their own vocabulary and grammar activities using freeware such as Hot Potatoes (http://hotpot.uvic.ca), which allows instructors to create different types of online activities (e.g., multiple choice, short answer, jumbled text, crossword) and post them to the Internet. Even as word processing has become more commonplace in the classroom, features such as tracking changes and embedding comments are now receiving more widespread attention as options for teacher or peer feedback (Ho & Savignon, 2007). Automated writing evaluation software programs offer options for individualized, immediate feedback to students as they learn to revise their essays (Warschauer & Ware, 2006); such programs are designed to promote formal writing within a relatively narrow range of genres and organizing structures, which may be more or less appropriate in different contexts and will manifest differently depending on the degree of integration into instruction (Warschauer & Grimes, 2008). While using these resources, it is important to keep in mind that EIL includes a multitude of legitimate grammatical and rhetorical variations, so teachers who are familiar with the local nativized variety may advise their students when it would be appropriate to use a particular grammatical feature or rhetorical pattern of the standard or the nativized variety (McKay, 2002).

Listening and speaking skills can be augmented using digital media through computer tools that provide individualized feedback on speaking and options for learner-controlled listening activities (Levy, 2009). Key to such tutorial approaches is the manner in which feedback is provided and the degree of sophistication of the computer-based feedback. Some programs, such as pronunciation software for Japanese learners of English studied by Tsubota, Dantsuji, and Kawahara (2004), target particular groups of native-language learners and are designed to identify cross-linguistic transfer areas that are particularly troublesome and in need of further practice. Many Internet-based listening supports are available in the form of websites that allow students to control the speed, to pause, or to repeat segments of speech. The Internet also offers access to a wide range of examples of English speakers that can provide learners with practice in listening to a variety of authentic intonation patterns, rhythms, stress, and segmentation (see, e.g., http://EnglishCentral.com).

In addition to these tutorial-based options, teachers use technology to help learners practice listening and speaking skills with more interactive tools. Podcasting, the creation and sharing of audio files on the web, has received much attention recently, as it can be used to promote listening and speaking skills (O'Bryan & Hegelheimer, 2007) by allowing students to download a wide variety of authentic materials or to create and upload their own files for audiences within and outside the classroom. Hegelheimer and O'Bryan (2009) recently reviewed many podcast resources available to teachers, such as ESLpod.com, which provides free files and help with listening skills in a range of areas from test preparation to academic listening for note-taking purposes. Digital media allow students to record and review their own speech, to speak with others at no cost via online voicemail and synchronous tools, to create audioblogs, and to participate in voiced bulletin boards. Such uses create a learner-centered environment that can enhance students' agency by making available listening content that would otherwise not be obtained, legitimizing diverse varieties of English, and allowing learners to contribute and critique their own content. In sum, these tools can be used to provide students with exposure to a wide range of pronunciation patterns to help them recognize the differences between accents and thus to enhance their receptive competence and their communicative competence in EIL.

The use of digital media, even within the context of more traditional practices, can resituate the goals of classroom instruction to be aimed not at mastery of a discrete set of English-language skills, but at the *use* of those skills within more meaningful, enriching contexts by offering local control of materials, individualized feedback, and personalization of learning. The classroom then becomes a place in which students are exposed to a rich set of autonomous learning tools for English development inside and outside the classroom, from audioblogs and automated software programs to hyperlinked dictionaries and podcasts.

Global Literacy: EIL Classrooms Inside a Changing World

We now examine more explicit attempts to foster global literacy. Such attempts respond to social and economic globalization, which has heightened the interdependence and interconnectedness among nations and people and has imposed a demand for an international means of communication. As Crystal (2003) has noted,

> there are no precedents in human history for what happens to languages in such circumstances of rapid change. There has never been a time when so many nations were needing to talk to each other so much … And there never has been a more urgent need for a global language.
>
> (p. 14)

English has taken up this role as the first global language, used worldwide for tourism, commerce, negotiation, and science, beyond its connection to individual countries and cultures (Alptekin, 2002; Crystal, 2003; Graddol, 2006; Paradowski, 2008). Although the 6.2% of the world population who speak English as their primary language is relatively small in comparison to the 20.7% who speak Chinese, the global influence of English is compounded by many factors, including the number of secondary speakers, the economic power associated with English, the social and cultural prestige of the language, and the distribution of English across areas of commercial activity and tourism (Weber, 2008). The shift to English as an international language is, arguably, both shaped by and a shaping force for globalization. As Graddol (2006) points out, "the phenomenon of English being a global language lies at the heart of globalization" (p. 12).

In particular, the development and diffusion of information and communication technologies have gone hand in hand with the spread of global English (Graddol, 1997; McKay & Bokhorst-Heng, 2008; Warschauer & De Florio-Hansen, 2003). In 2010, an estimated 27.3% of global total Internet usage was in English, followed by 22.6% in Chinese, dropping to single digits for all other languages (Miniwatts Marketing Group, 2010). Internet use among other languages, including Chinese, Arabic, and Russian, has also grown substantially in recent years. While the rapid growth of Internet use among other languages, together with the development of more sophisticated and efficient translation tools, may signal an eventual challenge to the rapid spread of English, English has already spread so extensively that its foothold as an international language is likely to be secure for a long time to come. There are still major incentives for individuals to learn English to send and receive information on the Internet and to interact with a global audience (see discussion in McKay, 2002). Currently, English, coupled with the communicative power of technology, is being used as a means for speakers to share ideas and cultures, and perhaps more importantly, to express their identity and to "make their voices heard" (Warschauer, 2000, p. 530), and this combined influence of English and digital media is likely to gain even more momentum in the coming years.

Just as digital media are helping shape the role of English as an international language, so too are they shifting EIL classrooms from a focus on mastery of skills to an emphasis on using English to communicate and engage with speakers of varieties of English using a wide range of media. English learners are now seen as global communicators, sharers of local cultures, arbiters of misunderstandings, and valued contributors to a growing global community. Communication skills therefore take on a new importance for English teaching (Cameron, 2002; Cortazzi, 2000), as the Internet provides a social environment that students enter with increasing frequency outside of the classroom. In this environment, many students typically use English rather than their first language for their interactions (Warschauer, 2001). When digital media are used to support integration of language skills within a larger communicative purpose, then other aspects of language use come to the fore: agency, identity, authenticity, and authorship (Kramsch, A'Ness, & Lam, 2000). Research exploring these aspects has primarily been conducted on non-institutional settings and provides a starting point in this chapter before we discuss implications for the EIL classroom.

Non-institutional Online EIL Communication

In many parts of the world and across a wide range of social classes, technology-mediated activity has become a part of everyday life. Apart from being used as a proxy or practice medium for real-world communication, electronic communication has become a high-stakes, high-frequency context for all kinds of professional, academic, and social activity (Thorne, Black, & Sykes, 2009). This means that, more often than not, technology-mediated EIL communication takes place outside, not inside, the classroom.

The link between the development of English as an international language and globalization is most evident in the business context.

English is regarded as the corporate language of many multinational companies, including a number that are headquartered outside official English-speaking countries. However, even though speakers of English in business settings share the international business culture, they usually differ in their personal, cultural, and linguistic backgrounds. Since ownership of English does not belong to any particular group (McKay, 2002), it becomes necessary for its users to appreciate a range of both English and discourse practices. Louhiala-Salminen, Charles, and Kankaanranta (2005) examined the discourse similarities and differences between Swedish and Finnish interactants by looking into the email communication between the two groups in a business context. Although they found generic similarities in terms of the form, content, communicative purpose, and linguistic characteristics in the email messages, they also uncovered that Finnish writers favored more direct requests, and Swedish writers used more indirect alternatives. For the two companies studied, the adoption of business EIL helped employees cope in the post-merger communication challenge. They suggested a construct called *culture three*, neither Swedish nor Finnish, that seemed to facilitate communication between the two groups in this context. In other words, online communication between EIL speakers of different nationalities provided opportunities to negotiate differences and to exercise communication skills.

The use of English for online communities in which interactants are global users is of course not limited to business contexts. For example, Cassell and Tversky (2005) examined the interaction that took place among 3,062 children from 139 countries in the Junior Summit '98, an international online community in which participants discussed global issues. The data set consisted of messages posted by the children who participated independently and chose English as their primary language of communication over a three-month period. Findings from word frequency counts (including singular and collective pronouns, apologies, references to the future, hedges, and WH questions) and content analyses indicated that the participants from very different cultural, linguistic, and socio-economic backgrounds in this online forum increasingly referred to themselves as a community; they spoke in the collective voice; and they concurred on the topics of conversation, the goals of the community, as well as their strategies for achieving them. In the meantime, the participants reported an increase in their appreciation for diversity, their ability to see different perspectives, and their positive reactions to one another.

Research examining such non-institutional contexts indicates that interacting in EIL can be different from interacting in other foreign languages because of English's lack of dominance by native speakers.

Through appropriation of English, EIL speakers often assert their sense of self and take ownership of the language (Ha, 2009), repositioning their own identity in the process. For example, Lam (2000) examined a Chinese immigrant teenager's correspondence with a transnational group of peers on the Internet and documented how this correspondence related to his identity formation and literacy development in ESL. Her findings reveal that although her Chinese-American subject, Almon, felt alienated in the classroom where standard American English was enforced, he obtained a newfound confidence and solidarity when communicating in his own variety of English with his multilingual Internet peers. Another study by Lam (2004) documents the socialization of two bilingual immigrant Chinese girls in a chat room in which participants developed a hybrid language variety that set them apart from both their English-only peers and their Cantonese-only peers. Similarly, Bloch (2004) has shown how Chinese students incorporate Chinese rhetorical forms in English when communicating in an online group, thereby creating a hybrid form of "world rhetoric" (p. 78). He concluded that the Internet provides a space in which EIL speakers can take control of discourse for their own purposes.

To summarize, digital media use outside the classroom provides learners with an additional source of global exposure to English as well as new resources to represent local identities and values (Canagarajah, 2006). Individuals socialize and construct online communities by appropriating the discursive and rhetorical styles commonly shared or deemed appropriate by members of the particular community. Identity construction and socialization are of course inherently intertwined with language. What shifts when using digital media is the focus on the skills of reading, writing, speaking, and listening in English to also include abilities to negotiate new roles and identities (Kern, 2006). In the EIL classroom context, this shift has most frequently occurred to date in online communication projects that cross geographic lines, opening the classroom up as a place for learners to have a global presence as they communicate with others using digital media, and it is to these international online projects within the classroom that we now turn.

Global Interaction: The EIL Classroom as Presence and Participation

In recent years researchers have examined the uses of digital media in bringing together language learners of different historical and cultural trajectories to meet and interact with each other (Alcón Soler, 2007). When these interactions take place through class-to-class partnerships among distally located students, they are commonly referred to as telecollaboration. Early research on telecollaboration often involved bilingual partnerships between two classes in which each side was learning the language of the partner class. This model followed tandem (Brammerts, 1996) learning principles that relied on learner autonomy and reciprocity in providing opportunities to practice language, provide feedback, and share personal and cultural information. Many studies discuss the purpose of such international partnerships not only as an opportunity to practice linguistic structures, but also as a venue for learners to "attempt to deal (sometimes successfully, other times less so) with specific communicative situations and with the linguistic, cognitive, social, and material resources available to them" (Kern, 2006, p. 189). Thus sharing personal ideas and developing intercultural competence may be more important in such exchanges than developing second language accuracy.

A second wave of research on telecollaboration is currently underway, in which telecollaboration is conducted in a lingua franca, often English, and preliminary findings from these projects suggest a promising direction for EIL classrooms. Two studies involving adult learners, for example, suggest that telecollaboration within an EIL context promotes student motivation, satisfaction, and intercultural learning. Fedderholdt (2001) linked a group of Japanese university students and a group of Danish students for online communication in English. The results showed that the interest levels of the students were high; interacting with someone from a different culture and learning about it was both enjoyable and rewarding to the participants. The students involved also reflected on how superficial and stereotypical their impressions had been about each other's cultures prior to the project. They reported that reading their counterpart's English was inspiring, as they mutually admired each other's English. Similarly, Keranen and Bayyurt (2006) found positive results in their English-language discussion board exchange between native Spanish-speaking in-service teachers and native Turkish-speaking pre-service teachers who engaged in conversations about features of their own cultures. Participants regarded the exchange positively, were well disposed towards the other culture, and demonstrated an interest and willingness to express personal opinions.

Positive results have been reported at the elementary and secondary levels. In a project called International Virtual Elementary Classroom Activities (IVECA), three classes of students in an American school and three classes in Korean schools engaged in online exchange to promote intercultural communication (O'Neill, 2007). Results showed that the students, particularly the more problematic ones, improved their intercultural competence, their motivation to learn at school, and their writing skills. In a mixed methods study linking young learners in an

English-language international blogging project, Ware and Rivas (2011) found that 12- and 13-year-old partners in Spain and in the United States made statistically significant gains in writing fluency and scored higher on a culture survey vis-à-vis a control group that did not participate in the project. Finally, in a recent project that focused on intercultural learning over linguistic accuracy, Liaw and English (2010) report on their multi-year, computer-mediated intercultural collaboration between French and Taiwanese EIL students. Their project used tasks designed to foster participants' awareness of cultural identities, their willingness to express personal opinions, and their knowledge of *self* and *otherness*. Participants noted that because both groups of learners would be using their imperfect English, they were less self-conscious about making errors and thus more engaged in active communication. Findings indicate an increase in communicative fluency as well as in students' intercultural competence as they engaged in tasks in which they openly compared and contrasted their cultures without much anxiety about making language mistakes.

While these examples show that telecollaboration can support EIL learner engagement, intercultural learning, and communicative fluency, other studies provide cautionary notes pertaining to logistical, institutional, and cultural constraints. Basharina (2007) reports on an ambitious post-secondary, multi-site EIL project among 52 Japanese students, 37 Mexican students, and 46 Russian students who communicated asynchronously through discussion boards for a 12-week period. Using an activity theory lens, she identified several contradictions that occurred as the result of various layers of difference pertaining to register, genre, topic choice, levels of participation, technological access, and instructional context. She concludes by discussing how such differences across multiple layers might be bridged. In another multi-site cross-cultural writing project, which involved college instructors and undergraduate students in Ukraine, Russia, and Saudi Arabia, Al-Jarf (2006) showed that the participants shared common interests and points of view on global culture, and they increased their respect through the project for differences in belief and tradition. However, the findings also acknowledge the tremendous effort made by the instructors to create and maintain the telecollaboration, due to the diverse levels of their students in language proficiency and computer skills as well as frequent obstacles in accessing computers and the Internet. Such challenges are widely documented in the literature on telecollaboration (cf. Belz, 2002; Kern, Ware, & Warschauer, 2004; O'Dowd & Ritter, 2006; Ware, 2005). They serve as reminders of the uneven access to digital media in different parts of the world and highlight the important roles of instructors in telecollaboration (Belz, 2005).

Pedagogical Implications: Instructors and Learners Using Digital Media

International English serves not only to conduct business and transmit information, but also to exchange ideas in a constant flow of movement and interaction across cultures (McKay, 2002). To help learners accomplish this kind of communication, McKay posits three overarching goals for the EIL teacher: help students analyze interactional language for its potential to confuse or criticize, build strategies for maintaining amicable relationships across discourse communities, and develop competencies across diverse genres and rhetorical styles. In using digital media, whether solely within the classroom context or as part of a telecollaborative project, teachers can promote all three of these goals as they show learners how to engage with, evaluate, and independently use new technologies to support autonomous learning, and as they help learners interpret, analyze, and maintain interaction across linguistic, cultural, geographic, and technological lines.

The instructor plays a key role in deciding how digital media are used. When using any of the new technologies discussed above that support skills instruction, for example, instructors must sometimes dedicate time to learn to use the new technologies involved. Materials development of any kind takes time, and weaving in new content or activities into existing syllabi requires creativity and conviction. When designing online interaction projects, intensive coordination is often required, including the alignment of partner class syllabi around shared information and the choice of media to support collaborative interpretive and investigative activities (Helm, 2009). Belz and Mueller-Hartmann (2003) have documented how instructors themselves must engage in intercultural encounters with other teachers as they develop telecollaborative projects. In this endeavor, teachers must constantly negotiate *faultlines* (p. 71), in which their own unarticulated assumptions about language, culture, expectations, and pedagogy may cause friction and require mediation and exploration. In addition to having expert knowledge of culturally specific discourse patterns for the successful negotiation of learning in telecollaboration, instructors may also need to overcome shortages in media resources and to ensure student readiness for online learning (Pillay, Irving, & McCrindle, 2006).

The power of digital media in the classroom stems in part from its potential to bridge in-class activities with out-of-class use, to blur the lines between formal instruction and informal learning, and to validate the wide range of registers and uses of English on the global scene. Researchers have documented the multiple ways in which language learners, including EIL learners, participate in out-of-school digital engagement, putting technology to use in personally meaningful ways so as to act upon the world (for reviews, see Thorne, 2006; Thorne, Black, & Sykes, 2009). Conole's study (2008) of two students and their technology use offers an illustration of the magnitude of new technologies in many learners' lives. The two focal students routinely used over 30 different technologies for both personal and educational purposes. These same two technology-savvy students can be imagined in a study by Canagarajah (1999), in which EIL students resisted the marginalization of Western-infused English textbooks by "glossing texts with drawings and words that clearly illustrate their opposition" (p. 95). Their resistance, if inscribed with digital media by a broadcast on a podcast or through writing in a blog, could have resulted in having a voice on a much more amplified scale.

When EIL classrooms move away from only teaching English language skills and toward also fostering attitudes and knowledge for global communication, then learners become ambassadors of their local contexts. Notions of intercultural citizenship (Byram, 2010) and of intercultural speakers (Belz & Thorne, 2006; Kramsch, 1998) become increasingly important as learners must develop a culturally sensitive, critical stance toward global literacy and interaction. As forums open up for instantaneous communication and multimodal production, learners in the EIL classroom grapple with real interactions, in which the messages they send and receive—the literal, linguistic meaning as well as the symbolic and cultural import underneath the words—position them as representatives of their communities and cultural groups. In this process, global agency is tied together with ethical responsibility and with the need to develop what Kramsch (2009) calls *symbolic competence*, a construct that "does not do away with the ability to express, interpret, and negotiate meanings in dialogue with others, but enriches it and embeds it into the ability to produce and exchange symbolic goods in the complex global context" (p. 251).

Conclusion

Given the diverse range of contexts in which EIL is taught, the options provided by digital media must acknowledge several challenges and constraints. First, access to technological tools and support differs across contexts in terms of the ratios of computers to students, access to technology outside of the classroom, and availability of broadband Internet connectivity. Second, there is a continuum of professional development that influences how teachers can integrate digital media, including the allocation of time for instructors to gain exposure to and expertise with particular tools through in-service training, the availability of technological and pedagogical support, and the existence of collegial support for sharing ideas and for developing collective expertise. Third, the degree to which instructors have control over their curriculum and their classroom logistics influences how and why digital media might become part of the classroom; some instructors, for example, might be assigned a focus on supporting the development of one or more discrete skills with an emphasis on preparation for high-stakes formal assessment, whereas others might teach an elective, integrated skills course focused on intercultural communication. Finally, the needs and backgrounds of students differ widely both across and within contexts, so instructors must situate their choices with an understanding of how much differentiation might be required.

Together, these four continua shape the choices that EIL instructors can make within their local contexts, and along these continua, digital media provide multiple options for teachers to draw upon as they shape their classrooms into places that prepare learners for global literacy in English and that provide them with a forum to have a global presence in English. Ultimately, digital media can help teachers enhance what they themselves view as appropriate pedagogy. Given the great diversity of contexts, resources, and challenges associated with teaching EIL, teachers must rely on what Prabhu (1990) has called their "sense of plausibility" (p. 172) as they discover how particular affordances and challenges of different forms of digital media might be integrated into the EIL classroom.

Exploring the Ideas

1 A recurring theme in this chapter is that traditional goals of skills-centered language instruction should be expanded to include the goal of fostering knowledge and attitudes that allow learners to purposefully communicate as global citizens. What might an emphasis beyond the traditional skills look like in practice? To what extent might traditional skills get folded into larger goals or instead be revised or replaced?

2 In discussions of how email and texting are changing traditional communication, individuals often point to shifting communication norms and to the gradual development of new rules about what is considered appropriate communication. In the global context, such discussions are arguably even more complex, in that locally shared cultural and social communication styles also influence rules of appropriateness. What do the ideas in this chapter suggest about how communication skills might be defined in the context of digital media use and EIL?

3 The chapter mentions that the growth of technology use across many languages may eventually pose a challenge to the rapid spread of

English as an international language. Why does the chapter suggest that such a shift is not likely to happen soon, and what are possible reasons why such a challenge may eventually arise?

Applying the Ideas

1 The chapter argues that, in the EIL classroom, teachers' development and use of original materials can provide students with opportunities for critical engagement with diverse content without solely relying on materials that reflect the culture and perspectives of a handful of English-speaking countries. In your own context, critically analyze the types of materials that you and your colleagues typically rely on and make suggestions as to how you might use digital media to offer more local control of materials development.

2 The chapter suggests some websites and other digital resources that can be used in instruction. Browse a selection of these resources to examine in greater detail what each has to offer, and then develop an instructional plan that demonstrates how you might integrate some of these resources into your teaching. Reflect on which types of resources you gravitate toward, then revisit the reasons suggested in the conclusion about why teachers might find integration of digital media challenging (e.g., time and opportunity for professional development, control over the curriculum, limited access to technology). Consider how, in your own teaching context, you might work to overcome any of these challenges in an effort to integrate digital media.

3 Research has given much attention to non-classroom and non-institutional contexts in which EIL is used. How can teachers learn more about their students' familiarity with and use of such non-classroom communication? How might teachers then utilize such knowledge about their students' English language uses outside of class in order to support within-classroom learning?

References

Alcón Soler, E. (2007). Linguistic unity and cultural diversity in Europe: Implications for research on English language and learning. In E. A. Soler & M. P. Safont Jordà (Eds.), *Intercultural language use and language learning* (pp. 23–40). Dordrecht, the Netherlands: Springer.

Al-Jarf, R. S. (2006). Cross-cultural communication: Saudi, Ukrainian, and Russian students online. *The Asia EFL Journal Quarterly, 8*(2), 7–32.

Alptekin, C. (2002). Towards intercultural communicative competence in ELT. *ELT Journal, 56*(1), 57–64.

Basharina, O. (2007). An activity theory perspective on student-reported contradictions in international telecollaboration. *Language Learning & Technology, 11*(2), 36–58.

Belz, J. A. (2002). Social dimensions of telecollaborative foreign language study. *Language Learning & Technology, 6*(1), 60–81.

Belz, J. (2005). The telecollaborative language study: A personal overview of praxis and research. In I. Thompson & D. Hiple (Eds.), *Selected papers from the 2005 NFLRC symposium: Distance education, distributed learning, and language instruction.* Honolulu, HI: University of Hawai'i National Foreign Language Resource Center. Retrieved December 20, 2010 from http://nflrc. hawaii.edu/NetWorks /NW44/belz.htm

Belz, J. A., & Mueller-Hartmann, A. (2003). Teachers as intercultural learners: Negotiating German-American telecollaboration along the institutional fault line. *Modern Language Journal, 87*(1), 71–89.

Belz, J. A., & Thorne, S. L. (2006). Internet-mediated intercultural foreign language education and the intercultural speaker. In J. A. Belz & S. L. Thorne (Eds.), *Internet-mediated intercultural foreign language education* (pp. viii–xxv). Boston, MA: Heinle & Heinle.

Bloch, J. (2004). Second language cyber rhetoric: A study of Chinese L2 writers in an online usenet group. *Language Learning & Technology, 8*(3), 66–82.

Brammerts, H. (1996). Language learning in tandem using the Internet. In M. Warschauer (Ed.), *Telecollaboration in foreign language learning* (pp. 121–130). Honolulu: University of Hawai'i Second Language Teaching and Curriculum Centre.

Byram, M. (2010). Linguistic and intercultural education for Bildung and citizenship. *Modern Language Journal, 94*(2), 317–321.

Cameron, D. (2002). Globalisation and the teaching of "communication skills." In. D. Block & D. Cameron (Eds.), *Globalisation and language teaching* (pp. 67–82). London: Routledge.

Canagarajah, A. S. (1999). *Resisting linguistic imperialism in English teaching.* Oxford, UK: Oxford University Press.

Canagarajah, S. (2006). Negotiating the local in English as a lingua franca. *Annual Review of Applied Linguistics, 26*, 197–218.

Cassell, J., & Tversky, D. (2005). The language of online intercultural community formation. *Journal of Computer-Mediated Communication, 10*(2).

Chun, D. M. (2006). CALL technologies for L2 reading. In L. Ducate & N. Arnold (Eds.), *Calling on CALL: From theory and research to new directions in foreign language teaching* (pp. 69–98). CALICO Monograph Series, 5. San Marcos, TX: CALICO Publications.

Coiro, J., Knobel, M., Lankshear, C., & Leu, D. (2008). Central issues in new literacies and new literacies research. In J. Coiro, M. Knobel, C. Lankshear, & D. J. Leu (Eds.), *Handbook of research on new literacies* (pp. 1–21). New York: Lawrence Erlbaum.

Conole, G. (2008). Listening to the learner voice: The ever-changing landscape of technology use for language students. *ReCALL, 20*(2), 124–140.

Cortazzi, M. (2000). Language, cultures, and cultures of learning in the global classroom. In K. Howah & C. Ward (Eds.), *Language in the global context:*

Implications for the language classroom. Singapore: SEAMEO Regional Language Centre.

Crystal, D. (2003). *The Cambridge encyclopedia of the English language*. Cambridge: Cambridge University Press.

Cummins, J. (2008). Technology, literacy, and young second language learners: Designing educational futures. In L. L. Parker (Ed.), *Technology-mediated learning environments for young English learners: Connections in and out of school* (pp. 61–98). New York: Routledge.

Fedderholdt, K. (2001). An email exchange project between non-native speakers of English. *ELT Journal, 55*(3), 273–280.

Graddol, D. (1997). *The future of English*. London: The British Council.

Graddol, D. (2006). *English next*. The British Council. Retrieved July 1, 2009 from http://www.britishcouncil.org/files/documents/learning-research-english-next.pdf

Ha, P. L. (2009). English as an international language: international student and identity formation. *Language and Intercultural Communication, 9*(3), 201–214.

Hegelheimer, V., & O'Bryan, A. (2009). Mobile technologies, podcasting, and language education. In M. Thomas (Ed.), *Handbook of research on Web 2.0 and second language learning* (p. 331–349). Hershey, PA: IGI Global.

Helm, F. (2009). Language and culture in an online context: What can learner diaries tell us about intercultural competence? *Language and Intercultural Communication, 9*(2), 91–104.

Ho, M.-C., & Savignon, S. J. (2007). Face-to-face and computer-mediated peer review in EFL writing. *CALICO Journal, 24*, 269–290.

Keranen, N., & Bayyurt, Y. (2006). International telecollaboration: In-service EFL teachers in Mexico and pre-service EFL teachers in Turkey. *TESL-EJ, 10*(3), 1–50.

Kern, R. (2006). Perspectives on technology in learning and teaching languages. *TESOL Quarterly, 40*(1), 183–210.

Kern, R., Ware, P., & Warschauer, M. (2004). Crossing frontiers: New directions in online pedagogy and research. *Annual Review of Applied Linguistics, 24*, 243–260.

Kramsch, C. (1998). *Language and culture*. Oxford: Oxford University Press.

Kramsch, C. (2009). *The multilingual subject. What language learners say about their experience and why it matters*. Oxford: Oxford University Press.

Kramsch, C., A'Ness, F., & Lam, W. S. E. (2000). Authenticity and authorship in the computer-mediated acquisition of L2 literacy. *Language Learning & Technology, 4*(2), 78–104.

Lam, W. S. E. (2000). Second language literacy and the design of the self: A case study of a teenager writing on the Internet. *TESOL Quarterly, 34*(3), 457–483.

Lam, W. S. E. (2004). Second language socialization in a bilingual chat room: Global and local considerations. *Language Learning & Technology, 8*(3): 44–65.

Levy, M. (2009). Technologies in use for second language learning. *The Modern Language Journal, 93*, 769–782.

Liaw, M-L., & English, K. (2010). *A tale of two cultures*. Paper session presented at the 2010 EUROCALL Conference, September, University of Bordeaux, France.

Louhiala-Salminen, L., Charles, M., & Kankaanranta, A. (2005). English as a lingua franca in Nordic corporate mergers: Two case companies. *English for Specific Purposes, 24*, 401–421.

McKay, S. (2002). *Teaching English as an international language: Rethinking goals and approaches*. Oxford: Oxford University Press.

McKay, S., & Bokhorst-Heng, W. D. (2008). *International English in its sociolinguistic contexts*. New York, NY: Routledge.

Miniwatts Marketing Group. (2010). Internet world stats: Internet world users by language. [Statistical report] Retrieved from http://www.internetworldstats.com /stats7.htm

O'Bryan, A., & Hegelheimer, V. (2007). Integrating CALL into the classroom: The role of podcasting in an ESL listening strategies course. *ReCALL Journal, 19*(2), 162–280.

O'Dowd, R., & Ritter, M. (2006). Understanding and working with "failed communication" in tellecollaborative exchanges. *CALICO Journal, 23*, 623–642.

O'Neill, E. J. (2007). Implementing international virtual elementary classroom activities for public school students in the U.S. and Korea. *The Electronic Journal of e-Learning, 5*(3), 207–218.

Paradowski, M. B. (2008). Winds of change in the English language: Air of peril for native speakers? *Novitas-ROYAL, 2*(1), 92–119.

Pillay, H., Irving, K., & McCrindle, A. (2006). Developing a diagnostic tool for assessing tertiary students' readiness for online learning. *International Journal of Learning Technology, 2*(1), 92–104.

Prabhu, N. S. (1990). There is no best method—Why? *TESOL Quarterly, 24*(2), 161–176.

Text Adaptor (2010). [Web-based support]. Ewing, NJ: Educational Testing Services.

Thorne, S. (2006). The pedagogy of internet-mediated intercultural foreign language education. In J. A. Belz & S. L. Thorne (Eds.), *Internet-mediated intercultural foreign language education* (pp. 2–30). Boston, MA: Heinle & Heinle.

Thorne, S. L., Black, R. W., & Sykes, J. M. (2009). Second language use, socialization, and learning in Internet interest communities and online gaming. *The Modern Language Journal, 93*, 802–821.

Tsubota, Y., Dantsuji, M., & Kawahara, T. (2004). An English pronunciation learning system for Japanese students based on diagnosis of critical pronunciation errors. *ReCALL Journal, 16*(1), 173–188.

Walker, S., Schloss, P., Fletcher, C. R., Vogel, C. A., & Walker, R. C. (2005). Visual-syntactic text formatting: A new method to enhance online reading. *Reading Online, 8*(6). Retrieved from http://www.readingonline.org/

Ware, P. (2005). "Missed" communication in online communication: Tensions in a German-American telecollaboration. *Language Learning & Technology, 9*(2), 64–89.

Ware, P., & Rivas, B. (2011). *Mixed method study of the impact of an international online exchange project on adolescent writing.* Paper session presented at the meeting of the American Educational Research Association, April, New Orleans, LA.

Warschauer, M. (1996). Computer-assisted language learning: An introduction. In S. Fotos (Ed.), *Multimedia language teaching* (pp. 3–20). Tokyo: Logos.

Warschauer, M. (2000). The changing global economy and the future of English teaching. *TESOL Quarterly, 34*(3), 511–535.

Warschauer, M. (2001). Millennialism and media: Language, literacy, and technology in the 21st century. In D. Graddol (Ed.), *AILA Review 14: Applied linguistics in the 21st century* (pp. 49–59). Oxford: Catchline/AILA.

Warschauer, M., & De Florio-Hansen, I. (2003). Multilingualism, identity, and the Internet. In A. Hu & I. De Florio-Hansen (Eds.), *Multiple identity and multilingualism* (pp. 155–179). Tübingen: Stauffenburg.

Warschauer, M., & Grimes, D. (2008). Automated writing assessment in the classroom. *Pedagogies, 3*(1), 22–36.

Warschauer, M., & Ware, P. (2006). Automated writing evaluation: Defining the classroom research agenda. *Language Teaching Research, 10*(2), 157–180.

Warschauer, M., & Ware, P. (2008). Learning, change and power: Competing frames of technology and literacy. In J. Coiro, M. Knobel, C. Lankshear, & D.J. Leu. (Eds.), *Handbook of research on new literacies* (pp. 215–240). New York: Lawrence Erlbaum.

Weber, G. (2008). *Top languages: The world's 10 most influential languages.* Retrieved from http://www.andaman.org/BOOK/reprints/weber/rep-weber.htm

Chapter 6

Linking EIL and Literacy
Theory and Practice

Constant Leung and Brian V. Street

Introduction

The widespread use of English as a medium of inter-communal and inter-lingual communication for a variety of commercial, educational, professional, and social purposes in different world locations has progressively raised questions about the validity and relevance of some of the fundamental assumptions about English in education and in society more generally. The use of English as an international language (EIL) for communication in an increasingly diverse range of contexts and purposes, involving complex participant language backgrounds and interests, has demanded re-visiting of some established and powerful conceptual certainties in the fields of language and literacy education. In this chapter we will focus on two of these "certainties": language competence and literacy standards. Terminologically there are several closely related terms for EIL—English as lingua franca (ELF) and Lingua Franca English (LFE), and so on. To keep in line with the theme of this book, we will adopt EIL in the discussion but use the related terms where appropriate, particularly in citations.

Language Competence

In the international field of English Language Teaching (ELT) a number of curriculum and pedagogic developments have been underpinned by the concept of communicative competence. This concept was first elaborated in the ethnographic work of Hymes some forty years ago (1972, 1977, 1994) who suggested that competence in language use is not just a question of an abstracted knowledge of grammar residing in the individual, it also involves social conventions of use in actual contexts of communication. The selection of appropriate grammatical and lexical choices for pragmatic purposes (e.g., politeness or formality) in specific contexts is an important dimension of effective language use. On this view communicative competence should be empirically derived—in Hymes' case often using an ethnographic perspective. The foregrounding of the social dimension in language use in this primarily research orientation was welcomed by the ELT profession (and other language educators) who were aware of the limitations of grammar-oriented pedagogies. However, the importation of this conceptualization of communicative competence from research to pedagogy has also been accompanied by an epistemic and ontological shift. Given that language teachers were more interested in practicable models and norms of language that are informed by examples of actual use than in a research-oriented community-by-community account of communicative practices, there was a tendency to abstract instances of observed culturally specific language use generally associated with "standard-variety" native English speakers from countries such as Australia, Britain, and the USA, and to transform them into universal pedagogic benchmarks. (For a more detailed account of this development see Dubin, 1989; Leung, 2005.) The various proficiency scales and levels within the politically powerful Common European Framework of Reference for Languages (Council of Europe, 2001) designed to inform language teaching and assessment, for instance, are linked to this concept of communicative competence. ELT curriculum and pedagogy (and language education more generally) continue to be strongly influenced by this somewhat reified notion of communicative competence (e.g., Brown, 2000; Kay & Jones, 2009; Leung, 2010a; Oxenden & Latham-Koenig, 2006). That said, in the past few years this orthodoxy has come under increasing scrutiny.

English in the Contemporary World

It is now commonplace to observe that the rapid pace of internationalizing of production of goods and commodities, trade and education (particularly in the university sector) in recent times has been accompanied by the spread of the use of English globally (see other chapters in this volume). Historically the spread of English was associated with imperial ambitions and colonial occupation. The English-ization of Australia and the North American continent (apart from Quebec), and the adoption of English as an official language in colonial Hong Kong and India are examples of this earlier phase of spread. In a colonial, or post-colonial situation of immigration into metropolitan countries, where English carries untrammelled political power and social prestige, it is not difficult to understand how the adoption of a particular set of native-speaker norms and practices is assumed to be part of the "natural order," particularly from the point of view of the metropolitan variety speaker. This native-speaker "superiority" continues to shape perceptions and practices.

For example, a recent speech by the British Prime Minister, David Cameron, was critical of "multiculturalism" and advocated what the SearchLight Educational Trust defined as a position favored by "cultural integrationists," who advocate a common national culture that immigrants should accept (Miliband, 2011). The implications of this stance for what counts as "English" seem like a throwback to earlier periods before the super diversity to which Vertovec (2007a), Blommaert (2010), and others refer, where it is recognized that language and culture operate in varied, complex, and "diverse" ways with global flows and movements that make it unhelpful to simply describe a single unique language or culture (cf. also Street, 1993a on "Culture is a Verb"). Another example is to be found in Arizona where the (state) Education Department has recently instructed schools to remove English as a Second Language teachers who speak English with non-acceptable "accents" (Nittle, 2010).

However, this historical domination-subjugation relationship does not *necessarily* hold in contemporary contexts in which English is used as a preferred common language for a variety of business, educational, professional, and social purposes by speakers from diverse language backgrounds. The widespread use of English in business organizations and political institutions in Europe (e.g., "English becomes Europe's second language," *Telegraph*, 2010) represents a good example of this development. The adoption of English as a medium of instruction in education in places such as Hong Kong and Singapore is another example. At the same time, within the metropolitan English-speaking societies the changing patterns of migration are beginning to impact on the ways in which English is perceived and used. For instance, citizens of the European Union are entitled to take up residence in the UK without restriction. The traditional notion of an "immigrant," associated with ex-colonial subjects and low-grade occupations in the 1950s and 1960s, is being transformed. Instead of seeing migration as a long-term up-rooting and re-settlement process, the relative ease of movement has given rise to the concept of circular migration (Vertovec, 2007b). An Estonian worker, for instance, can come and work in the UK for a short period of time, move on to other EU locations for a time, then come back to the UK when circumstances are suitable. Likewise students from other EU countries are entitled to apply to study in British universities as they are for all other universities in other parts of the EU; a French student may choose to do a first degree in France, a Master's degree in the UK, and a PhD in the Netherlands through the medium of English. Beyond the EU context, the continuing non-permanent cross-border relocation of technical and specialist staff in internationalized business and industrial enterprises has also contributed to this new form of migration.

Shifts in Values

Whether we are talking about the use of English in European Union institutions, or a business organization in Singapore, or the use of English by a Polish worker on a sojourn in London, or a French student in a British university, the voluntary nature of choosing and using English has begun to broaden the ways in which norms and values associated with English are understood. The unquestioned assumption that the language norms and practices associated with native-speaker varieties should be regarded as automatically relevant and legitimate has been considerably lessened. At a whole society level, Singapore has, for instance, set out to adopt English for its own national purposes (Dixon, 2009; McKay & Bokhorst-Heng, 2008), and to selectively embrace or reject aspects of cultural norms and practices associated with the metropolitan varieties (Chew, 1999). On a more local and individual level, Canagarajah (2007, p. 925), elaborating on some of the research studies investigating lingua franca communication (e.g., Dewey & Cogo, 2006; Meierkord, 2002; Seidlhofer, 2004), says:

> The speakers of LFE [lingua franca English] are not located in one geographic boundary. They inhabit and practice other languages and cultures in their own immediate localities. Despite this linguistic-cultural heterogeneity and spatial disconnect, they recognise LFE as a shared resource. They activate a mutually recognized set of attitudes, forms, and conventions that ensure successful communication in LFE when they find themselves interacting with each other.

A key operative phrase here is "they activate a mutually recognized set of attitudes, forms and conventions ...." At first sight this seems to suggest that EIL ushers in a sort of social convention-free space where participants in social interaction can create their own norms and rules in a case-by-case manner, a position that has been described as "Confident Multiculturalists" (see Miliband, 2011). Whether a-normic interactions are practicable and sustainable socially is a moot question; it would certainly be an important issue for further research. The developing literature in language education concerned with EIL communication, however, suggests that EIL interactions do not so much take place in an a-normic space as in a complex, in some contexts liminal, social space where multiple norms hailing from the participants' diverse language and cultural backgrounds are enacted and communicated (see Jenkins, 2007; Seidlhofer, 2009). So, we are not suggesting that EIL automatically confers on its speakers the tendency to use language in an a-normic and rule-free fashion; rather we are saying that EIL communication can be seen as a site where participants make meaning and negotiate understanding through a multiplicity of language (and other semiotic) resources, social expectations, and pragmatic moves in ways that may be different from conventionally observed norms based on metropolitan language varieties.

The idea that people from different language backgrounds with low English language proficiency fail to achieve successful communication outcomes (in English) is of course not new. In much of the commercially published ELT curriculum material the main emphasis is on the language learner to acquire and adopt requisite native-speaker inspired language forms and associated pragmatic meanings in order to communicate effectively. The early theoretical formulations of communicative competence within ELT were, perhaps by default, predicated on this perspective (e.g., see Canale & Swain, 1980, for a general framework; Thomas, 1983, on pragmatic failure). But in a changing EIL-medium communicative landscape where the privileging of native-speaker norms, values, and practices does not necessarily hold sway, a more dynamic perspective on participant enactment of their meaning is needed to understand how communication is achieved. Bremer, Roberts, Vasseur, Simonot, and Broeder (1996) provide an interesting discussion on how understanding is achieved in intercultural encounters. More recently Kramsch (2006, 2010) has discussed the notion of symbolic competence within what she refers to as "third culture" communication (see also Gutiérrez, 2008, on "third space"), which for the purpose of this discussion, can be understood in relation to EIL-mediated communication.

> ... the notion of third culture must be seen less as a PLACE than as a symbolic PROCESS of meaning-making that sees beyond the dualities of national languages (L1-L2) and the national cultures (C1-C2). The development of symbolic competence ... includes a systematic reflexive component that encompasses some subjective and aesthetic as well as historical and ideological dimensions that communicative language teaching (CLT) has largely left unexploited.
>
> (Kramsch, 2010, p. 2, original emphasis)

Symbolic competence, on this view, isn't something that can be fixed into a language learning point that can be reproduced in later use. EIL-mediated communication, by virtue of the fact that it is an intersection and interaction between speaker meanings shaped by diverse language and cultural practices, shows that the need and the possibility for negotiation and navigation are constantly present. Gee's (1990) notion of discourse is helpful here; it also provides a conceptual point of overlap with the field of New Literacy Studies (see below) in which his notions of discourse and social practice play a significant part. According to Gee, "discourse" is "a socially accepted association among ways of using language, of thinking, feeling, believing, valuing and acting that can be used to identify oneself as a member of a socially meaningful group or 'social network'" (Gee, 1990, p. 143). He aligns this view of discourse with a big "D" with an account of literacy "as social practice" (Gee, 1990, p. 137). He then brings these two accounts together in seeking to understand second language acquisition. For example, he challenges dominant perspectives on second language acquisition by arguing: "Research on second language acquisition both inside and outside classroom settings indicates that some speakers can have quite poor grammar and function in communication and socialisation quite well" (Gee, 1990, p. 139). It is through the combination of social literacies and Discourses as forms of identification, embracing an ideological model of literacy and "ideology in Discourses," that such communication is achieved. It is this bringing of participant agency to the fore, rather than simply focusing on "skills" and formal "correctness," that Kramsch (2010, p. 3) too emphasizes:

> It is ... a matter of looking beyond words and actions and embracing multiple, changing and conflicting discourse worlds, in which the circulation of values and identities across cultures, the inversions, even inventions of meaning, [are] often hidden behind a common illusion of effective communication ... while communicative competence was based on an assumption of understanding based on common goals and common interests, intercultural competence presupposes a lack of understanding due to divergent subjectivities and historicities. By defining culture as discourse, we are looking at the interculturally competent individual as a symbolic self that is constituted by symbolic systems like language, as well as by systems of thought and their symbolic power.

The key issue here is that the participants in interaction take hold of the communicative agenda in terms of both the meaning to be achieved and the way it is achieved. So what does this taking hold of the agenda look like in actual interaction? Here we will offer two examples of interaction between English speakers from different language backgrounds. The first example is concerned with the usage of the definite article, the second with pragmatic moves.

It has been observed that in English as lingua franca communication (ELF, now recognized as a field of study), conventional usages associated with metropolitan norms can be extended to carry communicative meaning. Conventionally established notions of "correctness" and "appropriateness" should now be applied with a degree of caution. For instance, Dewey (2007, p. 340) reports that the definite article "the" can be used to signal semantic prominence. The following extract provides an illustration of this observation:

S1:   Because they they know how to play(,) they know how to survive in *the nature* or in *the society* (,) instinct- un- unconsciously because they're children
S2:   yeah (,) they are very (xxx)
S1:   flexible
S2:   Yeah (.) they can catch up with the person who are edu- well educated in the city I think (,) they can catch up with them

S1 used the definite article "the" with two abstract nouns referring to two generic phenomena in this particular discourse context: nature and society. Dewey suggests that this particular use of the definite article can be related to other similar instances of usage in his data where the speaker uses "the" to foreground the "keyness" of the word/s (abstract generic nouns) in the context of on-going interaction and meaning making. In this case, it is argued that S1 inserted "the" to foreground the semantic importance of "nature" and "society" in this stretch of conversation.

Kaur (2009, p. 111) offers an example of pragmatic persistence in establishing a theme in conversation. In the following extract the participants, D and M, are both EIL speakers studying on an International Masters' program in Malaysia.

```
01  D:  an:d the problem is one of er:: my students in Indonesia
02  M:  uhhuh
03  D:  they make a research about the the effect of ... (1.9) oh no no no
04      the ::: relationship between :.... (0.8) future performance
05  M:  uhhuh=
06  D:  =an:d CEO change
07  M:  uhhuh
08  D:  CEO change: an:d future performance
09  M:  °yes°=
10  D:  =okay ... (1.3) the problem is ... (0.9) the sample is only
11  →   seventeen: firms ... (1.2) seventeen firms
12  M:  seventeen firms=
13  D:  =huh and also ... (0.6) we divide before an:d after
14      practice
```

Working with a Conversation Analysis (CA) perspective, Kaur suggests that participants in a conversation tend to signal their intention to take up the next available turn as early as possible. When this turn-taking procedure is interrupted, for instance, when there is no bidding from the "listening" participants when the next available turn is imminent, then the current-turn speaker may take action to ensure that there is no misunderstanding on the part of the other participants. Repeating or paraphrasing information already given is an example of this kind of repair strategy. In the data extract shown above D raised an issue about his student's research (small sample size) in 01. M, however, made minimal response in 02. D continued with his effort in 03, 04, 06, and 08; and M on her part continued with her minimal responses in 05, 07, and 09. Because M failed to use turn 09 to provide a fuller response, D then produced the key information (seventeen firms) in 10 and 11 which included a repetition of "seventeen," and he did so to make sure that M was given a further opportunity to follow the information. Kaur argues that this episode is consistent with an emerging theme in the ELF research literature which suggests that participants tend to make every effort to ensure that understanding is achieved. The key point here is that where speakers from diverse backgrounds cannot assume to be able to draw inferences from one another's utterances (meanings) based on shared knowledge, the need to negotiate and to ascertain meaning is more evident (for a wider discussion on this point see Scollon & Scollon, 1995).

Whilst these examples relate to spoken language, we would also like to see the issue in the broader context of Discourse, embracing both spoken and written communication. In the following section we summarize recent work in the field of Literacy Studies to which Gee referred above and then bring these insights to bear alongside the arguments presented above in addressing the understanding of EIL use in particular.

Literacy Studies

Literacy as Social Practice

Recent accounts of literacy as social practice have taken a similar direction to that pointed out above with respect to the diverse character of English in international settings. As with English, it is now recognized that the uses and meanings of literacy vary with context, there is not one single, uniform model—what Street (1984) terms an "autonomous" model (see below)—but rather there are multiple literacies whose definition and use are embedded in different cultural and ideological norms. As with the uses of English, the uses of literacy in specific contexts have to be negotiated— the "standard" norms are themselves products of particular ideological positions rather than being the neutral or universal variety that advocates of the "autonomous" model suggest. We can, then, provide similar examples of the variety and negotiation of different literacy practices as we have done regarding EIL. Before providing such examples, we will briefly outline the theoretical shifts and debates that underpin this view of literacy, some of them moving along similar trajectories and calling upon similar authors to those we encountered in the English language and communicative competence literature.

Just as recent studies of EIL have challenged the dominant assumptions of English as a single unified code and norms of interaction, and instead argue for English as fluid and varying across communicative settings, so in the field of Literacy, what has come to be termed New Literacy Studies (NLS) has established the importance of seeing literacy practices in their social contexts, rather than as autonomous and reified (Barton & Hamilton, 1998; Gee, 1999; Heath 1983; Street, 1984, 1993b). This approach has been particularly influenced by those who have advocated an "ethnographic" perspective, in contrast with the experimental and often individualistic character of cognitive studies, and the textual, etic perspective of linguistic-based studies of text evident in earlier accounts of English as Second/Additional Language (ESL/EAL). Much of the work in the NLS tradition, in contrast, focuses on the everyday meanings and uses of literacy in specific cultural contexts and links directly to how we understand the work of literacy programs for learning and teaching, which themselves then become subject to ethnographic enquiry (Robinson-Pant, 2004; Rogers, 2005).

Autonomous and Ideological Models of Literacy

In trying to characterize these new approaches to understanding and defining literacy, Street (1984) has referred to a distinction between an "autonomous" model and an "ideological" model of literacy. The "autonomous" model of literacy works from the assumption that literacy in itself—autonomously—will have effects on other social and cognitive practices. The model, he argues, disguises the cultural and ideological assumptions that underpin it and that can then be presented as though they are neutral and universal. Research in the social practice approach challenges this view and suggests that in practice dominant approaches based on the autonomous model are simply imposing Western, urban, or elite conceptions of literacy on to other cultures, whether non-western, "rural", or minority (Street, 2001). As we have seen above, the tradition of research and practice in ESL/EAL has likewise tended to adopt an "autonomous" approach that in effect imposes views of English rooted in specific cultural and historical contexts. The alternative, ideological model of literacy offers a more culturally sensitive view of literacy practices as they vary from one context to another, just as the approach to communicative language teaching described by Leung (2005; 2010b) is able to take account of local variations and meanings, and avoids the narrow cultural bias of earlier communicative approaches.

The ideological model starts from different premises than the autonomous model. It posits instead that literacy is a social practice, not simply a technical and neutral skill and that it is always embedded in socially constructed epistemological principles. The ways in which people address reading and writing are themselves rooted in conceptions of knowledge, identity, and being. Literacy, in this sense, is always contested, both its meanings and its practices, hence particular versions of it are always "ideological," they are always rooted in a particular world-view and a desire for that view of literacy to dominate and to marginalize others (Gee, 1999). The "autonomous" model is, then, itself a strongly ideological perspective, since it takes a firm view on what counts as literacy, its consequences for human social development. The argument about social literacies simply makes explicit what remains implicit in the autonomous model: that engaging with literacy is always a social event from the outset, even where educational policy perspectives attempt to describe such learning and practices as "neutral." The ways in which teachers or facilitators and their students interact is already a social practice that affects the nature of the literacy being learned and the ideas about literacy held by the participants, especially the new novice learners and their position in relations of power. It is not valid to suggest that "literacy" can be "given" neutrally and then its "social" effects only are experienced or "added on" afterwards. Many of these principles can also be applied to the teaching of English which, as we have seen, is then recognized as varying in different contexts, and often carrying hidden ideological assumptions about which version is more "correct" and more appropriate to be taught to second language learners.

Key concepts in the field of NLS that may enable us to overcome the problems evident in the autonomous model and that can help us to apply these new conceptions of literacy to specific contexts and practical programs include the concepts of *literacy events* and of *literacy practices*. Shirley Brice Heath (1983, p. 50) characterized a "literacy event" as "any occasion in which a piece of writing is integral to the nature of the participants' interactions and their interpretative processes." Street (1984, p. 1) employed the phrase "literacy practices" as a means of focusing upon "the social practices and conceptions of reading and writing." He later elaborated the term both to take account of "events" in Heath's sense and to give greater emphasis to the social models of literacy that participants bring to bear upon those events and that give meaning to them (Street, 1988). David Barton, Mary Hamilton, and colleagues at Lancaster University, have taken up these concepts and applied them to their own research in ways that have been hugely influential both in the

UK and internationally (cf. Barton, et al., 1999). The issue of dominant literacies and non-dominant, informal or vernacular, literacies is central to their combination of "situated" and "ideological" approaches to literacy.

"What's New" in New Literacy Studies?

More recently the concern with relations between local and global, of the kind that we suggest now frame our understanding of English as an international language, have been brought to bear on the study of literacy. Brandt and Clinton (2002), for instance, refer to "the limits of the local" in the accounts of literacy provided by NLS scholars. They and others (e.g., Collins & Blot, 2003) question the "situated" approach to literacy as not giving sufficient recognition to the ways in which literacy usually comes from outside a particular community's "local" experience, a feature common in adult literacy programs and also in the uses of English in many parts of the world. Street, in a paper entitled "What's 'new' in New Literacy Studies" (2003) summarizes a number of these texts and the arguments they put forward and offers some counter arguments from an ethnographic perspective, notably for present purposes that an ethnographic perspective does intrinsically take into account the dynamic links between "local" and "global" rather than just focusing parochially on "the local" as some critiques have argued. Building on this, Maddox (2007) has recently attempted to bring together the "situated" approach with that of NLS, using his own ethnographic field research in Bangladesh to explore the relationship between local and outside influences. Like Brandt and Clinton (2002), Maddox (2007) wants to recognize the force of "outside" influences associated with literacy, including the potential for helping people move out of "local" positions and take account of progressive themes in the wider world. He wants to "shift away from the binary opposition of ideological and autonomous positions that has dominated ... debates in recent years" and develop a "more inclusive theory that can link the local and the global, structure and agency and resolve some of the theoretical and disciplinary tensions over practice and technology" (2007, pp. 266–267). Stromquist (2006) also critiques aspects of the "social" perspective on literacy from the perspective of someone wishing to build upon literacy interventions for equity and justice agendas. She accepts the arguments put by NLS against the strong version of the cognitive consequences of literacy (Scribner & Cole, 1981), but does not believe that means entirely abandoning recognition of where literacy and cognition are associated:

> Understanding the contributions of literacy does not mean that one needs to see literacy functions as the only way to develop cognitive

> ability and reasoning powers, but rather that there be acknowledgement
> that literacy does enable people to process information that is more
> detailed, deliberate and coherent than oral communication.
>
> (Stromquist, 2006, p. 143)

For instance, "literacy enables people to participate in modern life
processes such as reading newspapers and maps, following instructions,
learning the law, and understanding political debates" (Stromquist,
2006, p. 143). Without returning to the now discredited claims of the
autonomous model, she and others in the field of adult literacy in the
international context want to hold on to some of the powers of literacy
associated with it. How these debates and challenges can be taken into
account in the discussion of local Englishes is currently at the heart
of both research and policy in the ELT field too, as Leung (2005) has
demonstrated (see also Dewey & Leung, 2010).

Applying NLS to Policy

Despite these objections, indeed mainly taking them into account, but
recognizing the failure of many traditional literacy programs (e.g., Abadzi,
2003), academics, researchers, and practitioners working in literacy in
different parts of the world are beginning to come to the conclusion that
the autonomous model of literacy, on which much of the existing practice
and programs have been based, is not an appropriate intellectual tool,
either for understanding the diversity of reading and writing around the
world or for designing the practical programs this requires which may
be better suited to an ideological model (e.g., Aikman, 1999; Canieso-
Doronila, 1996; Heath, 1983; Hornberger, 1997, 2002). The question
this approach raises for policy makers and program designers is, then,
not simply that of the "impact" of literacy—to be measured in terms of
a neutral developmental index—but rather of how local people "take
hold" of the new communicative practices being introduced to them,
as Kulick and Stroud's (1993) ethnographic description of missionaries
bringing literacy to New Guinea villagers makes clear. Literacy, in this
sense, is, then, already part of a power relationship and how people "take
hold" of it is contingent on social and cultural practices and not just on
pedagogic and cognitive factors. This raises questions that need to be
addressed in any literacy program. What is the power relation between
the participants? What are the resources? Where are people going if they
take on one literacy rather than another literacy? How do recipients
challenge the dominant conceptions of literacy?

That policy makers are indeed taking account of such a perspective is
evident from recent policy documents in a variety of fields. The Global

Monitoring Report on literacy (UNESCO, 2006) has ten chapters dealing with how progress in the Education for All worldwide agenda is being met and "why literacy matters" (Chapter 5) in this. Whilst a number of chapters address what may seem "traditional" views of literacy, rooted in an autonomous model, the volume does also pay considerable attention to a social practice view of literacy (cf. Chapter 6 "Understandings of Literacy") and the "future policy directions" (Chapter 9) recognize that "one size fits all" is no longer appropriate but instead "rich literate environments are necessary both for the acquisition and retention and uses of literacy" (p. 216). The policy directions also attend to "[m]ultilingualism as a crucial factor for literacy policy" (p. 216) and, in keeping with the arguments presented in this chapter, recognize the need for both mother tongues and "dominant languages," such as English. Similarly, the recent Programme for International Student Assessment (PISA) report (OECD, 2009) includes a section on reading that takes account of "understanding electronic texts" (p. 19) and the "motivational and behavioural elements of reading literacy." Whilst this is still mostly rooted in a more cognitive approach, the attention to new technologies and to "context and engagement" are newly added in ways that take more account of social literacies than previous reports. The new definition of literacy states: "Reading literacy is understanding, using, reflecting on and engaging with written texts in order to achieve one's own goals, to develop knowledge and potential and to participate in society" (OECD, 2009, p. 23). The phrase "and engaging with written texts" has been added to the previous, 2000 definition and perhaps indicates a shift in the direction that this chapter is concerned with, regarding the participation, engagement, and social interaction that language and literacy entail.

Implications for Research and Practice

As we apply some of these ideas to the teaching of English, new questions similarly arise, for example, which version of English is being privileged and what power assumptions are the pedagogy and program design based upon? The approach described here, embracing NLS and contemporary understandings of English and of EIL, has implications, then, for both research and practice. Researchers, instead of privileging the particular literacy practices familiar in their own culture, or the particular version of English with which they are familiar, now suspend judgment as to what constitutes literacy and English among the people they are working with until they are able to understand what these concepts mean to the people themselves—for instance which social contexts reading and writing derive their meaning from and what varieties of English are considered appropriate for different social purposes. For instance, many people labeled "illiterate" within the autonomous model of literacy may, from a more culturally-sensitive viewpoint, be seen to make significant use of literacy practices for specific purposes and in specific contexts. Indeed, studies suggest that even non-literate persons find themselves engaged in literacy activities so the boundary between literate/non-literate is less obvious than individual "measures" of literacy suggest (Canieso-Doronila, 1996).

Likewise, teachers and researchers of English language in different world locations can question the extent to which language norms and pragmatic conventions drawn from particular native-speaker varieties should be seen as benchmarks for communicative competence. It is not a question of wholesale rejection of everything to do with the metropolitan language varieties; rather it is a case of sensitively observing and examining how English as a set of linguistic resources has been taken hold of in local contexts, and how it is used to serve particular communication needs that may involve interlocutors from diverse ethnic and language backgrounds. On a conceptual level one may say that any attempt to adapt and extend norms and practices previously based on narrow metropolitan varieties of English is a move to the ethnographic perspective mentioned earlier. One may say that it is possible for many varieties of English to co-exist in any locale, some of which may enjoy greater prestige and status than others in the eye of some speakers.

This perspective would also help us understand that some speakers of local varieties of English may not always acknowledge the significance of what they already know and may respond instead to judgments that it is somehow inferior and secondary to some model of "proper" English. In that connection, it may be quite instructive to explore the social values and language ideologies that underlie the kind of views and judgments that would deem the use of the definite article in "they know how to survive in *the* nature or in *the* society" (example cited earlier) to be of questionable legitimacy, and yet would routinely accept *"The* skiing in Switzerland is good this year"* as part of idiomatically correct British English, albeit with certain social class affiliations. In the same vein, whenever one hears a pronouncement such as "We don't say 'I'm good' in English" (as opposed to "I'm well" in British English), it may be necessary to question the linguistic and socio-cultural bases of the claimed authority of "we."

These prejudices and misconceptions are not only apparent in the everyday world and in political contexts, but also we find that academics and researchers have often failed to make explicit the implications of such theory for practical work. In the present conditions of the world, such ivory-tower distancing is no longer legitimate, as work in both NLS and EIL has made apparent. But likewise, policy makers and practitioners have not always taken on board such "academic" findings, or have adopted one position (most often that identified with the autonomous model) and not taken account of the many others outlined here, although as we have indicated, a close search of recent policy documents can indicate evidence for some shift in perspective in the direction this chapter is pointing in. These findings, then, raise important issues both for research into English and literacy in general and language development and literacy in EIL in particular, and for policy in language-related education and training more broadly.

Exploring the Ideas

1 How should notions such as "correctness" and "appropriateness" be understood in EIL communication?
2 What criteria should teachers use to make judgments on "acceptable" and "unacceptable" English? How would New Literacy Studies criteria differ from the ones promoted by examination boards and/ or international language tests such as TOEFL or IELTS?
3 How does the shift in Literacy Studies concerning social practice relate to the shift in Language Competence concerning the international nature of English? Is it feasible to talk of an "ideological model" of EIL?

Applying the Ideas

1 Make an audio-video recording of a regular school subject lesson (e.g., English or Science) where EIL is used as the medium of instruction, and describe the forms/varieties of spoken and written English used by the teacher/s and students in different classroom activities (subject content-related teacher-fronted talk, teacher-led whole class question-and-answer session, teacher-student small group discussion, student group talk, etc.). How would you characterize the way/s in which the English language resources were used?
2 Describe the literacy activities in which students and teachers are engaging in a regular subject lesson (e.g., teacher writing on board; students taking notes, writing in exercise books; reading text books; displays on walls, etc.) and note the varieties of language (e.g., formal and informal English as understood locally, English, and other languages) being used. Relate your observations to the notion of literacy practice.
3 Ask students to discuss the different ways in which some of the words they use can be spelled, and try to work out the orthographic principles, e.g., light/lite (colloquial); pidgin/Tok Pisin (Papua New Guinea); activity/aktiviti (Malay); see you/ c u (texting). Examples

could be taken from different first languages and from electronic texts that students produce. Discuss literacy issues that this kind of oral-written relationship raises (e.g., correctness, Standard, vernacular).

References

Abadzi, H. (2003). *Improving adult literacy outcomes: Lessons from cognitive research for developing countries*. Washington, DC: World Bank.

Aikman, S. (1999). *Intercultural education and literacy: An ethnographic study of indigenous knowledge and learning in the Peruvian Amazon*. Amsterdam: Benjamins.

Barton, D., & Hamilton, M. (1998). *Local literacies: Reading and writing in one community*. London: Routledge.

Barton, D., Hamilton, M., & Ivanič, R. (Eds.). (1999). *Situated literacies: Reading and writing in context*. London: Taylor and Francis.

Blommaert, J. (2010). *The sociolinguistics of globalization*. Cambridge: Cambridge University Press.

Brandt, D., & Clinton, K. (2002). Limits of the local: expanding perspectives on literacy as a social practice. *Journal of Literacy Research, 34*(3), 337–356.

Bremer, K., Roberts, C., Vasseur, M., Simonot, M., & Broeder, P. (Eds.). (1996). *Achieving understanding: Discourse in intercultural encounters*. London: Longman.

Brown, H. D. (2000). *Principles of language learning and teaching* (4th ed.). White Plains, NY: Pearson Education (Longman).

Canagarajah, S. (2007). Lingua Franca English, multilingual communities, and language acquisition. *Modern Language Journal, 91*(Focus Issue), 923–939.

Canale, M., & Swain, M. (1980). Theoretical bases of communicative approaches to second language teaching and testing. *Applied Linguistics, 1*(1), 1–47.

Canieso-Doronila, M. L. (1996). *Landscapes of literacy: An ethnographic study of functional literacy in marginal Philippine communities*. Hamburg: UNESCO Institute of Education.

Chew, P. G. L. (1999). Linguistic imperialism, globalism, and the English language. In D. Graddol & U. H. Meinhof (Eds.), *English in a changing world (AILA Review 13)* (pp. 37–47). Oxford: Catchline.

Collins, J., & Blot, J. (2003). *Texts, power and identity*. London: Routledge.

Council of Europe. (2001). *Common European framework of reference for languages: Learning, teaching, assessment*. Cambridge: Cambridge University Press.

Dewey, M. (2007). English as a lingua franca and globalization: an interconnected perspective. *International Journal of Applied Linguistics, 17*(3), 332–354.

Dewey, M., & Cogo, A. (2006). Efficiency in ELF Communication: From pragmatic motives to lexico-grammatical Innovation. *Nordic Journal of English Studies, 5*(2), 59–93.

Dewey, M., & Leung, C. (2010). English in English language teaching: Shifting values and assumptions in changing circumstances. *Working papers in Educational Linguistics, 25*(1), 1–15.

Dixon, L. Q. (2009). Assumptions behind Singapore's language-in-education policy: Implications for language planning and second language acquisition. *Language Policy, 8*(2), 117–137.

Dubin, F. (1989). Situating literacy within traditions of communicative competence. *Applied Linguistics, 10*(2), 171–181.

Gee, J. (1990). *Social linguistics and literacies: Ideologies in discourses*. London: The Falmer Press.

Gee, J. (1999). The new literacy studies: From "socially situated" to the work of the social. In D. Barton, M. Hamilton & R. Ivanič (Eds.), *Situated literacies: Reading and writing in context* (pp. 180–196). London: Routledge.

Gutiérrez, K. D. (2008). Developing a sociocritical literacy in the third space. *Reading Research Quarterly, 43*(2), 148–164.

Heath, S. B. (1983). *Ways with words: Language, life and work in communities and classrooms*. New York: Cambridge University Press.

Hornberger, N. (1997). Indigenous literacies in the Americas. In N. Hornberger (Ed.), *Indigenous literacies in the Americas* (pp. 3–16). Berlin: Mouton de Gruyter.

Hornberger, N. (2002). *The continua of biliteracy: An ecological framework for educational policy, research and practice in multilingual settings*. Clevedon: Multilingual Matters.

Hymes, D. (1972). On communicative competence. In J. B. Pride & J. Holmes (Eds.), *Sociolinguistics* (pp. 269–293). London: Penguin.

Hymes, D. (1977). *Foundations in sociolinguistics: An ethnographic approach*. London: Tavistock Publications.

Hymes, D. (1994). Towards ethnographies of communication. In J. Maybin (Ed.), *Language and literacy in social practice* (pp. 11–22). Clevedon: Multilingual Matters in association with Open University.

Jenkins, J. (2007). *English as a lingua franca: attitude and identity*. Oxford: Oxford University Press.

Kaur, J. (2009). Pre-empting problems of understanding in English as a lingua franca. In A. Mauranen & E. Ranta (Eds.), *English as a lingua franca: Studies and findings* (pp. 107–123). Newcastle-upon-Tyne: Cambridge Scholars Publishing.

Kay, S., & Jones, V. (2009). *New inside out*. Oxford: Macmillan.

Kramsch, C. (2006). From communicative competence to symbolic competence. *The Modern Language Journal, 90*(2), 249–252.

Kramsch, C. (2010). The symbolic dimensions of the intercultural (Plenary speech). Retrieved 10 February, 2011 from http://journals.cambridge.org/action/displayFulltext?type=1&pdftype=1&fid=7931790&jid=LTA&volumeId=-1&issueId=&aid=7931788

Kulick, D., & Stroud, C. (1993). Conceptions and uses of literacy in a Papua New Guinean village. In B. Street (Ed.), *Cross-cultural approaches to literacy* (pp. 30–61). Cambridge: Cambridge University Press.

Leung, C. (2005). Convivial communication: Recontextualizing communicative competence. *International Journal of Applied Linguistics, 15*(2), 119–144.

Leung, C. (2010a). Communicative language teaching: Principles and interpretations. In C. Leung & A. Creese (Eds.), *English as an additional language: Approaches to teaching linguistic minority students* (pp. 1–14). London: Sage, in association with National Association for Language Development in the Curriculum.

Leung, C. (2010b). Language teaching and language assessment. In R. Wodak, B. Johnstone, & P. Kerswill (Eds.), *The Sage Handbook of Sociolinguistics* (pp. 545–564). London: Sage.

Maddox, B. (2007). What can ethnographic studies tell us about the consequences of literacy. *Comparative Education, 43*(2), 253–271.

McKay, S. L., & Bokhorst-Heng, W. D. (2008). *International English in its sociolinguistic contexts: Towards a socially sensitive EIL pedagogy.* London: Routledge.

Meierkord, C. (2002). "Language stripped bare" or "linguistic masala"? Culture in lingua franca conversation. In K. Knapp & C. Meierkord (Eds.), *Lingua franca communication* (pp. 109–133). Frankfurt: Peter Lang.

Miliband, D. (2011). Insecurity is fuel for hate. *Guardian*, February 27.

Nittle, N. K. (2010). Arizona targets teachers with accents, ethnic studies programs. Retrieved 11 April, 2011 from http://racerelations.about.com/b/2010/05/03/arizona-targets-teachers-with-accents-ethnic-studies-programs.htm

Organization for Economic and Cultural Development. (2009). *Programme for International Student Assessment: Assessment framework—key competencies in reading, mathematics and science* Strasbourg: OECD.

Oxenden, C., & Latham-Koenig, C. (2006). *New English file.* Oxford: Oxford University Press.

Robinson-Pant, A. (2004). *Women, literacy and development: Alternative perspectives.* Hamburg: UNESCO Institute for Education.

Rogers, A. (2005). *Urban literacy: Communication, identity and learning in urban contexts.* Hamburg: UNESCO Institute for Education.

Scollon, R., & Scollon, S. W. (1995). *Intercultural communication.* Oxford: Blackwell.

Scribner, S., & Cole, M. (1981). *The psychology of literacy.* Cambridge, MA: Harvard University Press.

Seidlhofer, B. (2004). Research perspectives on teaching English as a lingua franca. *Annual Review of Applied Linguistics, 24*, 209–239.

Seidlhofer, B. (2009). Common ground and different realities: world Englishes and English as a lingua franca. *World Englishes, 28*(2), 236–245.

Street, B. (1984). *Literacy in theory and practice.* Cambridge: Cambridge University Press.

Street, B. (1988). Literacy practices and literacy myths. In R. Saljo (Ed.), *The written word: Studies in literate thought and action* (pp. 59–72). Heidelberg: Springer-Verlag Press.

Street, B. (1993a). Culture is a verb. In D. Graddol (Ed.), *Language and culture* (pp. 23–43). Clevedon: Multingual Matters/BAAL.

Street, B. (1993b). *Cross-cultural approaches to literacy.* Cambridge: Cambridge University Press.

Street, B. (Ed.). (2001). *Literacy and development: Ethnographic perspectives.* London: Routledge.

Street, B. (2003). What's "new" in New Literacy Studies? Critical approaches to literacy in theory and practice. *Current Issues in Comparative Education, 5*(2), 1–14.

Stromquist, N. (2006). Women's rights to adult education as a means to citizenship. *International Journal of Educational Development, 26*, 140–152.

The Telegraph (2010) English becomes Europe's second language. October 27. Retrieved 11 February, 2011 from http://www.telegraph.co.uk/news/worldnews/europe/8041916/English-becomes-Europes-second-language.html

Thomas, J. (1983). Cross-cultural pragmatic failure. *Applied Linguistics, 4*, 91–112.

UNESCO. (2006). *EFA Global monitoring report: Literacy for life.* Paris: UNESCO.

Vertovec, S. (2007a). *Circular migration: The way forward in global policy?* Oxford: International Migration Institute.

Vertovec, S. (2007b). Super-diversity and its implications. *Ethnic and Racial Studies, 30*(6), 1024–1054.

Chapter 7

Identity and the EIL Learner

Lubna Alsagoff

Identity has become an important concept in language teaching and learning because of the way in which our understanding of language has changed. Increasingly, research within many branches of linguistics no longer positions language simply as a structured body of knowledge, comprising sets of rules and patterns that are to be acquired; rather, language is more currently understood as sociocultural practice, a means of meaning-making as well as membership and participation in discourse communities. Within the field of second language acquisition (SLA) and English language teaching, this move from structuralist understandings of language has meant a shift from a focus on the linguistic system to include the learner and processes involved in the learning of a language.

There has also been an expansion of focus in the SLA research literature, from a largely cognitive perspective which seeks to understand how learners gain knowledge and competence in a language to include sociocultural approaches that contextualize learning as socially situated practice that views the learner as a "complex social being" (McKay & Wong, 1996, p. 577). Consequently, the concept of identity has, in more recent research, played a larger role in the study of language learning, where psychologically-oriented suppositions such as personality, attitudes, and motivations once dominated. Research on identity in language learning highlights the transformative and discursive nature of language learning, in which issues are explored and re-articulated through concepts such as identity, agency, investment, and communities of practice.

In this chapter, I explore how this sociocultural approach to the study of identity in language learning, primarily developed in researching migrant learners learning English as a second language, can yield productive insights into the learning, and learners, of English as an international language (EIL). It demonstrates how a sociocultural perspective of identity as multiple, changeable, and subject to inequities of power is particularly salient to understanding the opportunities and challenges faced by learners of EIL. To provide background to this discussion, the chapter will begin with a historically positioned account of the developments relating to identity research within SLA that have led to understandings of identity as it is researched and studied from a sociocultural framework.

Identity and Learning in the Cognitive Framework

The topic of identity speaks to the very heart of language learning because it begins with a fundamental question: What does it mean to learn a language? For researchers working within a Chomskyan-influenced cognitive framework, learning a language is primarily about the gradual mental acquisition of knowledge about the patterns and rules of a language. Language is thought of as an idealized, objectified entity that is governed by a systematic set of rules, and the process of learning a language is consequently characterized in terms of mastering the linguistic system of the target language in increasing degrees of complexity, and where the L1, or "mother tongue" of the learner is considered as interfering with this process.

Other factors that were also seen as "interfering" or obviating the learning process were affective variables, such as attitude and motivation, anxiety, and self-confidence. Research into such variables was seen as key to understanding individual differences in learner performance. Krashen's affective filter hypothesis (Krashen, 1981) hypothesized that learner attributes such as low motivation, low self-esteem, and poor self-image can combine to "raise" the affective filter, thereby impeding the language acquisition process. Similarly, Gardner and his associates (Gardner, 1985; Gardner & Lambert, 1972) correlated success in language learning with a learner's motivation, which was defined in terms of the learner's desire to learn the language, the enjoyment they derive from learning the language, and effort which they put into the learning process. Gardner also distinguished between instrumental motivation and integrative motivation, in which he claimed the latter to be particularly salient to sustaining long-term success in language learning. Thus, Gardner saw a learner's positive attitude towards the target language group and the desire to integrate into the target language community as more important than their desire for pragmatic gains such as career advancement or academic success.

The learner's desire for affiliation with the target language group was also the basis of the Acculturation Model, in which Schumann hypothesized that acculturation, which he defined as "the social and psychological integration of the learner with the target language group" (Schumann, 1978, p. 29), was key to predicting the degree of success of language learning. He proposed that "the degree to which a learner acculturates to the TL [target language] group will control the degree to which he [sic] acquires the second language" (Schumann, 1978, p. 34). In much of SLA research, identity was therefore conceptualized as membership of social groups (Tajfel, 1974; Tajfel & Turner, 1979).[1]

Sociocultural Identity[2]

Unlike the cognitivists whose preoccupations with language learning revolved around understanding the psychological processes associated with language learning, socioculturally-oriented SLA researchers saw language learning as essentially a social process that involves the identity of learners. By the mid-1990s, there were clear signs that the cognitive approach in SLA studies was being challenged by a competing sociocultural perspective, with the emergence of publications (e.g., Duff & Uchida, 1997; Firth & Wagner, 1997; Norton, 1997; Norton Peirce, 1995; McKay & Wong, 1996; van Lier, 1994; among others) that indicated "a general uneasiness about a certain conceptual and epistemological narrowness in the field" and which advocated "open[ing] up SLA research beyond its roots in linguistics and cognitive psychology" (Block, 2007, pp. 863–864). Sociocultural theory therefore drew insights from fields outside linguistics, including anthropology, cultural studies, ethnology, and sociology in order to explore theoretically more productive approaches to the study of language. Instead of being motivated by a structuralist "search for unchanging universal laws of human behavior and social phenomena," sociocultural theory pursued "more nuanced, multi-leveled, and, ultimately, complicated framings of the world around us" (Block, 2007, p. 864).

The key difference between the sociocultural perspective and the cognitive paradigm to SLA lay fundamentally in the way language was conceptualized. While the cognitive paradigm saw language as an a priori system of symbols and rules, and language use as arising from an abstract idealized speaker competence, the sociocultural perspective conceptualized language as "a complex social practice in which the value and meaning ascribed to an utterance are determined in part by the value and meaning ascribed to the person who speaks" (Norton & Toohey, 2002, p. 587). Essentially, language is viewed not simply as a reflection of a fixed internal mental state, but as emergent structure (Bucholtz & Hall, 2005) arising out of socially-situated dialogic processes. Language and identity are seen to be "mutually constitutive" in which language is not only constructed by and through identity, but also constructs identity (Norton, 1997, p. 419).

A sociocultural perspective thus conceives of identity as essentially dynamic and shifting. Identity is no longer perceived as "a stable structure located primarily in the individual psyche or in fixed social categories" but is instead understood as "a relational and sociocultural phenomenon that emerges and circulates in local discourse contexts of interaction" (Bucholtz & Hall, 2005, pp. 585–586). Identity is also seen in more complex terms, and moves away from essentialized characterizations founded on the basis of group-based, long-term affiliations that are derived from language inheritance, ethnicity, religion, or national origin— what has been referred to in some of the research literature as "cultural identity" (Joseph, 2004). Instead, a constructionist approach sees identity as emergent, and focuses on "how people understand their relationship to the world, how that relationship is constructed across time and space, and how people understand their possibilities for the future" (Norton, 1997, p. 410).[3]

Here, Bakhtin's (1981) postmodern ideas of language as consisting of heteroglossic voices strongly influences the way in which sociocultural theories portray identity as multiple, complex, and often conflicting and contradictory. Norton's (Norton Peirce, 1995; Norton, 2000) ethnographic study of five immigrant women demonstrates the ways in which their multiple identities are discursively constructed through the classroom interactions as well as their work experiences. Similarly, McKay and Wong's (1996) investigations of the experiences of four Chinese-speaking high school students in an ESL program in California also reveal how the four immigrant learners have a range of identities within multiple discourses.

In framing learner identity as "a contingent process involving dialectic relations between learners and the various worlds and experiences they inhabit and which act upon them" (Ricento 2005, p. 895), sociocultural identity theory also highlights the ways in which the use of language is intimately tied to issues of power. McKay and Wong's (1996) study, for example, showed that the students' identities were affected by discursively-constructed images of Asians as model minorities (industrious, uncomplaining, academically successful) in contrast to views of other minority groups, such as Latin Americans, as inferior and contrary, in what McKay and Wong call "colonialist/racialized discourse" (p. 583). Such discursive constructions, as Pavlenko (2004) would argue, are evidence that language is "the locus of social organization and power, and a form of symbolic capital as well as a site of struggle where subjectivity and individual consciousness are produced" (p. 54).

All language use therefore presents opportunities for identity construction, in which negotiation and struggle take place in the contexts of differential power relations. Norton (Norton Peirce, 1995) also refers to Bourdieu's ideas of power as determining an individual's "right to speak" as well as his or her ability "to impose reception" (p. 18), i.e., to be heard.

Some of the immigrant women in Norton's study, for example, remained silent in certain social contexts—such instances might be interpreted as feelings of disempowerment, or conversely, such silences could be seen as instances of learner agency in which the immigrant women chose silence as "forms of resistance to inequitable social forces" (p. 20).

To capture the ways in which agency and identity are involved in the learning process, Norton (1997) uses the notion of *investment* to articulate the intricate ways in which learners' desires are bound up with the energies and effort they put into learning the target language. Norton defines investment as "the socially and historically constructed relationship of learners to the target language and their sometimes ambivalent desire to learn and practice it" (p. 411). She argues that the notion of investment gives a richer and more nuanced understanding of the ways in which the changing, multiple, and often conflicted identities of learners affect the way they participate in the learning process. Norton (Norton Peirce, 1995; Norton, 2000), for example, observed that although the immigrant women in her study were highly motivated, not all of them were willing to commit to the learning process.

Norton (Norton, 2001; Pavlenko & Norton, 2007) suggests that whether learners participate or not participate in the learning process is linked to their investment in particular imagined communities. Drawing on concepts from theories relating to imagined communities (Anderson, 1991) and communities of practice (Lave & Wenger, 1991; Wenger, 1998) Norton argues that imagination, which Wenger (1998, p. 176) defines as the creation of "new images of the world and ourselves," is essential to the learning process—second language learners' investments in learning are tied to the imagined images of the target language communities which they want to participate in. Norton's own study (2001) also demonstrates how learners may choose not to participate or invest in the learning process if they see this as being incongruent with their imagined communities.

Identity and EIL

The discussion in the two sections above has been organized around the different ways in which research on identity has influenced, or been influenced by, the way language is conceptualized, and our understanding of the ways in which it is acquired. We continue discussion of these concerns in this section by relating concepts of sociocultural identity with key issues relating to EIL research.

As used in this chapter, EIL refers to the way in which English has spread so rapidly and profusely across the globe such that it is now used by a diversity of people and communities around the world for a wide range of purposes and in a varied range of contexts. This dramatic increase in the number of people and communities around the world who have adopted English can be largely attributed to the effects of globalization, which, in the past thirty years, has been noticeably accelerated by the evolution of newer and better information and communications technologies. English has spread, fueled by the growth of social affordances of the Internet as well as through its role as the primary medium of communication for international travel, law, safety, health, and finance. The result of this rapid spread has meant that speakers of English who learn and use it as an additional language to their own mother tongues now considerably outnumber those who speak English as their L1. In addition, the use of English has also changed— English is now used more for global communication in multilingual contexts, across linguistic and cultural boundaries, rather than among L1 speakers in the traditional English-speaking countries such as the UK, the US, Canada, and Australia (Canagarajah, 2005). Crystal (2006), for example, estimates the current number of L1 English speakers at 400 million in contrast to the over 1 billion who speak it as an international language (see also McKay, this volume).

Ownership of English

The rapid spread of English as a global language has raised several issues in relation to English language teaching. The most fundamental of these relates to the ways in which it challenges basic assumptions of the links between language and identity, and in particular, what it means to "own" a language. As Rajagopalan (2004, p. 112) puts it, our normal understanding of a language is that it is "typically spoken by a country of native speakers, and [only] exceptionally, or marginally (that is to say, from a theoretical point of view, in a none-too-interesting sense) by a group of non-native speakers." Rajagopalan suggests then that the normative view of language ownership is one defined by linguistic inheritance (Rampton, 1990), which legitimizes the understanding that a language belongs to its native speakers. Furthermore, the assumption is that those who speak a language as "native speakers" will naturally outnumber those who use it only occasionally and for limited purposes. The phenomenal spread of English as an international language, however, clearly challenges such a perspective because those who speak English as a non-native language are clearly now the majority.

In response to this remarkable reversal in the profiles of English use and users, many researchers have proposed models to represent the pluricentricity of English. The most influential of these is Kachru's (1992) "Three Circle model" in which the spread of English is modeled using a tripartite distinction. At the center of his model, Kachru defines countries, e.g., Britain, the USA, Canada, Australia, and New Zealand, where English is spoken as L1, as the Inner Circle. In the second Outer Circle lie the postcolonial communities such as India, the Philippines, Singapore, Nigeria, and Malaysia for whom English is a nativized variety, by which is meant that these countries have policies that support the institutional and therefore widespread use of English in official domains such as government, law, and education. Such institutionalization of English in these communities has led to the development of locally-relevant varieties of World Englishes. The outermost circle in Kachru's model is the Expanding Circle where English is used in restricted contexts and for limited purposes; in these countries English is a foreign language for international communication with L1 speakers.

However, while the Kachruvian model of World Englishes in many ways expresses the multivocality and shared ownership of English as one tongue with many voices, it has been criticized for categorizing the different contexts of English use in terms of "norms." In particular, by positioning the Inner-Circle countries as norm-providing, the Three Circle model is seen to be perpetuating the misconception of the Inner-Circle countries as the rightful owners of English, since only they are the sanctioned providers of the linguistic norms of English. Furthermore, the model relegates the Outer-Circle countries as only norm-developing, which appears to characterize their Englishes as less than complete.[4] Similarly, the Expanding Circles are characterized as having norm-dependent learner-varieties of English which must rely on the Inner-Circle countries for standards of correctness.

Critically, the characterization of the English spoken in the Outer and Expanding countries, i.e., where English is spoken as an international language, with reference to the English spoken in the Inner Circle does not properly recognize the linguistic ownership of English by speakers of EIL. Three main areas of concerns with such a perspective are highlighted:

- First, it does not take into account that globalization has accelerated the adoption of English, not by individuals, but by whole communities and groups of people through what Brutt-Griffler (2002) calls "macroacquisition."
- Second, it fails to acknowledge that the widespread macroacquisition marks "the deterritorialization of the English language [in which] English has gained a life beyond its land of origins, acquiring an identity and currency in new geographical and social domains, as it gets localized for diverse settings and purposes" (Canagarajah, 2005, p. xxiii).
- Third, in comparing the norms by which EIL speakers use English with those of the traditional L1 English-speaking countries, it

perpetuates a deficit view of EIL learners. It implies that the goal of EIL learners in learning English is to emulate the speech patterns of English L1 speakers to achieve "native-like" competence. Here language learning is again equated with identifying with the target language group, and the subsequent loss of the EIL speaker's L1-associated identity.

In the following sections, we discuss each of these points in turn, ending each of these sections with reflections on the implications for EIL teaching and learning.

Global Discourse Communities

A distinguishing feature that characterizes English as a world language is the fact that it is used for communication across linguistic and cultural boundaries. EIL, defined in this broader manner, is a more inclusive definition that includes the use of English as a language of wider communication in both the Outer and Expanding Circles (McKay, 2002, p. 38). Such a definition contrasts with the term "English as a lingua franca" (ELF), which is generally reserved to describe the use of English in the Expanding Circles. EIL is a useful concept because it may not always be clear if a country should be considered an Outer or Expanding Circle. Take the changing linguistic profile of Malaysia, for example, which suggests its possible shift from the Outer to the Expanding Circle. Lee (2003) reports with the modifications to Malaysia's educational policies instituting Malay, in place of English, as the primary medium of instruction in schools, Malaysians under 30 years of age exhibit far less English use and knowledge than those whose basic education predates the policy initiatives. Conversely, McKay (2002) also discusses countries like Denmark, Norway, and Sweden where the intranational use of English is so prevalent that they might be considered Outer-Circle countries. Furthermore, as countries carve out new political and economic futures that involve new national identity options such as those of creating "citizens of the world," English, in its role as a global language, will be more prevalent in a greater number of nations (Pavlenko & Norton, 2007, p. 593).

For many EIL speakers, however, English is used to communicate ideas and information with people across national boundaries, rather than intranationally. In referring in this manner to the transnational communicative function of EIL, we recognize that it is a variety (or sets of varieties) that is (are) spoken by communities of speakers, rather than by isolated pockets of individual learners. This macroacquisition of English that Brutt-Griffler (2002) refers to can be seen not only in relation to countries or geographically bound communities, but also communities that are organized around specific interests or registers. We therefore now speak of EIL not only in terms of geographically-defined speech communities sharing a dialect, but also of the wide and varied range of global discourse communities, which are organized around specific registers, occupations, or social interest groups (McKay, 2002). These take especial advantage of global technologies which offer EIL users and learners new means of access to, and communication with, people across the globe who belong to these communities of practice, and who share their particular interests or registers. As the most used language of the Internet, English is naturally the primary medium of such engagement.

Such global discourse communities are useful resources for EIL teaching because they offer possibilities of imagined communities and hybrid identities that allow EIL learners to explore and engage with English in truly authentic EIL contexts outside the classroom. Lam's (2000) research on online fan practices demonstrates how technology-mediated affordances offer English language learners the representational resources to construct textually-mediated linguistic and cultural identities for themselves that extend beyond their classrooms, and beyond traditional geographical borders. Lam explores the identity development of a Chinese immigrant student who creates a website devoted to a popular Japanese singer. In authoring the site and responding to visitors to his site, Lam's learner engages in the online discursive practices through which he collaboratively shapes his identity as an EIL language user in his interactions with other English language learners who form a global community of fans from all around the world. Through such computer-mediated communication, learners are able to manage their investments in learning by focusing on clear goals that are meaningful to them, which may include membership of imagined global discourse communities that allow them to connect with people who share common histories, affiliations, and goals.

EIL as Global and Local

We need to recognize that English, in functioning as an international language, is "de-nationalized" (Smith, 1976 cited in McKay, 2002, p. 12) or "deterritorialized" (Canagarajah, 2005, p. xxiii) because it exists not just globally, but also locally, alongside local languages and cultures in multilingual communities of bilingual speakers (Brutt-Griffler, 2002). Consequently, English assumes a role as a local language, alongside its obvious position as a global language, to serve the diverse local needs of its multilingual, multicultural communities of EIL speakers and learners. Understood in this way, we see English as evolving and changing to suit local needs and identities. It is this "glocal" perspective that concerns research, especially of Outer-Circle English (e.g., Alsagoff, 2010 on Singapore English; Bhatt, 2005 on Indian English; Higgins, 2009 on the English spoken in East Africa), into the ways in which English, as part of the spectrum of EIL speakers' linguistic repertoire, is involved in "acts of identity" (Le Page & Tabouret-Keller, 1985), as speakers employ semiotic means such as code-switching, styling (Coupland, 2007), and crossing (Rampton, 1995) to index and enact their hybrid identities as EIL speakers.

In their appropriations of English as a resource for meaning-making and identity construction, EIL learners must also contend with conflicts relating to particular Western ideologies and practices that English is imbued with. The participants in Lee's (2003) and Gu's (2008) studies, for example, need to negotiate their orientations and stances with regard to English because of its associations with Christianity. In a study which examined how three university undergraduate EIL learners constructed multiple identities to position themselves in a Chinese educated urban community and an English speaking Christian community, Gu (2008) demonstrates how the perceived Western ideologies associated with English require learners to negotiate identities that allow them to manage local cultural discourses and beliefs. Gu's research participants reacted differently to the ideological connection to Christianity, resulting in differences in their investments in their use of English. Gu's study also demonstrates the association of English with urbanization, and the ways in which the learners re-examined and reframed their orientations and stances in developing investments and social participations congruent with their desired identities as worldly university students.

Lee's (2003) study of fourteen Malaysian speakers of English shows an interesting aspect of resistance in which her participants "mask" their identities as English speakers in order to be accepted as members of their religious or social communities. Lee's participants discuss their need to negotiate a gamut of multiple identities that balance their constructed multiple identities as educated persons, teachers, and professionals against more socially enforced identities as Muslim women. The investment of Lee's participants in English language is correspondingly nuanced—she argues that her participants see their identities and investment in English as sometimes needing to be hidden or disguised in order to discursively construct and claim more locally-relevant identities that allow them to manage the expectations of their interlocutors, and to participate in local discourse communities. These findings parallel those in Norton and Kamal's (2003) study, conducted on middle-school students in Karachi, Pakistan in the wake of 9/11, in which the authors similarly demonstrate that learning English must be understood in relation to a "politics of location" (Canagarajah, 1999) which sees English co-existing with vernacular languages, and where the learners exhibit multiple and hybrid identities, in negotiating balance between local needs and global imperatives.

McKay (2002), in suggesting that the "de-nationalization" of English ownership referred to by Smith in characterizing a world language be reframed as "re-nationalization" (p. 12), points to the role of culture in the teaching of EIL, where the teaching of the English language can be grounded in the local cultures and identities of its speakers. McKay (2002) suggests that in the teaching of EIL, culture be given attention to in the curriculum. She critically examines three primary sources of content for language teaching materials—cultural content from English-speaking countries, local cultural content, and international cultural content, suggesting a reflective approach to the teaching of culture in EIL teaching that develops an ethos of "interculturalism" (Byram, 1998). Interculturalism is an approach to teaching culture that seeks to develop learners as intercultural speakers or mediators who are able to understand and respect language users as individuals with complex multiple identities and avoid the stereotyping which accompanies identifying someone's person by their national or ethnic origins (Byram, Gribkova, & Starkey, 2002).

The Comparative Fallacy

The macroacquisition of English has an important consequence for EIL research: it suggests that focus on language learning should be turned to bilingualism, rather than language shift (McKay, 2002). Unlike immigrant learners whose goal in learning English is to integrate into the L1 community to which they have moved, EIL learners have very different and specific goals. Bilingual EIL learners learn English not as a replacement for their L1s, and not because they wish to integrate into an English L1 community. EIL learners use English as one of their many linguistic resources to gain access and membership into desired global discourse communities that may help them with their work or education, or with furthering their opportunities for interaction with people with similar social interests globally.

Cook (1999) therefore argues that it is a fallacy to compare EIL speakers' ways of speaking with those of native speakers. Instead, he offers a different kind of identity discourse in which EIL learner identities are constructed around the concept of a multicompetent user of English, who possesses rich multilingual repertoires that serve their communication needs. Cook's notion of the multicompetent user (1992, 1999) affords EIL learners alternative possibilities for multiple identities that may be constructed through their different languages.[5] Instead of being cast as imperfect native speakers, EIL learners are now re-imagined as multilingual agents in control of complex linguistic repertoires that serve their identity needs. Because EIL speakers learn English for specific purposes related to their jobs or business, their investments in learning English can be framed by an understanding of their desired participation into particular imagined communities. As a powerful global language, English is able to facilitate such participation—we are reminded of Kachru's (1986) comment that "knowing English is like possessing the fabled Aladdin's lamp, which permits one to open, as it were, the linguistic gates of international business, technology, science, and travel" (p. 1), offering learners access to cultural capital.

As the medium of globalization, English wields great power and prestige; so much so that Phillipson (1992) warns against the linguistic imperialism of English. In this respect, the hegemonic practices of the TESOL industry purposefully perpetuate the concept of the "native speaker," in which being an English speaker is linked with linguistic inheritance (Rampton, 1990) rather than need, use, or expertise. Rampton's proposal to move away from the notion of the "native speaker" by suggesting that identity as an English speaker should lie in linguistic expertise rather than linguistic inheritance is complicated when Western claims to the ownership of English are insinuated in the provision of "expertise" in the form of language teaching materials, textbooks, and "language teaching experts" from the West.

The imagined "native speaker" is a powerful myth— Jenkins (2009, p. 204) suggests that EIL learners and teachers may themselves be "complicit in the process of their own subordination" in conceptualizing their own learner identities in ways that are subordinate and stereotyped as the colonized "other," as revealed by their pejorative remarks in evaluating "non-native" English accents. What is perhaps most revealing is that the participants in Jenkins' report of her study comment positively on Swedish accents, but negatively on the Asian and Russian accents, signaling integral links between language and power, in which linguistic capital is measured in terms of perceived economic worth.

Jenkins' (2009) survey and interviews of research participants from Expanding-Circle countries show, however, that the EIL learners may realize the conflicts involved in this "othering." On the one hand, Jenkins reports that EIL learners want to "project their own local identity in their English, and [to feel] themselves to be part of a community of lingua franca English speakers, and to share a common identity with other ELF speakers" (p. 204), but on the other hand, still aspire to sound "native," as voiced by one of Jenkins' research participants:

> I really feel bad about this you know, I feel like I have to lose my identity. I'm a Taiwanese person and I should feel comfortable about

this, and I just feel that when I'm speaking English, I will want to be like a native speaker, and it's really hard you know.

(p. 205)

Such examples of learner attitudes demonstrate that identity construction for EIL learners is far from straightforward. The learners in Jenkins' study are conflicted in what they imagine their future selves to be and they struggle with their own desires to be "native," while wanting their locally-constructed identities to be recognized. Although agentive in their creations of imagined communities and their decisions whether to invest in learning, EIL learners are also subject to social forces that arise from the political realities of English as a valued commodity of globalization.

The literature on EIL, however diverse in opinion, is united in the desire to move away from teaching for native-speaker competence. In attempting to reconceptualize communicative competence in real and current sociocultural terms, Leung (2005) suggests that through developing teachers and learners as ethnographers and the adoption of different sets of intellectual sensitivities and sensibilities, we can begin to clarify our understandings of what it means to teach and learn English as an international language. Leung (2005, p. 138) proposes three such perspectives from Roberts, Byram, Barro, Jordan, and Street (2001):

- Epistemological relativity ... involves recognizing one's own assumptions about knowledge, and how it is legitimized in one's own society, so as to be able to view the knowledge of other societies with a more open mind ...
- Reflexivity ... refers to the ability to reflect critically on the way in which one's own cultural background and standpoint influence one's view of other cultures ...
- Critical consciousness ... views ethnography not simply as a convenient tool for studying and research but as itself a product of particular dominant societies at a particular period.

Swales (1990) similarly discusses an ethnographic approach to language teaching in relation to global discourse communities in which he sees knowledge of learner identities and understanding of the sociocultural contexts of learning distinct to each classroom situation as critical to the development of EIL appropriate strategies for the teaching of writing.

Conclusion

In this chapter, we have come to understand that identity is not a fixed or invariant attribute of the mind. Rather, identity is better viewed as a sociocultural phenomenon that is "co-constructed, negotiated and transformed on an ongoing basis by means of language" (Duff & Uchida, 1997, p. 452), which allows for an interrogation of the ways in which learning as a social process is mediated through language, and subject to "broader social discourses with their inscribed power relations" (Ricento, 2005, p. 895). The issues of ownership and identity, as we have seen, are key to understanding the ways in which EIL challenges our notions of what language is. Research on EIL learner identity is, however, in its infancy, and there are few ethnographic studies (e.g., Hirano, 2009; Lee, 2003; Rajadurai, 2010) that document the role that identity plays in pedagogic practice.

Exploring sociocultural identity in the teaching and learning of English as an international language is important because the highly diverse learning contexts as well as profiles of EIL learners pose a challenge for language education—as McKay (2002) observes, such diversity cannot be managed by any one teaching approach or method. Instead, this diversity is more wisely addressed by adopting postmethod practices (Canagarajah, 2005; Kumaravadivelu, 1994), in which the learner and the teacher are recognized as social agents who are able to act in locally appropriate ways. Central to such an approach therefore is the recognition of teacher and learner agency and identities to appropriate and shape English in ways that are congruent with their desires and purposes, that recognize their agency and participation, and which take into account their local understandings and cultures.

Exploring the Ideas

1 Do you believe that the concept of "native speaker" affects the way English is taught and learned in your country? Speak to five people who are learning English. Ask them about their textbooks and what methods their teacher uses in their English classes. Do they have a sense that they are expected to attain "native-speaker competence"? In what ways does this affect their sense of identity as learners?

2 Approach three learners and ask them to keep journals of their language learning for a period of three weeks. Have them write at least half a page twice or three times a week in which they discuss their experiences in their language classes. From their journals, can you pick out the ways in which the experiences that the learners write about reflect identity as changeable and multiple?

3 Write down five different ways in which your (or any of your friends') use of English may be different from what is found in the textbooks or dictionaries. Interview your friends to find out if they

are aware that they are using English differently, and if they can tell you why they do this. Do their reasons relate to notions of identity? If so how?

Applying the Ideas

1 In your opinion, should an English teacher strive to explore identity in their classrooms? Why or why not? Do you think your answer applies to all classrooms, learners, and teachers? If you think that identity is a useful concept to introduce in a language classroom, list three ideas you have as to how a teacher could do this successfully. Write down three possible problems teachers can face when trying to incorporate identity in language teaching.

2 If you use the Internet, keep a log for three days in which you document the English language used in three different social network sites or blog sites that you are familiar with. Record information about each site, who it is intended for, who it is used by, and what its purposes are. Examine the entries on such sites. Does the English used in these sites suggest the identities of its creator(s) or users? In what ways is the English different from what you find in your English language textbooks?

3 Examine at least three textbooks of English. List the ways in which people of different countries or races are depicted. What kinds of claims do these books make about the identities of such people? Are all the people represented in a similar way, or are there differences in the ways in which the books describe them? Examine how such descriptions affect the way you or your students might view yourselves or other language learners.

Notes

1 See McNamara (1997), for an extended discussion of the relevance of Tajfel's theories to current applied linguistics and SLA study.

2 I use the term "sociocultural" following Bucholtz and Hall (2005) in referring broadly to the "interdisciplinary field concerned with the intersection of language, culture, and society" (p. 586), rather than the more narrowly defined Vygotskyan framework. I refer to sociocultural identity rather than social or cultural identity as the latter two terms are associated with very different frames of thinking. "Social identity" can be confused with Tajfel's (1974) Social Identity Theory, and "cultural identity" with the univalent links that define language on the basis of national or ethnic identity.

3 Duff (2012) discusses how such sociocultural conceptualizations of identity have had a significant influence on current social-psychological theories of motivation and identity that now also seek to represent identity in terms of possible future selves rather than just current selves (e.g., as in Dörnyei & Ushioda, 2009).

4 Interestingly, however, it must be said that the Three Circle model has in fact been instrumental in giving prominence to the growing ownership of English by the Outer-Circle countries.

5 Duff (2012) also notes the ways in which researchers have shifted their characterization of EIL users and learners, from labels such as multicompetent users, interlanguage users, fossilized L2 users, limited (English) proficient users to lingua franca users/learners and advanced L2 users (rather than "learners").

References

Alsagoff, L. (2010). English in Singapore: Culture, capital and identity in linguistic variation. *World Englishes, 29*(3), 336–348.

Anderson, B. (1991). *Imagined communities: Reflections on the origin and spread of nationalism* (Revised ed.). London: Verso.

Bakhtin, M. M. (1981). *The dialogic imagination: Four essays by M. M. Bakhtin.* Ed. M. Holquist, Trans. M. Holquist & C. Emerson. Austin, TX: University of Texas Press.

Bhatt, R. M. (2005). Expert discourses, local practices, and hybridity: The case of Indian Englishes. In A. S. Canagarajah (Ed.), *Reclaiming the local in language policy and practice* (pp. 25–54). Mahwah, NJ: Lawrence Erlbaum.

Block, D. (2007). The rise of identity in SLA research, post Firth and Wagner (1997), *Modern Language Journal, 91*(5), 863–876.

Brutt-Griffler, J. (2002). *World English: A study of its development.* Clevedon: Multilingual Matters.

Bucholtz, M., & Hall, K. (2005). Identity and interaction: A sociocultural linguistic approach. *Discourse Studies, 7*(4–5), 585–614.

Byram, M. (1998). Cultural identities in multilingual classrooms. In J. Cenoz, & F. Genesee (Eds.), *Beyond bilingualism* (pp. 96–116). Clevedon: Multilingual Matters.

Byram, M., Gribkova, B., & Starkey, H. (2002). *Developing the intercultural dimension in language teaching: A practical introduction for teachers.* Strasbourg: Council of Europe Publishing.

Canagarajah, A. S. (1999). *Resisting linguistic imperialism in English teaching.* Oxford: Oxford University Press.

Canagarajah, A. S. (Ed.). (2005). *Reclaiming the local in language policy and practice.* Mahwah, NJ: Lawrence Erlbaum.

Cook, V. (1992). Evidence for multicompetence. *Language Learning, 42*(4), 557–591.

Cook, V. (1999). Going beyond the native speaker in language teaching. *TESOL Quarterly, 33*(2), 185–209.

Coupland, N. (2007). *Style: Language variation and identity.* Cambridge: Cambridge University Press.

Crystal, D. (2006). English worldwide. In R. Hogg & D. Denison (Eds.). *A history of the English language* (pp.420–39). Cambridge: Cambridge University Press.

Dörnyei, Z., & Ushioda, E. (2009). (Eds.). *Motivation, language identity and the L2 self.* Bristol, UK: Multilingual Matters.

Duff, P. (2012). Identity, agency and second language acquisition. In S. M. Gass & A. Mackey (Eds.), *The Routledge handbook of second language acquisition*. London and New York: Routledge.

Duff, P. A., & Uchida, Y. (1997). The negotiation of teachers' sociocultural identities and practices in postsecondary EFL classrooms. *TESOL Quarterly, 31*(3), 451–486.

Firth, A., & Wagner, J. (1997). On discourse, communication, and (some) fundamental concepts in SLA research. *Modern Language Journal, 81*, 285–300.

Gardner, R. C. (1985). *Social psychology and second language learning: The role of attitudes and motivation*. London: Edward Arnold.

Gardner, R. C., & Lambert, W. E. (1972). *Attitudes and motivation: Second language learning*. Rowley, MA: Newbury House.

Gu, M. (2008). Identity construction and investment transformation: College students from non-urban areas in China. *Journal of Asian Pacific Communication, 18*(1), 49–70.

Higgins, C. (2009). *English as a local language: Post-colonial identities and multilingual practices*. Bristol: Multilingual Matters.

Hirano, E. (2009). Learning difficulty and learner identity: A symbiotic relationship. *ELT Journal, 63*(1), 33–41.

Jenkins, J. (2009). English as a lingua franca: Interpretations and attitudes. *World Englishes, 28*(2), 200–207.

Joseph, J. E. (2004). *Language and identity: National, ethnic, religious*. Basingstoke: Palgrave Macmillan.

Kachru, B. B. (1986). *The alchemy of English*. Oxford: Pergamon Press.

Kachru, B. B. (Ed.). (1992). *The other tongue* (2nd ed.). Urbana and Chicago, IL: University of Illinois Press.

Krashen, S. (1981). The "fundamental pedagogic principle" in second language teaching. *Studia Linguistica, 35*, 50–70.

Kumaravadivelu, B. (1994). The postmethod condition: (E)merging strategies for second/foreign language teaching. *TESOL Quarterly, 28*(1), 27–48.

Lam, W. S. E. (2000). L2 literacy and the design of the self: A case study of a teenager writing on the internet. *TESOL Quarterly, 34*(3), 457–482.

Lave, J., & Wenger, E. (1991). *Situated learning: Legitimate peripheral participation*. Cambridge: Cambridge University Press.

Le Page, R. B., & Tabouret-Keller, A. (1985). *Acts of identity: Creole based approaches to language and ethnicity*. Cambridge: Cambridge University Press.

Lee, S. K. (2003). Multiple identities in a multicultural world: A Malaysian perspective. *Journal of Language, Identity, and Education, 2*(3), 137–158.

Leung, C. (2005). Convivial communication: Recontextualizing communicative competence. *International Journal of Applied Linguistics, 15*(2), 119–144.

McKay, S. L. (2002). *Teaching English as an international language: Rethinking goals and approaches*. Oxford: Oxford University Press.

McKay, S. L., & Wong, C. S. (1996). Multiple discourses, multiple identities: Investment and agency in second-language learning among Chinese adolescent immigrant students. *Harvard Educational Review, 66*(3): 577–608.

McNamara, T. (1997). Theorizing social identity: What do we mean by social identity? Competing frameworks, competing discourses. *TESOL Quarterly, 31*(3), 561–567.

Norton, B. (1997). Language, identity, and the ownership of English. *TESOL Quarterly, 31*(3), 409–429.

Norton, B. (2000). *Identity and language learning: Gender, ethnicity, and educational change.* London: Longman.

Norton, B. (2001). Non-participation, imagined communities, and the language classroom. In M. Breen (Ed.), *Learner contributions to language learning: New directions in research* (pp.156–171). Harlow: Pearson.

Norton, B., & Kamal, F. (2003). The imagined communities of English language learners in a Pakistani school. *Journal of Language, Identity, and Education, 2*(4), 301–318.

Norton, B., & Toohey, K. (2002). Identity and language learning. In R. Kaplan (Ed.), *Oxford University handbook of applied linguistics* (pp. 115–123). Oxford: Oxford University Press.

Norton Peirce, B. (1995). Social identity, investment, and language learning. *TESOL Quarterly, 29*(1), 9–31.

Pavlenko, A. (2004). Gender and sexuality in foreign and second language education: Critical and feminist approaches. In B. Norton & K. Toohey (Eds.), *Critical pedagogies and language learning.* Cambridge: Cambridge University Press.

Pavlenko, A., & Norton, B. (2007). Imagined communities, identity, and English language teaching. In J. Cummins & C. Davison (Eds.), *International handbook of English language teaching* (pp. 669–680). New York: Springer.

Phillipson, R. (1992). *Linguistic imperialism.* Oxford: Oxford University Press.

Rajadurai, J. (2010). "Malays are expected to speak Malay": Community ideologies, language use and the negotiation of identities. *Journal of Language, Identity and Education, 9*(2), 91–106.

Rajagopalan, K. (2004). The concept of "World English" and its implications for ELT. *ELT Journal, 58*(2), 111–117.

Rampton, B. (1990). Displacing the native speaker: Expertise, affiliation, and inheritance. *ELT Journal, 44,* 97–101.

Rampton B. (1995). *Crossing: Language and ethnicity among adolescents.* London: Longman.

Ricento, T. (2005). Considerations of identity in L2 learning. In E. Hinkel (Ed.), *Handbook of research on second language teaching and learning* (pp. 895–911). Mahwah, NJ: Lawrence Erlbaum Associates.

Roberts, C., Byram, M., Barro, A., Jordan, S., & Street, B. (2001). *Language learners as ethnographers.* Clevedon: Multilingual Matters.

Schumann, J. H. (1978). *The pidginization process: A model for second language acquisition.* Massachusetts: Newbury House Publishers.

Smith, L. (1976). English as an international auxiliary language. *RELC Journal, 7*(2), 38–43.

Swales, J. M. (1990). *Genre analysis.* Cambridge: Cambridge University Press.

Tajfel, H. (1974). Social identity and intergroup behavior. *Social Science Information, 13*(2), 65–93.

Tajfel, H., & Turner, J. C. (1979). An integrative theory of intergroup conflict. In W. G. Austin & S. Worchel (Eds.), *The social psychology of intergroup relations* (pp. 33–47). Monterey, CA: Brooks/Cole.

van Lier, L. (1994). Forks and hope: Pursuing understanding in different ways. *Applied Linguistics, 15*(3), 328–347.

Wenger, E. (1998). *Communities of practice: Learning, meaning, and identity.* Cambridge: Cambridge University Press.

Chapter 8

Assessing English as an International Language

Guangwei Hu

Introduction

The last few decades have witnessed significant changes in the users and uses of English as an international language (EIL) (McKay, 2002, this volume; Schneider, 2011). One change, grand in scale and far-reaching in consequence, is that the numbers of learners and users of English have risen staggeringly (Crystal, 2003). According to a recent estimate cited in Schneider (2011, p. 2), there are close to 2 billion English speakers today. Notably, the populations of native speakers (NS) of English in the Inner-Circle countries (see B. Kachru, 1986) are not only surpassed in number by non-native speakers (NNS) of English in the Outer-Circle countries but also far outnumbered by users of English as a foreign language (EFL) in the Expanding-Circle countries (Canagarajah, 2007; Crystal, 2003). Along with the geographical and demographical spread and diffusion of English at global and local levels, the domains of use have also expanded tremendously for English such that it is the de facto language for communication among people from different language backgrounds in a growing variety of political, economic, cultural, educational, intellectual, and social areas (Y. Kachru, 2011; McKay & Bokhorst-Heng, 2008; Murata & Jenkins, 2009; Svartvik & Leech, 2006).

The changing demographics of English language learners and users as well as the diverse contexts of English use have posed strenuous challenges to the assessment of English proficiency (Canagarajah, 2006a; Jenkins, 2006; Jenkins, Cogo, & Dewey, 2011). English proficiency tests, especially high-stakes ones, have huge consequences for English language learners and users.[1] Traditionally, two standard varieties of native-speaker English, namely American and British English, have been taken for granted in the definition of the construct of English proficiency for such tests (Davies, 2009; Hamp-Lyons & Davies, 2008; Lowenberg, 2002). However, the fundamentally changed landscape of EIL requires a critical examination of the established assessment practices. To that end, this chapter begins with an overview of the established approach to testing English proficiency, which is primarily concerned with the technical quality of the assessment procedures but gives little attention to ideological concerns arising from the choice of English norms for such procedures. This is followed by a discussion of some recent proposals for assessing EIL, World Englishes (WE), and English as a lingua franca (ELF) made in response to such ideological concerns. In particular, attention will be given to a "weak" approach to assessing English that allows test accommodations without changing the underlying test construct and a "strong" approach that defines the test construct not in terms of Standard American or British English but in terms of EIL/WE/ELF in its own right and/or competence criteria other than the traditionally dominant one of linguistic accuracy. The chapter concludes with a set of principles for developing valid and ethical assessments of EIL at international and intranational levels.

Established Practices and Principles for Assessing English

The established approach to developing English assessment instruments, especially standardized high-stakes English proficiency tests, consists of a variety of tasks and activities undertaken in four interconnected stages: conceptualization, construction, try-out, and operation (McNamara, 2000). What follows is an outline of the central considerations and core tasks that are addressed in each stage.

Test Design

The conceptualization or design stage typically begins with a consideration and specification of the purpose(s) of the assessment, that is, "the specific uses for which the test is intended" (Bachman & Palmer, 1996, p. 88). An English test may be intended primarily to assess learners' achievement of curricular goals, diagnose their strengths and weaknesses in specific domains of language learning, place them at the right level of instruction, or measure their proficiency for a specific purpose for selection decisions (Brown & Abeywickrama, 2010; Hughes, 2003). Once the main purpose of the assessment is determined, the target language abilities to be assessed, namely the construct underlying the assessment instrument, need to be defined theoretically and operationally (Bachman, 1990). The construct definition is often made in reference to one of those influential models/frameworks of communicative language ability (e.g., Bachman, 1990; Canale & Swain, 1980) that have been proposed. Notably, these models of communicative language ability are assumed, explicitly or implicitly, to be abstractions of the idealized monolingual native speaker's communicative competence (see Alptekin, 2002; Leung, 2005; Leung & Street, this volume).

Another important task of the conceptualization stage is the identification and description of the distinctive characteristics of "the tasks in the [target language use] domain to which we want our inferences about language ability to generalize" (Bachman & Palmer, 1996, p. 88). Such a specification is seen as providing the necessary basis for considering and ensuring the authenticity and situational appropriacy of target language use. Notably, authenticity and appropriacy are conceptualized with the native-speaker norms in mind (Alptekin, 2002; Rajagopalan, 2004). In this regard, Rajagopalan (2010) contends that "concepts like 'authenticity' and cultural or situational 'appropriacy' ... contribute toward ensuring special trading privileges for those who could claim the status of consummate native speakers (i.e. legal owners) of English" (p. 467). Other activities undertaken in the conceptualization stage include describing the prospective test takers' characteristics, inventorying available and required resources, planning the allocation and management of the available resources, and working out a plan for evaluating test usefulness. The conceptualization stage results in a "design statement" (Bachman & Palmer, 1996, p. 88) whose purpose is to provide principled guidance and input for the next stage of assessment development.

Test Construction

Informed by the design statement, a set of specifications for the intended assessment is developed at the outset of the construction stage. These specifications serve as a generative blueprint with detailed information on the structure of the assessment, the target candidates, the types and topics of texts to be included, the task types to be employed, the language skills and elements to be assessed, the test techniques to be used, time allotment, the criteria of performance against which candidates are evaluated, the scoring procedures to be adopted, etc. (Alderson, Clapham, & Wall, 1995; Hughes, 2003). Such a generative blueprint is paramount in that "testers should be able to compile new equivalent forms from the test specifications, and item writers should be able to write new items or tasks that have *congruence* with the item specifications" (Fulcher & Davidson, 2007, p. 377). Once the blueprint is in place, the specified content is sampled for inclusion in the assessment (Hughes, 2003). This is followed by the selection of materials for use in the construction of the assessment. Test items are then written in strict accordance with the specifications laid out in the blueprint. Also written in this stage are instructions for prospective candidates (Bachman & Palmer, 1996). The construction stage is usually rounded off with the moderating of the generated test items and instructions.

With regard to the fundamental considerations of the construction stage, it is important to note that the content of an English assessment as specified in the generative blueprint typically focuses on formal correctness as defined by a metropolitan native-speaker variety of English (Canagarajah, 2006a; Jenkins, 2006; Lowenberg, 2002) and that the criterial levels of performance adopted are often based on the linguistic and cultural norms of the idealized native speaker. Although sustained attention has been given to authenticity of language use in recent research on language testing in general and assessment of English proficiency in particular (Leung & Lewkowicz, 2006), authenticity per se is almost invariably conceived in terms of test tasks rather than language varieties or language norms. Furthermore, real-life tasks in EIL are often assumed to involve interactions primarily with native speakers of metropolitan varieties (Jenkins, 2006; Leung & Street, this volume). Thus, although there has been a growing emphasis on testing English ability and use in context, this has not taken account of EIL speakers' prevalent contexts of English use.

Test Try-out

In the development of a major test, the standard practice requires that the newly constructed instrument be tried out before it becomes operational (Alderson et al., 1995). The overarching purpose of the try-out stage lies in "collecting information about the usefulness of the test itself, and for the improvement of the test and testing procedures" (Bachman & Palmer, 1996, p. 91). The try-out may be conducted informally with a group of proficient users of the target language (Hughes, 2003), though it usually involves the trialing of the newly developed test on a sample of the learner population for whom the test is intended. The trialing results are then analyzed for validity and reliability evidence. Classical item analyses that involve the calculation of facility values and discrimination indexes for individual test items are conducted to determine how well particular items perform so that weak items can be identified and removed (Alderson et al., 1995). In major testing efforts, more sophisticated analyses based on Item Response Theory—for example, Rasch modeling (McNamara, 1996)—are performed to take the characteristics of the trial sample into account in estimating item parameters such as difficulty, discrimination, and threshold performance level (Fulcher & Davidson, 2007). If the assessment instrument in question requires the use of a rating scale, as in the case of a performance-based writing or speaking test, the try-out stage also involves scale calibration by expert raters (Hughes, 2003). In addition, both qualitative and quantitative feedback are collected by means of interviews, observations, questionnaires, and/or think-aloud protocols to identify problems with the testing environment, administrative procedures, and instructions; to discover test takers' perceptions of test tasks and test-taking processes; and to determine adequate time allocations (Bachman & Palmer, 1996). The collected information feeds back into the iterative process of revising and refining the test until its developers are confident that they "have reached the optimal design to release a working, crafted product, suitable for its intended purpose" (Fulcher & Davidson, 2007, p. 89).

Notably, native-speaker norms dominate the try-out stage, as is the case with the conceptualization and construction stages. This is evident in Hughes's recommendation that "items which have been through the process of moderation should be presented in the form of a test (or tests) to a number of native speakers—twenty or more, if possible" (2003, p. 63). In a similar vein, Alderson et al. (1995), though recognizing the controversial nature of trying out an English proficiency test on native speakers, believe that "the performance of suitably defined and selected native speakers is an important aspect of a test on which data ought to be gathered" because "there is always the danger that test writers may write items which follow the rules of the language, but do not reflect native-speaker usage" (p. 97).

Test Implementation

The next stage in the development of a test is the operation stage, in which the test is administered for the primary purpose of making inferences about the assessees' language ability. To facilitate valid inferences of this nature, materials (e.g., test syllabuses and operational manuals) need to be prepared for candidates, test users, and staff involved in the administration of the test (Hughes, 2003). By the same token, interviewers, scorers, proctors, and other testing staff are trained. In the case of assessments that involve subjective judgment, examiner reliability is monitored systematically and regularly. Other activities undertaken in the operation stage include the marking of the test, the reporting of scores to candidates and other stakeholders, and the preparation of post-test reports that provide evidence of the instrument's reliability, validity, and meaningfulness for different audiences, e.g., the institution responsible for producing the test, teachers who prepare candidates for the test, human resource personnel entrusted with the task of deciding whether the test is adequate for their purposes, and researchers working in language testing and other related fields (Alderson et al., 1995). The operation stage, however, is not the end of a test development project but is cyclically related to the other stages (McNamara, 2000). It involves the continuing collection of information on the test and its use that feeds back into the development cycle to improve the usefulness of the instrument (Bachman & Palmer, 1996).

Principles of Test Usefulness

As alluded to above, the overarching concern of a test development project in the established approach to language assessment is to increase test usefulness (Leung & Lewkowicz, 2006). According to Bachman and Palmer (1996), six assessment qualities contribute to test usefulness. These test qualities are:

1 reliability, i.e., consistency of measurement across parallel forms of a test, different administrations of the same test, and/or different raters;
2 construct validity, i.e., "the extent to which we can interpret a given test score as an indicator of the ability(ies), or construct(s), we want to measure" (p. 21);
3 authenticity, i.e., the extent to which the characteristics of a test task correspond to those of a target language use task;
4 interactiveness, i.e., "the extent and type of involvement of the test taker's individual characteristics in accomplishing a test task" (p. 25);
5 impact, i.e., the influences of a test on individuals (e.g., test takers and teachers), institutional practices, educational systems (i.e., washback), and society at large;
6 practicality, i.e., the extent to which the available resources exceed the resources required for developing and implementing a test.

With regard to these test qualities, three principles have been formulated and gained general acceptance in the established approach to test development. The first principle recognizes that "it is the overall usefulness of the test that is to be maximized, rather than the individual qualities that affect usefulness" (Bachman & Palmer, 1996, p. 18). The second principle stresses that "the individual test qualities cannot be evaluated independently, but must be evaluated in terms of their combined effect on the overall usefulness of the test" (Bachman & Palmer, 1996, p. 18). The last principle states that "test usefulness and the appropriate balance among the different qualities cannot be prescribed in general, but must be determined for each specific testing situation" (Bachman & Palmer, 1996, p. 18). While they are laudable for the emphasis on, and the effort to increase, test usefulness, these principles and the established practices in test development can be said to take a technological perspective, rather than an ideological one, on test usefulness and related issues (Ross, 2011). Although it can enhance the psychometric qualities of an English proficiency test, such a perspective ignores the fundamental changes that have been taking place in the sociolinguistic realities of EIL, and the profound implications these changes have for such crucial notions as the construct of English proficiency, the authenticity of target English use, and the impact of native-speaker normed English tests at the societal and individual levels. It is precisely these implications and issues of power relations inhabiting the choice of linguistic norms for EIL assessment that an ideological perspective is concerned with.

Recent Developments in Assessment of EIL/WE/ELF

The last decade has seen a growing awareness and questioning of the hegemony of native-speaker norms in English proficiency tests, especially standardized, high-stakes ones. Davidson (2006, p. 709), for example, notes that

> There is a well-established and legitimate concern that large, powerful English language tests are fundamentally disconnected from the insights in analysis of English in the world context. These exams set forth linguistic norms that do not necessarily represent the rich body of English varieties spoken and used in contact situations all over the world.

Similarly, Leung and Lewkowicz (2006, p. 228) observe that "in terms of English language testing, particularly high-stakes, large-scale proficiency testing administered by international bodies, it would be fair to say that, in terms of language norms, language functions, and pragmatics, the metropolitan native speaker varieties have held sway." This practice, however, is questionable because "the growing knowledge of English as lingua franca (ELF) in the past few years is beginning to make this self-imposed normative insulation untenable" (Leung & Lewkowicz, 2006, p. 228). Central to this newly acquired knowledge is the recognition that "Standard American or British English does not have any relevance to many communicative activities of millions of multilingual speakers outside the inner circle" (Canagarajah, 2006a, p. 233).

The "Weak" Approach

While the established approach to assessing English proficiency has been slow in responding to the changing sociolinguistic realities of EIL, some recent developments concerning several high-stakes international tests of English are noteworthy and suggestive. One such development concerns IELTS (International English Language Testing System), "the world's proven English language test" offered in more than 130 countries, recognized by over 6,000 organizations, and taken by

1,500,000 candidates each year (IELTS, n.d.). In recent years, several accommodations have been made to IELTS in terms of its development, content, and scoring. These include (a) the use of reading and listening texts that reflect social and regional (restricted to the Inner Circle) language variations; (b) the incorporation of material writers from the UK, Australia, and New Zealand; and (c) the inclusion of proficient non-native speakers as examiners for the oral and written tests (Taylor, 2002). As Uysal (2010) points out, the first two types of accommodation neither address non-native varieties of English around the world nor attend to cross-cultural variations in discoursal conventions, but are concerned only with the Inner-Circle native-speaker varieties of English, or the so-called "dominant host languages" (Taylor, 2006, p. 56). Thus, as Hall (2010) readily admits, IELTS "serves both to deliver and reinforce discourses which support native-speaker language norms" (p. 326). The involvement of non-native speakers of English as raters for oral and written tests, however, is an embryonic attempt to accommodate, in a limited manner, to non-native speaker candidates.

An attempt of a similar nature has also been made "as part of an effort to revise the TOEFL" (Major, Fitzmaurice, Bunta, & Balasubramanian, 2002, p. 174), the test of English as a foreign language that is claimed to be "the most widely respected English-language test in the world" (Educational Testing Service, n.d.) taken by nearly 1,000,000 candidates each year and recognized by over 8,000 universities and other institutions in more than 130 countries. The attempt was reflected in a study commissioned by the Educational Testing Service to examine whether inclusion of accented non-native speakers in the listening section of the TOEFL would affect the listening comprehension of native speakers of American English as well as non-native speakers from different first language backgrounds, including Chinese, Japanese, and Spanish. Despite the mixed findings and their inconclusive interpretations, the significance of this commissioned study lies, as Llurda (2004) comments, in its reflection of "a growing acknowledgement of the existence of the huge number of non-native English speakers and the need to incorporate their voices into mainstream English language teaching and language testing" (p. 315). Notably, the potential change considered in this study for the TOEFL, like IELTS' use of non-native speaker raters, represents a limited attempt to accommodate to non-native speakers of English without toppling the dominance of native-speaker norms in the tests.

The test accommodations discussed above are representative of what may be described as a "weak" approach to assessing EIL/WE/ELF. In such an approach, the target language norms of EIL tests are assumed to be a standard native-speaker variety or one based on such a variety.

To accommodate to candidates speaking non-native varieties of English, however, some modifications are made to

> the delivery and scoring of such tests on the grounds that the test population includes ELF users [or, for that matter, users of Outer- and Expanding-Circle varieties of English] whose speech or writing may deviate from the codified standard, not necessarily because they are deficient in English, but because they inhabit communities where English is acquired nonnatively and particular nonnative features have assumed the status of stable varietal differences.
>
> (Elder & Davies, 2006, p. 288)

Such accommodations are expected to make a native-speaker normed test "more accessible and fairer" to candidates from the Outer- and the Expanding-Circle societies without changing the test construct, that is, competence in an Inner-Circle variety of English (Elder & Davies, 2006; Uysal, 2010).

Accommodations in the "weak" approach are summarized by Elder and Davies (2006, pp. 289–290) as comprising the following:

1 Vet texts used in [Standard British or American English] tests for potential bias against [users of other English varieties] who might have limited opportunities to encounter particular topics or genre … and therefore lack the background knowledge needed to make sense of these texts.
2 Gloss or avoid altogether any lexical items or structures which are likely [to] be unfamiliar to NNS users.
3 Use interlocutors (either examiners or other candidates) who are expert NNS/ELF users and therefore have experience in ELF contexts and know how to adjust their speech in ways familiar to the test takers.
4 Train raters, whether NSs or NNSs, to ensure that only those errors which result in miscommunication are penalized.
5 Involve ELF users in standard setting exercises.

While such accommodations may represent progress for some quarters of the language testing community, they can give rise to several intractable problems, including the continued hegemony of native-speaker norms (Jenkins, 2006), irrelevance of the tests to multilingual test takers' communicative needs (Canagarajah, 2006a), different meaning for native and non-native English speakers of scores from the same test (Elder & Davies, 2006), and the possible reinforcement of a deficit view of non-native English users' competence by positive discrimination (Elder & Davies, 2006).

The "Strong" Approach

In contrast to the "weak" approach, a "strong" approach to assessing EIL/ WE/ELF involves a more radical reorientation towards the test construct. Such a radical rethink revolves around the contention that the Outer- and Expanding-Circle varieties of English are not dependent on the Inner-Circle varieties but are valid linguistic norms in their own right (Elder & Davies, 2006; Jenkins et al., 2011; Kirkpatrick, 2011). Consequently, they should be part and parcel of the test construct (Jenkins, 2006). According to Elder and Davies (2006), additional features of the "strong" approach may include the following:

1   Sample test items directly from domains relevant to EIL/WE/ELF communication.
2   Focus on performance tasks that are evaluated in terms of functional effectiveness or task fulfillment (see also Matsuda, 2003).
3   Give priority to strategic competence over formal accuracy (Jenkins, 2006; Jenkins et al., 2011).
4   Use pair or group tasks that allow candidates to assume various communicative roles and include peer assessment as a legitimate means of determining interlocutors' competence (Elder & Davies, 2006).

A number of benefits are expected to follow from the "strong" approach. These include a more egalitarian footing for the Outer- and Expanding-Circle varieties of English that would result from the subverting of the hegemony of the Inner-Circle varieties (Jenkins, 2006), the greater meaningfulness and relevance of the chosen language norms to test takers from communities outside the Inner Circle (Canagarajah, 2006a; House, 2003), "more valid representations of target language use domains" (Elder & Davies, 2006, p. 296), and positive washback on the teaching of endonormative standards (Jenkins et al., 2011). These anticipated benefits notwithstanding, there are several thorny problems with the "strong" approach. These problems are particularly obvious and acute in the assessment of ELF, "the common language of choice, among speakers who come from different linguacultural backgrounds" (Jenkins, 2009, p. 200), which "involves both common ground and local variation" (p. 201). For the sake of space constraints, only the three most intractable ones are discussed below.

First, for competence in ELF to become the construct of an English test, ELF itself needs to be sufficiently codified (Davies, 2009). Such an extent of codification, however, is far from being a reality (Suzuki, 2010). Despite Seidlhofer's (2001) call for research on the description of ELF, only a small set of pragmatic, grammatical, and phonological features of ELF have been identified (see House, 2003; Jenkins et al., 2011;

Seidlhofer, 2004). In fact, Jenkins (2009) admits that "at present there is insufficient evidence for researchers to be able to predict the extent of the common ELF ground" (p. 201) and that

> it is also likely that researchers working on ELF in different parts of the world ... will identify different branches of ELF, just as there are different branches of ENL [English as a native language] such as North American English, Australian English, British English and so on, and different sub-varieties within these.
>
> (pp. 201–202)

Second, the very enterprise of ELF codification poses a conceptual conundrum (Maley, 2010). As Canagarajah characterizes it, ELF

> is negotiated by each set of speakers for their purposes. The speakers are able to monitor each other's language proficiency to determine mutually the appropriate grammar, phonology, lexical range, and pragmatic conventions that would ensure intelligibility. Therefore, it is difficult to describe this language a priori. It cannot be characterized outside the specific interaction and speakers in a communicative context.
>
> (2007, pp. 925–926)

Last but not least, even if ELF eventually becomes structurally stable and codifiable, the choice of ELF norms for international English tests will raise the same old question of linguistic hegemony. As Saraceni (2008, p. 22) argues, "If a British or American ENL model was deemed exonormative for most learners of English around the world, so would be ... any other model that was intended to be suitable for users of English around the globe." A monolithic ELF model "would have the same power to demoralize, oppress, and disenfranchise" (Elder & Davies, 2006, p. 296) users of other English varieties as have the native-speaker norms dominating current international English tests (Berns, 2008). This problem would also plague any international tests based on a monolithic standard of WE, the varieties of English institutionalized in the Outer Circle.

Recommended Principles for Meaningful Assessment of EIL

The review above of the recent developments in the assessment of EIL indicates that to approach the many issues of EIL assessment simply in terms of accommodations vs. lack thereof or from a monolithic view of either native or non-native norms raises as many, if not more, questions as it seeks to address. Canagarajah (2006a, p. 234) makes the following perceptive observation:

> Posing the options as either "native English norms" or "new English norms" is misleading. A proficient speaker of English in the postmodern world needs an awareness of both. He or she should be able to shuttle between different norms, recognizing the systematic and legitimate status of different varieties of English in this diverse family of languages.

Thus, a more productive approach to EIL assessment is to develop a set of principles grounded in the present-day sociolinguistic realities of local and international English-using communities that can serve as useful macro-strategies to facilitate informed decision-making about what should go into a fair, relevant, meaningful, and valid test of EIL proficiency. What follows represents a preliminary endeavor to formulate several such principles.

Principle I: Determine Linguistic Norms for a Test According to its Intended Use

This cardinal principle recognizes not only the diversity of EIL uses and the social and cultural contexts in which these uses occur but also the diversity of the purposes that EIL tests can serve, and sees the intended purpose of a specific test as providing the primary basis for making an informed and realistic choice of language norms for that test. It underlies Canagarajah's (2006a) suggestion that "there is a need to develop tests in English according to local norms when the objective is the need to assess one's ability to use English as a second language in the local community" (p. 236). In other words, the target use of a test "should be the determining factor in deciding which English(es) will be used" (Brown, 2004, p. 319).

The principle on the primacy of a test's intended use in determining the appropriacy of specific linguistic norms resonates with the profound understanding that "it is the ways in which we *use* tests that is at the heart of language assessment" (Bachman, 2005, p. 2). "The intended uses and potential consequences of this use," Bachman points out, "are essentially specific local concerns in any assessment that need to be addressed regarding the stake-holders in that specific assessment—the various individuals who will be affected in one way or another by the assessment and by the way we use it" (p. 31). It is in the spirit of this overriding principle that Canagarajah (2006a) asserts that "although I am an outer-circle speaker, I do not mind doing the Test of English as a

Foreign Language [TOEFL] if I am planning to move to the United States for education or employment" (p. 235). The same principle of primacy of test use, however, rules out the same test as an invalid assessment of English proficiency for recruitment and promotion purposes in a Japanese company whose main clientele and business partners are based in India and Singapore. This is because TOEFL, as a test based on American English and developed to measure English skills to perform academic tasks in North American university settings (Educational Testing Service, n.d.), is not an appropriate measure of the Japanese candidates' English communication skills for international business with Indians and Singaporeans. By contrast, the wide use of the TOEIC (Test of English for International Communication)—another English test based on Inner-Circle English norms—by the business processing outsourcing industry in the Philippines to screen applicants (Bolton, 2008) is justifiable on the grounds that the industry serves mainly a North American clientele.

Principle 2: Choose a Standard Variety of English if More Than One Variety is Adequate for the Intended Test Use in a Society

This principle is based on three considerations. First, the standard variety of a society usually prevails and has the widest purchase in the local linguistic ecology. Consequently, it is very likely to be the variety that is adopted in local curricula, textbooks, teaching manuals, and other learning materials, i.e., the variety that is taught and learned in the classroom (Gupta, this volume; Matsuda & Matsuda, 2009). As a result, the choice of the variety as the linguistic norms for a language test can enhance the alignment between what is tested and what is taught/learned in the educational system.

Second, in contexts where the standard variety is not taught in the classroom, its adoption as the language standard for an important test can help to make the provision of instruction in this variety a moral obligation for the education authorities. Given the widely observed fact that the standard variety is a gatekeeper of opportunities and social wellbeing (Matsuda & Matsuda, 2009), this can contribute to the prospective test candidates' instrumental language rights, which

> aim at ensuring that language is not an obstacle to the effective enjoyment of rights with a linguistic dimension, to the meaningful participation in public institutions and democratic process, and to the enjoyment of social and economic opportunities that require linguistic skills.
>
> (Rubio-Marín, 2003, p. 56)

Third, as pointed out by Svartvik and Leech (2006), standard varieties of English in different societies, especially in their written forms, exhibit a level of homogeneity that makes them mutually intelligible. Similarly, Y. Kachru (2011) observes that "It has been demonstrated beyond controversy that all Outer Circle varieties have a standard, or 'acrolectal,' form, which is mutually intelligible among all English-using populations" (p.158). Thus, by directing prospective test takers' learning efforts to the development of proficiency in the standard variety used in their community, a test based on it can contribute to a greater intelligibility of their English than one based on a non-standard variety. It is important to point out, however, that the principle of testing a standard variety, when operating alone, may give rise to the same kinds of problems associated with the hegemony of native-speaker norms in current international tests of English proficiency. Therefore, it must be complemented by Principles 3 and 4 that follow.

Principle 3: Provide Candidates With Exposure to Multiple Native and Non-Native Varieties of English

This principle reflects a growing consensus about the need "to develop learners' proficiency in negotiating different forms of English to function effectively in international contexts" (Suzuki, 2010, p. 146; see also Flowerdew, this volume; Matsuda, 2003; Rajagopalan, 2004). This perceived need has arisen from the changing social conditions featuring what Canagarajah (2006a) has called "postmodern globalization" (p. 230). These conditions are characterized by (a) multilateral interactions between communities, (b) porous national boundaries that allow easy cross-border flows of people, goods, and ideas, and (c) the hybridization of languages, communities, and cultures (Canagarajah, 2006a). As a result, present-day communication in English is often carried out between people speaking different varieties of English (Rajagopalan, 2004). This is not only true of English users in the Outer- and Expanding-Circle communities but is also becoming increasingly common in an Inner-Circle society like the UK and the USA, whose nationals now have to communicate with users of different English varieties both outside and inside their border:

> Proficiency in Standard English cannot help American or British students engage in the transnational needs and relationships that they encounter today. They, too, need the facility to negotiate diverse varieties of English.
>
> (Canagarajah, 2006a, p. 241)

In response to the postmodern conditions for communication in English and subject to Principle 1 discussed above, an EIL test should, where feasible, provide candidates with exposure to multiple native and non-native varieties to foster their sociolinguistic awareness and sensitivity (Brown, 2004; Y. Kachru, 2011).

Principle 4: Broaden the Construct of EIL Tests to Incorporate Intercultural Strategic Competence

An emerging consensus in the recent scholarship on EIL pedagogy and testing is that the traditional exclusive focus on language form is anachronistic and fails to do justice to intercultural communicative competence in EIL (Canagarajah, 2006a; Matsuda & Matsuda, 2009). As Canagarajah (2006b) notes, there is cumulative research evidence that many culture-specific pragmatic and discourse strategies that multilingual users of EIL bring to communicative encounters "enable speakers to maintain their own varieties and still communicate without hindrance" (p. 204). Such research evidence lends support to the recognition that strategic competence—the ability to make effective use of various strategies of communicative negotiation, or what Canagarajah (2007) refers to as "the enabling pragmatic strategies" (p. 926), to enhance intelligibility and negotiate intercultural communication—should be a central component of the test construct (see Gu, this volume).

In a recent discussion of EIL pedagogy, McKay reviews previous research on EIL interactions and arrives at the following pragmatic goals for an EIL curriculum:

1 Explicit attention should be given to introducing and practicing repair strategies, such as asking for clarification and repetition, rephrasing and allowing wait time.
2 A variety of conversational gambits or routines should be introduced and practiced, including such items as expressing agreement and disagreement, managing turn-taking and taking leave.
3 The curriculum should seek to promote students' understanding of how pragmatic norms can differ cross-culturally.
4 Students should be free to express their own pragmatic norms but to recognize that, to the extent these standards differ from the norms expected by their listener, there may be cross-cultural misunderstandings. (2011, p.133)

With minor modifications, these same pragmatic goals can, and should, be included in the test construct of any EIL assessments, including those developed for Inner-Circle candidates (Maley, 2010). The challenge for EIL test developers, then, lies in how to devise appropriate language tasks to elicit, in a rigorous manner, those pragmatic strategies that facilitate effective communication and allow valid inferences about the test takers' strategic competence to attain interaction success in EIL (Davies, 2009).

Principle 5: Make Allowances for Individual Aspirations to Inner-Circle Norms

The worthwhile effort to incorporate non-native varieties of English in the test construct should not preclude a recognition that there are learners and test candidates from the Outer and the Expanding Circle who aspire to Inner-Circle English norms. In a survey study of 400 learners of English from fourteen different countries, Timmis (2002) found that as many as two-thirds of the students expressed a desire to conform to native-speaker norms in both pronunciation and grammar. Notably, this preference for native-speaker norms was not restricted to learners who used, or anticipated to use, English chiefly with native speakers. A preference for native-speaker norms, especially American English, was also identified in Young and Walsh's (2010) study of non-native speaker teachers' views. As Jenkins (2006, p. 48) acknowledges, "ELT examinations also have to provide for those students whose preferred goal remains, despite EIL developments, a near-native variety of English." Such allowances resonate with the understanding that "While it is clearly inappropriate to foist native-speaker norms on students who neither want nor need them, it is scarcely more appropriate to offer students a target which manifestly does not meet their aspirations" (Timmis, 2002, p. 249).

Conclusion

This chapter has conducted a critique of the established practices and principles for assessing English proficiency against the backdrop of the postmodern sociolinguistic realities of English as a language of global communication. It has been argued that while they help to ensure the technical quality of English assessments, these practices and principles do not take heed of the changing demographics of EIL users and the shifting geopolitical contexts of EIL uses. The chapter has also made a critical examination of recent developments in EIL assessment. Some of these developments represent a "weak" approach to assessing English language proficiency that attempts to accommodate test takers speaking non-native varieties by modifying the delivery and scoring system of the traditional, native-speaker normed tests without altering the test construct. Other developments represent a "strong" approach that involves a more radical rethink of Outer- and Expanding-Circle varieties of English as valid linguistic norms in their own right and an attendant redefinition of the test construct. These two approaches to EIL assessment, however, raise more thorny issues than they aim to solve. Instead of the oversimplistic dichotomies—i.e., accommodations vs. lack of accommodations to non-native varieties; Inner-Circle vs. Outer-/Expanding-Circle varieties of English as the norms underlying the test construct, it has been argued that a sociolinguistically more sensitive approach is to develop a set of macrostrategies grounded in a sound understanding of the postmodern conditions of EIL that can guide an informed redefinition of the test construct for a fair, relevant, and valid assessment of EIL proficiency.

Exploring the Ideas

1 Conduct a survey of the high-stakes English tests used in your society to answer the following questions. What are the predominant purposes of these tests? Whose linguistic norms prevail in these tests? How well are these norms aligned with the intended purposes of the tests?

2 Language assessments have a "fundamentally social character" (McNamara, 2001, p. 333) and are "instruments of social policy and control" (Davies, 2003, p. 361). What is the social meaning of English proficiency in your community? How are English tests used for various forms of social inclusion and exclusion?

3 Record ten minutes of your interaction with someone from a different cultural background and speaking a variety of English different from yours. Transcribe the recording and identify the pragmatic strategies used by you and your interlocutor to negotiate understandings successfully. Do you think the same pragmatic strategies can help other EIL users to negotiate communication with each other as well? Should such negotiation strategies be included in an EIL test?

Applying the Ideas

1 Choose a test of English proficiency that is used in your community. Consider how it may be modified to reflect the sociolinguistic realities of English use in your community and to better serve its intended use(s).

2 Canagarajah (2006a) points out that "to be really proficient in English today, one has to be multidialectal" (p. 233). In what ways can an English assessment be designed to capture the multidialectal nature of EIL proficiency?

3 To assess EIL users' ability to shuttle between different varieties of English, Canagarajah (2006a) argues that "we have to devise interactive and collaborative formats for testing one's proficiency

in strategies of language negotiation in context-bound situations of ongoing communication" (p. 238). What interactive and collaborative language tasks can be developed to test the negotiation strategies identified in Question 3 above?

Note

1 The language assessment literature distinguishes several key terms, including "assessment," "measurement," "test," and "evaluation" (see, for example, Brown & Abeywickrama, 2010). Of these terms, "assessment" is often used as a broad term to denote the process and product of "collecting information about a given object of interest according to procedures that are systematic and substantively grounded" (Bachman, 2004, p. 7). The other terms describe different types or uses of assessment. Because the issues discussed in this chapter apply equally to all types of English assessments, "assessment" and "test" are used more or less interchangeably.

References

Alderson, J. C., Clapham, C., & Wall, D. (1995). *Language test construction and evaluation*. Cambridge, UK: Cambridge University Press.

Alptekin, C. (2002). Towards intercultural communicative competence in ELT. *ELT Journal, 56*(1), 57–64.

Bachman, L. F. (1990). *Fundamental considerations in language testing*. Oxford, UK: Oxford University Press.

Bachman, L. F. (2004). *Statistical analyses for language assessment*. Cambridge, UK: Cambridge University Press.

Bachman, L. F. (2005). Building and supporting a case for test use. *Language Assessment Quarterly, 2*(1), 1–34.

Bachman, L. F., & Palmer, A. S. (1996). *Language testing in practice*. Oxford, UK: Oxford University Press.

Berns, M. (2008). World Englishes, English as a lingua franca, and intelligibility. *World Englishes, 27*(3/4), 327–334.

Bolton, K. (2008). English in Asia, Asian Englishes, and the issue of proficiency. *English Today, 24*(2), 3–12.

Brown, H. D., & Abeywickrama, P. (2010). *Language assessment: Principles and classroom practices*. White Plains, NY: Pearson Education.

Brown, J. D. (2004). What do we mean by bias, Englishes, Englishes in testing, and English language proficiency? *World Englishes, 23*(2), 317–319.

Canagarajah, S. (2006a). Changing communicative needs, revised assessment objectives: Testing English as an international language. *Language Assessment Quarterly, 3*(3), 229–242.

Canagarajah, S. (2006b). Negotiating the local in English as a lingua franca. *Annual Review of Applied Linguistics, 26*, 197–218.

Canagarajah, S. (2007). Lingua franca English, multilingual communities, and language acquisition. *The Modern Language Journal, 91*(5), 923–939.

Canale, M., & Swain, M. (1980). Theoretical bases of communicative approaches to second language teaching and testing. *Applied Linguistics, 1*(1), 1–47.

Crystal, D. (2003). *English as a global language* (2nd ed.). Cambridge, UK: Cambridge University Press.

Davidson, F. (2006). World Englishes and test construction. In B. B. Kachru, Y. Kachru, & C. L. Nelson (Eds.), *The handbook of World Englishes* (pp. 709–717). Malden, MA: Blackwell.

Davies, A. (2003). Three heresies of language testing research. *Language Testing, 20*(4), 355–368.

Davies, A. (2009). Assessing world Englishes. *Annual Review of Applied Linguistics, 29,* 80–89.

Educational Testing Service. (n.d.). *About the test.* Retrieved May 6, 2011, from http://www.ets.org/toefl/ibt/about/

Elder, C., & Davies, A. (2006). Assessing English as a lingua franca. *Annual Review of Applied Linguistics, 26,* 282–301.

Fulcher, G., & Davidson, F. (2007). *Language testing and assessment: An advanced resource book.* London and New York: Routledge.

Hall, G. (2010). International English language testing: A critical response. *ELT Journal, 64*(3), 321–328.

Hamp-Lyons, L., & Davies, A. (2008). The Englishes of English tests: Bias revisited. *World Englishes, 27*(1), 26–39.

House, J. (2003). English as a lingua franca: A threat to multilingualism? *Journal of Sociolinguistics, 7*(4), 556–578.

Hughes, A. (2003). *Testing for language teachers* (2nd ed.). Cambridge, UK: Cambridge University Press.

IELTS. (n.d.). *About us.* Retrieved on May 3, 2011, from http://www.ielts.org/about_us.aspx

Jenkins, J. (2006). The spread of EIL: A testing time for testers. *ELT Journal, 60*(1), 42–50.

Jenkins, J. (2009). English as a lingua franca: Interpretations and attitudes. *World Englishes, 28*(2), 200–207.

Jenkins, J., Cogo, A., & Dewey, M. (2011). Review of developments in research into English as a lingua franca. *Language Teaching, 44*(3), 281–315.

Kachru, B. B. (1986). *The alchemy of English: The spread, functions and models of non-native Englishes.* Oxford, UK: Pergamon.

Kachru, Y. (2011). World Englishes: Contexts and relevance for language education. In E. Hinkel (Ed.), *Handbook of research in second language teaching and learning* (Vol. 2, pp. 155–172). New York: Routledge.

Kirkpatrick, A. (2011). English as an Asian lingua franca and the multilingual model of ELT. *Language Teaching, 44*(2), 212–224.

Leung, C. (2005). Convivial communication: Recontextualizing communicative competence. *International Journal of Applied Linguistics, 15*(2), 119–144.

Leung, C., & Lewkowicz, J. (2006). Expanding horizons and unresolved conundrums: Language testing and assessment. *TESOL Quarterly, 40*(1), 211–234.

Llurda, E. (2004). Non-native-speaker teachers and English as an international language. *International Journal of Applied Linguistics, 14*(3), 314–323.

Lowenberg, P. H. (2002). Assessing English proficiency in the Expanding Circle. *World Englishes, 21*(3), 431–435.

Major, R. C., Fitzmaurice, S. F., Bunta, F., & Balasubramanian, C. (2002). The effects of nonnative accents on listening comprehension: Implications for ESL assessment. *TESOL Quarterly, 36*(2), 173–190.

Maley, A. (2010). The reality of EIL and the myth of ELF. In C. Gagliardi & A. Maley (Eds.), *EIL, ELF, global English: Teaching and learning issues* (pp.25–44). Bern, Germany: Peter Lang.

Matsuda, A. (2003). Incorporating World Englishes in teaching English as an international language. *TESOL Quarterly, 37*(4), 719–729.

Matsuda, A., & Matsuda, P. K. (2009). World Englishes and the teaching of writing. *TESOL Quarterly, 44*(2), 369–374.

McKay, S. L. (2002). *Teaching English as an international language.* Oxford, UK: Oxford University Press.

McKay, S. L. (2011). English as an international lingua franca pedagogy. In E. Hinkel (Ed.), *Handbook of research in second language teaching and learning* (Vol. 2, pp. 122–139). New York: Routledge.

McKay, S. L., & Bokhorst-Heng, W. (2008). *International English in its sociolinguistic contexts: Towards a socially sensitive EIL pedagogy.* New York: Routledge.

McNamara, T. (1996). *Measuring second language performance.* London: Addison Wesley Longman.

McNamara, T. (2000). *Language testing.* Oxford, UK: Oxford University Press.

McNamara, T. (2001). Language assessment as social practice: Challenges for research. *Language Testing, 18*(4), 333–349.

Murata, K., & Jenkins, J. (2009). Introduction. In K. Murata & J. Jenkins (Eds.), *Global Englishes in Asian contexts: Current and future debates* (pp. 1–13). Basingstoke, UK: Palgrave Macmillan.

Rajagopalan, K. (2004). The concept of "World English" and its implications for ELT. *ELT Journal, 58*(2), 111–117.

Rajagopalan, K. (2010). The soft ideological underbelly of the notion of intelligibility in discussions about "World Englishes." *Applied Linguistics, 31*(3), 465–470.

Ross, S. J. (2011). The social and political tensions of language assessment. In E. Hinkel (Ed.), *Handbook of research in second language teaching and learning* (Vol. 2, pp. 786–797). New York: Routledge.

Rubio-Marín, R. (2003). Language rights: Exploring the competing rationales. In W. Kymlicka & A. Patten (Eds.), *Language rights and political theory* (pp.52–79). Oxford, UK: Oxford University Press.

Saraceni, M. (2008). English as a lingua franca: Between form and function. *English Today, 24*(2), 20–26.

Schneider, E. W. (2011). *English around the world.* Cambridge, UK: Cambridge University Press.

Seidlhofer, B. (2001). Closing a conceptual gap: The case for a description of English as a lingua franca. *International Journal of Applied Linguistics, 11*(2), 133–158.

Seidlhofer, B. (2004). Research perspectives on teaching English as a lingua franca. *Annual Review of Applied Linguistics, 24,* 209–239.

Suzuki, A. (2010). Introducing diversity of English into ELT: Student teachers' responses. *ELT Journal, 65*(2), 145–153.

Svartvik, J., & Leech, G. (2006). *English: One tongue, many voices.* Basingstoke, UK: Palgrave Macmillan.

Taylor, L. (2002). Assessing learners' English: But whose/which English(es)? *Research Notes, 10,* 18–20.

Taylor, L. (2006). The changing landscape of English: Implications for language assessment. *ELT Journal, 60*(1), 51–60.

Timmis, I. (2002). Native-speaker norms and international English: A classroom view. *ELT Journal, 56*(3), 240–249.

Young, T. J., & Walsh, S. (2010). Which English? Whose English? An investigation of "non-native" teachers' beliefs about target varieties. *Language, Culture and Curriculum, 23*(2), 123–137.

Uysal, H. H. (2010). A critical review of the IELTS writing test. *ELT Journal, 64*(3), 314–320.

Part III

Implementing Change

Chapter 9

EIL Curriculum Development

James Dean Brown

Introduction

The purpose of this chapter is to explore what curriculum developers can learn from comparing the assumptions of traditional language curriculum development with the assumptions of English as an international language (EIL) curriculum development. To that end, the following issues are addressed: choosing the target language and culture; considering why people learn English; deciding who should be included in the curriculum; delimiting the curriculum; choosing the basic units of analysis in the curriculum; selecting from among the basic units of curriculum; as well as organizing and sequencing the curriculum. The chapter ends by suggesting procedures for developing EIL curriculum and directions for future EIL curriculum research.

Traditional Practices and Principles

Traditionally, curriculum developers have assumed (a) that students need to learn the English of native speakers (NSs), (b) that educated NSs of English should serve as the model and standard, (c) that *big* C American or British culture should be taught, and (d) that communicative language teaching is the most productive way to teach English. Curriculum developers have also assumed that students study English because (a) English is the principal means of communicating globally, (b) English helps foster internationalism, (c) English is important for gaining entry into higher education, and (d) English is the primary language for access to global information. Control of English language curriculum has typically been in the hands of NSs of English, who have either written the textbooks or guided local curriculum development, and the views of local students and teachers have often been belittled as so-called *outdated ideas*.

The overall goal of this chapter is to examine what curriculum developers can learn by contrasting their traditional assumptions with the relatively new set of assumptions emerging in the English as an international language (EIL) literature.

Comparing the Traditional and EIL Assumptions

In this section, I will use seven questions to compare traditional curriculum development assumptions with emerging EIL assumptions.

What Should the Target Language and Culture be?

Native-speaker models. Traditionally, curriculum developers have assumed that British or American English should be the target language in ESL/EFL curriculum. In the 1980s, other possible models emerged when Kachru (1985, 1986) distinguished among three circles of English that constituted "three distinct types of speech fellowships of English, phases of the spread of the language, and particular characteristics of the uses of the language and of its acquisition and linguistic innovations" (Kachru, 1986, p. 122): the *Inner Circle* (countries where English is the native language); the *Outer Circle* (countries where English is not the native tongue but does play an historical or institutional role, e.g., India, the Philippines, etc.); the *Expanding Circle* (countries where English is not the native tongue and does not play an historical/institutional role though it is widely studied as a foreign language).

More recently, Alptekin (2002) has directly criticized the NS target when he

> questions the validity of the pedagogical model based on the native speaker-based notion of communicative competence. With its standardized native speaker norms, the model is found to be utopian, unrealistic, and constraining in relation to English as an International Language.
>
> (p. 57)

Seidlhofer (2001, p. 151) notes that

> ... uncoupling the language from its native speakers and probing into the nature of ELF [English as a lingua franca] for pedagogical purposes holds the exciting, if uncomfortable, prospect of bringing up for reappraisal just about every issue and tenet in language teaching ...

Cultural content. Traditionally, British or American cultures have served as the target cultures for ESL/EFL curricula. However, what authors mean by *culture* is often far from clear. *Culture* can mean *big C culture* including the great literature, art, music, etc.; or what I call *almanac culture* dealing with the history, geography, politics, etc.; or *small c culture* focused on the "behavior and attitudes, and the social knowledge that people use to interpret experience" (Cortazzi & Jin, 1999, p. 197). Cortazzi and Jin (1999) shift their focus away from the UK and the USA when they distinguish among: *target culture* including the culture(s) of Inner-Circle countries; *international target cultures* involving a mixture of Inner- and Outer-Circle countries; and *source culture*, which is the students' culture (pp. 204–205). Why would anyone want to learn about their own culture in English? McKay (2003c) answers, reasonably enough, that students need to talk about their own culture when they talk to people from other cultures.

Culture of learning. Curriculum developers traditionally assume that CLT (communicative language teaching) is the most productive method for teaching ELT. This stance has several problems: (a) there is no empirical proof that CLT is the most productive method of ELT; (b) CLT is not nearly as common in actual practice as academicians would like to think; and (c) people were learning languages successfully for thousands of years before CLT emerged. As McKay (2003c) argues, the language teaching and learning assumptions of the local community should be taken into consideration especially with regard to the choices of target language, target culture, and culture of pedagogy.

Why do People Learn English?

People give many reasons for studying English, including global and local reasons. Traditionally, *global reasons* focus on the usefulness of English, arguing that it is:

1   The principal means of communicating globally
2   One way to foster internationalism or globalism
3   Important for gaining entry into higher education
4   The primary language for accessing global information.

Such lofty goals for learning English are often cited by governments and educational institutions.

Those advocating EIL would more likely assume that people have *local reasons* for learning English, which tend to focus on what people do with it:

1   Communicating locally with compatriots who speak other mother tongues
2   Working locally with foreign tourists
3   Gaining advantage over other local people in business dealings
4   Speaking with friends or family members who speak English
5   Acquiring the prestige locally of speaking English.

No doubt, some learners do want to learn native-like English for global purposes like studying abroad or immigrating to English-speaking countries, but other people need English mostly for local purposes, for both local and global purposes, or simply for meeting English requirements in school or work. It is the needs of this latter group that may best be described within an EIL framework.

Who Should be Included in the Curriculum?

Traditionally, NSs of English have controlled curriculum either by writing textbooks or guiding/controlling local curriculum development. In today's world, it has become clear that at least the following groups have a stake in any curriculum and therefore should be included in the curriculum development process, at least as sources of information:

1   Students
2   English teachers
3   Curriculum developers
4   Textbook writers
5   Content course teachers
6   Local communities in business, academia, the travel industry, etc.
7   Institutional administrators, politicians, etc.
8   External testers and testing organizations
9   Other influential people (culturally, economically, politically, etc.) from Inner-, Outer-, or Expanding-Circle countries.

Differences among these groups can prove problematic in any curriculum project, including differences in: (a) the English they use or perceive as important; (b) their views of what constitutes sound learning and education; (c) who they think should teach English; (d) how they think English should be taught; and so forth.

Actual control of EIL curriculum decisions should perhaps shift to local teachers and educational stakeholders. Llurda (2004, p. 314) states that

> the confluence of recent research on EIL, together with the increasing appreciation of NNS [non-native speaker] teachers—both in ESL and EFL contexts—are creating the right conditions for the gradual acceptance of English as a Lingua Franca, with the consequence of a decrease in the role of native-speaker teachers in setting the principles and norms on which this lingua franca will be taught in the future.

Since the local teachers and educational stakeholders are most often NNSs of English, McKay (2003a, pp. 140–141) contends that the field should recognize the strengths of "bilingual teachers of English" (note her use of the positive label *bilingual* in place of the negative *NNSs* that I used earlier in the sentence). The following list combines ideas from a number of authors (Arva & Medgyes, 2000; Kirkpatrick, 2007b; Llurda, 2004; Medgyes, 2001; McKay, 2003a; Seidlhofer, 1999) about the strengths of local bilingual teachers, who:

1   Know their students' culture
2   Know their students' first language
3   Know what it is like to have made the English their own
4   Can draw on the L1 for efficient explanations
5   Can code switch in class
6   Serve as models of successful second language learners
7   Know what it means to learn English because they have done it
8   Remember and understand the influences of L1 interference on learning English
9   Can simplify English (perhaps without even realizing it) for more comprehensible input
10 Understand the roles of English in the local community
11 Understand how local varieties of English have developed and how they compare linguistically
12 Understand that the different varieties are legitimate and complete linguistic systems
13 Can evaluate teaching methods and materials for local suitability
14 Know the educational expectations of students, parents, and administrators
15 May have more realistic expectations
16 May be more empathetic with students
17 May be able to better understand and attend to the students' real needs
18 Understand the local educational system and classroom culture
19 May be more committed to the local educational system
20 Can contribute to their institution's extra-curricular life.

As Seidlhofer (1999, p. 238) put it so eloquently, "One could say that native speakers know the destination, but not the terrain that has to be crossed to get there: they themselves have not travelled the same route." (For more on bilingual teachers, see Braine [1999] and Llurda [2005].) Given these strengths, local bilingual teachers or administrators seem to be the logical choice for guiding, informing, and controlling EIL curriculum development.

How Should the Curriculum be Delimited?

Since the 1970s, traditional ESL/EFL curriculum development has been integrally linked with English for specific purposes (ESP) in the belief that it is senseless to design curriculum that is "Teaching English for no Obvious Reason" (TENOR, after Carver, 1983, p. 131). The TENOR target is not only too vague to be of much use for curriculum development, but is also far too big. Learning any second language to a native-speaker standard is a very long and arduous process requiring decades of consistent work. As Kirkpatrick (2007a, p. 382) puts it, "The major problem for learners is that a native-speaker model is unattainable for the overwhelming majority of school-based language learners in expanding circle countries." It is no surprise then that ESL/EFL curriculum developers worldwide have instinctively chosen to delimit curriculum.

ESP has traditionally been used to delimit curriculum. ESP is often subdivided into English for Academic Purposes (EAP) and English for Occupational Purposes (EOP) (e.g., Brown, 2009, p. 274). But, EIL does not fit neatly into either EAP or EOP. What then is the purpose of EIL and how can we use it to delimit curriculum? There are at least three ways: world Englishes, English as a lingua franca, and locally defined EIL.

World Englishes. One way to delimit EIL involves world Englishes (WE). The awareness that different legitimate Englishes other than the native dialects exist and need to be understood by ESL/EFL learners has led to the possibility that variant dialects of native and non-native Englishes can and should be used as models in English language teaching. Thus WE is one form of EIL that can help inform and delimit course specifications, student learning outcomes, materials, assessments, and so forth.

ELF. A second way to delimit EIL curriculum is most often referred to as English as a lingua franca (ELF).[1] Jenkins (2009, pp. 200–201) defined ELF as

> English being used as a lingua franca, the common language of choice, among speakers who come from different linguacultural backgrounds. … ELF is thus a question, not of orientation to the norms of a particular group of English speakers, but of mutual negotiation involving efforts and adjustments from all parties.

As Maley (2010, p. 25) points out in his paper on the flaws of the ELF concept, more than one definition exists for ELF:

> On the one hand, there is the relatively "strong" version, … , which tends to emphasize the notion of ELF as an "emerging" or "emergent" variety of varieties. On the other, the term seems to be used virtually

interchangeably with English as an International Language (EIL), ... , where the emphasis is placed more on the diversity and complexity of the process of using English internationally.

Saraceni (2008) provides a discussion of the historical background of ELF and the sometimes mutually contradictory definitions provided for ELF concluding "that there has been too much emphasis on the *form* of English as a lingua franca and not enough on its *function*" (p. 26, italics in the original). From a curriculum perspective, the notions of ELF are attractive because, if they are accepted, the forms and functions of the strong version of ELF would provide a ready framework for delimiting the number and range of language features that need to be taught in a particular EIL curriculum.

Locally defined EIL. A third way to delimit EIL is what I call *locally defined EIL*, in which the choices of units of analysis, objectives, content, teaching strategies, resources, models, etc. are all based on carefully considered local needs for English including its international uses. Such local needs will typically be based on a thorough needs analysis of the EIL language and context involved in a particular local English learning situation (this will be discussed at length in the third paragraph of the section headed "Putting an EIL Curriculum Together"). Such locally defined EIL will tend to be found and needed in countries where English is not the native tongue.

All in all, delimiting EIL curriculum, whether based on *WE*, *ELF*, or *locally defined EIL*, or some combination of the three, will require that curriculum developers understand and examine the basic units of analysis that are important to the needs of the learners in a particular context. Examining the basic units of analysis through a WE, an ELF, and/or a locally defined EIL filter should ultimately help to limit the amounts and types of language that students will have to learn in the short amounts of time that are typically available.

What Should the Basic Units of Analysis be in Curriculum?

Traditionally, the curriculum development literature has focused on an ever-expanding list of syllabuses including structural, situational, topical, skills-based, functional, notional, lexical, and task-based syllabuses. Based on needs analysis, the units of analysis in these syllabuses have typically provided the pieces that are recombined into more complex syllabuses, materials, etc. As described in the EIL literature to date, the basic units of analysis in EIL appear to be mostly drawn from ELF notions of pronunciation, grammar, and vocabulary. Jenkins (1998, p. 124) focuses on ELF pronunciation and suggests that

> ... while approximation to the native model is probably essential for intelligibility in non-bilingual EIL contexts as regards core sounds, nuclear stress, and relevant articulatory setting, local non-native norms are likely to be both acceptable and intelligible in many other phonological areas.

She clarifies by saying that EIL teaching

> should concentrate the productive focus of pronunciation teaching on the three areas that appear to have the greatest influence on intelligibility in EIL, i.e. certain segmentals, nuclear stress (the main stress in a word group), and the effective use of articulatory setting, to the extent that it underpins the first two areas.

She fleshed out her ideas for ELF pronunciation syllabuses in Jenkins (2000, 2002, 2004).

In terms of ELF vocabulary and grammar, Seidlhofer and others provide ambitious first steps in describing how NNSs use English around the world by developing an ELF corpus known as VOICE (the Vienna–Oxford International Corpus of English). VOICE "is unscripted, largely face-to-face interaction among fairly fluent speakers from a wide range of first language backgrounds whose primary and secondary socialization (i.e., upbringing and education) did not take place through English" (Seidlhofer, 2004, p. 219). A rationale for VOICE is provided in Seidlhofer (2001), and the content of VOICE is described in Seidlhofer (2004, p. 219). (For more information, see http://www.univie.ac.at/voice/voice.php?page=what_is_voice)

Seidlhofer (2004) suggests that research on the "lexicogrammar" aspects of the ELF found in VOICE might be particularly productive (pp. 219–220), and she provides a synopsis of the lexicogrammatical patterns of ELF found so far (Seidlhofer, 2005). Beyond the VOICE project, Seidlhofer (2004, pp. 217–219) summarizes the considerable research to date on intercultural pragmatics that is generally relevant to EIL curriculum development (see also, McKay, 2003b; Nunn, 2005).

Hints of other possible units of analysis are found elsewhere. Lanteigne (2006) argues for using regionally specific non-western *tasks* where English is used. She does so for tests in her article, but tasks could certainly make sense as a unit of analysis in an EIL curriculum. McKay (2003a, p. 140) suggests that EIL should incorporate *topics* appropriate within the local context including topics that deal with local culture (see also, McKay, 2001, 2002, pp. 81–101).

Other units of analysis also show promise. Lin (2002, p. 3) suggests making *discourse* decisions about what to include in a syllabus, arguing that

"… discourse is the level of language that enables mutual comprehension in communication in spite of differences between varieties at the phonological, lexical and syntactical levels … Discourse, after all, is about achieving purposes with language." Derewianka (2003, p. 135) suggests using *genres*, which she defines as

> social practices [understood by all members of our social group or culture] that have evolved to enable us to achieve our goals. As we go about our daily lives, we engage in numerous situations that involve predictable and recurring patterns of language use, without which our interactions would be random and chaotic.

Where these patterns of language use occur in EIL locally, the patterns could usefully be isolated, analyzed, and included in curriculum. Nickerson (2005) suggests that *communicative strategies* would be useful in EIL, saying that there is "an increasing concern with language strategy, i.e., a concern with identifying those strategies that can be associated with effective communication in business, regardless of whether the speaker/writer is a native or non-native speaker" (p. 369).

In short, the fact that most of the attention to date in EIL has been on ELF phonological, structural, and pragmatic analyses does not preclude also analyzing the VOICE corpus (or other locally gathered data) for situations, topics, skills, functions, notions, tasks, discourse features, genres, communicative strategies, etc.

What Should be Selected From Among the Basic Units of Curriculum?

Typically, the *selection* of which structures, situations, topics, etc. to teach has been based on rationales like usefulness, salience, or importance. Even if these fairly fuzzy notions were clearly defined, which they usually are not, the question remains: useful, salient, and important to and for whom? Traditionally, such decisions have been left in the hands of educated NSs of English. In EIL curriculum, especially locally defined EIL, such decisions clearly should be in the hands of local bilingual teachers, administrators, students, etc.

Combining the ideas of a number of authors (Alptekin, 2002, p. 63; Deterding & Kirkpatrick, 2006, p. 392; Li, 2007, p. 14; McKay, 2002, pp. 128–129; Matsuda, 2003, p. 724; Mauranen, 2003, p. 516; and Pickering, 2006, p. 254), it appears that EIL curriculum developers, especially those developing locally defined EIL, should consider the following selection criteria:

1   Include successful bilinguals as English language and pedagogic models

2   Foster English language and cultural behaviors that will help students communicate effectively with others and achieve friendly relations with English speakers from any culture

3   Help students achieve intelligibility when they are among other English speakers

4   Enhance students' access to and capacity to contribute to the international body of information

5   Support learning English efficiently and help students feel better about their English learning

6   Provide students with awareness of linguistic and cultural differences in the various contexts in which English is learned and used, and furnish them with strategies for handling such differences

7   Use "global appropriacy and local appropriation" (Alptekin, 2002, p. 63) to help learners be "both global and local speakers of English" who can function both at home in their national culture as well as internationally (Kramsch & Sullivan, 1996, p. 211)

8   Respect the local culture of learning and promote a sense of ownership and confidence in the local varieties of English

9   Include materials and activities based on local and international situations that are recognizable and applicable to the students' everyday lives, pertaining to both NS–NNS and NNS–NNS interactions

10   Include models of Outer-Circle and Expanding-Circle users of English so students realize that English does not belong exclusively to the Inner Circle.

Naturally, locally defined EIL curriculum developers should only attend to those aspects of the above list that are appropriate for their local situation. However, incorporating even five or six of the above ten criteria would fundamentally change most curricula.

As discussed above, some authors argue for a universal approach to EIL, essentially taking the view that selection should focus on discovering a simpler, more general ELF that can be learned in all countries to help learners communicate with other ELF speakers from all of those countries. Thus, ELF would be an English that is acceptable and intelligible to NSs and NNSs alike (as described for pronunciation in Jenkins, 1998, p. 120). This would seem to be the goal of much of the research to date, where commonalities are being sought in the English used in many settings. Developments in the European Union described in Llurda (2004, p. 316) serve as an example: "If we look more closely at the European Union, proposals are being made on the progressive establishment of a common

lingua franca variety which some have already labeled Euro-English ..."
(For more on ELF in the European Union, see Seidlhofer, Breiteneder, &
Pitzl, 2006; Grzega, 2005, pp. 51–52.)

EIL is also sometimes viewed as a complex mixture of options, wherein
multiple NS and NNS models should be provided along with "teaching of
generalized norms according to individual learner need and choice, rather
than a narrow focus on a standard British or American accent" (Jenkins,
1998, p. 121). As Nunn (2005, p. 65) describes it,

> EIL competence, then, cannot be reduced to a single, limited,
> monolingual or mono-cultural concept. It is composed of a set of
> interlocking and interdependent competences that sometimes
> compensate for each other, sometimes counteract each other and
> sometimes reinforce each other.

Melchers and Shaw (2003, p. 39) differentiate in yet another way
among four types of EIL proficiency: internationally effective, nationally
effective, locally proficient, and ineffective.

Clearly, the *selection* of which structures, situations, topics, etc. to
teach will differ from context to context. One approach would be to base
selection decisions on information gathered from all relevant stakeholders.
Selection could still be justified on the basis of usefulness, salience, or
importance, but in this case, it would be based on the usefulness, salience,
or importance as perceived by the stakeholders.

How Should the Curriculum be Organized and Sequenced?

As mentioned above, syllabuses have traditionally been used to organize
and sequence language materials, courses, teaching, and learning. McKay
(1978) pointed to three types of syllabuses that predominated in the
1970s: structural, situational, and notional-functional. My list of potential
syllabuses grew to seven in Brown (1995a, pp. 6–14):

1 Structural
2 Situational
3 Topical
4 Functional
5 Notional
6 Skills
7 Task-based

Based on my recent reading in the EIL literature, I have extended my list
to include:

8   Lexical
9   Pragmatic
10 Discourse-based
11 Genre
12 Communicative strategies.

Naturally, other syllabuses will continue to surface as we expand our knowledge about language teaching and learning. Any of these syllabuses can be used singly, or in combinations that *alternate* (e.g., four chapters that are predominantly situational followed by a fifth review chapter that is topical, in repeated cycles) or are *layered* such that two, three, or more syllabuses are going on at the same time with one of them being the primary organizational unit (e.g., situational chapter headings like "At the Airport," "In a Taxi," etc. with structural and lexical syllabuses in subordinate roles across the chapters).

Sequencing is typically based on notions of easiness, frequency, salience, or chronology. For example, we tend to think we are teaching the easy grammar items first and then moving to more difficult ones. Or, when we realize the futility of the easy-to-difficult argument, we may think in terms of teaching the most frequent grammar items first. For situational syllabuses, the organization is usually chronological. After all, students will arrive at the airport first and then ride in a taxi to a hotel and then go to a restaurant to eat and so forth (or so we hope). Topics tend to be organized into macro and subtopics (e.g., a macro topic like American Cities might have upbeat subtopics like Crime, Drugs, Racism, etc.).

Shifting to examples of EIL teaching/learning sequences, Jenkins (2000, pp. 209–210) proposes a five stage sequence for learning pronunciation:

- Addition of core [i.e., Lingua Franca Core] items to the learner's productive and receptive repertoire
- Addition of a range of L2 English accents to the learner's receptive repertoire
- Addition of accommodation skills
- Addition of non-core items to the learner's receptive repertoire
- Addition of a range of L1 English accents to the learner's receptive repertoire.

Kirkpatrick (2008) briefly discusses phonological, syntactic, and communicative features of EIL that might be useful in the ASEAN countries, thereby suggesting another set of possibilities for sequencing a somewhat locally defined EIL curriculum for Southeast Asia.

Clearly more examples of actual EIL teaching/learning sequences, syllabuses, materials, etc. would be very useful for the entire EIL community.

Conclusion

In order to help curriculum developers learn from all of these comparisons between traditional and EIL curriculum assumptions, I will discuss how all these pieces can be fitted together into an EIL curriculum project and suggest some directions that further EIL curriculum research might usefully head.

Putting an EIL Curriculum Together

Until writing this chapter, I had assumed that systematic curriculum development (i.e., needs, objectives, assessment, materials, teaching, and program evaluation) is the most productive way to proceed (e.g., see Brown, 2006). I held this belief because I felt that:

1   Most teachers (a) think about what their students need to learn, (b) set goals for their courses, (c) adopt, adapt, or create suitable materials, (d) assess their students' progress, (e) help each other teach, and (f) try to determine whether they have succeeded. These steps are the same ones that I list for systematic curriculum development, so in my mind they form a common progression that teachers will recognize in any curriculum development project.
2   As I define them, these steps should be based on both language and situation needs throughout, so they tend to be highly sensitive to local context and thus may fit rather neatly in any curriculum project.
3   And, I have applied systematic curriculum development in a number of contexts around the world with a fair amount of success.

However, I now realize that this was one very big assumption, one that might not hold true everywhere. Given what I have read in the EIL literature, the most reasonable position I can take at this time within the EIL framework is that systematic curriculum development is one possible way of proceeding—one that can be adopted, adapted, or ignored as appropriate in any particular local context. Here I would like to consider blending these systematic curriculum development steps with the EIL assumptions in the hope that such a blending will provide one possible path to successful EIL curriculum.

Conducting EIL needs analysis could easily be mistaken to mean identifying the language forms that students should study in English. However, since there is more to language learning than just a set of language items, needs analysis might better be viewed as:

the systematic collection and analysis of all subjective and objective information necessary to define and validate defensible curriculum purposes that satisfy the language learning requirements of students within the context of the particular institutions that influence the learning and teaching situation.

(Brown, 1995a, p. 36)

Thus, needs analysis should take into account *language needs* (i.e., the linguistic items that students should learn) as well as *situational needs* (i.e., the local situational components of the teaching-learning process). Since students are not the only people involved in an EIL situation, the needs of the teachers, administrators, employers, parents, institutions, etc. should also be considered.

Because of its focus on the local context and the people in that context, locally defined EIL curriculum development naturally, and by definition, considers both the language *and* situational needs and is therefore likely to lead to a defensible curriculum that stands a reasonable chance of success. Indeed, since the target language and culture in the EIL curriculum must be defined in terms of all the factors discussed in this chapter, needs analysis must inevitably be responsive to many factors in the local context. Beyond simply shifting the target language and culture from the Inner Circle to whatever mix of Englishes from the Inner-, Outer- and Expanding-Circles is appropriate in the local context, EIL needs analysis must accommodate any and all local situational information and constraints on curriculum development. (For overviews on needs analysis, see Brown, 2009; Long, 2005.)

Setting goals and objectives for an EIL course is one way to maximize the usefulness of the information gained from a needs analysis. *Goals* are typically general statements of what the students need to learn (often related to the global reasons for learning English that I described above), whereas *objectives* (aka *student learning outcomes*) are comparatively precise statements of the content or skills the students will know or be able to use at the end of the course (often more appropriately related to the local reasons for learning English that I described above). Objectives come in many shapes and forms, which tend to vary in type and degree of specificity even within a specific course. To insure EIL curriculum success, local teachers and other stakeholders must be involved in setting the objectives so they feel a strong sense of ownership. (For more on language learning objectives, see Brown, 1995a.)

Assessing EIL objectives is an essential part of monitoring students' progress and providing feedback, but also a crucial part of determining the degree to which the objectives are appropriately defined. From a classroom-assessment perspective, diagnostic assessment helps at the beginning of a course by determining the students' relative weaknesses and strengths with regard to each of the course objectives, and achievement assessment helps at the end of the course by providing evidence for how much of each objective each student knows or can do. Naturally, achievement assessment can also be used for grading and pass/fail decisions. Any assessment procedures implemented in a locally defined EIL curriculum should be based on the needs analysis and objectives, and they should be respectful of assessment practices in the local community. (For more on classroom assessment, see Brown, 1995a, 2005; Brown & Hudson, 2002; Davidson & Lynch, 2003.)

Putting EIL materials in place is easier if they are based on a sound needs analysis, clear objectives, and useful classroom diagnostic and achievement assessments. Curriculum developers are then in an enviable position for adopting, adapting, or developing EIL materials and addressing the following questions: Should existing materials be adopted to fill the needs of the students? Or, would it be better to adapt existing materials to meet the students' needs? Or, if students' needs cannot be met by adopting or adapting of existing materials, should materials be developed from scratch? (For more on materials development, see Brown, 1995a, pp. 139–178; McDonough & Shaw, 2003; Tomlinson, 1998, 2002.)

Supporting EIL teachers in an EIL curriculum can take many forms, but common forms of support include orienting new teachers to the program; observing teachers (or organizing peer observations) and giving them feedback; providing in-service training opportunities; creating incentives for teachers to participate in professional improvement activities; and so forth. Forgetting to support teachers is likely to lead to grumbling, low morale, teacher burn-out, and even high levels of teacher turnover. At very least, teacher support can be fostered by involving them intimately in the EIL curriculum development and revision processes. In all cases, the goal of EIL teacher support should be to help teachers do what they do best—teach. (For more on teacher support, see Brown, 1995a, pp. 179–216; Farrell, 2008.)

Evaluating the overall EIL curriculum can be defined much like any curriculum evaluation as "the systematic collection and analysis of all relevant information necessary to promote the improvement of a curriculum and to assess its effectiveness within the context of the particular institutions involved" (Brown, 1995a, p. 218). True, this definition sounds a lot like a sort of on-going needs analysis. However, while needs analyses are typically conducted at the beginning of the curriculum development process, program evaluation takes place at a later stage, when information is available from all six curriculum components. The sort of continuing evaluation process called *formative evaluation* allows for the appraisal of the quality of all the curriculum components that are in place and for the ongoing maintenance of the curriculum as time passes, all of which is usefully applicable to EIL curriculum. (For more on language program evaluation, see Brown, 1989,

1995a, pp. 217–246, 1995b, 2001; Brown & Rodgers, 2002, pp. 227–256; Norris, Davis, Sinicrope, & Watanabe, 2009.)

Future EIL Curriculum Research

Curriculum development is hard work and may rely heavily on local teachers for talent and cooperation. Perhaps that is why curriculum development is relatively *rare* in the sense that most of the ESL/EFL teaching I have seen over the years around the world has been based on a single textbook. Textbook-based courses can be said to have curriculum, but only insofar as the textbook itself has curriculum. Since textbook authors tend to be NS, seldom know the students or the local context, and indeed are typically writing for the largest possible market, any resulting curriculum would be the opposite of locally defined EIL in almost all ways. Perhaps EIL textbooks are few and far between because they are doomed to failure by definition if they do not fit the EIL language and situation needs in the local context.

Part of the reason I find locally defined EIL so attractive is that its very definition requires that curriculum development be done in a particular context based primarily on the views of local stakeholders. As Cadman (2002, p. 87) put it,

> ... at whatever point we enter the discussion, there are recurring calls for contextualised research (Allison, 1996; Benesch, 2001; Pennycook, 1997). Each of us is encouraged to explore these crucial issues in relation to the specific institutional demands upon us and our students, and in particular to requestion the political as well as educational realities which we experience in the detail of our own learning and teaching commitments.

In writing this chapter, a number of EIL curriculum development questions occurred to me along the way (citations are for research already begun):

1 What does intelligibility mean in concrete terms (e.g., Deterding & Kirkpatrick, 2006; Kirkpatrick, Deterding, & Wong, 2008; Sewell, 2010)?

2 What are the components of ELF phonology (e.g., Jenkins, 2004), syntax (e.g., Seidlhofer, 2005) and lexis at various levels?

3 What EIL syllabuses, learning sequences, textbooks, or curriculum projects already exist? How do they compare with each other? Have they been successful? To what degree are they useful models for other curriculum projects?

4   What are teachers' attitudes toward the various features of EIL (e.g., Jenkins, 2009; Sifakis & Sougari, 2005)? What about the attitudes of students, parents, administrators, politicians, the general public etc.?

5   What EIL assessment techniques exist (e.g., Lanteigne, 2006)? How do they compare to traditional assessment and alternatives in assessment like portfolios, conferences, and self-assessments?

6   What are the effects on the EIL curriculum of students who have spent years in English speaking countries? Or on local students who want to study in or immigrate to English speaking countries?

Exploring the Ideas

1   What are the three most important differences between the assumptions of traditional curriculum development and EIL, and why are they important?

2   What are the five most important advantages that bilingual teachers have over NS teachers in EIL settings? What advantages might NS teachers have?

3   One set of steps for curriculum development includes: needs, objectives, assessment, materials, teaching, and program evaluation. Which step is the most important for shaping locally defined EIL?

Applying the Ideas

Answer the following questions for your particular EIL context (or one you know of):

- What should the target language and culture be?
- Why do people learn English?
- Who should be included in the curriculum?
- What other situational factors should be considered?
- How should the curriculum be organized and sequenced?

Note

1   Note that I use *EIL* in two ways in this chapter. The first is the general notion of EIL, which encompasses notions of *World Englishes* as content for curriculum, *ELF*, and *locally defined EIL*. The second is the narrower notion of *locally defined EIL*, which is EIL that is based on carefully considered local needs for English, particularly in Expanding-Circle countries. From this point on, I will differentiate between the general notion of *EIL* and what I am calling *locally defined EIL*.

References

Allison, D. (1996). Pragmatist discourse and English for academic purposes. *English for Specific Purposes, 15*(2), 85–103.

Alptekin, C. (2002). Towards intercultural communicative competence in ELT. *ELT Journal, 56*(1), 57–64.

Arva, V., & Medgyes, P. (2000). Native and non-native teachers in the classroom. *System, 28*(3), 355–372.

Benesch, S. (2001). *Critical English for academic purposes: Theory, politics and practice.* Mahwah, NJ: Lawrence Erlbaum.

Braine, G. (Ed.) (1999). *Non-native educators in English language teaching.* Mahwah, NJ: Lawrence Erlbaum.

Brown, J. D. (1989). Language program evaluation: A synthesis of existing possibilities. In K. Johnson (Ed.), *The second language curriculum* (pp. 222–241). Cambridge: Cambridge University Press.

Brown, J. D. (1995a). *The elements of language curriculum: A systematic approach to program development.* New York: Heinle & Heinle.

Brown, J. D. (1995b). Language program evaluation: Problems and solutions. *Annual Review of Applied Linguistics, 15*, 227–248.

Brown, J. D. (2001). *Using surveys in language programs.* Cambridge: Cambridge University Press.

Brown, J. D. (2005). *Testing in language programs: A comprehensive guide to English language assessment* (New ed.). New York: McGraw-Hill.

Brown, J. D. (2006). Second language studies: Curriculum development. In K. Brown (Ed.), *Encyclopedia of language and linguistics* (2nd ed.; Volume 11, pp. 102–110). Oxford: Elsevier.

Brown, J. D. (2009). Foreign and second language needs analysis. In M. H. Long & C. J. Doughty (Eds.), *The handbook of language teaching* (pp. 269–293). Oxford: Wiley-Blackwell.

Brown, J. D., & Hudson, T. (2002). *Criterion-referenced language testing.* Cambridge: Cambridge University Press.

Brown, J. D., & Rodgers, T. (2002). *Doing second language research.* Oxford: Oxford University Press.

Cadman, K. (2002). English for academic possibilities: The research proposal as a contested site in postgraduate genre pedagogy. *Journal of English for Academic Purposes, 1*(2), 85–104.

Carver, D. (1983). Some propositions about ESP. *The ESP Journal, 2*, 131–137.

Cortazzi, M., & Jin, L. (1999). Cultural mirrors: Materials and methods in the EFL classroom. In E. Hinkel (Ed.), *Culture in second language teaching* (pp. 196–219). Cambridge: Cambridge University Press.

Davidson, F., & Lynch, B. K. (2003). *Testcraft: A teacher's guide to writing and using language test specifications.* New Haven, CT: Yale University Press.

Derewianka, B. (2003). Trends and issues in genre-based approaches. *RELC Journal, 34*(2), 133–154.

Deterding, D., & Kirkpatrick, A. (2006). Emerging South-East Asian Englishes and intelligibility. *World Englishes, 25*(3/4), 391–409.

Farrell, T. S. C. (2008). *Reflective language teaching: From research to practice.* New York: Continuum International.

Grzega, J. (2005). Reflections on concepts of English for Europe: British English, American English, Euro-English, Global English. *Journal for EuroLinguistiX, 2,* 44–64.

Jenkins, J. (1998). Which pronunciation norms and models for English as an international language? *ELT Journal, 52*(2), 119–126.

Jenkins, J. (2000). *The phonology of English as an international language.* Oxford: Oxford University Press.

Jenkins, J. (2002). A sociolinguistically based, empirically researched pronunciation syllabus for English as an international language. *Applied Linguistics, 23*(1), 83–103.

Jenkins, J. (2004). Research in teaching pronunciation and intonation. *Annual Review of Applied Linguistics, 24,* 109–125.

Jenkins, J. (2009). English as a lingua franca: Interpretations and attitudes. *World Englishes, 28*(2), 200–207.

Kachru, B. B. (1985). Standards, codification, and sociolinguistic realism: The English language in the outer circle. In R. Quirk & H. Widdowson (Eds.), *English in the world: Teaching and learning of language and literature* (pp. 11–30). Cambridge: Cambridge University Press.

Kachru, B. B. (1986). The power and politics of English. *World Englishes, 5*(2/3), 121–140.

Kirkpatrick, A. (2007a). Setting attainable and appropriate English language targets in multilingual settings: A case for Hong Kong. *International Journal of Applied Linguistics, 17*(3), 376–391.

Kirkpatrick, A. (2007b). *World Englishes: Implications for international communication and English language teaching.* Cambridge: Cambridge University Press.

Kirkpatrick, A. (2008). English as the official working language of the Association of Southeast Asian Nations (ASEAN): Features and strategies. *English Today, 24*(2), 27–34.

Kirkpatrick, A., Deterding, D., & Wong, J. (2008). The international intelligibility of Hong Kong English. *World Englishes, 27*(3/4), 359–377.

Kramsch, C., & Sullivan, P. (1996). Appropriate pedagogy. *ELT Journal, 50*(3), 199–212.

Lanteigne, B. (2006). Regionally specific tasks of non-western English language use. *TESL-EJ, 10*(2), 1–19.

Li, D. C. S. (2007). Researching and teaching China and Hong Kong English. *English Today, 23*(3/4), 11–17.

Lin, B. (2002). English as an international language: Discourse as an answer to what to teach and how to teach it (pp. 1–16). *Conference proceedings of the 7th annual Conference of Pan-Pacific Association of Applied Lingustics.* Retrieved January 7, 2011 from http://www.paaljapan.org/resources/proceedings/PAAL7/pdfs/01benedict.pdf

Llurda, E. (2004). Non-native-speaker teachers and English as an international language. *International Journal of Applied Linguistics, 14*(3), 314–323.

Llurda, E. (Ed.) (2005). *Non-native-speaker teachers: Perceptions, challenges, and contributions to the field*. New York: Springer.

Long, M. H. (Ed.) (2005). *Second language needs analysis*. Cambridge: Cambridge University Press.

Maley, A. (2010). The reality of EIL and the myth of ELF. In C. Gagliardi & A. Maley (Eds.), *EIL, ELF, global English: Teaching and learning issues* (pp. 25–44). Bern: Peter Lang.

Matsuda, A. (2003). World Englishes in teaching English as an international language. *TESOL Quarterly, 37*(4), 719–729.

Mauranen, A. (2003). The corpus of English as lingua franca in academic settings. *TESOL Quarterly, 37*(3), 513–527.

McDonough, J., & Shaw, C. (2003). *Materials and methods in ELT: A teacher's guide* (2nd ed.). Oxford: Blackwell.

McKay, S. (1978). Syllabuses: Structural, situational, notional. *TESOL Newsletter, 12*(5), 11.

McKay, S. L. (2001). Teaching English as an International Language: Implications for cultural materials in the classroom. *TESOL Journal, 9*(4), 7–11.

McKay, S. L. (2002). *Teaching English as an international language: Rethinking goals and perspectives*. New York: Oxford University Press.

McKay, S. L. (2003a). Teaching English as an international language: The Chilean context. *ELT Journal, 57*(2), 139–148.

McKay, S. L. (2003b). Toward an appropriate EIL pedagogy: Re-examining common ELT assumptions. *International Journal of Applied Linguistics, 13*(1), 1–22.

McKay, S. L. (2003c). EIL curriculum development. *RELC Journal, 34*(1), 31–47.

Medgyes, P. (2001). When the teacher is a non-native speaker. In M. Celce-Murcia (Ed.), *Teaching English as a second or foreign language* (pp. 429–442). Boston: Heinle & Heinle.

Melchers, G., & Shaw, P. (2003). *World Englishes*. London: Arnold.

Nickerson, C. (2005). English as a lingua franca in international business contexts. *English for Specific Purposes, 24*(4), 367–380.

Norris, J. M., Davis, J. McE., Sinicrope, C., & Watanabe, Y. (2009). *Toward useful program evaluation in college foreign language education*. Honolulu, HI: National Foreign Language Resource Center.

Nunn, R. (2005). Competence and teaching English as an international language. *Asian EFL Journal, 7*(3), 61–75.

Pennycook, A. (1997). Vulgar pragmatism, critical pragmatism, and EAP. *English for Specific Purposes, 16*(4), 253–270.

Pickering, L. (2006). Current research on intelligibility in English as a lingua franca. *Annual Review of Applied Linguistics, 26*, 219–233.

Saraceni, M. (2008). English as a lingua franca: Between form and function. *English Today, 24*(2), 20–26.

Seidlhofer, B. (1999). Double standards: Teacher education in the Expanding Circle. *World Englishes, 18*(2), 233–245.

Seidlhofer, B. (2001). Closing a conceptual gap: The case for the description of English as a lingua franca. *International Journal of Applied Linguistics, 11*(2), 133–158.

Seidlhofer, B. (2004). Research perspectives on teaching English as a lingua franca. *Annual Review of Applied Linguistics, 24*, 209–239.

Seidlhofer, B. (2005). English as a lingua franca. *Oxford advanced learner's dictionary of current English* (7th ed., p. R 92). Oxford: Oxford University Press.

Seidlhofer, B., Breiteneder, A., & Pitzl, M. (2006). English as a lingua franca in Europe: Challenges for applied linguistics. *Annual Review of Applied Linguistics, 26*, 3–34.

Sewell, A. (2010). Research methods and intelligibility studies. *World Englishes, 29*(2), 257–269.

Sifakis, N. C., & Sougari, A.-M. (2005). Pronunciation issues and EIL pedagogy in the periphery: A survey of Greek state school teachers' beliefs. *TESOL Quarterly, 39*(3), 467–488.

Tomlinson, B. (1998). *Materials development for language teaching.* Cambridge: Cambridge University Press.

Tomlinson, B. (Ed.) (2002). *Developing materials for language teaching.* New York: Continuum International.

Chapter 10

Teaching Materials in EIL

Aya Matsuda

Introduction

In foreign language classrooms, regardless of the language, textbooks and other teaching materials play an important role. Brown (1995) acknowledges their significance by positioning it as one of six components of a language curriculum, along with needs analysis, goals and objectives, testing, teaching, and program evaluation. Dubin and Olstain (1986) argue that, because the process of curriculum design is sometimes not clear to teachers and most likely unknown to learners, "the tangible element that gives a language course face validity to many learners and teachers is the textbook" (p. 167).

One obvious way the teaching materials contribute to foreign language teaching is as a source of input. Because the contact with the target language is limited outside the classroom, the quality and quantity of the language input in class is critical in acquiring the language. Textbooks and Audio Visual (AV) materials enrich the classroom input by providing language samples that differ from the voice and style of the teacher, and even serve as the exclusive source of input when the teachers themselves are not fluent in the target language. Consequently, they are often regarded as a high prestige source of input by foreign language students (Bardovi-Harlig, 1996).

Besides providing valuable language input, teaching materials also express, reinforce, and construct a certain view of the world. Hino's study (1988a) of Japanese English-as-a-foreign-language (EFL) textbooks, for example, showed how the representation of nationalism changed over time, reflecting the political climates of the country in each period. In other words, teaching materials do not only disseminate knowledge but may also play a vital role in the construction of students' perception of and beliefs about the target language.

Since most English learners who are learning the language for international communication are in contexts where English is taught as a foreign language, everything discussed above is likely to apply. In fact, teaching materials may hold an even more important place in English-as-an-international-language (EIL) classrooms, for both teachers and students. A goal of teaching EIL is to prepare the learners to use English to become part of the globalized world, which is linguistically and culturally diverse, and thus EIL courses naturally strive to incorporate such diversity and to represent English as a pluralistic and dynamic entity rather than a monolithic and static one. Few teachers, however, have a rich enough knowledge of and personal experience with all of the varieties and functions of Englishes that exist today, and thus they need to rely on teaching materials in order to introduce students to the linguistic and cultural diversity of English. In other words, EIL courses and teachers depend on well-designed teaching materials that include ample linguistic samples of world Englishes[1] as well as metalinguistic discussions on and comprehensive representations of the global spread of English.

The availability of published teaching materials, the amount of freedom an individual teacher has in selecting the materials, and the level of support, resources, and expectations to create original ones vary greatly from one context to another. In some contexts, all teachers in a program are expected to use the same textbook, and thus occasional short readings or audio/video clips may be the only supplemental materials teachers can incorporate into their lessons. In other contexts, teachers may be expected to select one textbook among all that are available world-wide without any guidelines or guidance for selection. Some programs (or students) cannot afford textbooks. Others may require teachers and students to use the same textbooks every year. Although such variation makes it difficult to discuss EIL materials in a general way, there are some common issues to be kept in mind, regardless of the context, as we explore the role of EIL teaching materials.

This chapter focuses on the evaluation, selection, and development of teaching materials in EIL classrooms. Teaching materials can be defined as "any systematic description of the techniques and exercises to be used in classroom teaching" which is "broad enough to encompass lesson plans and yet can accommodate books, packets of audio-visual aids, games, or any of the other myriad types of activities that go on in the language classroom" (Brown, 1995, p. 139). These materials can take a variety of forms, including books, workbooks, teachers' resource books, realia, and various audio-visuals. Ideally, the process of materials development—including evaluating and selecting existing materials as well as adapting or creating materials from scratch for a particular group of students—is guided by the overall orientation of the language curriculum (e.g., theoretical approaches) as well as other components of curriculum such as students' needs or goals and objectives. In some cases, however, teachers find themselves in a situation where the orientation is neither clearly articulated nor consistent, or the inadequate analysis of needs has led to goals and objectives that do not match the actual needs of students. In such cases, careful selection of published materials and creation of original materials become particularly critical as they allow teachers to strengthen the curriculum.

The primary focus of this chapter is on what teachers and administrators regularly do: select published materials and develop their own. However, most issues raised and criteria presented can also be used to design materials for publication. The chapter first identifies the limitations of traditionally available materials, and then suggests ways to make them more suitable for EIL curricula. Specifically, the chapter presents (1) criteria for selecting and developing teaching materials for EIL classrooms, (2) steps for modifying or supplementing teaching materials currently in use, and (3) possible sources for the supplemental materials.

Traditional Practices and Principles

One characteristic of English used in international settings is its heterogeneity. Although linguistic variation is found in all natural human languages, English is unique in that it is a language with "multiple norms and diverse systems" (Canagarajah, 2006, p. 199). The world-wide spread of English through migration, colonization, and globalization has resulted in the institutionalization of the language in multiple countries, where the language has become nativized and a new norm for the localized English has emerged (Kachru, 1986).

Consequently, in the contexts of international communication, different varieties of English are represented. That is, rather than switching to a distinct international variety of English, each speaker uses a variety of English he or she happens to know, while using various communicative strategies to achieve successful communication. Although we talk about EIL as though it is a uniform and homogeneous entity, in practice, implicit rules about appropriate forms and usage of English are negotiated for each communicative event and thus there is a great deal of formal and pragmatic variation across situations (Friedrich & Matsuda, 2010; Matsuda & Friedrich, 2011). What this suggests is that in EIL classrooms, one of the important goals is to develop awareness of and sensitivity toward differences—in forms, uses, and users—and learn to respect (or at least tolerate) those differences. EIL teaching materials must support and promote this.

Traditional ELT teaching materials, however, especially textbooks and other materials specifically developed for classroom use, tend to focus on the "standard" varieties from the UK and the US. This is because the EFL curricula, by default, have focused almost exclusively on these varieties of English (Matsuda, 2002). These varieties have dominated the ELT profession for a long time, and thus seem "natural" to most teachers and students. The existence of multiple legitimate varieties of English is rarely represented in ELT textbooks.

The dominance of the Inner Circle[2] (Kachru, 1985), particularly the UK and the US, is also apparent in representations of English *users*. In the analysis of seven 7th-grade textbooks used in Japan from 1997–2002, it was found that the majority of the non-Japanese main characters in these textbooks were from Inner-Circle countries, specifically the US, Canada, Australia, and Scotland, and they tended to play more significant roles, producing more words and contributing more substantially to the dialogues (Matsuda, 2002). The number of characters from the Outer Circle and the Expanding Circle other than Japan constituted less than 10% of the total, and the use of English exclusively among non-native speakers,[3] which in reality is increasing (Crystal, 1997; Graddol, 1997), was rarely present in the dialogues: most were between native and non-native speakers of English and some were even exclusively among Inner-Circle speakers. This study focused specifically on English textbooks used in Japan, but anecdotes shared by teachers from other Expanding-Circle countries suggest that the tendency to focus on US/UK English and English users seems to be prevalent in various contexts.

Overall, materials published specifically for classroom use—as opposed to "authentic" materials individual teachers choose to bring in—tend to be based on and reinforce a common assumption in the field of ELT that English is the language of the Inner Circle, particularly that of the US and the UK, and the reason for learning English is to interact with native English speakers, which often is equated with those from the UK and the US.

One problem of such representation of the English language and users vis-à-vis the present-day use of EIL is that it is incomplete and may result in a limited and skewed understanding of who speaks English and for what purposes. Such a limited perception of the English language may lead to confusion or resistance when students are confronted with different types of English users (e.g., users from the Outer Circle). Students may be shocked by varieties and uses of English that differ from Inner-Circle English, view them as deficient rather than different, or be disrespectful of such varieties and uses.

Current representations of English as the language of the Inner-Circle speakers, as already stated, also fail to acknowledge the increased use of English among non-native speakers of English. This is also problematic because if students do not understand the significance of the uses of English among non-native speakers, they may not fully take advantage of the opportunities that accompany the use of EIL. Instead, students may assume that English belongs to the Inner Circle, and that others are expected to conform to Inner-Circle norms and remain in a peripheral position in international communication in English (e.g., Matsuda, 2003).

The relationship between teaching materials' representations and the construction of students' language ideology is yet to be empirically verified, but it is at least safe to say that representations that do not accurately capture the reality of EIL use are inadequate in preparing learners for such use of the language. A language is not merely a combination of discrete linguistic and metalinguistic knowledge, but rather a dynamic system embedded in a social context (Berns, 1990; Halliday, 1978). Therefore, the awareness of the context of English, including its worldwide spread, diversity in its forms and functions, and the increased use among non-native speakers, is crucial for understanding and acquiring English. Fortunately, however, there is increasing attention and research on world Englishes and EIL that we can draw from in order to make teaching materials more comprehensive and useful for both teachers and students of EIL.

Practices and Principles for an EIL Framework

How accurately the textbook and other teaching materials represent the complex reality of English today is one of many questions one must ask in evaluating, selecting, and developing materials. The appropriateness of levels, integration of skills being taught in class, and quality and amount of exercises are some examples of questions teachers ask, regardless of their commitment to bringing in the EIL perspective to their pedagogy. But for those who are interested in the EIL perspective, there are some additional questions to ask in order to gauge the comprehensiveness and appropriateness of an EIL representation in teaching materials.

For the rest of the chapter, I will present those questions and why they are relevant in teaching EIL. I will then present steps a teacher can take to determine what is needed to be modified or added to the materials currently used. At the end, some sources one can turn to for supplemental materials are discussed.

Criteria for Evaluating Teaching Materials

Which Variety of English is the Material Based on? Is it the Variety my Students Should Learn?

Multiple varieties of English are used successfully in international communication contexts in English, which implies that we have a wide variety of Englishes to choose from when selecting an instructional model for English instruction. The dominant instructional model(s) of the course should be selected according to the goal of the curriculum and the needs of students, and the varieties of English represented in the teaching materials should match the focus of the course. For instance, if the central goal of the course is to prepare students to study in the UK, the textbooks and other materials must introduce students to British (academic) English and its culture(s). Similarly, if the course is to prepare business professionals to relocate to Hong Kong, ideal materials would expose learners to a kind of Hong Kong English used in business as well as for social purposes (see Matsuda & Friedrich, 2011, for further discussion on the selection of instructional models).

In many cases, American or British English—the two most popular choices for instructional models—may be a reasonable choice. They are considered legitimate and respected in many international contexts—i.e., they may not be the most preferred in all contexts but are acceptable in many. After all, there is nothing *wrong* per se with these varieties.

One key issue here, however, is that such a selection must be made after much consideration and should not disregard the need for students to be aware, appreciative and somewhat prepared for the encounter with other varieties. And in unfortunate cases where such consideration has not already taken place as part of the curriculum design, such gap may need to be filled through the process of careful selection and development of teaching materials.

Does it Provide Adequate Exposure to Other Varieties of English and Raise Enough Awareness about the Linguistic Diversity of English?

It is reasonable for a course or textbook to focus predominantly on one variety of English because, even in an EIL course, it is neither possible nor necessary for students to become fluent in multiple varieties of English. Most people who successfully use English for international communication, whether native or non-native speakers of the language, are fluent in only a limited set of English varieties anyway (mostly a combination of different social and situational dialects, rather than multiple regional varieties of English). However, students must understand that the variety they are learning is one of many and may differ from what their future interlocutors use. If the variety serving as the instructional model is the only variety presented in class, an impression might be formed that it is the only correct variety. Such an impression is not only inaccurate but could also lead to negative attitudes toward other varieties of English and students' confidence in successful communication involving multiple varieties of English (Matsuura, Chiba, & Fujieda, 1999). Furthermore, their ability to interpret interactions in various Englishes correctly may also be compromised (Smith & Nelson, 2006).

There are several ways to increase students' awareness of English varieties using appropriate materials. One is to use pre-packaged teaching materials that already include multiple varieties of English. CDs that accompany textbooks, for example, may include samples of different varieties of English. The listening section of the current TOEIC (Test of English for International Communication) test includes speakers from Britain, Australia, New Zealand, and North America. While the selection is still limited to Inner-Circle varieties, this change in the TOEIC test makes it possible—and even desirable—to introduce varieties other than American and British English even in test preparation courses which tend to be rigid about norms and standards.

Another way to expose students to different varieties of English is through supplemental materials—both those created for pedagogical purposes (but not part of the pre-packaged materials adopted by the course) and non-pedagogical purposes (e.g., movies)—that include textual, audio, and visual samples of other varieties of English. Luckily, these materials are now widely accessible through the use of the Internet. If students are starting a chapter on Native American cultures in the US, for instance, why not bring in a short documentary of Native American culture that also features speakers of Native American Englishes (e.g., Navajo English)? If they are learning about English in India, how about introducing an article or two from an English language newspaper from India such as *The Times of India*? This would allow students to see that English varieties are not only a matter of different pronunciation features or vocabulary, but rather a much more encompassing manifestation of cultural, linguistic, and other values.

Finally, yet another way to increase students' meta-knowledge about Englishes is by making it a lesson focus. In Japan, for instance, there are several textbooks and readers that are entirely based on the discussion of the global spread of English (e.g., *English Across Cultures* by Honna, Kirkpatrick, & Gilbert, 2001); those that include a chapter on different national varieties of English (e.g., a chapter on Singlish in *Crown English Series II* by Shimozaki et al., 2004); as well as popular magazines featuring articles on these issues. Such materials allow teachers to explicitly teach students about the use of English as an international language and its linguistic, cultural, and political implications.

Does it Represent a Variety of Speakers?

The world-wide spread of English has also changed the demographics of English users. English is not used exclusively among native English speakers or even between native and non-native English speakers anymore, but also often for communication exclusively among non-native speakers of English (Graddol, 1997; Smith, 1983; Widdowson, 1994). Accordingly, the assumption that non-native English speakers learn English in order to communicate with native English speakers does not always hold true anymore.

Given this reality of English, it is important that the materials used in class represent both native and non-native speakers, particularly those similar to learners themselves. Such an inclusive representation represents the profile of English users more accurately and helps learners develop a more realistic expectation about their future interlocutors.

Additionally, the inclusive representation of speakers, especially those similar to themselves, fosters the sense of ownership of English. One characteristic of English today that has been pointed out by several applied linguists is that English no longer belongs exclusively to native speakers of English (Graddol, 1997; McKay, 2002; Widdowson, 1994). Graddol wrote in his book, *The Future of English*, "Native speakers may feel the language 'belongs' to them, but it will be those who speak English as a second or foreign language who will determine its world future" (p. 10). Widdowson (1994) also wrote, "How English develops in the world is no business whatever of native speakers in England, the United States, or anywhere else. They have no say in the matter, no right to intervene or pass judgement" (p. 385). In other words, the process of learning to use EIL involves a process of claiming ownership of the language. Such sense of ownership may be fostered through a variety of ways, from having an opportunity to use English for authentic communication to meeting someone with a similar background using English effectively to having explicit discussions in it. But if the teaching materials continue to portray only Inner-Circle users of English, it will send a message that the language nonetheless belongs to the Inner Circle, and that the learners are using the language to talk only to those people.

This actually leads to the third reason to argue for an inclusive representation of speakers. The inclusion of people who are similar to the learner is important because they serve as the role model. Specifically, it allows learners to see themselves as someone who can become a legitimate user of the language. EIL learners rely on English textbooks and other teaching materials to create an imagined community (Pavlenko & Norton, 2007) where English is used as a medium of communication. Textbook characters that are similar to themselves makes it easier for students to imagine themselves as legitimate members of the community, and thus brings English closer to them. It allows them to take the ownership of not only the language but also the experience of language learning.

Whose Cultures are Represented?

Language classes often incorporate the teaching of culture as part of their content because language and culture are considered inseparable. Language constructs and reflects culture. Rules about the appropriateness of language use are culture-specific. Although the concept of culture is rather difficult to define, there seems to be a consensus among language teaching specialists that culture holds a legitimate space in language teaching, and consequently, in materials we teach with.

While some scholars of the global spread of English argue that English has become de-anglicized (Kachru, 1992), it does not necessarily mean that English has become de-culturalized. Rather, it is now intricately intertwined with a wide variety of cultures, including national and regional cultures that were not traditionally associated with English (see Canagarajah, 2006, for further discussion on the complicated relationship between English as a lingua franca and the local culture).

In courses for English for Specific Purposes (ESP) in international contexts, the content of the teaching materials is naturally tied to the specific purpose for which students are prepared. For example, textbooks on English for international business may include readings on principles of cross-cultural business negotiation or cultural differences in business ethics. A teacher of a medical English course may incorporate a video clip of movie scenes that depict conversation between a doctor and patient in English, preferably from diverse English-speaking contexts involving different types of English speakers. In other words, the culture taught in such a course may be specific to the professional and discipline-specific community that the learners are attempting to enter.

In general English courses, where learners are preparing themselves for the use of English in international contexts, culture is defined much more broadly. And for teaching materials to capture such broadness, their cultural content must be drawn from multiple sources.

The first source of cultural content is global culture, which includes topics that cut across national boundaries and are relevant to the global society as a whole. Topics such as world peace and environment conservation are already popular in ELT teaching materials, and they continue to provide appropriate content for readings, class discussions, and course assignments in EIL classrooms, as they help foster the sense of global citizenship among students. This is particularly useful in contexts where inter-subject/departmental collaboration and coordination is encouraged. For instance, English teachers and science teachers may collaboratively develop a unit on world ecology, allowing students to study the topic from multiple perspectives and reinforce learning in two languages. Another example of a global topic is that of the role of EIL itself. Students can read, write, discuss, or conduct research on such topics as the spread of English, multilingualism, language ecology, and language rights. Materials targeted for particular grades and language levels can assist teachers in presenting these topics in a way that is meaningful to students.

The second source would be the culture(s) of their future interlocutors. In today's global world where English is the most common lingua franca, any culture of a person who uses English as such is already part of the English-speaking world as much as members of American and British cultures are. The challenge here, of course, is that who those interlocutors may be is unknown, and it would be impossible to touch upon every single country and culture within each country. One way to address this challenge is to strategically diversify the content to include countries and regions from various parts of the world in the teaching materials. Such coverage can illustrate not only the geographical spread but also the functional diversity of the language (e.g., the dominant language of the society, its use for performing specific functions while co-existing with local languages, and as perceived and used as the language for international communication).

The third possible source of cultural content for EIL materials is the learner's own culture. When English was considered as the language of the UK and the US and merely as a tool to access information, knowledge, and resources only available in the language, the knowledge of a narrowly defined "English-speaking culture" may have been adequate. Today's use of EIL is not limited to exchanges between native and non-native speakers of English, and there is often a desire to establish and maintain an equal, mutually-respectful relationship with others. In those cases, the ability to perceive and analyze the familiar from an outsider's perspective is critical and needs to be part of our teaching goals as well. Culture is not limited to traditional—and often stereotypical—culture, such as "sushi" for Japan and "soccer" for Brazil. Any beliefs and practices in which the students' experience is situated—e.g., school, family, community—also constitute local culture. From this perspective, any materials that engage students to explain local culture, to critically reflect upon what they take for granted, and to work on skills to describe local culture in English can be legitimately incorporated into EIL classrooms.

Is it Appropriate for Local Contexts?

Another issue that has been overlooked in the past but has attracted more attention in recent years is the question of the appropriateness of curriculum, methodology, and teaching materials for local teaching contexts (McKay, 2002). Some scholars, for instance, have argued that we cannot automatically assume certain teaching methodologies that are well received in the western contexts work equally well with students and teachers in other parts of the world (e.g., Hino, 1988b; Hu, 2002). Each culture has a way of teaching and learning that is historically situated in the local context. Although there is nothing wrong with introducing a new pedagogical approach, it cannot be expected to work well without any adjustments in a new context and should not be assumed to be *more* effective or better than the local practices. The same argument applies to the appropriateness of teaching materials. That is, materials should be based on—or compatible with—the way of teaching and learning that teachers and learners are familiar with, and ideally should draw from the strength of approaches they are already accustomed to.

While users often have a view of teaching materials (especially published ones) as an objective collection of information, they are indeed a cultural artifact that represents and promotes certain values, whether intentional or unintentional (Hino, 1988a). Thus, values represented in teaching materials could potentially come into direct conflict with that of teachers and students. Dissonance created by such conflict itself is not necessarily a bad thing: the exposure to different values broadens one's perspective and provides a learning opportunity. Furthermore, the increased access to the global community through English is likely to introduce conflicting values anyway, and thus students may appreciate it if the initial encounter to new values takes place in a language classroom, in an insulated community with the support of teachers and peers.

Introducing unfamiliar values, however, requires some careful planning and responses. For instance, a mixed-gendered dialogue in a professional context may seem strange or unrealistic to students in a society where gender roles are rigidly defined and clearly divided, and thus may require some explanation. Similarly, we must ensure that students are not offended and alienated by representations in the textbooks, to the point that their commitment to learning is adversely affected. In some cases, teachers themselves may be confused or put off by the values and practices presented in the textbooks, and thus need extra time to figure out how to position themselves in the discussion.

It is also important that the content of teaching materials is relatable and meaningful to learners, as educational research suggests that students learn better when they can relate to the material and find the material real and meaningful to themselves (e.g, Howard, 2003; Ladson-Billings, 1995). It could be a matter of a simple thing, like climate—children from a place with a long winter and lots of snow are likely to relate to a story about sledding and fireplaces more easily than those living in the tropical weather would. It could also be more subtle issues, such as gender roles as discussed above. An editorial article about working conditions for women may be hard to relate to for those in a society where women typically do not work outside the home.

Again, this is not to suggest that we should avoid stories about snow when teaching in tropical countries. It is, in fact, a great learning opportunity if the story serves as the window to parts of the world and ideas children have never considered before. What it means, however, is that the children may need extra preparation to be able to engage in the story. The class may need to spend some time learning about cold weather and snow, playing with artificial snow, or even making and enjoying snow-themed snacks before students begin to feel that the story is relevant to them. It would be unfortunate if students do not learn a language well merely because they found the reality created in the teaching materials to be too foreign to them.

Steps for Supplementing Materials

In most cases, teachers need to supplement the core textbook. The above criteria may help material writers create materials that are more applicable for EIL teaching, but no textbook works for everyone without any modification because the goals of students and the availability of other kinds of teacher resources vary from one context to another. Here is a step-by-step approach to identify what supplemental materials are needed.

Question 1: What are the Needs of Learners?

Before evaluating the teaching materials, the learners' needs must be revisited. A needs analysis should have been completed as part of the curriculum development, but in some cases, it may need some careful re-examination. In the context of EIL specifically, this starts with the question: where, with whom, and for what purposes will they be using English?

Question 2: Does the Teaching Material in Question Meet the Needs of the Learners Adequately?

Once the needs are identified, any gaps between the learners' needs and what the materials provide can be explored by asking further questions. For example,

- Does it expose students to English varieties they are likely to be exposed to in real situations where they use English for international communication?

- Does it represent English users that are similar to the learners themselves as well as their future interlocutors?
- Does it include content information that is relevant to the learners and would be useful in accomplishing their communicative goals?
- Does it help students develop an awareness of the linguistic and cultural diversity of English and a sense of the linguistic ecology that English is part of?

Question 3: How can the Identified Gaps be Filled?

Once the gaps are identified, the materials that would fill the gaps can be found. Advancements in instructional media, including the Internet, allow teachers to easily access various kinds of materials that can be used to support teaching and learning. The following are some examples of where supplemental materials may be found.

Possible Sources for Supplemental Materials

Other Textbooks and Pre-packaged Materials

Although the representation of English in published teaching materials traditionally focused more on the US and the UK, there are recent materials that include explicit and implicit references to the kinds of diversity discussed above. Also, many textbooks that are used in language programs in the Inner-Circle countries also have global and multinational representations, both in terms of topics and users. A section from such materials can be incorporated as the supplemental materials.

Audio-Visuals: CD, DVD, and Audio and Movie Clips Available on the Internet

Clips from a radio and TV program or DVD that specifically addresses the issues related to the spread of English, globalization, or any of the "global topics" discussed above can be used for the warm-up and wrap-up as well as for the main activity in the lesson. There are also movies not necessarily *about* EIL, but which include scenes that illuminate the use of EIL and potential challenges associated with it.

Media: Newspapers and News Scripts

English newspaper articles and news scripts from different countries can be brought in for linguistic analysis, as well as to serve as the base for a class discussion. Comparing and contrasting articles from different countries about the same event helps students understand the competing perspectives that exist in the world (see Hino [in press] for a more detailed discussion of such pedagogy). In addition, news program websites often have broadcast news clips, script of the news clip, and links to related articles or websites all on one page, creating a multimedia packet.

Official Websites: Countries and Cities, International Organizations, etc.

Websites are also a great resource for information about other communities. For example, official websites created by a government, particularly for the international tourist, are a good starting point to learn about a particular country or city. They not only provide factual information about them but also often represent a local perspective on the place, which may help alleviate some stereotypes held by outsiders. For a unit on a "global topic," a website of international organizations devoted to the issue would be useful (e.g., UNESCO for education; WWF for environment and wildlife conservation). In many cases, having students research those websites and report back what they found is a meaningful activity since one benefit of learning EIL is to gain access to information that is not available without English.

Personal Websites, Blogs, and Social Networking Sites (SNS)

One area where students may out-experience their teachers is in social networking and blogging. Teenagers and older students in countries where the Internet is readily accessible may already be participating in such SNS programs like Facebook or Myspace. They may also maintain their own blogs or read others, or participate in fan sites and other interactive online communities. Such interactive space on the web provides authentic international and multilingual communicative situations, and teachers may be able to take advantage of them by having students participate in them or bringing in an aspect of it to class (i.e., creating a Facebook page for the class).

Such personal and social websites often include social, regional, and situational dialects that differ from what is perceived as the standard variety, which students are exposed to in the classroom. There are also utterances that are incomplete or contain errors, unlike "cleaned-up," artificial dialogues found in many textbooks. While these discrepancies may create some confusion for learners at first, those are the same kind of confusions—and learning opportunities—that learners would encounter when they start using English to interact with others. Exposure to different styles and registers allows students to understand that English is as heterogeneous and dynamic as their own language. It also provides an opportunity to discuss dialects, different levels of formalities coded in language, and the appropriateness of certain language use for particular situations.

Conclusion

The chapter discussed the role of teaching materials in EIL curricula. Specifically, the chapter introduced a series of questions one can use to assess how accurately and comprehensively the material represents the characteristics of EIL use. It also presented steps a teacher can use to identify what needs to be supplemented, and examples of supplemental materials that can be used to fill the gap between what students need to know and what the materials in place already provide.

What this chapter did not address is the question of what makes good teaching materials in general. When selecting and modifying materials, there are basic criteria such as the compatibility with the orientation of the curriculum, quality of exercises, and the difficulty level of English, and other issues that teachers and administrators look for in the content (e.g., Brown, 1995, p. 161). They also need to be mindful of practical issues such as the price or size of the textbooks. These factors were not addressed in this chapter, but they continue to play an important role in how we think about teaching materials for EIL courses. The selection criteria and modification suggestions presented in this chapter are not meant to replace, but rather complement existing criteria by explicitly directing the decision maker's attention to the sociolinguistic complexity of the English language today.

Exploring the Ideas

1 Do you agree that ELT materials typically focus on English, users, and cultures from the US and/or the UK? What evidence do you have to support your belief?

2 What are some challenges you might face in creating teaching materials that introduce varieties of English that you are not fluent in or familiar with? What can be done to alleviate those challenges?

3 How can the awareness of respect toward different varieties of English be promoted? Is mere exposure enough? If not, what else needs to be done?

4 What are the pros and cons of incorporating social media (e.g., Facebook, blogs, fan site) into classroom instruction? How should teachers address the use of "nonstandard" language in such spaces?

Applying the Ideas

1 Select a textbook you are currently using or may be interested in adopting in the future. Using the five criteria presented under "Criteria for evaluating teaching materials," assess the appropriateness of the textbook for an EIL course. Specifically:

   a. Identify examples of how the textbook already does what is discussed under each criterion (you may be surprised how much "good practice" is already in place).

   b. What are areas that particularly need to be supplemented?

2 Find an ELT textbook that was published in a country different from where your students come from. Review the content and identify topics, visual representations, and other information that may be unfamiliar to your students. Is there anything that may be misinterpreted or be off-putting or offensive to your students? What kind of scaffolding is needed to help students understand them and find the material relevant to them?

3 Find a TV or movie clip that includes "scenes that illuminate the use of EIL and potential challenges associated with it" (p. 180, this chapter). Create a lesson plan that incorporates the showing of the clip. What points about EIL does the lesson illustrate?

Notes

1 In this chapter, the term "world Englishes" is used to refer to varieties of English found world-wide today, including not only "new Englishes" from post-colonial countries but also those from the Inner- and Expanding-Circles (Kachru, 1985).

2 I am using the terms from the concentric circle model (Kachru, 1985) to efficiently describe different ways English is acquired and used in each country: the Inner Circle (i.e., where English is acquired as the first language of the majority of its population and used as the dominant language of the society), the Outer Circle (i.e., where English is acquired as an additional language and performs specific functions in domestic communication while co-existing with local languages), and the Expanding Circle (i.e., where English is learned as a foreign language and perceived as and used as the language for international communication). It does not suggest the centeredness of the Inner Circle over other contexts or homogeneity within each circle, as critically pointed out by some scholars (e.g., Bruthiaux, 2003; Canagarajah, 2006).

3 In this chapter, "native English speakers" refers to people who have learned the language as the first language and use it as the dominant language, typically found in the Inner Circle, while "non-native English speakers" refers to people who did not acquire it as the first language, for the lack of better alternatives. It should be noted that the concepts of "native" and "non-native speakers" in general have been problematized in applied linguistics literature (e.g., Davies, 1991, 2003), and particularly in reference to English

as there are many users of English who do not comfortably fit in these two categories. Sometimes the word "multilingual speakers" is used to refer to English users who have acquired English as an additional language ("second" or "foreign"); it is not useful in this context since there are also "native" speakers of English who are also multilingual.

References

Bardovi-Harlig, K. (1996). Pragmatics and language learning: Bringing pragmatics and pedagogy together. *Pragmatics and Language Learning, 7,* 21–39.

Berns, M. (1990). *Context of competence: Social and cultural considerations in communicative language teaching.* New York: Plenum Press.

Brown, J. D. (1995). *The elements of language curriculum.* Boston, MA: Heinle & Heinle.

Bruthiaux, P. (2003). Squaring the circles: Issues in modeling English worldwide. *International Journal of Applied Linguistics, 13*(2), 159–178.

Canagarajah, A. S. (2006). Negotiating the local in English as a lingua franca. *Annual Review of Applied Linguistics, 26,* 197–218.

Crystal, D. (1997). *English as a global language.* Cambridge, UK: Cambridge University Press.

Davies, A. (1991). *The native speaker in applied linguistics.* Edinburgh: Edinburgh University Press.

Davies, A. (2003). *The native speaker: Myth and reality.* Clevedon: Multilingual Matters Ltd.

Dubin, F., & Olstain, E. (1986). *Course design.* Cambridge, UK: Cambridge University Press.

Friedrich, P., & Matsuda, A. (2010). When five words are not enough: A conceptual and terminological discussion of English as a Lingua Franca. *International Multilingual Research Journal, 4,* 20–30.

Graddol, D. (1997). *The future of English?* London: The British Council.

Halliday, M. (1978). *Language as social semiotic: The social interpretation of language and meaning.* Baltimore, MD: Edward Arnold.

Hino, N. (1988a). Nationalism and English as an international language: The history of English textbooks in Japan. *World Englishes, 7*(3), 309–314.

Hino, N. (1988b). Yakudoku: Japan's dominant tradition in foreign language learning. *JALT Journal, 10*(1 & 2), 45–55.

Hino, N. (in press). Participating in the community of EIL users through real-time news: Integrated practice in TEIL (IPTEIL). In A. Matsuda (Ed.), *Teaching English as an international language: Principles and practices.*

Honna, N., Kirkpatrick, A., & Gilbert, S. (2001). *English across cultures.* Tokyo: Sanshusha.

Howard, T. C. (2003). Culturally relevant pedagogy: ingredients for critical teacher reflection. *Theory into Practice, 42*(3), 195–202.

Hu, G. (2002). Potential cultural resistance to pedagogical imports: The case of communicative language teaching in China. *Language, Culture and Curriculum, 15*(2), 93–105.

Kachru, B. B. (1985). Standards, codification and sociolinguistic realism: The English language in the outer circle. In R. Quirk & H. Widdowson (Eds.), *English in the world: Teaching and learning the language and literatures* (pp. 11–30). Cambridge: Cambridge University Press.

Kachru, B. B. (1986). *The alchemy of English: The spread, functions and models of non-native Englishes.* Oxford: Pergamon.

Kachru, B. B. (1992). Teaching world Englishes. In B. B. Kachru (Ed.), *The other tongue: English across cultures* (2nd ed., pp. 355–365). Urbana, IL: University of Illinois.

Ladson-Billings, G. (1995). Toward a theory of culturally relevant pedagogy. *American Educational Research Journal, 32*(3), 465–491.

Matsuda, A. (2002). Representation of users and uses of English in beginning Japanese EFL textbooks. *JALT Journal, 24*(2), 80–98.

Matsuda, A. (2003). The ownership of English in Japanese secondary schools. *World Englishes, 22*(4), 483–496.

Matsuda, A., & Friedrich, P. (2011). "So, what are we supposed to teach?": A blueprint for an EIL curriculum. *World Englishes, 30*(3), 1–13.

Matsuura, H., Chiba, R., & Fujieda, M. (1999). Intelligibility and comprehensibility of American and Irish Englishes in Japan. *World Englishes, 18*(19), 49–62.

McKay, S. L. (2002). *Teaching English as an international language.* Oxford, UK: Oxford University Press.

Pavlenko, A., & Norton, B. (2007). Imagined communities, identity, and English language learning. In J. Cummins & C. Davison (Eds.), *International Handbook of English Language Teaching* (Vol. 15, Section 1, pp 669–680). New York: Springer.

Shimozaki, M., Iida, R., Iwasa, Y., Kuroiwa, Y., Sasaki, H., Kanno, A., Tsujimoto, C., Matsubara, K., Mochizuki, N., Yui, R., Watanabe, Y., Deaux, G., & Taylor, G. (2004). *Crown English series II.* Tokyo: Sanseido, 2004.

Smith, L. E. (1983). English as an international language: No room for linguistic chauvinism. In L. Smith (Ed.), *Readings in English as an international language* (pp. 7–11). New York: Pergamon.

Smith, L. E. & Nelson, C. (2006). World Englishes and issues of intelligibility. In B. B. Kachru, Y. Kachru, & C. L. Nelson (Eds.), *The handbook of world Englishes* (pp. 428–445). Malden, MA: Blackwell.

Widdowson, H. G. (1994). The ownership of English. *TESOL Quarterly, 28*(2), 377–389.

Chapter 11

Teaching Oral Skills in English as a Lingua Franca

Juliane House

In this chapter I will first briefly characterize the nature of English as an international language, World Englishes, and English as a lingua franca. While I refer in this chapter predominantly to recent empirical research on English as a lingua franca, I suggest that since interactions in English as a lingua franca are found to differ on the levels of discourse and pragmatics from Inner-Circle English talk, they may well also be relevant for speakers of English as an international language and World Englishes.

I will propose several ways of applying these research results to improving ways of teaching oral skills in English as a global lingua franca and concentrate on making suggestions about the development of "pragmatic fluency" and intercultural competence in order to heighten speakers' oral English competence and their interactional awareness

Characteristics of English as an International Language, World Englishes, and English as a Lingua Franca

While "English as an international language" (EIL), "World Englishes" (WE) , and "English as a lingua franca" (ELF) all refer to the global nature, spread, and use of the English language, it is important to tease them apart. In this chapter, as in this volume as a whole, WE can be defined as institutionalized second-language varieties of English in the sense of Kachru (1986). These nativized varieties of English have a long (often colonial) history of linguistic and cultural adaptation to new geographical contexts, and they fulfill many different and important functions in the respective local legal, administrative, and educational system.

EIL is here defined as the use of English between L2 speakers of English regardless of whether they share the same culture or not, and between L2 and L1 English speakers. Since EIL includes both WE speakers' interactions in their own country and interactions in ELF, it is the most comprehensive term and also the linguistically most complex use of English, as it captures the vast formal and functional plurality of English indicating national, regional, local, cross-cultural variation, the distinct identities of these varieties, their degrees of acculturation and indigenization, and their embeddedness in a multilingual and multicultural context.

ELF provides a kind of "global currency" for people from a great variety of backgrounds who come into contact with one another and use the English language as a default means of communication. ELF as a contact language is often used in short contact situations, such that fleeting English norms are in operation, with variation being one of the hallmarks of ELF (Firth, 2009). Thus ELF does not function as a territorialized and institutionalized "second language," nor can it be described as a variety with its own literary or cultural products, as is the case with the English language used for instance in Singapore, Nigeria, Malaysia, or India, where WE have emerged in different ways from much longer contact situations.

Since the research presented in this chapter refers to ELF use, I will now try to describe in some more detail what ELF has come to mean, and what the notion of a lingua franca implies.

In its original meaning, a lingua franca—the term comes from Arabic *lisan al farang*—was simply an intermediary or contact language used, for instance, by speakers of Arabic with travellers from Western Europe. Its meaning was later extended to describe a language of commerce, a rather stable variety with little room for individual variation. This meaning is not applicable to today's most important lingua franca: global English, whose major feature is its enormous functional flexibility and spread across many different linguistic, geographical, and cultural areas, as well as its openness to foreign forms. In both its international and intra-national use, ELF can best be described as a special type of contact language and intercultural communication where each combination of interactants, each discourse community, negotiates their own lingua franca use in terms of code-switching, discourse strategies, negotiation of forms and meanings.

In its role as an auxiliary language, English can be compared to Latin at the time of the late Roman Empire, or French in the 17th and 18th centuries. When the so-called Western world in the second half of the 20th century came to depend on border-crossing communication, political, economic and scientific cooperation, and supranational organization, it so happened that English was in the right place at the right time (Crystal, 1997). By then English had spread to so many ethnically diverse societies, and had acquired a considerable cultural distance from its original British culture. It therefore offered itself as a convenient language for communication. Another more linguistic factor that helped propel English into a position of first choice for an auxiliary language is the fact that English has long been, especially in its lexical repertoire, a rich mixture of Romance and Germanic languages, languages of supra-regional importance in their own right.

ELF is not in any sense a restricted language, but a means of communication showing full linguistic and functional range. Users of ELF are not "learners," but rather multilingual individuals possessing "multicompetence" (Cook 1992; Bassetti & Cook, 2011), which is to be taken as a yardstick for describing and explaining ELF communication. Relevant here is the rich literature on bilingualism, where the notion of a "simultaneous activation" of speakers' native tongue and ELF in the cognitive structures of bilingual subjects is widely accepted today (Grosjean, 2001).

A major characteristic of ELF is its multiplicity of voices. ELF is a language for communication, a medium that can be given substance with many different national, regional, local, and individual cultural identities. When English is used in interactions between, say, German, Chinese, and Korean native speakers, the differences in native interactional norms, standards of politeness, feelings of cultural and historical tradition may remain intact. These norms are not shared, nor need they be. Localized or regionalized ELF varieties—whose linguistic surface is English, but whose speakers creatively perform pragmatic shifts in using ELF—have taken over the linguistic landscape. Non-native speakers of English anywhere in the world have been developing their own discourse strategies, speech act modifications, and communicative styles in their use of ELF.

ELF is no more and no less than "a contact language between persons who share neither a common native tongue nor a common national culture, and for whom English is the chosen foreign language of communication" (Firth, 1996, p. 20). How do speakers make this type of communication work? In what follows, a number of studies that have examined ELF speakers' interactional behavior in both general conversational and institutional academic settings will be discussed.

Pragmatics and Discourse-related Studies of ELF: Some Research Findings as a Basis for Developing Oral Competence in Global ELF

An important early work on ELF pragmatics is Meierkord's (1996) analysis of audiotaped English dinner-table conversations elicited in a British student residence from subjects of many different L1 backgrounds. She examined opening and closing phases, gambits, topic management, politeness, turn-taking, overlaps, and hesitation phenomena, and found surprisingly few misunderstandings. Trouble spots were usually not overcome by negotiations but by often abrupt topic changes. Further results include a reduced variety of tokens, shorter turns than in native English talk, frequent use of non-verbal supportive back-channeling, especially laughter, and little interference from L1 discourse norms.

Some of Meierkord's findings were confirmed by Firth (1996) and Wagner and Firth (1997) who analyzed telephone conversations between employees of Danish companies and their foreign partners. The authors stress the "fleeting" nature of ELF talk, the fluidity of norms, and participants' attempts at conversational attuning resulting in overtly consensus-oriented interactional behavior and in interactants' attempts to "normalize" potential trouble sources in a preventive way, rather than attend to them explicitly, via repair initiation, reformulation, or other negotiating behaviors.

As long as a threshold of understanding is achieved, ELF participants adopt a "Let-it-pass" principle (Firth, 1996), an interpretive procedure that makes the interactional style "robust," "normal," and consensual. This ordinariness is a joint achievement of interactants, who manage to sustain the appearance of normality despite being exposed to relatively "abnormal" linguistic behavior. Achieving ordinariness is the direct outcome of the "Let-it-pass" procedure, to which interactants resort whenever understanding threatens to become difficult. The "ordinariness" of ELF discourse is also achieved via a "make-it-normal" orientation: when ELF speakers are faced with interlocutors' marked lexical and phonological selections, unidiomatic phrasings, morphological vagaries, and idiosyncratic syntactic structuring, they deliberately divert attention from these infelicitous forms. This behavior is also evident in the surprising absence of "other repairs" and requests for information or confirmation, as these might expose interlocutors' linguistic "deficits" and threaten their face. They appear to be competent enough to be able to monitor each others' moves at a high level of awareness, preventing a breakdown in communication through helping each other in collaborative action and joint discourse production.

An important general characteristic of ELF talk is its enormous inherent variability (Firth, 2009). This variability is not to be equated with ELF speakers' failure to fulfill native norms, and their widely varying levels of competence in English. Rather it lies at the core of ELF discourse, where speakers creatively exploit, intentionally appropriate, locally adapt, and communicatively align the potential inherent in the forms and functions, items and collocations of the English language they use in their performance as the need arises.

If ELF interactants do not seek to adjust to some real or imaginary native-speaker norm, they conceive of themselves as individual ELF users united in different "communities of practice" (see Wenger, 1989; House, 2003a for applying the concept to ELF research). The notion "community of practice" is most appropriate for ELF in that the constitution of a community of practice is governed by a joint purpose, i.e., to communicate efficiently in English as the chosen and agreed means of communication without, however, heeding or being constrained by English native norms.

A project specifically concerned with discourse pragmatics is the Hamburg ELF project (cf. Baumgarten & House, 2010a, 2010b; House, 2002, 2008, 2009; House & Lévy-Tödter, 2010). Here we have collected a corpus of everyday ELF interactions between international students of many different L1s, institutional ELF discourse between students and faculty as well as post hoc interviews.[1] The analyses of this data essentially confirm previous findings. However, several other characteristics of ELF interactions have also emerged. They will be discussed in what follows.

Recourse to L1: Pragmatic Transfer and Code-switching

Pragmatic transfer from the L1 occurs frequently in ELF discourse. Thus, Asian speakers often employ cyclical topic management, i.e., there is no strictly linear progression of a chosen topic as tends to be the case in Inner-Circle English but rather a series of introducing and re-introducing a particular topic in a cycle. This often results in turns-at-talk that lack sequentiality—a phenomenon, however, that tends to be consistently ignored by other participants, such that the talk remains "robust," "normal," and never breaks down (House, 2002). Another example of pragmatic transfer is the use of L1-specific conventions of directness. For instance, speakers of L1 German use speech acts with the high directness level conventionalized in German (Blum-Kulka, House, & Kasper, 1989), but not in English. In the post hoc interviews we conducted with interactants, they themselves ascribed such an interactional style to native discourse norms. The frequent use of the discourse marker *Represent,* with which speakers repeat (parts of) previous speakers' turn, serves to support speakers' working memory and ease processing (see below). But Represents can however also be interpreted as pragmatic transfer from Asian languages and be understood as a sign of politeness, because explicitly verbalized acknowledgment of other speakers' talk can be considered to support one's interactional partner and to aim at consensus-building.

Another important L1 related strategy is Code-Switching, frequently used in ELF talk mostly to overcome speakers' linguistic limitations (House & Lévy-Tödter, 2010). A case in point is the use of L1 discourse markers (such as for instance the German gambit *ja*), in particular "uptakers" and "go-ons" (Edmondson & House, 1981). Uptakers usually occur as second-pair parts of exchanges, and go-ons are used as back-channel devices, both expressed with reduced self-monitoring, i.e., automatically, "off-guard." That switching into one's mother tongue should occur in this particular interactive slot is thus easily explained. Similar findings of the frequent use of code-switching in ELF talk are reported in Pölzl and Seidlhofer (2006) with reference to the use of Arabic gambits and other L1 derived discourse phenomena, and by Jenkins (2009) who found many instances of code-switching by ELF speakers of Asian L1s. Cogo (2009) also documents code-switching in ELF discourse. Interestingly, she also found that interactants sometimes switch not to their respective L1s but to a third shared language.

Here are two examples of code-switching taken from the Hamburg corpus of ELF interactions in academic advising sessions (cf. e.g., House & Lévy-Tödter, 2010; House, 2010), where code-switching occurs from ELF into one of the interactants' German mother tongue. The interaction takes place between a professor (P), his assistant (WM), and a Spanish exchange student in a German university. In these and all the following excerpts a simplified transcription is used for ease of comprehension. Italics are used in these excerpts to highlight the respective forms and phenomena under discussion.

Excerpt 1

P: And then you may put everything like in this drawing and then afterwards we can think whether to find some (.) simplified equation (.) erm (speaking to WM) *macht das Excel ? so irgendwie* I I don't know what do you know wh whether whether Excel makes something ap approximation? maybe?
S: I think uhhh

In Excerpt 1 P switches into German in the middle of his lengthy turn to quickly request some information from his assistant in a routine exchange that functions as a sort of side sequence to the primary interaction. Such side sequences are often unconsciously and automatically conducted in speakers' mother tongue. This is a natural occurrence, and it should not be discouraged but rather be recommended to ELF users as a useful aid in maintaining the smooth flow of the conversation.

Excerpt 2

P: The printing is is wrong only the printing or?
S: I think only the printing [because]
P: [*ja ja ja*]
S: in my file is okay

P: Strange
S: In in your file is okay in computer?
P: I didn't look I didn't look but it (mumbles unintelligibly)
WM: But if it is a pdf document
P: must be must be=
WM: =then we have the same in the document we have the
P: *Na ja na ja*

In Excerpt 2 the professor uses the German gambit *ja* as a *Go on* and the *Uptaker na ja* as signs of little conscious control, occurring off-guard as it were. Again this is a perfectly ordinary occurrence in ELF interactions whenever one of the interactants is familiar with the other's L1—and as such this brief recourse to speakers' L1 should be promoted and not discouraged. Similar interactions in which participants can practice their oral skills in ELF can be used in the classroom for instance by using provocative trigger text to stimulate conversations. These conversations will be taped, transcribed, and used by the teacher in post hoc discussions of students' own productions. In this way, insights into the reasons for students' linguistic choices can be elicited. In this reflective process in which teachers and students jointly engage, students will develop an increased awareness of their own competence in ELF and their degree of pragmatic fluency (House, 1996).

Accommodation: Re-presenting Information and Co-constructing Utterances

In ELF talk, (parts of) previous speakers' moves are frequently "represented" (House, 2002). *Represents* (Edmondson, 1981) are multifunctional gambits used to support speakers' working memory; to create coherence via the construction of lexical-paradigmatic clusters; to signal receipt, and confirm comprehension. All of these uses can be interpreted as a deliberate accommodative strategy to ELF speakers' particular needs. Represents are also known in the literature as "echo," "mirror," or "shadow" elements that typically occur in psycho-therapeutic interviews, instructional discourse, and aircraft control discourse—genres in which information is deliberately and routinely restated to ensure understanding. The fact that ELF speakers exploit this convention for their own benefit shows that their strategic communicative competence is well developed. Cogo and Dewey (2006) and Cogo (2009) also document many instances of accommodation and strategic repetition in their analyses of ELF talk. Here are two examples of the use of Represents as powerful instruments for securing understanding. They are taken from the Hamburg corpus of ELF interactions (for details see House, 2002, 2008, 2009).

Excerpt 3

Mauri: But the grammar *is quite different very different*
Wei: *Is very different*
Mauri: between Chinese and Japanese

Excerpt 4

Joy: And you mean that English (2 sec) is really getting important or taken for the education because the grammar is syntactical erm the grammar *is very easy*
Wei: *Is easy is very easy*

In Excerpt 3 and 4 we notice how the use of the Represents results in a kind of stalling of the interactional flow—similar to speakers' L1 interjections discussed above—and provides support for themselves and for their interlocutors whenever more time is needed for planning, verbalization, and articulation. Another interpretation of the function of the use of Represents is that it is a sign of pragmatic transfer from Wei, the Chinese participant's mother tongue where Represents function as a sign of Asian politeness and acknowledgment of one's interlocutor's message. But Represents as signs of accommodating to one's interlocutor's needs also occur in interactions featuring European ELF interactants (French, Czech, Croatian) as in the following example:

Excerpt 5

Hilda: If you start speaking English in France they will answer you in French
Anne: Answer you in French *that that's true*
Sue: *That's true*

Here again the use of the Represent acts is a useful strategy for helping self and others formulate further thoughts.

ELF speakers also consistently demonstrate solidarity and consensus in the face of marked linguistic and cultural differences. For instance, speakers often help one another in cases of formulation problems, joining forces to gradually and jointly build up the discourse in a series of scaffolding moves (House, 2003a, 2008). Participants' attempts to negotiate what it is that each one of them wants to convey leads to a feeling of community, solidarity, and group identity.

Another useful means for enhancing pragmatic fluency in ELF talk is to encourage ELF learners' and users' competence in the art of co-constructing utterances in order to show solidarity when their interlocutors are faced with formulation problems. Here are two examples of such useful supportive scaffolding activity:

Excerpt 6

Joy: I recently read an article in a Korean erm (2sec) Moment (4sec)
Brit: *Newspaper? Internet?*
Joy: Yes thank you @ erm the article is about new foreign language education in Japan

Excerpt 7

Mau: I think it begins erm of course with the colonialism I think too because the history of this if this development how the language in the very early period erm (3 sec)
Joy: *Build up this basis*
Mau: Yes
Joy: *To be a world language*
Mau: Yes

In Excerpts (6) and (7) ELF speakers successfully join forces to finish an interlocutor's turn at talk. In both cases the recipient of this support explicitly acknowledges it.

Re-interpretation of Discourse Markers: You Know, Yes/Yeah, So

ELF speakers' use of the discourse markers *you know, yes/yeah*, and *so* has been found to differ from English native discourse, as will be shown in the examples of each of these markers below.

You know is often described as an interpersonally-oriented marker used as a hedge and signaling politeness. House (2009) reports that ELF speakers tend to re-interpret *you know* as a much more self-referenced way of highlighting formulation difficulties and providing coherence in speakers' own turns. *You know* frequently co-occurs with the conjunctions *but, and, because*, even taking over their functions in stand-alone position. It is also used when speakers reveal planning difficulties by fumbling for an appropriate formulation. In such cases, *you know* is used in mid-utterance, often inside nominal, verbal, and adverbial groups to help speakers process and plan their own output, and to link stretches of discourse.

Here is an example of the typical use of *you know* as a strategy for self-help and plugging any gaps or pauses in a conversation.

Excerpt 8

M: No matter how many people speak in the university some of them speak very well English but erm (1sec) *you know* the real life it's different and you have to learn English

S: Yeah erm

M: This institution where you're working at is this the only possibility to erm learn better English

The gambit *yeah/yes* is used in ELF talk with a variety of different functions (Spielmann, 2007; Baumgarten & House, 2010b) such as uptaking, back-channeling, agreeing, and discourse structuring. All of these uses are potent tools for making the discourse (appear) "normal." The inherent face-saving feature of *yeah/yes* and its overall inoffensive accommodating undertone make it particularly suitable for ELF talk, where interactants are well aware of the precarious nature of their intercultural interaction. ELF speakers therefore often exploit the positive import of *yeah/yes* to tone down objections. *You know, yeah* can also serve as a self-supporting strategy. But the frequent use of *yeah/yes* in ELF discourse is probably best explained with its polyfunctionality, which renders it "communicatively effective" because a lot of pragmatic content is packed into minimal verbal form. Findings in Baumgarten and House (2010b) and House and Lévy-Tödter (2010) also point to an interesting systematic variation in the use of the tokens *yes, yeah*, and German *ja: yes* is primarily used as an agreement marker, *ja* as a back-channeling device, and *yeah* as an uptaking and structuring signal supporting speakers' own moves and turns.

Excerpt 9

P: There there is erm one week where the building companies come to to to the university and they make some presentation and =

S: Ahh this week (.) *yeah* (1 sec)

P: This one week erm *yeah* but I cannot do it I have to go here this week

S: Yeah the week of civil engineering *yeah*

In Excerpt 9 the gambit *yeah* is used strategically to gain time, plug gaps in the conversation, and take the time it takes to come to terms with what one's interlocutor has said and to generally monitor each other's moves and plan one's next productions while at the same time giving the interaction a tone of agreement and approval through the meaning of *yeah*—in other words a highly useful strategy, which should be taught to and practiced by learners and users of ELF.

The marker *so* also functions as a speaker-supportive element in ELF discourse. *So* is here used as a deictic element to both support the planning of their upcoming moves and help them sum up and "seal" the preliminary outcome of previous discourse stretches. *So* functions as a complex double-bind element, a (mental) hinge between what has come before and what will occur next. It certainly does not index other-attentiveness, and is not used with a strong interpersonal function. Rather *so* takes on a text structuring, self-attentive, and self-monitoring function, acting for instance as a stop-gap "fumble" (Edmondson, 1981) to help speakers bridge formulation problems. In the majority of occurrences, *so* follows hesitation markers such as "erm" or "hmm," or pauses, and it also often collocates with the connector *and*. All these co-occurrences show that *so* in ELF talk acts as a self-prompting strategy to monitor own output and mark the resumption of speech after being "bogged down" both turn-initially and in mid-turn.

Excerpt 10

S: I actually better take some notes
P: Mhm (1 sec) *so* there is one one man erm he is working for erm for (company 1)
S: Mhmm
P: And erm *so* he is in the erm working in with the design and calculation of (company 1)

In Excerpt 10 P uses the marker *so* following the hesitation marker *mhm* and the conjunction *and* in order to get himself going again, to resume the train of thought he had begun in his previous move—another useful gambit in ELF conversation which should be taught to and practiced with learners and users of ELF.

Given the linguistic potential of the English language available for creative appropriation and local re-interpretation, ELF speakers are found to effectively engage in self-help interactional behavior both for their own and their interlocutors' benefit, deliberately supporting each other's speech production, tolerantly letting others' oddities and infelicities pass, and generally managing to make interactions robust and normal. As indicated above, ELF users are multilingual speakers who have more than one language at their disposal, and they demonstrate this in the way they mark identity, attitudes, and alliances, signal discourse functions, convey politeness, create aesthetic and humorous effects, or pragmatic ambiguity. In ELF research, a radical rethinking of the norm against which speakers' pragmatic discourse behavior is matched, has taken place. This norm is never the monolingual native speaker, but rather the expert multilingual user. ELF users' pragmatic fluency (House, 1996) and their strategic competence enables them to engage in meaningful effective communication, and to alternatively adhere to their L1 discourse pragmatic norms as a strategy of identity maintenance or construct new ELF norms to foster a sense of group identity in their local communities of practice. Both strategies are effective and contribute, in their different ways, to ELF users' increasing independence from English native-speaker usage.

On the basis of the results of the ELF research discussed above, oral competence in ELF might be developed using a variety of different scenarios that reflect students' interests, the domains in which they operate, and their level of proficiency. In such a scenario-based training, students will be made aware of the fact that, in real life, ELF speakers often make use of the let-it-pass principle and also engage in code-switching as useful strategies for overcoming formulation difficulties in the English language. However, in the world of the classroom active use of these principles have of course a lesser role to play. Here I am merely pleading for making students aware of these strategies and for changing their attitudes vis-à-vis code-switching away from the traditional interpretation as a sign of a lack of competence in English towards looking upon it as a natural exploitation of a multilingual speaker's linguistic repertoire.

Improving the Practices and Principles of Teaching Oral Skills in ELF

Given the above results of empirical studies of the use of ELF in oral interaction, I would now like to propose several ways of improving the practices and principles of teaching spoken English in its lingua franca use. Before doing this, I want to briefly sketch some traditional ways of teaching oral skills in English. During the classic grammar-translation approaches, the teaching of speaking played a negligible role. In the Reform movement around 1900, the Direct Method and later the Audio-Lingual Method, speaking was considered central in the foreign language classroom. Speech as the medium of face-to-face dialogues was and is also central in functional and communicative language teaching. However, this popularity of the spoken language in the communicatively oriented classroom has never implied a special methodology particularly geared to the characteristics of spoken language. Nor was the teaching of oral skills considered to be an important sub-domain of communicative competence in its own right which was given an independent value.

Oral skills have thus not been central in syllabus development, and have not addressed the important questions as to the nature of oral skills, the types of speaking activities that need to be taught, the route of development envisaged, and the particular learning problems they might afford (cf. Bygate, 2009). What thus often happens in secondary and tertiary educational contexts is the incidental, non-explicit teaching of oral skills for instance in so-called conversation classes. These classes are often organized in a series of discussion groups with the structure of the course being determined by the topics which are handled in turn. These are generally matters of moment, taken from newspapers, magazines, and other sources, and it is hoped that the input materials will somehow generate interest and "engagement" thus stimulating good discussion. This model widely used all over the world in the teaching of oral skills in English as a global language is, I would submit, of limited effectiveness in terms of improving oral skills of those who participate for the following four reasons:

- Participating in organized discussions is a highly marked type of oral language behavior, which is not very common, except in formal instructional settings, debating clubs, and so on.
- As only one speaker can speak at one time, opportunities for a turn at talk are limited, especially if the native-speaker teacher leading the discussion is an active member of the discussion.
- Those learners who are most confident regarding their oral skills (or who have the strongest feelings about the topic under discussion) dominate the talk such that the participants who may in fact most need the practice tend to get fewer opportunities to talk.
- The problem of feedback, and indeed the problem of learning, is not focused on in any systematic way, but rather ad hoc. The assumption seems to be simply that it is good for you to talk English, and the acquisition of communicative oral skills will somehow occur incidentally.

To remedy this situation it seems necessary first and foremost to heighten learners' awareness of the nature of the spoken language in general and the nature of ELF in particular and to use an interactional approach where individual learners are exposed to interactions in ELF, taught to become experts in the use of ELF in interaction and become aware of their own and others' interactional behavior. In this context it is important to provide ELF learners and users with an appropriate meta-language with which to describe interactional moves and strategies. For this a brief introduction to interaction and intercultural pragmatics is essential.

Here I would recommend introducing students to the important notion of a speech act, provide them with examples of a (simplified) typology of speech acts, mentioning e.g., apologies, requests, complaints, promises, etc. and the notion of illocutionary force as well as the usefulness of gambits or discourse markers as strategic support for the use of speech act sequences. Further, the concept of discourse structure in terms of consecutive phases in an interaction: opening phases, central "business phases," closing phases. Students will be alerted to the fact that both opening and closing phases tend to be heavily ritualized, and specific tokens of typical utterances in all three phases will be introduced, explained, and practiced in a variety of simulations and scenarios. Students will also be introduced to the usefulness of discourse strategies, with which speech acts such as e.g., a request, an apology, or a complaint can be prefaced, grounded, expanded upon, or modified in degrees of politeness and directness. Other important concepts are turn-taking, feedback, initiating, and responding moves, the notion of face, face-threat, and face saving as well as politeness, impoliteness. All these basic concepts of oral discourse will also need to be considered from a cross-cultural pragmatic perspective, and they need to be embedded in particular social situations such that students are aware of how the choice of form for the enactment of a particular speech act greatly depends on the particular context-of-situation.

The point of this introduction to the make-up and the functioning of oral discourse is to provide students with a useful meta-language with which to capture, describe, and explain what it is they and their interlocutors are doing when they are engaging in oral English communication. To be able to put a name to what happens when speakers interact with one another is a prerequisite to raising students' awareness about their own and others' speech.

But for students to become pragmatically fluent in ELF talk, it is not only commendable to teach, and provide practical experience in, the use of linguistic-pragmatic strategies such as the ones discussed above, it is also important to develop intercultural competence because ELF, as noted above, is a hybrid multicultural and intercultural mode of talk.

Developing Intercultural Competence in ELF

Three points need to be stressed for the teaching of intercultural communicative competence to students of English as a lingua franca:

First, learners and users of ELF, who are interested in using English mainly for communication purposes, should be enabled to keep their individual discourse styles, their individual capacity for wit, humor, social charm, or repartee, in other words their very own social persona in the medium of the English language. This can be achieved not through proclaiming such lofty and vague intercultural objectives as tolerance, empathy, and mutual understanding, but through the acquisition of rather more mundane, practical communicative-linguistic skills such as the ones discussed above with which misunderstandings might be minimized.

Second, for developing intercultural competence in English as a lingua franca, it is essential to intensify and make more effective the teaching of interactional phenomena so as to enable learners to manage turn-taking smoothly through sensitizing them to points of transitional relevance, to use a multitude of different discourse-"lubricating" gambits and discourse strategies, and generally to provide learners with the linguistic means for realizing their full interpersonal competence, i.e., achieve their own goals *and* remain polite. These goals can best be reached by increasing speakers' meta-pragmatic knowledge and awareness, i.e., by developing learners' insights into their own communicative potential—their communicative strengths and deficiencies—in realizing their communicative intentions. Useful activities for achieving such insights include collaborative sessions where students' taped and transcribed naturalistic or role-play interactions will be discussed, jointly interpreted, and problematized.

It is important to both heighten ELF speakers' sensitivity to others' communicative needs and to enable them to formulate their own questions and reply appropriately to questions posed by others, to realize their own communicative intentions in a less superficial manner, and to reach a deeper understanding of others' communicative intentions. One way of doing this is to use open role-play scenarios in which students interact in pairs (cf. Edmondson & House, 1981). These scenarios will be taped and transcribed, distributed to the students, and jointly analyzed and discussed. In particular, rich points in the interactions, cross-cultural comparisons, and a discussion of what students may have meant but could not express the way they had intended will be a fruitful undertaking. As mentioned before, for such in-depth discussions of an interaction the provision of a meta-language is essential.

For developing intercultural competence in ELF, I suggest a pragmatics oriented approach be given preference: in promoting knowledge about and awareness of the functions and uses of linguistic forms, speech acts, and speech act sequences in situated discourse, one will at the same time foster a heightened linguistic and cultural awareness.

Third, in dealing with intercultural misunderstanding (House et al., 2003) both in the classroom and outside, we must not forget to highlight the moral implications of what I have called "strategic misunderstandings," i.e., those manipulative practices found in deliberately deceitful talk, propaganda, and demagogy as well as in some types of advertising. Further, one should be wary of the possibility of intentionally conflictual, confrontational discourse, where misunderstanding seems to be built into participants' communicative practices. And it is only these "strategic misunderstandings" which can be, and for ethical reasons should be, avoided. All other types of intercultural misunderstandings can at least be attenuated in their consequences if one simply acquires more knowledge about one's interactants. An increase in knowledge will also make one more aware of the consequences of acting out one's own discourse style in ways that might give offence to one's hearer. And for the extension of knowledge we need interdisciplinary work informing in-depth analyses of authentic ELF interactions in different contexts as well as introspections, where interactants' own voices can be heard. But, alas, knowledge is not enough given the nature of language and the nature of human beings.

Meaning is never laid out clean and neat in any language but must be inferred, and since inferences in the fast give and take of spoken discourse tend to be quick, automatic, and fixed when they really need to be slow, flexible, and readily revisable, we also need a kind of attitude that might be characterized as "an openness of mind." To counteract the damaging personal recriminations and emotional upsets in many intercultural misunderstanding events, such an openness would imply taking things more slowly, keeping them in abeyance to avoid premature judging or prejudice. Handling misunderstanding in the classroom is of prime importance as we are here focusing on using language in a sensitive, informed, and reflexive way.

Teaching Activities for Developing Intercultural Competence in ELF

On a practical level, I would suggest the following "types" of teaching and learning approaches for developing intercultural competence in ELF and for making ELF users aware of misunderstandings in intercultural interactions conducted in ELF:

Cognitive teaching: Here I suggest introducing students to the importance of cognitive and meta-cognitive learning strategies, communication strategies, and a variety of reflexive activities and guided "noticing" (on the basis of taped and transcribed interactions) in order to increase awareness of interculturally "rich points" and to develop systematic knowledge about culture- and language-conditioned differences in communicative styles and preferences that characterize the way ELF speakers use the English language. As an example of such cognitive teaching activities I suggest students be introduced to the mechanism of oral ELF discourse, which would imply explanations of such basic concepts as speech acts, discourse strategies, phases, markers, turns and moves, cross-cultural variation in realizing politeness, directness turn-taking, the introduction and sequences of topics, and so on. As mentioned above, such an introduction to the nature of oral ELF discourse is principally designed to raise students' awareness of the diversity of language use underneath the apparent uniformity of the English Language. For such an awareness, the provision of a meta-language based on a theory of discourse and interaction is absolutely essential. There is nothing more practical than a good theory!

Process teaching: Here I recommend actively promoting students' learning process of ELF using a variety of ethnographic activities such as asking students to keep diaries in which they are to record their personal experiences and reflections on their learning process. On the basis of their entries in these diaries, teachers can help students formulate their very own "subjective theories" about their individual learning routes. Further process activities might include asking students to engage in taking field notes and teacher-guided observation of ELF interactions in their environment. I also suggest teachers engage in regular personal conferencing with students to monitor their individual learning process and progress.

Experiential teaching: Here I suggest teachers resort to using multimedia modules, treating intercultural misunderstandings in the medium of ELF as "critical incidents" using simulations, scenarios, and open role plays. Critical incidents should stem from learners' own personal experiences and not pre-fabricated, stereotyped, prejudice-promoting so-called "culture standards." Learners' own authentic intercultural ELF interactions should be taped, transcribed, and then collaboratively interpreted, discussed, and problematized in class.

Critical teaching: In this teaching activity teachers might encourage discussions of stereotypes and prejudices. These can be based on the teacher's own construction of humorous multiple choice tasks, in which well-known (linguistic and cultural) stereotypes about particular local, regional, and national groups of ELF speakers will be unmasked and satirized as human foibles.

Interactional sensitivity training: making learners observe general rules of interaction by for example giving them the following advice:

- Watch out for misunderstandings.
- Use checks to immediately clarify nascent problems.
- Use repair strategies whenever you suspect a misunderstanding, but make sure to avoid loss of your own and your interlocutor's face.
- Delay interpreting your interlocutor's moves as long as possible, and be always prepared to revise your preliminary interpretations.
- Be flexible and move back and forth from a micro- to a macro-perspective in your cumulative discourse interpretation.
- And finally: Never assume that others understand you.

Conclusion

Given the nature of ELF as a "plurilingual" means of communication whose speakers do not feel the need to adhere to any native Inner-Circle English norm, attempts to improve oral English skills should focus on interactional phenomena and the achievement of pragmatic fluency. Phenomena handled in this chapter include awareness of ELF speakers' default recourse to their mother tongue in transfer and code-switching and the encouragement of the strategic employment of gambits to safeguard the flow of talk, monitor their own and others' output, and generally increase interactional awareness and competence. This interactional pragmatic focus might well be complemented by attempts to improve intercultural competence including the effective handling of imminent intercultural misunderstanding via the employment of a variety of different teaching approaches.

Exploring the Ideas

1 In your opinion, is there a difference between the notions of English as an international language, World Englishes, and English as a lingua franca? If you feel there are differences, what exactly are they, and how do you think they might affect teaching principles and practices?

2 How important are Inner-Circle standard English norms and native speakers of this norm in your particular teaching context? What in your opinion are the differences between these Inner-Circle speakers and speakers in Outer and Expanding Circles and in English as a lingua franca constellations?

3 What are the major advantages of using an interactional, pragmatics-discourse approach to the teaching of English as a lingua franca? In your opinion, how useful is an introduction to basic concepts of interaction and the provision of a theory-based meta-language? Do you think it could enable students to talk about what happens in oral discourse in a more informed manner?

Applying the Ideas

1 Research different ways of describing mechanisms of oral discourse in your library and the Internet. Are the different approaches you found equally useful for the practice of teaching in the classroom? Useful sources are Edmondson's (1981) spoken discourse model, Edmondson and House's (1981) pedagogic interactional grammar of English, as well as House's (2003b) more recent application of these. Try to come up with your own eclectic model which you think is most useful for your academic background, particular teaching situation, your institution and your students!

2 Collect your own corpus of students' role-play transcriptions complete with your notes on the ensuing discussions. This should enable you to come up with a profile of each student's particular interactional strengths and weaknesses. These profiles can then be

discussed with students as a means of heightening their awareness of their very own oral expression potential.

3 Conduct a small study about intercultural misunderstanding in oral discourse in the medium of the English language. You might do this using a questionnaire and interviewing your students as well as asking your students to collect intercultural misunderstandings in ELF using ethnographic observation of rich points, diaries, and examining plays and dialogues in novels for the portrayal of one particularly salient intercultural misunderstanding.

Note

1 This is a small special domain corpus. The biggest available source of ELF data to date is VOICE, the Vienna Oxford International Corpus of English.

References

Baumgarten, N., & House, J. (2010a). I think and I don't know in English as a lingua franca and native English discourse. *Journal of Pragmatics, 42*(5), 1184–1200.

Baumgarten, N., & House, J. (2010b, May). Discourse markers in high-stakes ELF academic interaction: Oral Exams. Paper presented at the 3rd International ELF Conference, Vienna.

Bassetti, B., & Cook, V. (2011). Relating language and cognition: The second language user. In V. Cook & B. Bassetti (Eds.), *Language and Bilingual Cognition* (pp. 143–190). New York: Psychology Press.

Blum-Kulka, S., House, J., & Kasper, G. (Eds.). (1989). *Cross-cultural pragmatics: Requests and apologies.* Norwood, NJ: Ablex.

Bygate, M. (2009). Teaching the spoken language In K. Knapp & B. Seidlhofer (Eds.), *Hand book of foreign language communication and learning* (pp. 401–438). Berlin, New York: Mouton de Gruyter.

Cogo, A. (2009). Accommodating differences in ELF conversations: A study of pragmatic strategies. In A. Mauranen & E. Ranta (Eds.), *English as a lingua franca: Studies and findings* (pp. 254–273). Newcastle: Cambridge Scholars Press.

Cogo, A., & Dewey, M. (2006). Efficiency in ELF communication: From pragmatic motives to lexico-grammatical innovation. *Nordic Journal English Studies, 5*(2), 59–94.

Cook, V. (1992). *Linguistics and second language acquisition.* New York: St. Martin's Press.

Crystal, D. (1997). *English as a global language.* Cambridge: Cambridge University Press.

Edmondson, W. J. (1981). *Spoken discourse. A model for analysis.* London: Longman.

Edmondson, W. J., & House, J. (1981). *Let's talk and talk about it: A pedagogic interactional grammar of English.* Munich: Urban and Schwarzenberg.

Firth, A. (1996). The discursive accomplishment of normality on "lingua franca" English and conversation analysis. *Journal of Pragmatics, 26*(2), 237–259.

Firth, A. (2009). The lingua franca factor. *Intercultural Pragmatics, 6*(2), 147–170.

Grosjean, F. (2001). The bilingual's language modes. In J. L. Nicol (Ed.), *Language processing in the bilingual* (pp.1–22). Oxford: Blackwell.

House, J. (1996). Developing pragmatic fluency in English as a foreign language. Routines and metapragmatic awareness. *Studies in Second Language Acquisition, 18*, 225–252.

House, J. (2002). Communicating in English as a lingua franca. In S. Foster-Cohen (Ed.), *EUROSLA Yearbook 2* (pp. 234–261). Amsterdam: Benjamins.

House, J. (2003a). English as a lingua franca: A threat to multilingualism? *Journal of Sociolinguistics, 7*(4), 556–578.

House, J. (2003b). Misunderstanding in intercultural university encounters. In J. House, G. Kasper, & S. Ross (Eds.), *Misunderstanding in social life: Discourse approaches to problematic talk* (pp. 22–56). London: Longman.

House, J. (2008). (Im)politeness in English as a lingua franca discourse. In M. Locher & J. Straessler (Eds.), *Standards and norms in the English language* (pp. 351–366). Berlin/NY: Mouton de Gruyter.

House, J. (2009). Subjectivity in English as lingua franca discourse: The case of *you know. Intercultural Pragmatics, 6*(2), 171–194.

House, J. (2010). The pragmatics of English as a lingua franca. In A. Trosborg (Ed.), *Pragmatics across languages and cultures* (pp. 363–390). Berlin/New York: Mouton de Gruyter.

House, J., Kasper, G., & Ross, S. (Eds.). (2003). *Misunderstanding in social life: Discourse approaches to problematic talk*. London: Longman.

House, J., & Lévy-Tödter, M. (2010). Linguistic competence and professional identity in English medium institutional discourse. In B. Meyer & B. Apfelbaum (Eds.), *Multilingualism at work* (pp. 13–46). Amsterdam: Benjamins.

Jenkins, J. (2009). Explaining attitudes towards English as a lingua franca in the East Asian context. In K. Murata & J. Jenkins (Eds.), *Global English in Asian Contexts* (pp. 40–58). Houndsmill: Palgrave Macmillan.

Kachru, B. B. (1986). *The alchemy of English*. Oxford: Pergamon Press.

Meierkord, C. (1996). *Englisch als Medium der Interkulturellen Kommunikation. Untersuchungen zum Non-Native-Non-Native Speaker Diskurs*. Frankfurt: Peter Lang.

Pölzl, U., & Seidlhofer, B. (2006). In and on their own terms: The "habitat factor" in English as a lingua franca interactions. *International Journal of the Sociology of Language 177*, 151–176.

Spielmann, D. (2007). *English as lingua franca: A simplified code?* (Unpublished MA thesis). University of Hamburg, Germany.

Wagner, J., & Firth, A. (1997). Communication strategies at work. In E. Kellerman & G. Kasper (Eds.), *Advances in research on communication strategies* (pp. 323–344). Oxford: Oxford University Press.

Wenger, E. (1989). *Communities of practice*. Cambridge: Cambridge University Press.

Chapter 12

Lexical Innovation in English as an International Language

Implications for English Teaching

Wendy D. Bokhorst-Heng

Introduction

As we begin this chapter, take a moment to reflect: What are some new words or phrases that have been coined recently? Or perhaps new meanings and uses of "old" words? For in many respects, the processes of lexical innovation in EIL are no different from what occurs in all languages. However, what lexical innovation signals in EIL is the dismantling of the simplistic notion of the imperial and hegemonic spread of ENGLISH as some kind of monolithic entity. Such a narrative suggests so-called non-native speakers can at best only imitate the language. However, while many users do not regard English as their mother tongue, it is nevertheless their language, an expression of their unique identity, histories, and socio-cultural contexts (McKay & Bokhorst-Heng, 2008). Notably as well, there has been a dramatic paradigm shift from monolingualism to bi-/ multi-lingualism as the defining feature of English language learners and users: they are mostly bilingual speakers, learning English in addition to their mother-tongue language(s), and using English in interaction with their other language(s); and they are using English in multilingual contexts, where English serves a very specific purpose in their linguistic repertoire. What this means is that English in its international contexts is dynamic as its speakers continually transform the languages they speak. This transformation is especially pertinent as it relates to vocabulary. Such lexical innovations are increasingly codified and accepted as standard— and not just in Kachru's Outer-Circle countries, but also, as Lowenberg (2002) documents, in many Expanding-Circle nations as well, where English actually functions as a second language and often develops nativized norms.

This chapter begins with examples of how lexical innovations are formed from borrowing and from word-formation processes found in all languages (e.g., compounding). The intent of this discussion is to demonstrate the impact of lexical innovations, as an on-going activity on EIL. The significance of these innovations lies in their cultural embeddedness, and the ways in which they serve what Kachru (1981) calls the "acculturation" of the English language in its international sociocultural contexts. As such, consideration will be given to the pragmatic functions of many innovations, as well as at their cultural embeddedness. The conversation then turns to an overview of traditional pedagogical practices in the Lexical Approach, and a proposal to familiarize instructors of English, and through them their students, with the resulting multi-normative nature of the lexicon of English as an international language.

Processes of Innovation

In his book entitled *The Vocabulary of World English*, Stephan Gramley (2001) identifies three aspects of lexical innovation: through *borrowing*; *semantic shift*, or a change of meaning; and *word formation*. These, he argues, occur in the context of three "background" factors: the first, which was mentioned earlier, is the ways in which English has interacted with differing linguistic backgrounds. Second is the impact of the varying social features of its speakers on lexical innovation—features such as age, class, gender, ethnicity, and so forth. In Singapore, for example, English is the medium of instruction in all schools. In such a situation where the majority of English speakers are bilingual, if not multilingual, the choice of language may depend on user characteristics such as gender, age, level of education, or social status. But it may also depend on domains, which brings us to a third factor, and that is how the language is used. For example, language use could follow diglossic patterns with a fairly domain-specific formulation. Or, language use could be characterized by code-switching and code-mixing. It is worth noting here as well that these background factors also give rise not just to variation *between* countries but also *within* countries. Bamgbose (1992, pp. 149–150) for example, describes four different varieties of Nigerian English, distinguished by the varying degrees to which they embody unique characteristics/innovations in relation to Standard British English and their degree of international intelligibility.

Forms of Lexical Innovation

Referring back to Gramley's (2001) framework of lexical innovation, we consider here examples of *borrowing*, *semantic shift*, and *word formation*. However, rather than use the term "borrowing," I prefer Mesthrie and Bhatt's (2008) use of *retention*. "The term 'borrowing' for these terms is not entirely appropriate," they argue, "since speakers have not been adopting a new word or acquiring a new concept" (p. 110); rather, it is part of the ancestral languages of the territory and part of their repertoire.

Retention (Gramley, 2001; Jenkins, 2003; Mesthrie & Bhatt, 2008)

Many vocabulary retentions concern local customs and culture, such as food, clothing, and politics.

Food Items

- akaru (bean cake) (Nigerian English)
- haleem (thick broth of meat and lentils or wheat) (Pakistani and Indian English)
- makan (eat; food) (Singaporean and Malaysian English)
- braai (fry) (South Africa).

Clothing

- akwete (a type of cloth) (Nigerian English)
- shalwar kameez (baggy pants and long shirt) (Indian and Pakistani English).

Music, Customs

- mela (fair, festival) (Indian English)
- adowa (Akan dance) (Ghanaian English)
- kundiman (love song) Philippine English.

Political Terms

- bumiputra ("son of the soil"; patriot) (Malaysian English)
- ujamaa (familyhood, African socialism) (East African English, especially Tanzania).

Semantic Shift (Bamgbose, 1992; Gramley, 2001)

A semantic shift occurs when a word or phrase from a well-established variety is adopted into a New English, and given new meaning or use, but with no structural change.

- cockpit (type of valley) (Jamaican English)
- beverage (referring just to lemonade) (Jamaican English)
- maiden name ("given name" when applied to males) (Ghanaian English)
- stranger (guest) (Sierra Leone English)
- take-in (become pregnant) (Sierra Leone English).

Word Formation (Baumgardner, 1993, 1998; Crystal, 2003; Jenkins, 2003)

Locally coined words/expressions arise usually in one of two ways: by compounding from English elements, or by hybrid compounds; and by the addition of a prefix/suffix to an existing word.

Compounding From English Elements

- wheelcup (hub-cap) (Pakistani English)
- side-hero (supporting actor) (Pakistani English)
- lifter (cf. shoplifter): car lifter, luggage lifter, book lifter (Pakistani English)
- walla (one who does something): exam-centre-walla, coachwalla (Pakistani English)
- peelhead (a bald-headed person) (Jamaican English)
- dry coffee (coffee without milk and sugar) (East African English)
- basket-women (coarsely behaved woman) (Lankan English).

Hybrid Compounds (Baumgardner, 1993, 1998; Crystal, 2003)

The following are examples from Pakistani English, using Urdu and English elements to create new hybrid compounds:

- khas deposit (special deposit)
- double roti (bread).

Prefixation (Gramley, 2001; Jenkins, 2003)

- enstool (to install a chief) (Ghanaian English)
- destool (to depose a chief) (Ghanaian English)
- co-wives (wives of the same husband) (West African English).

Suffixation

Baumgardner (1993, 1998) and Crystal, (2003) give examples of suffixation in Pakistani English, using both English and Urdu bases:

- ruinification
- cronydom
- wheatish
- scapegoatism.

Jenkins (2003) gives examples from other forms of English:

- teacheress (female teacher) (Indian English)
- jeepney (a small bus—army jeeps converted to buses) (Philippine English)
- heaty (foods which make the body hot, e.g., durian) (Singapore/ Malaysian English).

Word-class Conversion

Baumgardner (1993, 1998) and Crystal (2003) give examples of word-class conversion found in Pakistani English:

- to aircraft
- to slogan
- to tantamount
- the injureds
- the deads.

Collocations

A collocation is two or more words that co-occur habitually. They are combinations that just "sound right" to the users of the language. An example would be *heavy drinker*. Gramley regards collocations as "one of the most distinctive domains of varietal differentiation" (2001:162).

Baumgardner (1993, 1998) and Crystal, (2003) provide examples of collocation in Pakistani English which involve English/Urdu combinations:

- commit zina (adultery)
- recite kalam (verse)

Idioms

Like collocations, idioms comprise more than one word form. However, unlike collocations, "their meanings are opaque, which means their meaning cannot be derived from their single components" (Gramley, 2001, p. 163). An example would be *that takes the cake* (wins the prize). Jenkins (2003) provides examples that demonstrate the formation of idioms through direct translation from indigenous languages, such as:

- to shake legs (from Malay idiom, "goyang kaki," meaning "to be idle") (Singapore English).

Or by combining elements from English and indigenous forms, such as:

- to put sand in someone's gari ("to threaten someone's livelihood" [gari is a type of flour]) (Nigerian English).

Kamwangamalu's (2001) analysis of South African English provides some rich examples of idioms that make reference to various parts of the body to convey personal feeling. This practice of "body symbolism," (Kamwangamalu, 2001, p. 56), has its roots in the indigenous languages:

- I wrote it down in my head (from Dangarembga, 1988)
- Snakes started playing mini soccer in my spine (I became very excited).

Lexical Innovation and the Processes of Acculturation

One of the key principles presented in this book is that the form and functions of EIL must be analyzed according to the "context of situation which is appropriate to the variety, its uses, and users" (Kachru, 1983, p. 215). Kachru calls this the process of "acculturation," which Bhatt further describes as follows: "Nonnative English speakers ... created new, culturally-sensitive and socially appropriate meanings—expressions of bilingual's [and multilingual's] creativity—by altering and manipulating the structure and functions of English in its new ecology" (2005, p. 534).

And so the question to be asked is: How can such lexical innovation be understood? And what is the significance of lexical innovation for the teaching and learning of English in EIL contexts? To answer these questions, we turn to the work by Lowenberg (1986) and Kamwangamalu (2001). Lowenberg (1986, p. 71) developed his analysis of acculturation and lexical innovation in critique of two related biases in SLA (second language acquisition) research: one, a tendency to regard all "deviations" from native-speaker norms by non-native speakers of a language as deficient approximations of that language; and two, the view that non-native varieties are nothing but "approximate systems" or "interlanguages"—that is, native-speaker varieties were originally the target, but along the way became "fossilized" due to insufficient contact with native speakers of English. Lowenberg maintains that English in its different socio-linguistic contexts has gone through processes of acculturation that privilege the development of local norms. Lexical innovation is one strategy of acculturation.

Lowenberg's analysis of the pragmatic functions of lexical transfer (i.e., retention) provides an example of such acculturation strategies. The most obvious function of retention would be to fill *lexical gaps* for which there are no pre-existing words in English. Monetary terms would often fall into this category (Malaysian *ringgit*, Japanese *yen*), as would names for indigenous condiments and dishes (e.g., *sambal belacan*, a Malay name for a spicy dish, in Malaysian English). However, Lowenberg (1986, p. 75) argues, stronger evidence of retention as a strategy of acculturation arises from "lexical shifts" whereby a word from a local language replaces a known English word. He draws examples from Malaysia, where the establishment of Bahasa Melayu as the national language has been a key strategy used by the government towards developing a national identity. Where Bahasa Melayu retention occurs is enormously significant for how it participates in these processes of identity formation. For instance, the use of *bumiputera* rather than "Malays" within the nation's pro-Malay affirmative action policies vis-à-vis the Chinese, Lowenberg argues, "neutralizes this deliberate inequity in official policy, while also lending it nationalistic legitimacy" (1986, p. 76). He provides the following example:

Excerpt 1

> The special issue of 12.85 million shares to Bumiputera investors approved by the Trade and Industry Ministry at $1.40 per share is to increase Bumiputera shareholders to about 20 per cent of the enlarged capital.
>
> *(New Straits Times, 6/22/83:23)*

Such linguistic retention thus raises "the relative status of ethnic groups through the language of the politically most powerful group" (Lowenberg, 1986, p. 76).

Kamwangamalu (2001) offers similar analyses of the cultural embeddedness of South African English. Noteworthy in his discussion is the dialectic relationship between the socio-cultural context and lexical innovation. Consider the following two excerpts:

Excerpt 2

> I went to see my sister, same father same mother.
>
> (from Chisanga, 1987, p. 53)

Excerpt 3

> My aunt Gladys, the one who is my father's womb-sister, older than him but younger than Babamukuru (old father), came first ... The next minute he was drowned in a sea of bodies belonging to uncles,

aunts and nephews; grandmothers, grandfathers and nieces; brothers and sisters of the womb and not of the womb. The clan had gathered to welcome its returning hero.

(from Dangaremgba, 1988, p. 53)

According to Kamwangamalu (2001), kinship terms have been prone to retention in South African English. For many South African communities, the word sister is used for any female, regardless of her relationship to the speaker. Speakers will therefore qualify the term same father same mother, or, womb sister. The use of the term *Babamukuru*, which also appears in its translated form "old father" is in reference to an uncle, but is seen to be more affectionate than simply "uncle."

The new socio-political circumstances of post-apartheid South Africa have also given rise to new lexical innovations. One illustrative example is the creation of the rainbow-X compound. The phrase refers either to the "coming together of people from previously racially segregated groups," or to something that affects or benefits these people. Kamwangamalu provides the following example from the *Sunday Times*:

Excerpt 4

Mrs van Reenen has taken her two older children ... to the rainbow-nation school across the road, where she teaches Standard 2.

(*Sunday Times*, July 1996, p. 54)

Other compounds cited by Kamwangamalu include rainbow gathering, rainbow swimming pools. Kachru and his colleagues (2006) refer to this form of lexical innovation as "international lexical creativity"—lexical changes that develop as a result of social changes, rather than simply a result of contact between languages.

Given what has been learned here about the cultural embeddedness of language and such processes of acculturation, the question of, "What does it mean to know a word?" which is central to vocabulary pedagogy, becomes suddenly complex. Gardner (2007) explores this question in depth, considering pronunciation, definition(s), lexical category (noun, verb, etc.), collocation (fast car, tall man, soft breeze), derivations (walk, walks, walked), synonyms, and antonyms. Scrivener (2005, pp. 247–248) identifies thirty-two dimensions involved in knowing a lexical item, including how it is spelled to its connotations, synonyms, lexical families, colligation, and collocations. But the cultural embeddedness of language suggests much more is going on. We will come back to this discussion; but first, a look at one of the key approaches that has dominated traditional practices of lexical instruction.

Traditional Practices and Principles

"Vocabulary is the single, strongest predictor of success for EL students," contend Feldman and Kinsella (2005). Yet, the early approaches to Communicative Language Teaching in the 1960s tended to give vocabulary instruction minimal attention, focusing instead on the functional uses of language and allowing vocabulary learning to occur incidentally with little explicit instruction. This began to change in the 1990s, with the introduction of several approaches to language learning that viewed vocabulary and lexical units as central in language learning and teaching. These include *The Lexical Syllabus* (Willis, 1990), *Lexical Phrases and Language Teaching* (Nattinger & DeCarrico, 1992), and *The Lexical Approach* (Lewis, 1993). Concurrently, advances in computer-based studies of language, corpus linguistics, developed to provide an extensive resource for lexically-based inquiry and instruction.

What lexically-based language teaching looked like varied between the authors. For Willis, the emphasis was on word frequency, which was modeled in his 1989 *Collins COBUILD English Course*. The COBUILD computer analyses of text indicated that "the 700 most frequent words of English account for around 70% of all English text" (Willis, 1990, p. vi). The syllabus was thus based on word frequency, while also focusing on their most common patterns of usage. Nattinger and DeCarrico (1992) developed a slightly different approach, using a lexically-based functional schema for organizing instruction—"distinguishing lexical phrases as social interactions, necessary topics, and discourse devices" (1992, p. 185).

Lewis has been perhaps the most influential in terms of his attempt to develop a coherent framework for lexically-based teaching, and it is his work that encapsulates "the Lexical Approach." The most relevant assumptions and principles put forward in his approach as they apply to our discussion here include:

Principle 1: Grammaticalized Lexis

While traditional language teaching methods worked with vocabulary lists, definitions, written and oral drills, flash cards, the Lexical Approach places emphasis on the *lexis*, and the need to see lexis in naturally occurring language. The concept of lexis refers to a kind of internal database of words and ready-made combinations of words that speakers recall frequently, without having to construct new phrases word by word. Thus, lexis includes single word vocabulary items, but also frequent combinations of words known as collocations (e.g., *traffic jam*; *moved to tears*) and even longer combinations, or chunks, such as *go against the grain*, or, *figment of his imagination*.

Principle 2: Differentiated Instruction

A second key principle in Lewis's Lexical Approach is the view that the materials and methods used in language teaching need to be differentiated according to level; what is appropriate at the beginner or elementary level is radically different from the strategies and materials used for upper-intermediate or advanced students. For example, he stressed the importance of an early emphasis on receptive skills, and de-contextualized vocabulary learning for lower-level students. At the lower levels, teachers are encouraged to talk extensively to their students, while requiring little or no verbal response from learners (Lewis, 1997, p. 49). Similarly, extensive writing should be delayed until the advanced levels.

Principle 3: Maximally Useful Language

According to Lewis, what is deemed maximally useful is not something inherent to the language, but has to do with particular courses, and even particular students. This is where some of the emphasis on corpus studies in the development of course content can fail. Many practitioners take Willis' (1990) assertion mentioned earlier about 700 most frequent words covering 70% of text to use the *frequency* of lexis in a corpus to determine its priority in the syllabus. While this may hold some validity in the early stages of language learning, this quickly falls apart at the higher levels. Any consideration of a core lexicon of expressions for learners, Lewis argues, needs to consider several factors (1997, p. 186). Where and with whom are they likely to use their English? What is their current general level and what is their target level? Are there social restrictions on the language that make it unsuitable for EFL use? Do the learners need ESL, in-country EFL, or EFL in the learners' home country?

Along the same lines as what we have been arguing throughout this book (although using different terminology), Lewis notes that, as more and more users of English come to use English alongside one or more other languages, their use of English will be significantly different from monolingual speakers of English. For example, EFL is used much less in intimate situations, and is more likely to be used with strangers than friends. Furthermore, "the vast majority of person-to-person encounters where English as a foreign language is the medium do not include a native speaker at all" (1997, p. 185). And because bilingual speakers of English frequently have different purposes in using English than do monolingual speakers, it is unwarranted to assume that bilingual speakers necessarily want or need to attain native-like competence: "Teachers must constantly remind themselves that native-speaker-like productivity ability is rarely the target" and that "vast numbers of learners will remain intermediate throughout their lives, and that they are both happy with this and derive enormous benefits from their, albeit partial, mastery of English" (1997, p. 185).

This broadened approach to vocabulary and vocabulary instruction has had a significant impact on pedagogy and curriculum. Activities used to develop learners' knowledge of lexical units include the following (summary taken from Moudraia, 2001):

- Intensive and extensive listening and reading in the target language.
- First and second language comparisons and translation (chunk-for chunk, rather than word-for-word), aimed at raising language awareness.
- Repetition and recycling of activities, such as summarizing a text orally one day and again for a few days to keep words and expressions that have been learned active.
- Guessing the meaning of vocabulary items from context.
- Noticing and recording language patterns and collocations.
- Working with dictionaries and other reference tools.
- Working with language corpuses created by the teacher for use in the classroom or accessible on the Internet to research word partnerships, preposition usage, style, etc.
- The use of authentic materials, rich in collocations.

The focus of the lexical approach in Lewis' work is thus to direct students' attention toward naturally occurring language and of the lexical nature of language.

There are other key players to consider in discussions about lexical instruction, including Hunt and Beglar (2002) and Nation (2003). Hunt and Beglar (2002) discuss three approaches to vocabulary instruction: incidental learning, explicit instruction, and independent strategy development. They present these three approaches as seven teaching principles. Along the same vein, Nation (2003) talks about four strands in language pedagogical practices: (1) learning from meaning-focused input (learning through listening and reading); (2) deliberate language-focused learning (learning from being taught sounds, vocabulary, grammar, and discourse); (3) learning from meaning-focused output (learning by having to produce language in speaking and writing); and (4) developing fluency. These two are mapped against each other in Table 12.1.

There are a number of possibilities offered by the Lexical Approach for the teaching of English in EIL contexts. However, application requires an expansion of what Lewis himself advocates. For, while he acknowledges the bilingual contexts of much English language learning and usage today, he is silent on the variation of English in EIL contexts, and on how different varieties of English can influence lexical choices in syllabus

Table 12.1 Approaches to Vocabulary Teaching and Learning

Hunt & Beglar's Approaches to Vocabulary Teaching and Learning	*Hunt & Beglar's Seven Principles*	*Nation's Four Strands in Language Instruction*
Incidental Learning	Principle 1: Provide opportunities for the incidental learning of vocabulary, especially through extensive reading and listening	Learning from meaning-focused input
Explicit instruction	Principle 2: Diagnose which of the 3,000 most common words learners need to study	
	Principle 3: Provide opportunities for the intentional learning of vocabulary	Deliberate language-focused learning
	Principle 4: Provide opportunities for elaborating word knowledge	Learning from meaning-focused output
	Principle 5: Provide opportunities for developing fluency with known and high-frequency vocabulary	Fluency
Independent Strategy Development	Principle 6: Experiment with guessing from context	
	Principle 7: Examine different types of dictionaries and teach students to use them	

design and instruction. Furthermore, he tends to focus on the degree of proficiency (e.g., some learners are content to remain at the intermediate levels), and thereby reaffirms the native-non-native continuum.

Practices and Principles for an EIL Framework

In the remainder of this chapter, I pose a number of questions to guide our conversation about what lexical teaching within an EIL framework looks like. The following quote from Bhatt (2005) sets the tone: "The creative use of language variation, representing plural identities, must find a space in the local pedagogical practices, in the English teaching curriculum generally, and more specifically in the construction of instructional materials" (p. 49).

What Lexis?

The Lexical Approach presented by Lewis opens the possibility for many of the considerations suggested by Matsuda in this volume. That is, a guiding principal in determining what lexical items to include in the curriculum for the teaching and learning of English in EIL contexts is that they need to correspond with the learning needs of the students and match the focus of the course. A key question in addressing "what lexis" is: what do we mean by real English and real lexis? And where does the English of the millions of speakers of EIL fit in? But in addition, and something Lewis does not give explicit attention to, there is the need to expose students to the linguistic diversity of English.

Lexical teaching in the EIL framework is based on the assumption of plurality. Learners need to be made aware of the various forms of English available to them, and understand their use in different contexts. This suggests something other than a single textbook or curriculum for all situations. As Harwood (2002, n.p.) reminds us,

> it is well for the teacher to bear in mind that issues like world Englishes and intercultural pragmatics are complex: being acutely aware that the real lexis will vary immensely depending on the user should help ensure the classroom atmosphere is not one of small-minded prescriptivism.

An incomplete (and hence inaccurate) understanding of the English language could potentially lead to confusion or even resistance when students are confronted with different types of English users or uses, with a possibility that they view such differences as deficient. However, an endonormative understanding of language would challenge such a deficit model, and dismantle the myth of the native speaker. As a practical example, Baumgardner (1987) used contrastive analysis (utilizing their own local or national variety of English and international English) when teaching grammar to university students in Pakistan. In her chapter in this volume, Matsuda suggests a number of sources that would foreground the diversity of English in different EIL contexts.

Furthermore, to make learning authentic and meaningful, it would be important to involve the learner in the design of the materials used and lexis selection. In this way, students can bring their own linguistic practices into the classroom to bear on language learning. And in this way, their own purposes and contexts are intimately incorporated into the learning process, based on the assumption of plurality, and privileging the socio-cultural location of language.

When is a Word a Word?

Put another way, this question asks: when is an innovation considered a norm? This question is important in lexical teaching, particularly in EIL contexts where, as was discussed earlier in this chapter, lexical innovation is a central characteristic. However, if the diversity of English is to be part of the core curricula, it needs to be clear what innovations are indeed normative of the English used in that context, and what would be considered errors, or aberrations. Bamgbose (1998) suggests the following assessment model in answering this question, taking into account the pragmatic and communicative appropriateness of language usage. He identifies five "internal measures" of innovation that determine when an innovation can be considered a norm: (a) demographic (how many people use the innovation?); (b) geographical (how widely dispersed is it?); (c) authoritative (who uses it?); (d) codification (where is the usage sanctioned?); and (e) acceptability (what is the attitude of users and non-users to it?). Of these, Bamgbose argues, codification and acceptance are the most important factors.

What Does it Mean to Know a Word?

From the previous discussion, it is clear that learning individual vocabulary words does not represent true comprehension of the meaning of a word. It is about using the word appropriately to do things in a variety of contexts. Ching (2011) identifies a number of semantic concepts relevant to ESL instruction and learning, including:

- *Sense*: not just linguistic sense (the literal meaning of the word), but also speaker-sense (the meaning intended by the speaker).
- *Reference*: not just linguistic reference (what is actually said by the speaker) but also speaker-reference (who the speaker is actually referring to).
- *Lexical ambiguity*: multiple meanings for a word (e.g., bank could refer to a financial institution, the side of a river, a pile of snow).
- *Synonyms*: some words have the same meanings (e.g., big and large), yet may also have different connotations in different contexts (e.g, consider the different between my big sister and my large sister).
- *Overlap*: words that overlap are ones that share some, but not all, semantic values. For example, the words father, son, brother, uncle,

and nephew all refer to males and to relatives, but differ in other significant ways. Important comparisons can be made between the different varieties of English. For example, Ching notes how in many cultures, your father's brothers are all referred to as father, and your mother's sisters as mother. In other cultures, such as Singapore, the word for uncle refers to any male a generation older (similarly aunt/auntie for females).

He also talks about idioms and words that have no L1 equivalent. All of these concepts allow for discussion concerning the socio-cultural contexts of language, and for unpacking variety in EIL lexis. Students at the upper levels would be able to bring into the conversation their own experiences with language, and their own "knowing" of words.

What are Some of the Strategies for Teaching Lexical Items in EIL?

The underlying principal of EIL pedagogy is that, just as EIL is defined by its acculturation and cultural embeddedness, so too the methodology of teaching English is linked to the local culture of learning. As put by McKay (2003), "an appropriate EIL methodology presupposes sensitivity to the local cultural context in which local educators determine what happens in the classroom" (p. 17). Therefore, any sound pedagogy for teaching EIL must be sufficiently complex to account for this diversity.

Many of the strategies discussed earlier in the work of Lewis (1997), Nation (2003), and Hunt and Beglar (2002), such as semantic mapping, lexical phrases, vocabulary notebooks are all relevant to the teaching of EIL. What would be different is the content and intent of the lexical items introduced. As a simple example, a semantic map for a phrase in Excerpt 4 would necessarily entail mapping the socio-political meanings embedded in the rainbow collocations. The pragmatic contexts of language use—which, in EIL contexts often involves an awareness of the bilingual langscape—would similarly inform all of these strategies.

The use of comphuter corpora profiled in the Lexis Approach is also very relevant to the teaching of EIL, particularly with the development of EIL corpus data bases. Nelson (2006) describes the International Corpus of English (ICE)—a project conceived in the late 1980s by Sidney Greenbaum. The ICE project involves researchers from a wide array of countries in Inner- and Outer-Circle countries; and a further ancillary project involves countries in the Expanding Circle. Each ICE team is compiling (or has already compiled) a 1-million-word corpus of their own variety of English, produced by adults (aged 18 and over) after 1989. Importantly, the greater part of its contributions come from spoken samples of English (as compared to writing), and primarily from face-to-face conversations. This makes the ICE corpora unique in the emphasis placed on the spoken medium, and in particular on informal, conversational English. These corpora are of course incredibly useful for comparative analysis. Students will be made more aware about the use of English as an international language and the implications of EIL linguistically, culturally, and politically. In addition, the cultural embeddedness of language and of lexical innovation provides students an opportunity to learn more about their own culture and the development of their own language, as well as that of other varieties of English. Such discussion would dismantle the "native/non-native" speaker dichotomy and any notion that "English" belongs to only the Inner Circle. It also opens up the possibility for teaching and learning strategies of negotiation, as learners understand the socio-cultural and political positioning of language.

Along the same vein, using international target culture materials would be the inclusion of cross-cultural encounters in which all interlocutors are bilingual users of English. The use of such materials could exemplify the manner in which bilingual users of English are effectively using English. Texts could include examples of lexical (and other) variation in present-day use of English. This would provide a basis for students to gain a fuller understanding of the diversity of English and its uses in a broad range of contexts. Such an approach of course challenges the model of English-only classrooms, and rather presupposes appropriate language behavior in the classroom to include bilingual, if not multilingual, exchanges.

In the section below, I will talk about the importance of incorporating the culture of learning into EIL pedagogy. By way of simultaneously concluding this current section and introducing the next, I provide an example of a vocabulary lesson taught in a Vietnamese classroom (taken from McKay, 2002, drawn from the work by Kramsch and Sullivan). The Vietnamese culture of learning has three central characteristics: the notion of classroom-as-family, teacher-as-mentor, and language-learning-as-play. These characteristics are evident in a vocabulary lesson on character: "What sort of person are you?" According to the curriculum, students were to write "Yes," "No," or "Sometimes" as they answered questions about their behavior. In a western classroom, students would probably be asked to answer the questions individually and then discuss their responses in small groups. In this classroom, however, the class as a whole went through the list, with individual students calling out their responses and other students commenting on these responses, and sometimes, with considerable laughter, simultaneous responses. This teacher thus creatively transformed the curriculum through locally relevant pedagogy—which brings us to the question of "who should teach" in an EIL classroom.

Who Should Teach?

Even though about 80% of English language teaching professionals are bilingual users of English, a so-called "native speaker fallacy" prevails, privileging Inner-Circle curriculum and teaching methodologies (McKay, 2003). Yet, in light of the socio-cultural embeddedness of language and the need for the teacher to respond to the needs of students, the perceived need for teachers to model Inner-Circle texts, curricula, and teaching methodologies undermines the true value that such teachers can bring to the classroom (McKay, 2003). The answer to "who should teach" is thus: local professionals who are bilingual users of English, *and* who are empowered to appropriate local cultures of learning.

In the first place, bilingual professionals are intimately aware of how English fits into the linguistic repertoire of their students. They are also familiar with the different varieties of English spoken within the country and the contexts of their use. While there is indeed a Standard form that may be promoted through the education system, it is rarely the *only* form of English used in many Outer-Circle countries. Recall Bamgbose's (1992) earlier description of at least four varieties of Nigerian English as just one example. An effective bilingual teacher is aware of this diversity and the pragmatic rules that govern their use, and incorporates them in decisions about instruction and learning. Finally, bilingual teachers have nuanced understanding of the local culture, which is so important in designing learning in accordance with the goals of the learners themselves. The purposes for learning and using English in EIL contexts are different than those of immigrants to English-speaking countries who may eventually use English as their dominant language. For example, many current learners of English may learn English to promote trade and tourism, to participate in international scholarly exchange, or to share with others their culture. Bilingual teachers native to the local culture are able to incorporate such goals and purposes into their curriculum and pedagogy. Hearkening back to the example of the Vietnamese classroom, Kramsch and Sullivan's suggested motto (in McKay, 2003) is: "global thinking, local teaching"—which McKay describes as an approach that recognizes "the use of English as a global language" yet at the same time, considers "how English is embedded in the local context" (p. 17).

Conclusion

The focus of this chapter was on lexical innovation in English as an international language, and the implications that such processes of acculturation have for the teaching and learning of English. A key argument in this chapter is that language is embedded in culture, and innovation needs to be seen as processes of acculturation. This discussion set the stage then for a pluricentric view of language, in contrast to a "native/non-native" model. An overview of the main tenets of the Lexical Approach, which characterizes much of the lexical teaching today, suggested both possibilities and limitations for its application to the EIL framework. The possibilities were that it allowed for an approach to lexical teaching that prioritizes language in its context of use and is responsive to the needs and goals of the learners. However, it fell short of fully appreciating and incorporating the diversity of the English language into its pedagogy and curriculum. The chapter ended with discussion around some key questions pertaining to principles around lexical teaching in the EIL framework to address those gaps, and to suggest ways forward in developing a lexical pedagogy within the EIL framework.

Exploring the Ideas

1 Do you agree with Bamgbose's criteria for determining when an innovation is a norm? Provide evidence from innovations you are aware of in the form of English that you are familiar with to support your answer.

2 One argument made in this chapter is that there is no single core lexical syllabus that can be used in all language learning situations around the world; rather, the lexical syllabus needs to emerge through involvement with learners and with the input of individual teachers. What challenges do you think you might face in developing such a lexical syllabus? What might be some ways you can address these challenges? What are some of the strengths you see in this approach?

3 One of the principles of the Lexical Approach is that the teaching of grammar and lexis cannot be separated, that the two are inherently intertwined. Once you have read the chapter in this book on Grammar teaching and standards, consider this claim by comparing the arguments presented in these two chapters (Grammar and Lexis). How does the teaching of grammar and lexis inform each other?

Applying the Ideas

1 What role do you think dictionaries of nativized English can play in assisting vocabulary development? Consult at least one dictionary of a nativized variety of English (e.g., South African English, Caribbean English) and then develop one classroom task that could be used with it.

2 Examine an ELT textbook series to see how vocabulary is dealt with. What vocabulary targets does the series teach? On what basis do you think the vocabulary was chosen? Why do you think so?

3 Examine a Vocabulary lesson plan that has been developed by an Inner-Circle publishing company. What might you change if you were to use this lesson in an EIL classroom in an Outer-Circle country? Identify the country and context, including a description of its landscape and key characteristics of the culture of learning in that context.

References

Bamgbose, A. (1992). Standard Nigerian English: Issues of identification. In B. B. Kachru (Ed.), *The other tongue* (pp. 148–161). Chicago: University of Illinois Press.

Bamgbose, A. (1998). Torn between the norms: Innovations in World Englishes. *World Englishes, 17*(1), 1–14.

Baumgardner, R. J. (1987). Utilizing Pakistani newspaper English to teach grammar. *World Englishes, 6*(3), 241–252.

Baumgardner, R. J. (1993). *The English language in Pakistan*. Karachi: Oxford University Press.

Baumgardner, R. J. (1998). Word-formation in Pakistan English. *English World-Wide, 19*(2), 205–246.

Bhatt, R. M. (2005). Expert discourses, local practices, and hybridity: The case of Indian Englishes. In A. S. Canagarajah (Ed.), *Reclaiming the local in language policy and practice* (pp. 25–54). Mahwah, NJ and London: Lawrence Erlbaum.

Ching, G. (2011). An introduction to teaching language. (Unpublished paper). New Brunswick, NJ: Crandall University.

Crystal, D. (2003). *English as a global language* (2nd ed.) Cambridge: Cambridge University Press.

Feldman, K., & Kinsella, K. (2005). *Narrowing the language gap: The case for explicit vocabulary instruction*. New York: Scholastic Inc. Retrieved from http://teacher.scholastic.com/products/authors/pdfs/Narrowing_the_Gap.pdf

Gardner, D. (2007). Validating the construct of word in applied corpus-based vocabulary research: A critical survey. *Applied Linguistics, 29*(2), 241–265.

Gramley, S. (2001). *The vocabulary of world English*. London: Arnold.

Harwood, N. (2002). Taking a lexical approach to teaching: principles and problems. Retrieved from http://privatewww.essex.ac.uk /~nharwood / lexapproach.htm

Hunt, A., & Beglar, D. (2002). Current research and practice in teaching vocabulary. In J. C. Richards & W. A. Renandya (Eds.), *Methodology in language teaching: An anthology of current practice* (pp. 258–266). Cambridge: Cambridge University Press.

Jenkins, J. (2003). *World Englishes: A resource book for students*. London and New York: Routledge.

Kachru, B. B. (1981). The pragmatics of non-native varieties of English. In L. Smith (Ed.), *English for cross-cultural communication* (pp. 15–39). New York: St. Martin's Press.

Kachru, B. B. (1983). *The Indianization of English: The English language in India*. New York: Oxford University Press.

Kachru, B. B., Kachru, Y., & Nelson, C. (Eds.). (2006). *The handbook of world Englishes*. Malden, MA: Blackwell Publishing.

Kamwangamalu, N. M. (2001). Reincarnations of English: A case from South Africa. In E. Thumboo (Ed.), *The three circles of English* (pp. 45–66). Singapore: UniPress.

Lewis, M. (1993). *The lexical approach: The state of ELT and a way forward*. Hove, UK: Language Teaching Publications.

Lewis, M. (1997). *Implementing the lexical approach: Putting theory into practice*. Hove, UK: Language Teaching Publications.

Lowenberg, P. (1986). Non-native varieties of English: Nativization, norms and implications. *Studies in Second Language Acquisition, 8*, 1–18.

Lowenberg, P. (2002). Assessing English proficiency in the expanding circle. *World Englishes, 21*(3), 431–435.

McKay, S. L. (2002). *Teaching English as an international language: Rethinking goals and approaches*. Oxford and New York: Oxford University Press.

McKay, S. L. (2003). Toward an appropriate EIL pedagogy: Re-examining common ELT assumptions. *International Journal of Applied Linguistics, 13*(1), 1–22.

McKay, S. L., & Bokhorst-Heng, W. D. (2008). *International English in its sociolinguistic contexts: Towards a socially sensitive EIL pedagogy*. New York: Routledge.

Mesthrie, R., & Bhatt, R. M. (2008). *World Englishes: The study of new linguistic varieties*. Cambridge and New York: Cambridge University Press.

Moudraia, O. (2001). Lexical approach to second language teaching. *ERIC Digest*. EDO-FL-01-02. Washington, DC: ERIC Clearinghouse on Languages and Linguistics, Center for Applied Linguistics.

Nation, P. (2003). Vocabulary. In D. Nunan (Ed.), *Practical English language teaching* (pp. 129–152). New York: McGraw Hill.

Nattinger, J., & DeCarrico, J. (1992). *Lexical phrases and language teaching*. Oxford: Oxford University Press.

Nelson, G. (2006). World Englishes and corpora studies. In B. Kachru, Y. Kachru, & C. Nelson (Eds.), *The handbook of world Englishes* (pp. 733–750). Malden, MA: Blackwell Publishing.

Scrivener, J. (2005). *Learning teaching: A guidebook for English language teachers* (2nd ed.). Oxford: Macmillan.

Willis, J. D. (1990). *The lexical syllabus*. London: Collins COBUILD.

Willis, J. D., & Willis, D. (1989). *Collins COBUILD English Course*. London: Collins.

Chapter 13

Corpora in Language Teaching from the Perspective of English as an International Language

John Flowerdew

Introduction

The use of corpora in the classroom has developed alongside the exponential growth in the use of personal computers. Pedagogical applications of corpora developed out of corpus linguistics. That is to say corpus linguistics findings and methodologies were applied to language teaching. More recently, however, as Römer (2008, pp. 7–8) points out, pedagogical concerns have come to influence corpus linguistics as well as vice versa; insights from corpus studies are being incorporated into pedagogy, but also pedagogical requirements are providing impetus for work in corpus linguistics.

While the first corpora relied on main-frame computers, nowadays anyone with a laptop computer can work with corpora. Indeed, with the advent of online corpora, it is now possible to work with corpora on mobile phones or tablet computers. From the point of view of English as an International Language (EIL) (and EIL is understood here to be "a means of communication across national and linguistic boundaries" [Jenkins, 2006, p. 160]), while, in the early days, developments in corpus techniques were mainly limited to highly developed countries or projects with international funding, now, with the spread of computer technology throughout the world, more and more teachers and learners internationally have the possibility of using corpora inside and outside classrooms in one form or another.

We can define EIL learners as individuals who are learning English in order to communicate with others who use English as a language of international communication. This is the definition that will be used for the purposes of this chapter. This community of EIL speakers has been described by Burns (2005, p. 24) as an "international communicative network."

Corpora and Language Teaching: Principles and Practice

What is a Corpus?

A corpus is a large data-base of language. The first corpora were relatively small. The Brown corpus (developed at Brown University, USA in the early 1960s), for example, consisted of 1 million words and was considered huge at the time. There now exist, however, corpora consisting of hundreds of millions of words, e.g., *British National Corpus* (100 million words), *Bank of English* (http://www.collinslanguage.com/wordbanks/) (over 500 million words), and *Corpus of American Contemporary English* (http://corpus. byu.edu/coca/) (over 400 million words). At the same time, however, much smaller corpora with as few as 100,000 words or less are being created all the time for individual and specialist applications (Ghadessy, Henry, & Roseberry, 2001). While some corpora are kept in a "raw" state (e.g., *Bank of English*, *Corpus of Contemporary American English*), many are "tagged" (i.e., coded, according to parts of speech) and "parsed" (i.e., analyzed for grammatical structure) (e.g., *British National Corpus*).

Corpora are useful for investigating patterns of lexis, grammar, semantics, pragmatics, and textual features (e.g., Aijmer, 2009; Biber, Conrad & Reppen, 1998; L. Flowerdew, 2012; Hunston, 2002; Kennedy, 1998; McEnery & Wilson, 1996; Sinclair, 2004). Most work in corpus linguistics to date has relied on word frequency lists, which provide criteria upon which to base a search, and keyword in context (KWIC) concordances, the presentation of every instance of a selected word, phrase, or particle in the corpus presented down the middle of the page with a limited amount of linguistic context on either side. Figure 13.1 provides

	Your query "as time goes by" returned 42 hits in 39 different texts (98,313,429 words [4,048 texts]; frequency: 0.43 instances per million words), sorted on node word (42 hits)		
1	Simply because we live in inflationary times	**as time goes by**	everything will cost more. Your protection
2	as far as the client's concerned. But it can be altered	**as time goes by,**	if a client can afford extra premiums, their salary
3	re-use of data involves published summary tables.	**As time goes by,**	more and more information is being routinely
4	audlts nearby will rush over to see what is wrong.	**As time goes by,**	the mother seems to become a little blasé about
5	self-confidence can be further enhanced. Inevitably,	**as time goes by,**	the necessity to recod one's ideas and thoughts
6	out in one of the small number of ordered states.	**As time goes by,**	the system will evolve according to the laws of
7	descendants that come to dominate the population.	**As time goes by,**	the world becomes filled with the most powerful
8	a comment which becomes more fully justified	**as time goes by,**	though Leonard's anarchism remained personal
9	he says. 'Like VAT, it seems complicated, but	**as time goes by,**	we will accommodate its requirements without
10	ideas of replication servers and so on and so forth	**as time goes by,**	we will be able to exploit that technology or
11	the maintenance of the house and estate, And	**as time goes by,**	your staff will likely decrease, for the age limits
12	tend to become more rather than less aggresive	**as time goes by.**	Aggression has its own rewards, which leads to
13	systems which are acheiving Posix compliance	**as time goes by.**	Even IBM have stated that OS Four Hundred
14	Only very slightly at first, but increasingly	**as time goes by.**	Even in the few years since Volumes I and
15	focus on those, and no doubt we will focus on those	**as time goes by.**	My feeling is that while focusing on those we
16	as any form of fear or negativity feeds upon itself	**as time goes by.**	Perhaps as a child Joyce simply knew that

Figure 13.1 Example of Concordance Extract for the Phrase *as time goes by* (Source: BNC Web)

part of a concordance of the phrase *as time goes by* downloaded from the British National Corpus (BNC) (http://bncweb.lancs.ac.uk/bncwebSignup/user/login.php). Most concordancers nowadays also allow the researcher to select the key word or phrase of a given concordance and show its wider context in the overall corpus.

Corpus Applications to Language Teaching

In terms of application to language teaching, knowledge of linguistic and discoursal features and their relative frequency can be helpful in deciding what items to teach and when to teach them, as well as, importantly, providing input for reference materials. Corpora provide empirical data and do not depend on introspection about the language, which is notoriously unreliable. Even where individuals are confident about their intuitions, in fact, corpus evidence often proves them to be wrong (e.g., Biber et al., 1998). To give a simple example, many L1 and L2 users of English believe that the word *research* is always a non-count singular noun and therefore not used in the plural. However, a search of the BNC reveals many uses of *researches* as a noun.

Corpus-based approaches have also given rise to what is referred to as the "lexical approach" to language teaching. The lexical approach is based upon the understanding that words typically do not occur in isolation, but in prefabricated chunks, or collocations. Speakers of the language have a huge store of these prefabricated chunks, which are essential for fluent production. Such collocations are not reliably accessed by intuition, but can be identified by the computer. Typically, course books are based on intuition, however, and therefore do not present language as prefabricated patterns and thereby fail to provide an accurate representation of the language, according to proponents of the lexical approach. According to Michael Lewis (1997), who coined the term lexical approach, the language of most course books is "not what people really say" (Lewis 1997, p. 10) and, indeed, empirical studies of course books have been conducted to demonstrate this to be the case (e.g., Flowerdew & Miller, 1997; Holmes, 1988; Hyland, 1994). It follows that the way to avoid such inauthenticity is to base teaching and learning materials on corpus-based lexical chunks, on what is referred to as "real" English, in other words.

In discussing the application of corpora to language teaching, one may distinguish between indirect and direct applications (Flowerdew, 2009; Leech, 1997; Römer, 2008). With indirect applications, the findings of corpus analysis are used in the preparation of dictionaries, grammar and usage books, and teaching materials. Römer (2008) has described direct applications of corpora as follows:

Instead of having to rely on the researcher as mediator and provider of corpus-based materials [indirect applications], language learners and teachers get their hands on corpora and concordancers themselves and find out about language patterning and the behaviour of words and phrases in an "autonomous" way.

(p. 118)

Indirect Applications

To begin with indirect applications, space allows for just one example to be provided of each type.

Dictionaries

Traditionally, dictionary entries were created by informants who wrote definitions for words and made up examples. The *Collins Cobuild English Dictionary* (Sinclair, 1995) was the first dictionary to be based on a corpus, the latest version using the *Bank of English* corpus, which consists of hundreds of millions of words. The corpus data provides full sentence examples to show how a word or phrase is typically used and is a source of data on frequency distribution and other variation across registers, as well as pragmatic features. Following the pioneering work of *Cobuild*, today, many international publishers use corpora in their dictionary-making.

Grammar and Usage Books

The *Longman Grammar of Spoken and Written English* (Biber, Johansson, Leech, Conrad, & Finegan, 1999) is based on a corpus of 40 million words. The grammar is derived from four main registers: transcribed conversations, fiction, news, and academic prose; in addition, there are smaller samples of non-conversational speech and general prose. The corpus allows for frequency data to be provided based on these registers, a feature which had not been possible with earlier grammars. The use of the corpus means that real examples can be given where previously non-corpus-based grammars relied on made-up examples.

Coursebooks

Collins Cobuild English Course (Willis & Willis, 1988) is the first course book to be based on a *lexical syllabus*, focusing on "the commonest words and phrases in English and their meanings" (Willis, 1990, p. 124). The course is based on insights from corpus linguistics which have revealed how language is patterned around repeated lexical collocations and how lexis and grammar work together. It is worth noting, however, that this course was not particularly popular. There are signs though that a more recent course, the *Touchstone* series of course books (McCarthy, McCarten, & Sandiford, 2005), which is also based on a lexical syllabus, will be more popular.

The above examples have been prepared by international publishers and have involved the investment of considerable financial support. Not all indirect applications need to be limited to large enterprises, however. Already, in the first book on concordancing for teachers, Tribble and Jones (1990) showed how to prepare teaching materials based on corpus outputs. In an early report, Flowerdew (1993/2001) showed how a small team of teachers created a corpus, developed a syllabus, and designed materials in an English for Specific Purposes (ESP) situation in the Middle East. In her book on corpora in ESP, Gavioli (2005) describes how she used corpora that she created from academic articles downloaded from the Internet.

Direct Applications

One basic function of corpora as far as the teacher is concerned is that they provide a means for teachers to enhance their own knowledge of English (Barlow, 1996). As Barnbrook (1996, cited in Römer, 2008, p. 120) has put it, corpora may function as "tireless native-speaker informant[s], with rather greater potential knowledge of the language than the average native speaker." More will be said on this topic in the second part of this chapter.

Corpus examples can also be used to support teachers' explanations. Suppose the teacher finds that learners are using forms such as *as the time goes by, *with the time goes by, *with the time goes on, instead of *as time goes by*. Rather than the teacher just correcting such uses and providing the standard form, the computer can be used to provide a set of concordances, as in the extract presented earlier in Figure 13.1 above. As well as highlighting the standard pattern, this concordance also shows some other interesting features of *as time goes by*. For example, there are only 42 occurrences of this pattern in nearly one million words of the BNC corpus, so the teacher may draw attention to the fact that learners may be overusing this item. In addition, we can see from this concordance that a number of the examples have *as time goes by* in clause-final position (easily identified by full stops), where many learners typically only use it in clause-initial position. This can also be pointed out to learners.

In addition to using corpora as linguistic informants, teachers may use corpora to create learning materials for their own classroom use (see e.g., Gavioli, 2005), corpus data ensuring that "real" language is being used.

Further possibilities are opened up as regards direct applications with two other types of corpora: learner corpora and parallel corpora. A learner corpus is a corpus of language data produced by learners of a language, while a parallel corpus is a corpus of text aligned with its translation in another language, i.e., the L1 and English.

One of the most productive areas in corpus applications in language learning, in fact, has been with learner corpora. The best known work in this area is that of Sylviane Granger and colleagues at the University of Louvain in Belgium. This group of researchers has put together a suite of learner corpora from a range of language backgrounds: *The International Corpus of Learner English* (http://www.uclouvain.be/en-cecl.html) (Granger, Dagneaux, Meunier, & Paquot, 2009). This corpus contains sub-corpora from a wide range of mother-tongue backgrounds (at the time of writing, Bulgarian, Chinese, Czech, Dutch, Finnish, French, German, Italian, Japanese, Norwegian, Polish, Russian, Spanish, Swedish, Turkish, and Tswana). For teachers who may not know the language(s) of their learners, learner corpora are of value in demonstrating difficulties that learners from particular language backgrounds experience. (Learner corpora are also of value in indirect applications: in syllabus and materials design.)

Although not receiving as much attention as learner corpora, parallel corpora, which as stated, are bi-lingual corpora and which are specially formatted for side-by-side comparison, are also of much potential as a source for individual learners for translation equivalents in the target language for units of language in their first language. (Parallel corpora may also be of value for indirect applications [e.g., Teubert, 2004].)

In the 1970s, Tim Johns, working at the University of Birmingham, UK, an early pioneer in corpus-based approaches, started to use corpora in ESP teaching to overseas university students. He put his students in the role of "language detectives" and asked them to consider concordance outputs directly. This approach, where the students themselves become linguistic researchers, became known as *data-driven learning* (DDL). DDL works on the principle that learners have an innate inductive capacity to identify, classify, and generalize on the basis of language experience (Bernardini, 2004, p. 17). DDL may take one of two forms: the student may work with the corpus directly or the corpus outputs may be mediated by the teacher, who first prepares (and also has the opportunity to edit, if she or he so wishes) the outputs, and then presents the material to the student.

To take an example where students work on their own, suppose learners have difficulty with the various forms of the verb *give* as a phrasal verb. They can be asked to concordance the various patterns—e.g., *give away, give off, give out, give up, give way*—and notice the differences in meaning of each of the different patterns, which are derivable from the context of the concordance output. To take another example, students of English for Academic Purposes (EAP) may be asked to investigate the use of count vs. non-count nouns such as *research, data, study,* and *equipment* in an academic corpus such as MICASE or BAWE (see below for details of these corpora). Bernardini (2004, p. 17) gives as a further example for DDL that of article usage, describing this feature of English as follows:

> Its intricacies make this aspect of English little amenable to neat classifications, where corpus work, on the contrary, can provide enough evidence and stimuli for the learner to arrive at developmentally appropriate generalisations.

An innovative approach to DDL is reported in Lee and Swales (2006) in an advanced EAP context where international doctoral students created personalized corpora of their own writing and compared them with other corpora that they created of published papers in their field. Given the tremendous international demand for ESP, there is, indeed, a wealth of corpus-based linguistic research on a whole range of academic and professional genres (see e.g., any issue of *English for Specific Purposes* or *Journal of English for Academic Purposes).* In addition, learner corpora are beginning to be used to highlight specific ESP/EAP issues where learner usage does not correspond to what is found in expert specialist corpora (e.g., Flowerdew, 2006, 2010).

Principles and Practice for an EIL Framework

Having reviewed briefly a range of principles and practices for corpora from the traditional perspective, attention will now be given to seeing what these principles and practices might look like from an EIL perspective. Given the embryonic state of corpus work for EIL contexts—the fact that there are not many EIL corpora and the work that has been done on them is limited—this section will be somewhat speculative. Each section will discuss an issue and current practice and conclude with a potential general principle.

The Issue of Standards

With the use of English internationally, an immediate question is that of which variety to teach. What should be the standard? Should it be American English, British English, or another "Inner-Circle" variety? Should it be Indian English, Nigerian English or another "Outer-Circle" variety? Or should it be Korean English, Chinese English, French English, or another "Expanding-Circle" variety? Then again, might not English as a Lingua Franca (ELF), which can be defined as "a common means of communication for speakers of different first languages" (http://www. univie.ac.at/voice/page/faq), be a valid variety? On the other hand, should not learners be exposed to more than one variety? As Burns (2005, pp. 5–6) has written,

> limiting learners' exposure to only one or two of the infinite variations of L1 and L2 varieties and representing them as universal norms denies the realities of the repertoires of World Englishes learners encounter when they go out into the real world.

Indeed, it can also be argued that limiting learners to a single variety when they may want access to other varieties is an infringement of their rights as learners.

If learners are to be helped to acquire English that can be used in international contexts, it needs to be intelligible to the largest number of possible interlocutors (Burns, 2005; McKay, 2002; McKay & Bokhorst-Heng, 2008). Learners need to acquire a widely intelligible variety or varieties of English. Traditionally, this would be modeled on one of or a hybrid of the Inner-Circle varieties: American, Australian, British, Canadian, etc. At the same time, if learners come from an Outer-Circle country, they may already have acquired one of the newer varieties of English: Indian English, Malaysian English, Nigerian English, etc. Given the distinctiveness of some of these emerging varieties, it can be argued that, for international communication, speakers of these varieties still need to acquire (at least certain features of) an Inner-Circle variety (or ELF, see below). At the same time, EIL users from the Inner-Circle countries, if they interact with Outer-Circle speakers of English, may need to develop familiarity with one or more of these emerging varieties. As Crystal (1988) has written:

> We may, in due course, all need to be in control of two standard Englishes—the one which gives us our national and local identity, and the other which puts us in touch with the rest of the human race. In effect, we may all need to become bilingual in our own language.
>
> (p.265)

This may be over-emphasizing the diversity and mutual unintelligibility of different varieties. As well as forces pulling language in different directions, there are other forces pulling them together (Bakhtin, 1981), EIL itself being an important contributor to the latter. There is an important role for educational systems here in maintaining norms of mutual intelligibility. As McKay (2002) has written:

> [T]here is no question that many varieties [of English] will develop, each with its own norms. Yet the fact that many bilingual users of English acquire the language in an educational context in which particular standards of use are emphasized will likely ensure some unifying norms.
>
> (p.53)

This may be more expected for formal written situations than for informal speech, it is worth pointing out. It is the case in Hong Kong, for example, where government policy favors Inner-Circle standards. In the universities, dissertations and theses target Inner-Circle norms, but lectures and seminars exhibit more localized forms, including code switching (Flowerdew, Miller, & Li, 1998; Flowerdew, Li, & Miller, 2000).

Whichever of the suggested possible standards is/are the target(s)—Inner-Circle standard varieties, Outer-Circle varieties, or Expanding-Circle varieties—the implications for corpus applications are clear: there is a need for corpora consisting of data from these different varieties. To date, the single most important endeavor to create corpora of international Englishes is the *International Corpus of English* (ICE) (http://ice-corpora. net/ice/), a project which includes over twenty countries or groups of countries from the Inner and Outer Circle where English is the first language or an official second language. Each ICE sub-corpus is made up of a million words of spoken and written English (60% spoken). Linguists are working internationally to provide linguistic descriptions of national varieties, most of which have to date not been systematically described. Such descriptions, when available, no doubt, can be used for pedagogic application.

Principle: Consider corpora from more than one variety for EIL.

The "Real" English Question

As indicated in the first part of this chapter, one of the core tenets of corpus-based teaching, the lexical approach, has been that such an approach ensures that "real" English is presented to learners and that their English does not sound "artificial" or "non-native-like." If one takes an EIL perspective, however, then a question arises as to what "real" English actually is. Following what has already been said in this chapter, EIL varieties of English would be as equally "real" as center varieties. Moreover, learners may not want to sound like native speakers; they may want to preserve their cultural identity as non-native speakers (Harwood, 2002). These problems might easily be overcome, therefore, if corpus data used in lexical approaches to teaching were based on EIL corpora instead of Inner-Circle ones. At the same time, however, corpus data based on Inner-Circle corpora will still be of value where the approach is a pluralistic one, i.e., including both Inner-Circle as well as other corpora. Learners will not be denied access to "real" native-speaker English when they want it and, indeed, teachers who do not speak Inner-Circle varieties will be more confident in any statements that they may want to make about the language and feel at less of a disadvantage in this area with regard to their native-speaker counterparts.

Principle: "Real" English is not just Inner-Circle English.

Applications

The indirect applications briefly reviewed in the first part of this chapter raise some important issues regarding EIL. With many indirect applications, such as those commercial publications described above, considerable financial support is inevitable because such enterprises require large teams of researchers and writers. As such, they need to be aimed at an international market and as a consequence of this are based on Inner-Circle standard varieties (American and/or British English). There are issues of hegemony here, created by the international English Language teaching industry. Local initiatives, on the other hand, open up the possibility of using local corpora consisting of Outer- and Expanding-Circle varieties for indirect applications such as dictionaries, grammars, coursebooks, and teaching materials. Such uses of local corpora thus allow a move away from what Tollefson (1991, cited in McKay & Bokhorst-Heng, 2008, p. 51) refers to as the "modernization" model of curriculum development, where Western models are applied by Western experts (Inner-Circle countries) to (non-Western) Outer- and Expanding-Circle contexts.

Where corpora are constructed for specific pedagogic applications, it is worth noting that written data are much more easily collected than spoken. This is significant for EIL corpora, because Outer- and Expanding-Circle varieties tend to exhibit more distinctive features in their spoken forms than in their written ones.

Learner and parallel corpora, in particular, based as they are on the learner's L1, offer potential for locally based models in terms of EIL provision. Where learner and parallel corpora have been used to date, however, there is a tendency to conform to what has been referred to as the "native speaker fallacy," a belief that the educated native speaker and

Inner-Circle models of English are used as the desired standard against which judgments of learner appropriacy are made (Phillipson, 1992).

There is an issue here, however, with regard to learner corpora. A distinction needs to be made between what is a feature of a given variety and what is an interlanguage "error" made by learners. Where EIL varieties are not clearly defined, then this is a distinction which it is not easy to answer. Only substantial corpora of the relevant variety spoken or written by educated users can answer this question.

> Principle: Make use of local corpora, including learner and parallel corpora, for application to teaching materials.

English as a Lingua Franca

An alternative model that has been put forward in place of the Inner- (and Outer-) Circle varieties as a goal for international communication is that of ELF. ELF can be defined as a functional variety of English which is acquired as an addition to the speaker's first language in order to communicate with other speakers for whom English is not their first language (Hülmbauer, Böhringer, & Seidlhofer, 2008). It is a hybrid variety. Users of ELF concentrate on communicative efficiency more than linguistic accuracy. The argument for using ELF as a target, as put forward by one of its proponents (Jenkins, 2004, p. 65), is that "this is the most likely situation for the majority of learners in the 21st century."

In spite of its hybrid nature, researchers have identified common features which tend to be shared by speakers of ELF, such as, in the area of grammar, omission of third-person singular "s," shifts in article usage, and invariant question tags; for pronunciation, Jenkins (2000) has identified a "common core" of (reduced) phonological features of ELF which vary from "standard" models (e.g., "t" and "d" may replace "th" sounds as in "thin" and "this"), without impairing intelligibility. Kirkpatrick (2007) has identified a set of core features for ELF users in the ASEAN region. It is to be noted, however, that ELF is not a single variety of English, but rather a set of accommodative strategies.

A key point about ELF is that it can be appropriated by speakers of any L1. This is significant because it implies equal communicative rights for all of its users (Hülmbauer et al., 2008). At the same time, L1 speakers of standard varieties may use ELF, so long as they are interacting with speakers from other language and cultural backgrounds (hence Crystal's point quoted above about everyone having to become bilingual in their own language). Two corpus projects are particularly prominent in the context of ELF research: the VOICE project (www.univie.ac.at/voice) in Vienna (e.g., Seidlhofer, 2010) and the ELFA project (www.eng.helsinki.fi/elfa)

in Finland (e.g., Mauranen, Hynninen, & Ranta, 2010). Mauranen et al. (2010) have written as follows regarding ELF:

> ... the dominance of the ENL [English Native Language] speaker model is likely to diminish, because the determinants of language use lose their connections to any national basis. Instead, the influence of professional and disciplinary communities may well be on the increase. ... It is no longer sufficient to point to the "educated native speaker" for a model. The successful use of ELF demands new skills from its speakers, native or non-native, compared to those which traditional language education has prepared people for.
>
> (p. 189)

In terms of application to pedagogic practice, it is still early days for ELF, however.

> Principle: Consider ELF corpora as models for EIL.

Academic and Business English

ELF has been studied mostly in academic contexts, both the VOICE and ELFA consisting of academic language. Academia and business are the two contexts where EIL is probably most prevalent. For a considerable time now already, English has been the international language of academic research and, whether it is international student exchange visits, international degree programs taught in English, or whole universities adopting English as the medium of instruction, English is being increasingly used for study at all levels. Indeed, this is not only at the level of the university. English is also increasingly being used as the medium of instruction at primary and secondary school, the CLIL (Content and Language Integrated Learning) movement in Europe and elsewhere being indicative of this trend (http://ec.europa.eu/education/languages/language-teaching/doc236_en.htm). In addition to the ELF corpora, various academic corpora are available to researchers and teachers, the most notable ones being the *Michigan International Corpus of Academic Spoken English* (MICASE) (http://micase.elicorpora.info/) and its written counterpart, *Michigan Corpus of Upper Level Student Papers* (MICUSP) (http://micusp.elicorpora.info/), and *British Academic Spoken English Corpus* (BASE) (http://www2.warwick.ac.uk/fac/soc/al/research/collect/base/) and its written counterpart, *British Academic Written English Corpus* (BAWE) http://www2.warwick.ac.uk/fac/soc/al/research /collect/bawe/). These corpora can be considered EIL corpora insofar as the data they use were collected from both L1 and L2 users of the language, a reflection of the international make-up of the student bodies of the universities concerned.

The other primary field where English is used internationally, business, also has a range of corpora, although perhaps less readily accessible than those for academia. Bargiela-Chiappini, Nickerson, and Planken (2007) describe a number of corpus-based business teaching and learning projects, but unfortunately most of the corpora referred to are not freely available. Warren (2010), however, describes two corpora of Business and Academic English created in Hong Kong and which are freely available on the Internet: *Hong Kong Engineering Corpus* (HKEC) (http://rcpce. engl.polyu.edu.hk/HKEC/) and *Hong Kong Financial Services Corpus* (HKFSC) (http://langbank.engl.polyu.edu.hk/HKFSC/).

Another freely available Hong Kong corpus (Cheng & Warren, 2000) is the *Hong Kong Corpus of Spoken English* (HKCSE) (http://rcpce. engl.polyu.edu.hk/HKCSE/). This corpus consists of three sub-corpora: everyday conversation, spoken academic discourse, and spoken business discourse. In their initial analysis of the HKCSE, Cheng and Warren (2000) note differences in tag questions, discourse markers, inexplicitness, and vague language between the two types of speakers.

Cheng and Warren (2000) highlight a number of pedagogical implications for language learning from working with this data. First, they state that they now use the corpus as their source of authentic examples in their teaching, being able to compare the two types of usage. Second, they state that they are using the findings to make their students aware of some of the intercultural implications of, for example, the use of tag questions, discourse markers, inexplicitness, and vague language. Third, their students are using the corpus in DDL, as autonomous learners "able to identify, offer explanations, and learn from the characteristic patterns that they find in the data" (p. 144).

Principle: Make use of academic and business EIL corpora.

Cultures of Learning

An important issue that arises with EIL, where people are interacting across borders, is that of cultural compatibility. Some have claimed that EIL is culturally imperialistic (Phillipson, 1992, is the seminal text). EIL carries with it, according to this claim, cultural values associated with the Inner-Circle countries. For corpora, this means consideration of the fact that the choice of corpus may carry with it cultural implications. Inner-Circle corpora will carry certain cultural assumptions and discourse patterns (such as allusions to Shakespeare and the Bible), while Outer-Circle and Expanding-Circle corpora will carry other such assumptions.

This is one of the reasons for advocating ELF, in so far as it is free from L1 cultural influences (although this has been disputed by e.g., Phillipson, 2003, p. 170).

Another alternative is to propose a hybrid model, as already mentioned, where students are exposed to different varieties: Inner-Circle, Expanding-Circle, Outer-Circle, and ELF. At the same time, learners can be encouraged to develop an awareness of some of the cultural implications of the different varieties. Consideration might also be given to code-switching (e.g., McKay & Bokhorst-Heng, 2008, p. 165), an important feature of local varieties.

Principle: Be aware of the cultural implications of corpus selection.

Critical Language Awareness

The foregoing leads on to critical language awareness, as mentioned by McKay (this volume), but specifically from a corpus-based perspective. In a corpus-based critical EIL awareness program, students might be encouraged to compare features of different language varieties or differences between spoken and written corpora of a given variety. McKay's example of Singapore (this volume) is relevant here, where she argues that Singaporean users of English need to be made aware about the differences between Standard Singapore English and the more colloquial spoken variety, sometimes referred to as *Singlish*.

The following set of questions, adapted from Burns (2005, p. 8) for teachers, might serve as a useful starting point for a corpus-based critical EIL awareness program:

- What notions of the standard for English are dominant in your learning context? Are they different for spoken and written English?
- Why is this standard considered to be the most appropriate in your learning context?
- What attitudes exist in your local context toward varieties that are considered to be nonstandard?
- Are these varieties introduced into the classroom in any way? What kinds of discussions (might) take place in your context in relation to these varieties?
- What repertoires of standard and nonstandard English do you and people in your society use? What relative values and relevance do these repertoires have?

All of these questions can be investigated with regard to corpora. A further question which might be posed is the following:

- What strategies can you use for deciding which corpus to use for a given EIL application?

Principle: Promote critical language awareness from a corpus-based perspective.

Conclusion

This chapter has suggested an approach to corpus-based pedagogy for EIL which corresponds to the needs and wants of learners and which at the same time takes account of the sociolinguistic reality of EIL in the 21st century. While practical examples have been given, a lot of what was said is rather programmatic. This is due to two main factors. First, as many writers on EIL have noted, there remains a lot of bias in favor of L1 models of English. This bias is particularly noticeable among corpus practitioners, many of whom still subscribe to a native-speaker fallacy, where the educated native speaker is the desired standard. More awareness is needed in the field of corpus-based pedagogy about the role of English in the world today and its plurality. Second, there remains a tremendous amount of work to be done in the creation of corpora and linguistic description based on those corpora so as to represent the myriad varieties that exist. That is not to say that what has been achieved is inconsiderable.

Exploring the Ideas

1 Which model do you think should be taken as the target corpora for the learners you work with or are familiar with? Give your reasons.
2 What do you think about data driven learning (DDL)? Have you any experience of it? Do you think it would work/works in your context?
3 What is your attitude to English as a Lingua Franca? Do you think it is a valid standard for international communication? What would a Lingua Franca corpus look like in your context? How would it compare with the ELFA and VOICE corpora?
4 How important do you think it is for learning materials such as dictionaries and course books to employ corpus-based examples?

Applying the Ideas

Go online and find one or more of the corpora listed in this chapter and investigate their potential. List at least two of the advantages and disadvantages of each corpus you investigate from an EIL perspective.

References

Aijmer, K. (Ed.). (2009). *Corpora and language teaching*. Amsterdam: John Benjamins.

Bakhtin, M. M. (1981). *The dialogic imagination: four essays* (edited by M. Holquist) (C. Emerson & M. Holquist, Trans.). Austin, TX: University of Texas Press.

Bargiela-Chiappini, F., Nickerson, N., & Planken, B. (2007). *Business discourse*. Basingstoke: Palgrave Macmillan.

Barlow, M. (1996). Corpora for theory and practice. *International Journal of Corpus Linguistics, 1*(1), 1–37.

Bernardini, S. (2004). Corpora in the classroom: An overview and some reflections on future developments. In J. Sinclair (Ed.), *How to use corpora in language teaching* (pp. 15–36). Amsterdam: Benjamins.

Biber, D., Conrad, S., & Reppen, R. (1998). *Corpus linguistics: Investigating language structure and use*. Cambridge: Cambridge University Press.

Biber, D., Johansson, S., Leech, G., Conrad, S., & Finegan, E. (1999). *Longman Grammar of Spoken and Written English*. New York: Longman.

Burns, A. (2005). *Teaching English from a global perspective: Case studies in TESOL series*. Alexandria: TESOL.

Cheng, W., & Warren, M. (2000). The Hong Kong corpus of spoken English: language learning through language description. In L. Burnard & T. McEnery (Eds.), *Rethinking language pedagogy from a corpus perspective* (pp. 133–144). Frankfurt: Peter Lang.

Crystal, D. (1988). *The English language*. London: Penguin.

Flowerdew, J. (1993). Concordancing as a tool in course design. *System, 21*(2), 231–244. [Reprinted in *Small corpus studies and ELT: Theory and practice*, pp. 71–92, by M. Ghadessy, A. Henry, & R. L. Roseberry (Eds.), 2001, Amsterdam, Philadelphia: Benjamins]

Flowerdew, J. (2006). Use of signalling nouns in a learner corpus. *International Journal of Corpus Linguistics, 11*(3), 345–362.

Flowerdew, J. (2009). Corpora in language teaching. In M. H. Long & C. J. Doughty (Eds.), *The handbook of language teaching* (pp. 327–350). Wiley-Blackwell: Oxford.

Flowerdew, J. (2010). Use of signalling nouns across L1 and L2 writer corpora. *International Journal of Corpus Linguistics, 15*(1), 34–53.

Flowerdew, L. (2012). *Corpora and language education*. Basingstoke: Palgrave Macmillan.

Flowerdew, J., Li, D. C. S., & Miller, L. (2000). Chinese-speaking lecturers' perceptions, problems and strategies in lecturing in English to Chinese-speaking students. *RELC Journal, 31*(1), 116–138.

Flowerdew, J., & Miller, L. (1997). The teaching of academic listening comprehension and the question of authenticity. *English for Specific Purposes Journal, 16(*1), 27–56.

Flowerdew, J., Miller, L., & Li, D. C. S. (1998). Attitudes towards English and Cantonese among Hong Kong Chinese university Lecturers. *TESOL Quarterly, 32*(2), 201–259.

Gavioli, L. (2005). *Exploring corpora for ESP learning*. Amsterdam and Philadelphia: John Benjamins.

Ghadessy, M., Henry, A., & Roseberry, R. L. (Eds.). (2001). *Small corpus studies and ELT theory and practice*. Amsterdam: John Benjamins.

Granger, S., Dagneaux, E., Meunier, F., & Paquot, M. (2009). *International Corpus of Learner English*, Vol. 2. Presses Universitaires de Louvain: Louvain-la-Neuve, Belgium.

Harwood, N. (2002). Taking a lexical approach to teaching: principles and problems. *International Journal of Applied Linguistics, 12*(2), 139–155.

Holmes, J. (1988). Doubt and certainty in ESL textbooks. *Applied Linguistics, 9*(1), 21–44.

Hülmbauer, C., Böhringer, H., & Seidlhofer, B. (2008). Introducing English as a lingua franca (ELF): Precursor and partner in intercultural communication. In C. Cali, M. Stegu, & E. Vetter (Eds.), *Enseigner apprendre utiliser le français langue internationale en Europe au jour d'hui pour une perspective comparatiste Synergies Europe 309* (Vol. 3, pp. 25–36). Retrieved from http://ressources-cla.univ-fcomte.fr/gerflint/Europe3/hulmbauer.pdf

Hunston, S. (2002). *Corpora in applied linguistics*. Cambridge, Cambridge University Press.

Hyland, K. (1994). Hedging in academic writing and EAP textbooks. *English for Specific Purposes, 13*(3), 239–256.

Jenkins, J. (2000). *The phonology of English as an international language*. Oxford: Oxford University Press.

Jenkins, J. (2004). ELF at the gate: The position of English as a lingua franca, *European Messenger, 13*(2), pp.63–68.

Jenkins, J. (2006). Current perspectives on teaching world Englishes and English as a lingua franca. *TESOL Quarterly, 40*(1), 157–181.

Kennedy, G. (1998). *An introduction to corpus linguistics. Studies in language and linguistics*. London: Addison Wesley Longman Ltd.

Kirkpatrick, A. (2007). *World Englishes: Implications for international communication and English language teaching*. Cambridge: Cambridge University Press.

Lee, D., & Swales, J. (2006). A corpus-based EAP course for NNS doctoral students: Moving from available specialized corpora to self-compiled corpora. *English for Specific Purposes, 25*(1), 56–75.

Leech, G. (1997). Teaching and language corpora: A convergence. In A. Wichmann, S. Fligelstone, A. M. McEnery, & G. Knowles (Eds.), *Teaching and language corpora* (pp. 1–23). London and New York: Addison Wesley Longman.

Lewis, M. (1997). *Implementing the lexical approach: Putting theory into practice*. Hove: Language Teaching Publications

Mauranen, A., Hynninen, N., & Ranta, E. (2010). English as an academic lingua franca: The ELFA project. *English for Specific Purposes, 2*(9), 183–190.

McCarthy, M. (2004). *Touchstone: From corpus to course book*. Cambridge: Cambridge University Press. Retrieved from http://www.cambridge.org/other_files/downloads/esl/booklets/McCarthy-Touchstone-Corpus.pdf

McCarthy, M., McCarten, J., & Sandiford, H. (2005). *Touchstone 1–4: From corpus to course book*. Cambridge: Cambridge University Press.

McCarthy, M., & O'Dell, F. (2010). *English vocabulary in use* (2nd ed.). Cambridge: Cambridge University Press.

McEnery, T., & Wilson, A. (1996). *Corpus linguistics*. Edinburgh: Edinburgh University Press.

McKay, S. A. (2002). *Teaching English as an international language*. Oxford: Oxford University Press.

McKay, S. A., & Bokhorst-Heng, W. (2008). *International English in its sociolinguistic contexts: Towards a socially sensitive EIL pedagogy*. New York and London: Routledge.

Partington, A. (1998). *Patterns and meanings*. Amsterdam: John Benjamins.

Phillipson, R. (1992). *Linguistic imperialism*. Oxford: Oxford University Press

Phillipson, R. (2003). *English-only Europe? Challenging language policy*. London: Routledge.

Römer, U. (2008). Corpora and language teaching. In A. Lüdeling & M. Kytö (Eds.), *Corpus linguistics. An international handbook* (Vol. 4, pp. 112–130). [HSK series] Berlin: Mouton de Gruyter.

Seidlhofer, B. (2010). Lingua franca English: The European context. In A. Kirkpatrick (Ed.), *The Routledge handbook of world Englishes* (pp. 355–371). Abingdon: Routledge.

Sinclair, J. (Ed.). (1995). *Collins Cobuild English Dictionary*. London: Collins.

Sinclair, J. (Ed.). (2004). *How to use corpora in language teaching*. Amsterdam: John Benjamins.

Teubert, W. (2004). Units of meaning, parallel corpora, and their implications for language teaching. In U. Connor & T. A. Upton (Eds.), *Applied corpus linguistics: A multi-dimensional perspective* (pp. 171–189). Amsterdam: Rodopi.

Tribble, C., & Jones, G. (1990). *Concordances in the classroom*. Harlow: Longman.

Warren, M. (2010). Online corpora for specific purposes. *ICAME Journal, 34,* 169–188.

Willis, D. (1990). *The lexical syllabus: A new approach to language teaching*. London: HarperCollins.

Willis, J., & Willis, D. (1988). *Collins COBUILD English course*. London: Collins.

Chapter 14

Grammar Teaching and Standards

Anthea Fraser Gupta

Introduction

Wherever English is taught, either to people who already speak it or to people who do not, Standard English is the dialect that is taught and assessed. Standard English is the dominant dialect of English and is already a global variety. The Standard English that is taught and learned all over the world differs very little from place to place, particularly in the area of grammar. It is a single world-wide variety, but many people think—wrongly—that there are large differences in Standard English as it is used in different English-using countries. Paradoxically, because Standard English is so important, it is almost invisible—until we see something we don't like. As a result, much grammar teaching focuses on relatively rare and unimportant features of grammar about which users of English disagree, rather than on the many more areas on which they all agree.

It is essential for English, everywhere, to be taught in a way that accepts the fact that English is used all over the world, within and between communities. A global perspective is needed whoever the students are, whether they are native speakers or not, and whether or not they live in a place where English is used in daily life. Teachers and students of English need to take a global perspective, because all users of English (to varying degrees) experience English in a global context. The particular challenges for teaching Standard English are:

- How can it be established what is correct in Standard English?
- How can teachers help students to learn from the English that they see and hear?
- How can students be made to feel confident in using English and yet be corrected when they make mistakes?

In this chapter I will discuss these questions only as they apply to grammar, and will illustrate my answers by using real texts.

Definition of Standard English

"Standard English" is usually defined by its contexts of use (see Trudgill, 1999). I will begin with a definition of this sort:

> Standard English is the variety of English normally used in edited written texts. What is and what is not considered correct in Standard English is determined by the general consensus of those of its writers who are in a position to influence it.

This is a vague definition for a problematic concept. Standard English is a living dialect: something is standard if Standard English writers around the world more or less agree that it is. It is not pre-defined: usages regarded as non-standard now may become standard in 20 or 200 years from now (and vice versa).

Definition is not enough. Teachers, students, and writers need to know what the grammatical rules of Standard English are. When we see a text, we see spelling and vocabulary as well as grammar, and the whole can give a quick impression of a text's being targeted on Standard English, even if there are some mistakes—spellings or grammatical structures that the writer thinks are Standard but which are not. We can say that a text is "in Standard English" as a whole. But if a group of people look at any text closely, each of them is likely to identify some structures that they disapprove of. Different users of English will pick out different things (try it on this paragraph).

Dictionaries and grammar books both include information on grammar. Their guidance is based on the description of how English is used: rules are inferred from the texts. Reliable reference grammars based on this principle are difficult to use, however (for example, Jespersen, 1909 etc.; Quirk et al., 1972; Biber et al., 1999; Carter & McCarthy, 2006). To check whether what we have written (or read) is correct is hard for grammar. The only method that most writers have for checking that their grammar is correct is to give it to someone else to read, ideally someone regarded as especially skilled in Standard English. Many of the grammatical features that an editor changes will be those about which different users of English will disagree. Other changes will be to correct mistakes and therefore necessary to make a text correspond with agreed rules of Standard English.

If we compare the written Standard English of writers from around the world, we can see that there is general agreement about most of the grammar of Standard English. And the areas of disagreement vary more from one individual to another than they do from one region to another. There are some features of Standard English grammar that all users should be able to learn to identify. At the heart of Standard English are features of grammar that are clearly defined and easy to identify, which characterize Standard English and about which there is no disagreement. I refer to these features as being "criterial" of Standard English.

Most people seem to think that Standard English is something very remote from their own experience, the most "perfect" and most formal kind of English there is. For me, as for most linguists, the central concept of a standard variety is that it is something that English writers are all, in some circumstances, expected to do, and on which they will accept correction. It is a variety that English users are expected to have some skill in; the most common dialect of English; the only global dialect of English; the dialect taught and examined in all formal education of native and non-native speakers; the dialect that is nearly always used in writing. Far from being remote, it is ordinary English, and seen as ordinary.

Here are the opening words of two well-known texts:

> In the light of the moon a little egg lay on a leaf. One Sunday morning the warm sun came up and—pop!—out of the egg came a tiny and very hungry caterpillar. He started to look for some food. On Monday he ate through one apple. But he was still hungry.
> (Eric Carle, *The Very Hungry Caterpillar*)

> The basic chemical formula of DNA is now fairly well established. It is a very long chain molecule formed by the joining together of complex monomeric units called nucleotides. Four main types of nucleotides are found in DNA, and it is probable that their sequence along a given chain is irregular.
> (Crick & Watson, 1954)

The children's story has shorter, simpler sentences than the article in the academic journal. In the Carle extract, all but one verb (*to look*) is simple past tense (*lay, came, started, ate, was*), while the academic article has a greater variety of types of verbs, including four passives (*is … established, formed, called, are found*). The differences we see here—and would see more of if we compared the full texts—are differences of choice within Standard English. It is vital to understand that differences of frequency (such as the proportion of verbs that are passives) have nothing to do with determining whether or not a text is written in Standard English. What matters is whether the choices are among those that are possible in Standard English.

Nothing in these extracts indicates the geographical origin of the authors, or the place of publication. Many Standard English texts do give such information, though sparingly, and seldom through grammar. There are almost no categorical grammatical differences among the Standard English writing of different regions of the world. What is Standard English grammar in Nigeria is (almost entirely) Standard English grammar in Canada (and vice versa).

There is, however, considerable variation within Standard English depending on the text type. The most extreme grammatical differences in grammar are found in some written text types that use an abbreviated form of Standard English. These include newspaper headlines, SMS messages, postcards, and small advertisements in which the grammar is very different indeed from what I could call "ordinary Standard English grammar" ("Leaving soon"; "Car for sale"; "Add asparagus; stir-fry until crisp-tender"). Most users of English are well aware of these abbreviated text types and know how they are related to ordinary Standard English. The most common grammatical features of abbreviated texts are:

- omission of first person subjects;
- omission of articles: *the* and *a(n)* are not used;
- omission of BE from contexts where it is required in other Standard English text types.

There has been a great deal of publicity given to the use of abbreviated English in SMS messages, but abbreviated English is nothing new. It just so happens that SMS is a new text type that uses abbreviated grammar, as telegrams once did. Students need to know that it is appropriate in some contexts but not others. The rest of my discussion is about ordinary Standard English.

Regional Variation in Standard English Grammar?

Sociolinguists began to study English as a world language in the 1960s, at a time when the United Kingdom of Great Britain and the United States of America were seen as the sources of Standard English. Even Australian and New Zealand English had to fight for legitimacy. Features associated with the English of places like Singapore, India, and Nigeria were seen as "interference" errors. This view is not entirely absent from the world today, but it is now widely accepted that the English of former colonies, where the population are mostly not of European ancestry, has its own legitimacy and a right to its own standards of language use.

Most of the sociolinguists (such as Moag, 1982; Kachru, 1985, 1992) who first considered English as a global language wanted to raise the status of the English of Britain's former colonies. We analyzed texts from various countries and identified what we thought were differences from "British" or "American" Standard English (e.g., Gupta, 1986). We often argued for local acceptance of these features as Standard. We tended to refer to Standard English*es*, and attempted to identify and promote, for example, Nigerian Standard English, New Zealand Standard English, or Indian Standard English. We focused on the differences that we thought existed between the Standard English in one place and that in another. (Gupta [2010] explains why I have rejected this earlier approach.)

Since those days the Internet has made available to everyone a wide range of written texts of all types, from most of the world. Two things have become apparent:

1 Many of the differences we once thought were categorical are in fact differences of frequency: we were comparing real texts from one place with an imagined ideal grammar from the UK or the USA.
2 The differences that are identified in descriptions of, for example, Standard Singapore English, account for a very small proportion of the total text.

When we do make a direct comparison, using a large corpus or database, or using the web as a corpus, we find that the grammar of the Standard English of one place is virtually identical to the grammar of the Standard English of another. There are statistical differences in terms of preferences: for example, the present perfective (e.g., "I have seen her") is more frequent in proportion to the past tense ("I saw her") in UK English and Australian English than in US English. But it is almost impossible to identify grammatical features that are regarded as correct in one place and incorrect in another (examples of texts taking this approach include Schmied, 1997; Biber et al., 1999, many papers in Modiano, 2002; Gupta, 2006a, 2006b, 2010).

Standard English is so assumed it is almost invisible to most readers. As a result, a single mistake will be highly salient. For instance, in the sentence "As I was watched her in the kitchen, she fried the chicken meat first and set it aside," the mistake ("was watched") will take on more importance than the other 277 words of entirely Standard English in the text from which it comes. Readers will also notice choices within Standard English that differ from the choices they would make themselves, some of which will also loom larger than is warranted.

It is common to read about "American Standard English" and "British Standard English." This refers to little more than a small number of spelling differences (e.g., *colo(u)r*), amounting to less than 0.5% of words in most texts. In grammar, there are almost no real differences. By focusing on features they regard as distinctive, or the small number of things that vary from one place to another, sociolinguists have also given the impression that countries like Nigeria and Singapore use a Standard English that is more different from (for example) British Standard English than it actually is. The intention was to raise the status of former colonies, but in some cases this impression has given both locals and foreigners the impression that the English in such places is far from Standard English, and has created a negative impression (e.g., "He's Indian. So his English will be a bit off.").

Many of the differences identified as being grammatical features of local varieties of Standard English turn out either to be present more widely world wide (perhaps with varying rates of frequency). The differences in grammar between the (written) Standard English of different countries is not sufficient to justify there being several Standard Englishes: it is better for all teachers and learners to think of Standard English as a single dialect. In the next section I will indicate some of the areas of grammar where Standard English is clearly defined.

Criterial Features of Standard English

For teacher and student alike, a sound knowledge of four areas of grammar will help in developing a clear idea of what is and what is not Standard:

1 Inflectional morphology
2 The structure of the verb
3 Interrogatives with DO
4 Negation.

In these areas Standard English is strict and unified across the world.

1 *Inflectional morphology.* Changes in the shape of the word depending on the grammatical role. In English there are such changes in form in nouns, pronouns, and verbs. For example: *Cat / cats / cat's / cats'; Child / children / child's / children's; I / me / my / mine; dance / dances / danced; see /sees / saw / seeing / seen.*
2 *The structure of the complex verb.* The verb is at the heart of every clause. One verb group in Standard English can have from none to four auxiliaries before the lexical verb. The verbs in the chain must be arranged in a specific order and each of them must have a specific form. For example: *was eaten; can swim; is finding; had seen; might have watched; should have been being monitored.*
3 *Interrogatives with DO.* In Standard English the way in which interrogatives are created is unusually complicated, involving changing the order of part of the verb and the subject (inversion) and, in most cases, inserting a particular form of the verb DO. For example: *are you; can you swim; did you swim.* Note that this is not the only way of forming questions in Standard English.

4 *Negation.* Negation with *not* is complex in Standard English, and also involves inserting a particular form of DO in some types of verb group (for example: *I swim* negates to *I do not swim*). Standard English negation is also linked with a change of *some* to *any*, so that "I want some" negates to "I do not want any." Many languages, and many other dialects of English, use multiple negative words to emphasize negativity (as in "I don't want none, nohow") but Standard English does not reinforce negativity in this way.

In all of these areas there is almost no variation within Standard English. The only variation of which I am aware is in a few irregular verbs where there is choice in the form of either the past tense or the past participle or both (for example, *learned / learnt; got / gotten; dived / dove*). Both forms can be found in many regions, though particular places may have a preference for one or the other. For example, *dove* is more popular as the past tense of *dive* in the USA than in most other places, but both forms can be found side by side in many single locations.

Teachers in areas with a vigorous local dialect need to be aware of the non-standard grammar in their own region and will need to explain to the students what the differences are in these areas. Students should be encouraged to use their local dialect forms in appropriate contexts, such as in dialogue or poetry. Even learners of English living in a place where English is not used will come across examples of non-standard dialects. As soon as they can, most learners, even very young ones, will start using English and will see and hear varieties of English other than Standard English. They need to know that other dialects are not wrong and that creative writers often use non-standard dialects in addition to Standard English. Many songs have lyrics and titles that are entirely or partly in dialects other than Standard English. A clear understanding of what the basic structures of Standard English are will allow students to learn from what they read and hear.

Students should get ample opportunity to create and analyze texts, and, wherever they are from, should be exposed to non-standard grammar too, so that they can learn what is and what is not Standard. The following examples (all real ones) are definitely Standard English:

- I've seen him.
- The engine is turning over.
- She should arrive soon.
- We have been attacked.
- Who did you see?
- I did not have any problem.
- What did you think of it?
- They did not have any bananas.

The following (also real ones) definitely do not follow the grammar of Standard English (parts that do not follow the rules are italicized):

- I have *went* off on quite a few related tangents.
- You *might could* have a problem.
- I *was watched* her.
- He has *finish*.
- We *done* it for the kids.
- Where did she *went*?
- They *never* had *no* future.
- Who *say mi done*?

If you are aiming for Standard English and you do not get the rules right in these four areas, you will have made a mistake. A sentence with "I have went off ..." *might* be a mistake or not. Sometimes writers are not aiming for Standard English. Anyone who writes "Who say mi done?" is *certainly* not aiming for Standard English: Cutty Ranks made a conscious effort to write his song in Jamaican Patwa.

Learning from speech presents even more problems than learning from reading. Speakers have greater freedom than do writers. The grammatical structures of speech are very different from the grammar of writing (more about this in recent accounts of the grammar of English, such as Biber et al., 1999; Carter, 2004; Carter & McCarthy, 2006). Some structures that are used in speech are seldom or never used in writing, and vice versa. For example, in speech there are discourse markers (including expressions like *thank you, yes, OK, you know, isn't it, Well, ...*) that are rare in most written text types (except those that represent dialogue). Some grammatical structures are impossible in writing, like this example (collected by Sarah Castell in the UK during research for MA degree):

> the good ones you want to dance and the bad ones you just want to like cut yourself off

If we translated this into written Standard English grammar it would be something like "You want to dance to the good ones and you just want to cut yourself off from the bad ones" or "When you hear the good ones you want to dance and when you hear the bad ones you just want to cut yourself off." In the spoken version, the two noun phrases ("the good ones"/"the bad ones") have been put in the prominent first position, so that they become the topic of the sentence, functioning almost as a heading—"this is what I'm going to talk about." This kind of topic-comment structure is seldom used in written English, but is common in speech. In speech too, there is more regional variation, including some in grammar, than there is in writing. The freedoms found in speech make it harder for those learning English to learn from what they hear than to learn from what they read. Students need to be warned to expect a wide range of grammar in speech. However, the criterial features discussed above are shared with what we might call Standard English speech.

My focus in this section has been on the criterial structures of Standard English, which do not allow for variation. However, there are areas where there is choice and variation, and also areas where there is disagreement about what is and what is not Standard. It is to these areas I will move on next.

Areas of Dispute Within Standard English

Because users of English are so much agreed on the grammar of Standard English, they tend to discuss most those areas where they are not in agreement. In this section, I outline two areas (not entirely separate from each other) in which there is dispute:

1 Verb group choice
2 The purist tradition.

It is my view that in the past we have paid too much attention to these areas at the expense of those areas on which there is agreement.

The form of the verb is strict in Standard English. But there is another issue relating to the verb which is less clear cut, and where there is choice within Standard English. In this area, not all users of Standard English agree on what is right and what is wrong. When does a speaker or writer use a present perfective (*has/have*+past participle) rather than a past tense? What about the choice between a present continuous (*am/is/are* + present participle) and a present tense?

The longest possible verb phrase is of five verbs, as in this real example, from a medical journal published in Chicago:

all patients should have been being managed under SARS precautions

The very long verb group in the example above is not the only one that could have occurred in the same context: another writer might have written "all patients *should have been managed* under SARS precautions." The original writers chose to add the progressive aspect (*being managed*), but it is not required. Both choices are probably available to most writers of Standard English, and no-one would regard either alternative as wrong. It is essential for all students, and especially for non-native learners of English, to realize that there are areas of choice within Standard English.

I will give just a few examples of some of the contexts where many users of English have a choice in the type of verb group. All the verb groups here are constructed following the criterial rules for form. In some cases, some individuals may be able to use all the alternatives. In other cases, different people may regard one or more as impossible for them. Some people will disapprove of the use of some of the alternatives in particular contexts. All seem to be present to lesser or greater extents across the English-using world. I supply them in what seems to be the order of frequency on the web, using the precise words that I have supplied in quotation marks in Google searches: Note that different sentences may give different frequencies for the same grammatical alternatives. I would urge all readers to try out a few alternatives of this sort and reflect on the validity of the findings.

- I have a cold. (clearly the most common)
- I have got a cold.
- I am having a cold.

- Did they give you a map? (the most common)
- Have they given you a map? (a strong runner up)

- This is the first time I am wearing it. (the most common world wide, probably because of the high frequency of captions on photographs)
- This is the first time I have worn it. (good runner up and most common alternative in some places)
- This is the first time I wear it. (rare)
- This is the first time I wore it. (rare—occasionally used when describing a photograph)

- I go there tomorrow. (all alternatives very common: patterns differ in main and dependent clauses)
- I'll go there tomorrow.
- I'm going to go there tomorrow.
- I'll be going there tomorrow.
- I'm going there tomorrow.

- Can I watch television? (the most common)
- May I watch television? (a strong second)
- Could I watch television? (also common)
- Might I watch television? (rare)

In a situation where there is choice, the differences in meaning (if any) between alternatives can be subtle. These choices are paid a lot of attention in language learning where, in some curricula, the rules for using them are made to seem much clearer than they are in real use. This can lead to students being surprised when they see real texts that appear to violate the grammar they have been taught at school. For instance, many learners of English are taught that the past tense must be used after "since" in sentences like "It is a long time since I saw her." Using the past tense in this context will seldom result in an incorrect sentence, but the present perfect ("It is a long time since I have seen her") is frequent and equally standard. Other students may (wrongly) be taught that "Did you bring a map?" is incorrect in British English. This is an area where teaching needs to come up to speed with reality.

There are some choices that are more frequent in the English of South Asia than in other regions (e.g., "I am having a cold"). I see no reason to reject such choices as part of Standard English. Notice that the grammar of the verb is the same as it is all over the world: the only difference is the context in which that structure might be used.

The purist tradition in English has caused a good deal of confusion in classrooms and has been criticized by many linguists (such as Wardaugh, 1999). All over the world in English classrooms, too much attention is paid to a few usages that are regarded as incorrect by some users. The rules are linked to the normative or purist tradition of English, which is an effort (going back to the 1700s) to give Standard English a stricter grammar than it actually has. For many native speakers of English, this is what "grammar" is. A great deal of attention is paid to invented rules such as "A sentence must not begin with *but*" and "do not split an infinitive." Sentences beginning with *but* can be found in the most formal and carefully written texts all over the world as can sentences with so-called "split infinitives," such as "We need to slowly decrease the amount." Purists may not like them, but they are Standard English, and students should not be told they are incorrect. A fourteen-year-old British pupil may be able to repeat "You should not start a sentence with 'but'" yet be unable to articulate the rule for choosing between "forget" and "forgets." But in Standard English sentences can begin with "but," while the choice between "forget" and "forgets" is a strong rule. Advanced students should discuss the purist tradition and need to know that it exists, but when it comes to teaching and marking, the focus should be on Standard English as it is, not as some people think it ought to be.

All teachers of English need to pay the greatest attention to areas of grammar where the rules are clear and the same across the world. They also need to tell their students that there are many areas of choice within Standard English. At an advanced level, they need to make their students aware of the nature of some of the disputes within Standard English.

In the Classroom

In all formal education, Standard English is taught and examined. English is not unusual in this: standard dialects emerge when languages are written. Standard dialects are functional in that they help communication over wide areas and neutralize many social features that we cannot help but convey in speech (especially regional origin). The tradition is that children who come to school knowing English (speakers of English) must learn to read and write Standard English, whatever dialect(s) they speak, and that those who do not yet know English (learners of English) are taught to speak Standard English as well as to read and write it. I am not aware of any serious suggestion from either political or academic sources to cease teaching Standard English. Many sociolinguists (including myself) have called for non-standard dialects to have a place in education, and to be respected. This is not to suggest that they would replace Standard English in schools. Standard English has wide currency and prestige and a student who was denied access to it would be cheated.

The main focus of formal teaching of Standard English grammar, even to learners, is generally on the written language, which is understandable given the very different grammar of speech. It is appropriate that learners of English in places where English is not locally used are taught a plain Standard English style for both writing and speech. Where a learner is in an educational setting alongside speakers, that learner will acquire local forms of English from schoolmates. As long as there is adequate opportunity for such a learner to socialize with speakers of English, it should not be the responsibility of formal instruction to teach the grammar of any local dialect.

Many speakers of English are exposed to both Standard and non-standard dialects. For example, I studied Singaporean children acquiring English as a native language (Gupta, 1994), who were initially exposed mainly to a non-standard dialect of English, commonly called Singlish. But their parents and other family members knew Standard English as well as Singlish, and were in the habit of reading aloud to them in Standard English. As their children began formal schooling (from the age of three years) the parents began to use more Standard English in the home, especially in contexts they saw as educational. The children clearly demonstrated that they distinguished the non-standard dialect from the standard dialect in their own usage by the age of four. Other studies of children growing up in other societies where a non-standard dialect of English operates alongside Standard English have shown a similar early awareness and use of Standard English. In Trinidad, Youssef's subjects demonstrated this kind of switching before their third birthday (Youssef, 1991, 1993). Children can be bidialectal, and it is likely that virtually all children who are exposed to a non-standard dialect are also exposed to Standard English, because Standard English is so pervasive that it is a part of every community of English speakers, and every home where English is spoken. I know of no English-using community from which Standard English is absent: such a community would have to have no-one in it who was literate in English, no books, no visual, or sound media. Speakers acquire skills in English from formal and informal teaching and from exposure to the Standard English in ordinary life.

Where pupils are either native speakers of English or live in a community where English is widely used, they do not seem to find it hard to separate the grammar of Standard English from that of their local dialect, if there is one. Children are also learning the very different text types associated with writing, and seem to associate the written forms with the text type. The written forms of the local dialect seldom appear as errors in children's writing. For example, a child (or adult) in Leeds (UK) may always say "He were" rather than the Standard English "He was"; the same child will almost always write "He was." Similarly, in Singapore, children who use the very different grammar of Singlish in much of their speech ("kena flu") almost never write with its distinctive grammar when targeting Standard English ("I caught flu"). Speakers of other dialects should not be told that their grammar is "bad." Even young children can understand local dialects have their own grammar which is different from that of Standard English and can learn to discriminate them.

Students need to know what is a hard and fast rule for Standard English and what is not. The reason English is so successfully learned today is that learners want to use it. Most learners (especially if they have access to a computer) have the opportunity to use English in a real situation once they have the basics. Even very young children outside the Anglophone world rapidly gain access to the world of English use. Learners are often able to access books, online activities, and entertainment media that use English.

This is to be encouraged. But once learners are in the real world of English use, they will be exposed to a range of usages and they need to be navigated through the complexities of usage. They may find it hard to understand that what is appropriate in one context is not appropriate in another. Students need to be encouraged towards a confident use of English, so that they can use English without feeling that they have to write perfectly. On the other hand, the teacher is responsible for correcting their errors, and for guiding them to write in styles appropriate for context.

Students should not experience a gap between situated and social learning and the learning of the classroom. The classroom must be flexible enough to cope. Students cannot and should not be protected from real English. Having an opportunity to speak and write in a context where the focus is not on correctness, but on getting the message across, will stretch students to produce more and to experiment with language. Their English will improve as a result of use and adventure. Wherever English is taught, there should be some classroom opportunity to use English in a context where effort rather than correctness will be rewarded. Students can also reflect on what they have written and compare what they have written to the writing of others.

It is appropriate for textbooks for learners of English to teach rules similar to the one about verb choice after "since." Such rules can help learners to avoid errors. It is appropriate too to drill students in correct sentences and to ask them to select between correct and incorrect choices in an assessment. But in these pedagogic contexts, it is essential that Standard and disputed alternatives should never be marked "wrong," even if they are not the structure that has been taught. If alternatives are supplied, only one should be Standard English, such as:

Complete the sentence with the verb that is correct:

It is a long time since I _____ *her.*

    is seeing

    have saw

    saw

    seen

If learners of English are too inhibited by a focus on correctness, they may be afraid of using the language. This applies to all kinds of learners, from monolingual native speakers of English in (for example) Sydney, through bilingual English and Tamil speakers in Chennai, to learners of English outside Anglophony in São Paulo. They must learn from their experience in the ocean of English. If the "school English" is different (more purist, perhaps) than the real English that they see, students will be confused. They may reject their teaching.

There should be some scope in the classroom for analyzing real texts, and especially for discussing the grammatical differences between different text types. One thing speakers and learners alike need to learn is that correctness matters more in some contexts than in others. The tools of grammatical analysis should be used to identify patterns in texts and differences between different kinds of text types. It is vital to know that there are choices for all speakers.

Educators and older students can explore alternatives (not just those in verb choice) in order to try to discover the patterns of use. Students can be guided in their exploration, the aim being to show them where variation within Standard English is possible and where it is not. The analysis of abbreviated Standard English can be valuable because the insertion of elements to convert an abbreviated text into ordinary Standard English helps develop analytic skills.

The texts that are analyzed should be situated in the real world of English. Children should be exposed to literature for children and to factual writing. They should be encouraged to interact socially in the international world of English. It is pointless to require students to follow rules that they see violated all around them, and is damaging to "correct" students when they write sentences that they see in use in Standard English texts. It is also unnecessary and unhelpful to teach learners English in a way that suggests that they will use English only in specific restricted contexts or places. No-one can predict where and to whom a learner will use English now or in the future. For many learners the global world of English is right there on their phones.

Conclusion

All teachers should have a clear focus on the criterial areas of Standard English grammar. It is important to know from an early stage of learning that there are also zones of choice within Standard English. Every time a teacher marks as incorrect a usage which is actually Standard English, that teacher has failed the student. Students can be helped to learn from what they read and hear by the guided analysis of texts. They should be taught basic grammatical analysis and then shown how to analyze texts of different types in order to identify differences and similarities. They should be told that writers and speakers are often playful, and that this playfulness includes the deliberate use of non-standard English. Understanding the areas of choice and having some analytic tools to identify Standard English grammar will help them to produce texts appropriate for their context.

Exploring the Ideas

1 What dialects of English other than Standard English are your students likely to see or hear? Where? How does the grammar of these dialects differ in the four criterial areas of grammar discussed in this chapter?
2 Would you wish to show your students Standard English texts from a variety of regions? What are the advantages and/or disadvantages of doing this?
3 To what extent have your students mastered the four criterial areas of grammar discussed in this chapter? What mistakes do they make? What other areas of grammar do you consider need close attention?

Applying the Ideas

1 *Different styles for different text types.* Select a picture or a very short sequence of pictures that tell a story. Students imagine that they experienced the events portrayed and then have to write about what they saw—for two different readerships. For example, in a workshop with 14-year olds I presented a picture of a man falling off a bicycle and an x-ray image of a broken arm. The students had to imagine that they had seen the incident on the way to school. They were told to write (a) a text message to a friend and (b) a letter to the school principal explaining why they were late to school that day. The class then discussed the differences in the language used in the two text types.

2 *Developing analytic skills and identifying non-standard features.* In a question where the teacher supplies a text, questions should always be specific and directed, and should relate to what has been taught. The focus should always be on specific features. Select a text that includes a large number of categorical non-standard features. There are many such texts online, which you can find by targeted online searches. Some of them are texts carefully written in a specific dialect. To find these either try a search for "dialect poetry," or search for words or phrases that you know to be used in a specific dialect, such as (for Singlish) *kiasu* and *kena*. Others are texts written by learners of English in international online forums. It is important to emphasize to students that communication by learners can be good even if the English is not perfect. It is easy to come across these either by searching for subjects of international interest (such as travel, gardening, dog-breeding, motorbikes) or by searching for errors of the kind commonly made by learners of English, such as "didn't came" or "was finish soon": where one of these errors is made, a text will usually have several. In both kinds of texts, ask the student to (a) identify and classify the non-standard features, and (b) explain why these non-standard features are used.

References

Biber, D., Johansson, S., Leech, G., Conrad, S., & Finegan, E. (1999). *Longman grammar of spoken and written English*. London: Longman.

Carle, E. (1969). *The very hungry caterpillar*. New York: Collins.

Carter, R. (2004). *Language and creativity: The art of common talk*. London: Routledge.

Carter, R., & McCarthy, M. (2006). *Cambridge grammar of English*. Cambridge: Cambridge University Press.

Crick, F. H. C., & Watson, J. D. (1954). The complementary structure of deoxyribonucleic acid. *Proceedings of the Royal Society of London Series A, Mathematical and Physical Sciences, 223*, 80–96.

Gupta, A. F. (1986). A standard for written Singapore English? *English World-Wide, 7*(1), 75–99.

Gupta, A. F. (1994). *The step-tongue: Children's English in Singapore*. Clevedon: Multilingual Matters.

Gupta, A. F. (2006a). Standard English in the world. In R. Rubdy & M. Saraceni (Eds.), *English in the world: Global rules, global roles* (pp. 95–109). London: Continuum.

Gupta, A. F. (2006b). Standard English and Borneo. *Southeast Asia: A Multidisciplinary Journal 6*(1), 79–94 (Special Volume of Selected Papers from The Tenth Conference on English in Southeast Asia).

Gupta, A. F. (2010). Singapore standard English revisited. In L. Lim, A. Pakir, & L. Wee (Eds.), *English in Singapore: Unity and utility* (pp. 57–89). Hong Kong University Press.

Jespersen, O. (1909 etc.) (repr 1948). *A modern English grammar on historical principles* (Vols. 1–7). London/Copenhagen: George Allen & Unwin/Munksgaard.

Kachru, B. B. (1985). Standards, codification and sociolinguistic realism: The English language in the outer circle. In R. Quirk & H. G. Widdowson (Eds.), *English in the world: Teaching and learning the language and literatures* (pp. 11–30). Cambridge: Cambridge University Press.

Kachru, B. B. (1992). World Englishes: Approaches, issues and resources. *Language Teaching, 25*, 1–14.

Moag, R. (1982). English as a foreign, second, native and basal language: a new taxonomy of English-using societies. In J. B. Pride (Ed.), *New Englishes* (pp. 11–50). Rowley, MA: Newbury House.

Modiano, M. (Ed). (2002). *Studies in mid-Atlantic English*. Gävle: University of Gävle Press.

Quirk, R., Greenbaum, S., Leech, G., & Svartvik, J. (1972). *A grammar of contemporary English*. London: Longman.

Schmied, J. (1997). Beyond recipes, beyond Maks, beyond Africa. Texts, text-types, text collections and African realities. In E. W. Schneider (Ed.), *Englishes around the world: Studies in honour of Manfred Görlach. Volume 2: Caribbean, Africa, Asia, Australasia* (pp. 141–158). Amsterdam/Philadelphia: John Benjamins.

Trudgill, P. (1999). Standard English: what it isn't. In T. Bex & R. Watts (Eds.), *Standard English: The widening debate* (pp. 117–128). London: Routledge.

Wardaugh, R. (1999). *Proper English*. London: Blackwell.

Webster, N. (1789). An essay on a reformed mode of spelling. Appendix to *Dissertations on the English language: with notes, historical and critical*. Boston, MA: for the author. Retrieved from *Eighteenth Century Collections Online*. Gale Group. 0-galenet.galegroup.com. wam. leeds .ac.uk:80/servlet/ECCO

Youssef, V. (1991). Variation as a feature of language acquisition in the Trinidad context. *Language, Variation and Change, 3*, 75–101.

Youssef, V. (1993). Children's linguistic choices: audience design and societal norms. *Language in Society, 22*, 257–274.

Chapter 15

Principles and Practices for Teaching English as an International Language
Teaching Critical Reading

Catherine Wallace

Introduction

What is the role of reading within an English language teaching pedagogy tailored to the demands of the 21st century? This chapter examines the role of critical reading in the teaching of English for the global age, charting the development from skills based views of reading to those which take a more sociocultural emphasis. This leads in turn to what we might mean by "critical reading." I shall argue that the position of English as the world's major language for the foreseeable future means that it becomes ever more important to teach English language learners worldwide to read critically. Robert Scholes (1985) noted more than twenty years ago that

> in an age of manipulation, when our students are in dire need of critical strength to resist the continuing assaults of all the media, the worst thing we can do is foster in them an attitude of reverence before texts.
>
> (p. 16)

Since then English language texts—now including online English-medium print media—have achieved global reach. Currently, the UK newspaper the *Daily Mail* is the most widely read online newspaper in the world. One consequence of this commercial domination is a need to alert students to the option of resistance to powerful and pervasive texts.

Reading English language texts is one means for second language learners of English to access and develop critical and creative competence, with a view to participating in the global debates of the age. And in taking a critical perspective to the teaching of reading in English, we need to attend to discourse as much as to the forms and everyday uses of the language. Following Foucault (e.g., 1972), I use the term discourse here to refer to the uses of language which typify social situations, phenomena, and values linked to the institutional bases of a society. Thus there are culturally recognizable ways of talking/writing about marriage, the relationships between men and women, the family, work, medicine, and education. These discourses are routinely embedded in texts of all kinds, including the English language textbook which, for many learners of English, may be the first introduction to the supposed values, attitudes, and behavior of members of English speaking societies. Gray (2002) talks about the course book as "an ambassador" for a particular way of life, in its implicit claim to typify the mores of the countries of "the center" which continue to feature in textbooks, marketed and used globally, even while grounded in the topics and discourses emanating from the center. If one scrutinizes this material, it is striking that the anodyne images of Britain, or of other center countries, bear little resemblance to a grittier reality. Gray (2010, p. 102) notes, for instance, how in *Headway*, the archetypal global English language course book, the world of work is represented as entirely a matter of personal choice. While the latest version of *Headway* (Soars & Soars, 2009) makes passing reference to low paid work, the difficulty of gaining any work at all for many social groups around the world is not contemplated. The key reading text in the unit on "the working week" is "The Life of a Hard-Working Future King," referring to Prince Charles, which says little about what most of us would call work. In general, the discourses within such texts operate to privilege the wealthy over the poor, the young over the old, white people over black, and the cultural insider over the outsider, often the foreigner.

Artifacts such as *Headway* perpetuate the Western dominance of the traditional textbook even in an age when English language users internationally look to forms and uses of English that reflect local settings and local cultural values and practices. This is not to propose a narrow focus on the local, exclusively privileging students' familiar cultural practices and English language use; rather I want to argue that our language teaching practices and materials can aim to span the local and the global. In short, with the world-wide flow of information, discourses and the phenomena they represent may be locally inflected but have global reach. These include political protest, changes of national government and regimes, and the environment. One global discourse relates to immigration, as people cross borders in the pursuit of work and the escape from injustice or persecution; another relates to the supply of global resources, such as water, clean air, and land which are unequally distributed world-wide. Critical reading pedagogy, the theme of this chapter, centers around the texts and discourses which embody these global events and phenomena. Because critical reading aims to challenge conventional choices of texts for teaching and ways of reading which privilege the center-based native speaker, it has particular resonance for the teaching of English internationally, where both texts and readers are coming from a range of different perspectives and where learners have different needs, knowledge, and cultural assumptions.

In this chapter I shall discuss some of the ways in which learners of all levels of English can be supported in their critical reading of globally oriented texts and discourses. In doing so, while I shall continue to talk of "reading" as the act of engaging with particular texts, I see reading, especially critical reading, as situated within sets of sociocultural practices which are covered by the broader term "literacy."

Traditional Practices and Principles in the Teaching of Reading

An Incremental View

Learning to read has tended to be seen as an incremental process both in first and second language reading. Conceptualized as a development from decoding to comprehension, early reading instruction has traditionally focused on form and meaning as evidenced in the grapho/phonic form of words or sentence structure; with more advanced learners of English this gives way to the so-called four skills view of language teaching, which is predicated on a natural teaching sequence with the oral skills, listening and speaking, having priority over reading and writing. Neglected is the fact that reading may be acquired in advance of speaking in some learning contexts and that experience of reading and writing has a washback effect on spoken English, especially for formal use.

Skills and Strategies

Skills and strategies are differently conceptualized by reading educators. Those of a more holistic turn favor an emphasis on strategies as the intentional use by readers of cognitive, metacognitive, and linguistic resources over the teaching of skills learned transmissively and in fairly mechanical ways (see, for example, the discussion in Goodman, 1996). In L2 reading theory, the dichotomy is presented differently: Skills tend to be characterized as developing out of strategies. Influential reading theorists, such as Grabe, posit a progression from strategies to skills. As Grabe puts it: "strategies are cognitive processes that are open to conscious reflection but that may be on their way to becoming skills" (Grabe, 2009, p. 221).

The Strategic Reader

If we see the use of strategies as not merely a staging post to automatization, but as suggestive of greater agency for the reader, then reader strategies are continually in play by both emerging and proficient readers. Readers who are new to the second language and in some cases to reading itself, may be working harder as language processers, drawing on all the cues in text, graphophonic, structural, semantic, and pragmatic (Goodman, 1967, 1996). More proficient readers will draw on macro strategies such as scanning or skimming, the use of headings, titles, and indices. In language teaching materials, since the 1980s, a strategy approach has been implemented through pre- and while-reading activities which prime or prompt readers with linguistic and world knowledge to approach the text initially and, in the course of reading, to maintain an active engagement with it (see, for example, Wallace, 1992). Seeing reading as the deployment of strategies, albeit in rather different ways, fits with a critical orientation to text, as I set out later in this chapter.

The Sociocultural Challenge

Earlier versions of the teaching of reading, whether focused on strategies or skills, envisaged the lone reader engaged with the print text. In the 1980s, this view was challenged by literacy ethnographers, most notably Shirley Brice Heath (1983), who investigated the literacy practices of three socioeconomic communities in the United States, documenting their diverse, culturally inflected "ways with words." On this view, reading and writing are seen as social, culturally variable practices, embedded in everyday activities and social need. We read as members of communities. Influenced by the ground breaking work of Heath, Street (1984) and others, such as Barton and Hamilton (1998), shifted the focus away from reading and writing processes in formal instructional contexts to anthropological investigations of literacy as situated practice within communities of use.

Social Practices and Social Roles

The New Literacy Studies, as the literacy ethnography movement came to be known, offered a fresh way of looking at the reader in a sociocultural context, and continues to develop powerful studies of literacy as practice (see, for example, Baynham & Prinsloo, 2009). Nonetheless, the need remained for a model of reading which looked at the sociocultural *processes* involved in the actual act of reading and learning to read. Freebody and Luke (2003) provide this through their conceptualization of the reader as taking on sets of social roles, as they make use of four key resources for tackling text. They call these the roles of code breaker, text participant, text user, and text analyst. That is, readers need to decode—to make sense of the marks on the page—

participate in the text by drawing on knowledge of the world, and, as users of text, to see texts as having a range of practical uses beyond those of schooling. The fourth role, of particular relevance here, is that of the reader as text analyst. One feature of critical reading, as I set out below, is the ability and willingness to *analyze* the intentions and effects of texts.

A Social View of Text: Genre

At the same time as the reader is socially located within a particular community and society, he or she is also responding to texts as artifacts which are themselves socioculturally configured. Genres, whether spoken or written, are socioculturally recognizable. Reading the opening of the text below we immediately recognize its source, purpose, and context.

> With your help, we can bring the gift of friendship to an isolated and lonely older person who could be spending the festive season with only the television for company.

With only three lines of text we are able to recognize the genre of this text, that is its sociocultural purpose. Genre relates to the job a text is doing, which members of the reading community recognize. So we are able to recognize whether a text is a recipe, a report, or a short story. In this case we have little difficulty seeing that this is a request from a charity. Moreover, genre is tied to context of situation. We expect a ticket collector to give us a ticket and not a theater program. Thus the charity appeal is part of a deluge of mail which reaches our homes at certain times of the year, such as at Christmas, in western Christian societies.

Finally, genres are culturally specific. Though some may cross cultural boundaries, genres are usually defined and categorized differently in different cultural contexts. The genre of charity appeals is familiar to those who live in prosperous societies and who are part of perceived well-off communities within these.

Practices and Principles for an Alternative Framework for the Teaching of Reading in International Contexts

Reading as a Sociocultural, Interpretative Process: Identity, Disposition, and Stance

While building broadly on a social view of reading, I want to propose a more nuanced, flexible role for the reader, as enacting a complex and shifting set of identities, dispositions, and stances by which reading becomes more a matter of interpretation than comprehension, as traditionally conceived. This view of the reader, first sits better with an understanding of the reader of English in international contexts as coming from a wide range of cultural settings, and with diverse purposes and reader identities. Second, it offers a useful bridge into a conceptualization of what we might mean by the *critical* reader.

Reader identities link with social identities. One may read as a Muslim, member of the Green Party or a professional trade union, as an expert or novice in the field of knowledge. Identity allegiances, linked to gender, nation, social class, or religion, come into play both in what we opt to read in the first place and how we process text. What is salient for a reader is in part related to the identities invoked. In a study of literacy and identity in an urban London school, two boys of Sri Lankan Tamil heritage were asked about their interpretation of the *Merchant of Venice* (see Wallace, 2008). Asked whether they might sympathize with the character of Shylock, they noted by way of reply the moment when Bassanio encourages Shylock to eat pork as of particular significance. What was memorable for the boys, and likely to elude the majority readership, is what they appeared to see as insensitivity to dietary observance in religion. Their identities as observant Hindus where dietary matters were important seemed to color their interpretations of texts.

Disposition, while linked to identity, will also be affected by factors, such as personal taste, life experience, and cultural expectations. Learners develop and maintain dispositions shaped by motivation and aspiration as well as current membership of particular social groups. Dispositions are a matter of temperament but are also socioculturally influenced by assumptions regarding what boys and girls or men and women should read, what counts as suitable school texts, what are culturally desirable literacy acts, in short, where, what, and how one should read.

While we bring a set of identities and dispositions to all the reading we undertake, it is important to note that both identity and disposition are open to adjustment and even radical change in the course of reading. We talk of the books that change lives. At the same time, we take up a stance to the particular text we are faced with. Stance is dynamic. It is an orientation to text which shifts from moment to moment and recalls Goffman's notion of footing, which he describes as "an alignment we take up to ourselves and the others present as expressed in the way we manage the production or reception of an utterance" (Goffman, 1981, p. 28). Goffman has oral communication in mind but reading as communication also involves a constant adjustment of alignments, by both the reader and writer in the interactive reading event.

In broad terms then, critical reading involves drawing on a set of identities and dispositions which come into play as we adopt a stance to the text which confronts us. For instance, faced with the charity text, rather than reaching for my cheque book or credit card I might choose to reflect on the immediate context of the text, how it reaches my address and, beyond that, what kinds of social circumstances occasion the need for such appeals to strangers. In short I can opt to read "against the grain of the text," not in the way the text demands to be read. The exercise of such choice takes us into consideration of what a *critical* stance might involve.

What we Mean by Critical: Two Views of Criticality

Just as there are different views of reading, so there are different understandings of the critical. Some use the term "critical" to refer to ways of reading which address the logical coherence of texts and the credibility of argument. This is part of a broader emphasis on "critical thinking" (see, for instance, Paran, 2002). A second interpretation of criticality, explored in detail in recent work by Janks (2010), considers texts from a perspective of power, drawing on a discourse view of reading. The discourses within texts assume that the reader of the text will align him/herself with shared views about the events or phenomena described; one strand of critical reading is being able to "read the reader," especially relevant when the actual reader, in our case the international learner of English, differs from the model, mainstream reader who is also frequently a native speaker of Standard English.

This stronger view of "critical" involves a preparation to challenge existing views of the relationship between the self and "the other." The other is the social outsider, perceived as different from the mainstream and, within texts, variously interpreted as the victim or the villain, both roles often embodied in the "foreigner" or "the immigrant." Part of a critical stance in this second view of criticality is an awareness of a likely difference between a text's actual and implied or model reader.

In adopting the role of reader as analyst (see Freebody & Luke, 2003), the critical reader aims for some critical distance from the conventionally compliant, cooperative reader stance. However, this should not be taken to mean a fixed pre-determined position of antagonism unsupported by argument. Drawing on Giroux (1983) one might distinguish between *opposition* and a more considered position of *resistance*. Resistant, as opposed to oppositional reading, means testing initial reactions against a set of rational principles. Without the preparedness and ability to offer a reasoned defence of one's views, critical reading becomes a futile exercise of having one's existing prejudices confirmed.

From Principles to Practice: Tools for Critical Reading

A Freirean Perspective

Many who espouse the stronger version of critically orientated pedagogy have turned for inspiration to Paulo Freire (see for example Freire, 1972), the Brazilian educator who famously saw reading the word as "reading the world." Freirean literacy programs are built around the notion of key or generative words which encode politically and socially significant events, objects, or phenomena in people's lives. Participants are presented with an image, visual, or key word which acts as a trigger or prompt for participants in the teaching group to explore aspects of their reality. The ultimate aim is enhanced reflexivity, especially around issues of social justice.

In a century where globalization has resulted in greater stratification and inequality world-wide, Freire's work has continuing resonance. A Freirean literacy project, developed by Action Aid in 1996 (Archer & Cottingham, 1996) and known as Regenerated Freirean Literacy through empowering community techniques or REFLECT, has now been implemented in more than twenty countries world-wide, including the United Kingdom where it is known as the REFLECT for ESOL project (REFLECT for ESOL 2007). Written for a North American context, the teaching material of Auerbach and Wallerstein (2004), also Freirean inspired, offers texts as codes which problematize aspects of social life. Codifications take the form of pictures, photos, simple texts, or strip cartoons, as shown in Figure 15.1, which capture problems or contradictions in people's lives. Codes are not mirrors which directly reflect back our learner's lives; rather, they are thinking tools which invite learners to consider wider aspects of social injustice than those which might affect them personally.

A Critical Discourse Analysis Perspective

While Freire's work frames critical education in its widest sense, critical discourse analysis provides some tools to dig deeper into texts, helping to answer the question *how* we might teach texts as discourse, in the sense described in the introduction to this chapter. Critical Discourse Analysis draws on linguistic tools to show how texts are not and cannot be ideologically impartial, that they inevitably privilege certain social groups over others, and certain ways of looking at the world over others.

Many critical discourse analysts draw on Halliday's systemic functional grammar (Halliday, 1994). Halliday's view that grammar is socially

Activity 15.1

How might you adapt or adopt the approach taken in the material in Figure 15.1?

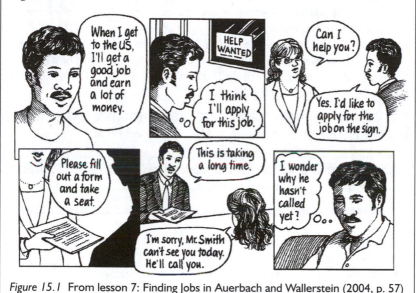

Figure 15.1 From lesson 7: Finding Jobs in Auerbach and Wallerstein (2004, p. 57)

motivated meshes with a view of language which is permeated with the social and cultural values and dispositions of its users, in both intended and unintended ways. Grammatical choice is not merely an exercise of individual preference but reveals discourse choices which link to wider ideological tendencies. Moreover such tendencies can be particularly striking to EIL readers as they may be positioned outside the model readership and so less likely to succumb to the taken for granted world view of the writer and the model reader, who will frequently share a language, history, and ideological perspective.

Halliday characterizes all spoken and written texts as involving three parameters: field, tenor, and mode. Field is what we are talking about, tenor relates to how we establish communication with an addressee, and mode relates to how the text is put together as a whole. At the same time, field encodes propositional or ideational meaning, tenor encodes interpersonal meaning, through such features as modality and personal pronouns, and mode is linked to textual meaning, that is how the text is put together as a text through cohesion and coherence and an overall organization. This is represented in Figure 15.2.

- Field, linked to *ideational* meaning, is realized by features such as nouns (participants), verbs (processes), and adverbs.
- Tenor, linked to *interpersonal* meaning, is realized by such features as modal verbs, personal pronouns, and mood, e.g. affirmative statements, imperatives, or questions.
- Mode is linked to *textual* meaning or the organization of the text. It is realized by features such as the use of tenses (present and past), how much information is presented, the use of direct or indirect speech, and cohesion.

Figure 15.2 Halliday's Three Parameters of Field, Tenor, and Mode

We can draw on Halliday's framework to ask questions of texts related to key features of field, tenor, and mode. Figure 15.3 offers an example.

■ *Aspects of field*
- Who are the major participants?
- What kind of processes collocate with the participants?
- Are there invisible participants?

■ *Aspects of tenor*
- How is the reader addressed? (What kind of reader identity is assumed?)
- What language tells us the attitude of the writer to the reader and the subject matter?

■ *Aspects of mode*
- What information comes first?
- Is the information relevant?
- What is the effect of the use of tenses?

Figure 15.3 Key Critical Questions Related to Field, Tenor, and Mode

We might note the significance of language choice in these two extracts from reports of a series of student protests in London in late 2010, by asking some of the questions in Figure 15.3.

Compare Text A with Text B, written about a similar event, a few days later.

School's Out
Children take
to the streets

- Student protests across UK
- Isolated breakouts of violence
- Clegg's "regret" over fees pledge

Tens of thousands of students and school pupils walked out of class, marched and occupied buildings around the country yesterday in the second day of mass action within a fortnight to protest at education cuts and higher tuition fees.

From *The Guardian* (25 November 2010)

Text A

Shop staff in fear
For their lives as
Student protesters
Try to smash doors

Shop staff in Trafalgar Square told today how they feared for their lives during the student protest.
It came after thousands of students descended on central London in the third demonstration against plans to triple university fees.

From *The Evening Standard* (1 December 2010)

Text B

Text A and B

In Text A and Text B we can readily see the difference of field as indicated by the use of participants and processes. In Text A, the students are the major participants, given strong agency with a series of simple active verbs: "walked," "marched," and "occupied," whereas in Text B the shop staff become the major actors with the students relegated to the role of, largely ineffective, participants suggested by a verb of weaker agency "descended" (inanimate things can "descend," such as fog). Tenor is not strongly marked in either extract although the story in Text B is told from the point of view of the shop staff. If we turn to consideration of mode, cohesion is of some interest in Text B as, in a typical newspaper strategy, two events are juxtaposed in "staff in fear of their lives" as "student protestors try to smash down doors." While the writers avoid attributing direct intention of the students to put shop staff in fear of their lives, there is an implied linkage of the two events and a suggestion of irresponsible behavior on the part of the students.

It is important to emphasize that there is no one "correct" way of interpreting either text, which needs to be seen in the context of other texts and discourses which circulate in social life. There will be a range of interpretative possibilities. However, the process of noticing language choice and of making metalinguistic judgments about why certain nouns or verbs are selected over others, allows second language students to exercise both knowledge of grammar and their own critical judgment.

Text C

One might note that although the major participants in Text C are "immigrants" in that they are thematized in the headline, subsequent paragraphs offer little agency to the immigrants, dealing rather with the consequences of the immigrants' presence in Britain, mainly in terms of benefit or gain to Britain or the British. Immediately a tension is set up, a "them" and "us" between the immigrants as the outsiders, as "the other" and "us," presumed to refer to the model reader who is one of the indigenous British population. To a large extent the immigrants are invisible certainly as agents of their own actions or destiny. In terms of tenor, the use of "us" in the headline immediately assumes a reader which excludes the "immigrant"—the "us" is presumed to be the "native" UK readership. This is in spite of the reality that the readership of *The Metro* is likely to include as many "immigrants" as British born people. Finally the organization of the information privileges the views of "Migration Watch"—a campaign expressly committed to curtailing immigration—over the very different views, if we read deeper into the text, of the then Foreign Secretary, the CBI (Confederation of British Industry) and the Home Office. Thus we can see the significance of the ordering of information.

The Hallidayan framework is a flexible instrument which can be introduced incrementally. Thus for early learners one might, under "tenor" look simply at the use of pronouns, such as incidences of "I" or "you." With more advanced learners one can build in work on grammar at deeper levels, such as features of modality and modulation. In the next section I set out some practical procedures which might be used for learners with varying degrees of language proficiency.

Activity 15.2

Use the questions in Figure 15.3 to analyze the way in which Text C, an article from the free London daily newspaper *The Metro*, uses field, tenor, and mode to create a particular effect.

Immigrants worth '4p to each of us'

THE financial benefit brought by immigrants to Britain amounts to just 4p per week per person, it was claimed yesterday.

The gain would allow each person to buy just a third of a Mars bar every month, said Migrationwatch, which campaigns against mass immigration.

The group's chairman, Sir Andrew Green, said: 'Of course, many immigrants make a useful contribution to the economy but, taken in total, the economic benefit is, at best, marginal.

'The main beneficiaries are the immigrants themselves, who are able to send home about £10million a day, not the host nation.'

The claim comes after Foreign Secretary Margaret Beckett insisted Britain stands to benefit from Romanian and Bulgarian membership of the EU, as the two countries acceded on Monday.

The CBI's Susan Anderson criticised the report. She said: 'Migrationwatch is seeking to score a few

Claim: Margaret Beckett

cheap political points with these figures but the benefits of migration need to be looked at more deeply.

'Migrants to the UK bring valuable skills and ideas with them and help to fill job vacancies where Britons are unable or unwilling to do so.

'Their taxes help pay for our public services and our pensions, long after many migrants have returned home.'

A Home Office spokesman said: 'Overall, migration is good for employment and good for the economy.'

From *The Metro* (3 January 2007)

Notes on text:

4p is the equivalent of about 5cents in US money

A Mars bar is a popular chocolate bar in the UK

The CBI is the Confederation of British Industry

Text C

Applying a Critical Reading Pedagogy at Different Levels

Beginner Learners of English

As noted earlier, part of the task of creating critical readers is encouraging a critical disposition and stance; in short, a different kind of orientation to text. This is potentially available to early and/or younger readers. Below are some suggestions for critical literacy with early learners of English.

1   One can encourage learners to explore uses of English, both written and spoken in their own environments. In societies where English is used as one of the official languages it is particularly fruitful to investigate the different forms and uses of English language texts in the local environment. Within these wider settings learners can then explore the particular domains of home, school, or the street to conduct literacy inventories by noting who reads what, to whom, and why. This helps to take reading away from the classroom, legitimizing the everyday practices of our learners' own communities. We might call this critical consciousness raising.

2   Teachers of young children can also use a critical orientation through activities around fiction and non-fiction texts which highlight the way in which gender stereotypes are presented in texts. O'Brien notes how, in her teaching of 6 year olds, she encouraged them to critique the story of *Fantastic Mr Fox*, and present an alternative version with the words: "In this story Roald Dahl shows Mrs Fox to be weak and scared. Draw a different Mrs Fox helping to save her family" (O'Brien, 1994, p. 38).

3   One can use simple texts or visuals to generate key words, in the Freirean spirit of encouraging learners to read the world through reflecting on key words which represent aspects of their experience. One text which I have used for critical reading begins with the single word SINGAPORE, presented in a large banner headline, much as it appears in the original article from which it is taken. The key question I have asked of students from such countries as Sweden, China, Germany, Singapore, and the United Kingdom is "what does this word suggest to you?" A range of responses typically follow, depending on reader identity; not surprisingly students from Singapore or neighboring countries will make different bids from the model readers of this text, namely young British women (the text is from the British version of the international magazine *Marie Claire*). Few students, however, predict the actual continuation of this text: "where the state chooses your partner" (see Wallace, 2003, p. 38 for a fuller discussion of this text).

4 To encourage students to be aware of the intended readership of texts and how it varies in different cultural contexts, we can ask students to bring into class a range of text genres, such as newspapers, magazines, advertisements, political leaflets, and appeals from charities. A possible procedure then is to:

- divide the class into groups and give each group a mixed set of texts
- ask each group to sort its texts into genre categories, such as "advertisements" or "public information leaflets"
- when the students have identified five or six broad types of texts they attempt to answer the following questions for each type:
  - Who is the producer of the texts?
  - For whom are they produced?
  - Why have they been produced?
  - Is this type of text of relevance or interest to you?

Once sets of texts have been brought into class one can work with a set of basic critical questions of the kind given above.

More Advanced Learners of English: Critical Pre/While/ Post-reading

As noted earlier, reading texts for the teaching of L2 learners are frequently accompanied by pre- and while-reading activities, emphasizing the on-going strategies readers draw on in processing text. These can be re-shaped as *critical* pre-, while-, and post-reading activities. So while a standard pre-reading question invites the reader to link the text with her or his background knowledge, a *critically* oriented pre-reading question might ask why the text has been written in the first place. The aim is to encourage a critical stance to a text, one which draws on a disposition to challenge rather than take at face value the topic, readership, and emphases of the text and which invites reflection on omissions and distortions. Below I consider some critical pre-, while-, and post-reading questions which might accompany the reading of texts in the classroom.

Critical Pre-reading Activities

1 Students pose their own questions of a text, after a quick survey of the text and its context. The aim is not to "find answers" to questions but to consider the significance of the omission or inclusion of information or to raise further questions which the initial reading of the text suggests.

2 One can encourage students to consider the range of discourses available to describe the issue in hand. For instance in the case of

the text "Immigrants worth '4p to each of us'" one could provide learners with the basic premise of the text to be read along the lines of "immigrants bring benefits to the UK economy." If asked "what could the writer choose to write about," students might offer:

- the nature of these benefits to the UK
- the nature of the benefits to the immigrants
- some of the negative impacts
- views of the immigrants and of the host community.

They can later, as post-reading, check out their options with those actually exercised in the text.

3 Intercultural pre-reading activities can encourage learners to reflect on how universal phenomena and accompanying discourses are differently inflected across different cultural settings. This kind of pre-reading activity might accompany a set of texts which look at a universal theme or a particular event from different perspectives. For instance, the reporting of public protest, whether by students or other groups, might be couched in different kinds of discourse, in keeping with wider public attitudes among the particular national or cultural group about appropriate ways of expressing dissent.

Critical While-reading Activities

1 To reveal the differential treatment of participants in texts, we can ask students to complete a simple grid which lists the major participants (i.e., who or what the text is about) and any collocating adjectives or verbs, for example in the case of Text C "Immigrants worth '4p to each of us'" we might produce something like:

Immigrants   —main beneficiary

                              —worth 4p = the cost of half a Mars bar

Migration Watch   —campaigns against mass immigration

                              —said that the gain would allow each
                               person to buy just a third of a Mars bar
                               every month

The Foreign Secretary   —insisted that Britain stands to benefit.

Such a grid provides a starting point for students to reconstruct the text, as they reflect on other ways to describe the main characters in the story.

2 One can identify parallel discourses in some texts. This is notable in Text B above where the shop staff and students arguably constitute two sets of participants in this version of the story of the protests. The result may be something like:

Shop staff	*Students*
in fear for their lives	try to smash doors
told (the story is from their point of view)	descended on central London

3 Cloze or gap filling activities are common for while-reading. A *critical* cloze activity might involve learners actively thinking of how changing the choice of words, particularly their connotative value, will impact on the overall effect. Taking the example of Text C we might have:

> "The financial ... brought by ... to ... amounts to ... 4p per week per person, it was claimed yesterday. The gain would allow each ... to buy ... every ..."

The facts are not changed but the effect is, if we imagine something like:

> "The financial advantage brought by newcomers to the society amounts to as much as 4p per week per person, it was claimed yesterday. The gain would allow each citizen to buy as many as two paperback books every year."

Critical Post-reading Activities

1 Students might be asked to revisit the text to consider how it might have been written. A rewrite of the text from the point of view of one of the invisible or near invisible participants can be revealing.
2 Following a lesson, students can be asked to collect texts on the same theme but written from a different perspective for a different context and readership. Anne Cardwell (2008), teaching in Poland, used two sets of texts in one critical reading project: those written in Poland about the English (especially young people visiting Prague or Krakow for heavy drinking weekends) and those written in England about the Poles who had come as migrant labor to the United Kingdom (and who constitute one of the largest groups alluded to in Text C). Such readings allow students to gain a clear sense of the "othering" of texts.

3 There are a number of global stories which appear as culturally variable versions of the same essential narrative. Many of these traditional stories have been changed to challenge the typically sexist or racist discourse within them. In the classroom students might be presented with post-reading activities which highlight different features of contrasting versions of such stories (see for instance Mellor, Hemming, & Leggett, 1984).

Conclusion

In this chapter I have set out some of the principles of critical reading in the context of teaching English as an international language. It is important to emphasize that there are no easy steps to critical pedagogy. The acknowledgment of resistance means that students may well resist our own forms of critical pedagogy, as McKinney (2003) discovered in a course on prescribed literacy texts which focused on issues of social inequality in South Africa. McKinney's students found it painful to deal with the legacy of apartheid and the implied sense of guilt which the critical study unearthed. Nonetheless, handled flexibly, a critical reading pedagogy has the potential to support second language learners' access to the global debates of the age. To participate meaningfully in these, they need tools to challenge the dominant discourses which frame the uses of English in a whole range of settings and genres: in newspapers, often, these days, online rather than in print, in advertising and in the glossy, multimodal English language teaching packages themselves.

Teachers will come to different judgments about what kind of critical reading pedagogy suits their own disposition and their students' circumstances and aspirations. Much will depend on the language level and age of the students. With more advanced learners it is possible to introduce students to quite sophisticated linguistic tools for talking about, critiquing, and reconstructing texts and discourses. With learners new to English, including children, we can plan critical consciousness raising activities which involve simple observations of literacy practices and discourse tendencies in texts, rather than full-scale language analysis. But for all language learners, critical reading, in its invitation to textual scrutiny, allows readers of English to develop their overall language competence cognitively and critically. As I argued at the start of this chapter, this is a pre-requisite for membership of international English language-using communities in a global age.

Exploring the Ideas

1 What obstacles might you face from the institution or the school you teach in or your national curriculum in taking a critical orientation to the teaching of reading?

2 What kinds of reader identities and dispositions typify language learners in your teaching context? Do your learners for instance read widely in their first language? What are some of the implications for approaches to critical reading?

3 Consider how far you might want to adopt a critical thinking approach to teaching reading as opposed to a discourse view of critical reading which attends to issues of power and ideology. What factors affect your decision?

4 The chapter set out two broad orientations to critical literacy, those indebted to the work of Paulo Freire and those which draw on systemic functional grammar. Which one is more in keeping with the current approaches to English teaching in your country?

Applying the Ideas

1 With reference to the idea of encouraging students to be literacy ethnographers, how might you set up an activity which encourages your learners to investigate the uses of English language literacy in their own immediate context? If English is not widely used, what findings would emerge if students were encouraged to investigate the literacy practices conducted in the *home* language, which are part of public and social life in your teaching context?

2 In this chapter I have noted the narrow range of discourses which might feature in the global English language textbook. Often, however, we have no choice but to use a textbook, often a global one. However, in such a case you might ask teachers to take a chapter from an English textbook they are familiar with and show how they could approach it from a critical literacy perspective. Consider ways you could approach this task.

3 Compare the coverage of a news item of global import in your local media, whether this is in English-medium or in another local language, with the coverage of the same item in a different English-medium context. How could these contrasting texts form the basis of a critical reading activity?

4 Bearing in mind the approach taken by Cardwell in her teaching of students in Poland, how might you collect and exploit sets of texts which feature contrasting discourses about people, places, or phenomena?

References

Archer, D., & Cottingham, S. (1996). *Regenerated Freirean literacy through empowering community techniques*. London: Action Aid.

Auerbach, E., & Wallerstein, N. (2004). *Problem-posing at work: English for action* (2nd ed.). Edmonton, Alberta: Grass Roots Press.

Barton, D., & Hamilton, M. (1998). *Local literacies.* London: Routledge.

Baynham, M., & Prinsloo, M. (Eds.). (2009). *The future of literacy studies,* Basingstoke: Palgrave Macmillan.

Cardwell, A. (2008). *Critical reading: An introductory course for Polish students in an EFL context.* A report as part of an MA in Teaching English to Speakers of Other languages. Unpublished MA report. Institute of Education, University of London.

The Evening Standard. (2010). Shop staff in fear for their lives as student protesters try to smash doors. December 1.

Foucault, M. (1972). *The archaeology of knowledge.* New York: Tavistock Publications.

Freebody. P., & Luke, A. (2003). 'Literacy as engaging with new forms of life: the "four roles" model'. In G. Bull & M. Anstey (Eds.), *The literacy lexicon* (pp 51–66). Frenchs Forest, NSW: Pearson.

Freire, P. (1972). *Pedagogy of the oppressed.* Harmondsworth: Penguin.

The Guardian (2010). School's Out, November 25.

Giroux, H. (1983). Theory of reproduction and resistance in the new sociology of education: A critical analysis. *Harvard Educational Review, 3*(53), 257–293.

Goffman, E. (1981). *Forms of talk.* Philadelphia, PA: University of Pennsylvania Press.

Goodman. K. (1967). Reading: A psycholinguistic guessing game. In F. K. Gollasch (Ed.), *Language and literacy: The selected writings of Kenneth S. Goodman Vol 1: Process, Theory, Research* (pp. 19–31). London: Routledge, 1982.

Goodman, K. (1996). *On reading. A common-sense look at the nature of language and the science of reading.* Portsmouth, NH: Heinemann.

Grabe, W. (2009). *Reading in a second language: Moving from theory to practice.* Cambridge: Cambridge University Press.

Gray, J. (2002). The global coursebook in English language teaching. In D. Block & D. Cameron (Eds.), *Globalization and language teaching* (pp. 151–167). London: Routledge.

Gray, J. (2010). *The construction of English culture, consumerism and promotion in the ELT global coursebook.* Basingstoke: Palgrave Macmillan.

Halliday, M. A. K. (1994). *An introduction to functional grammar* (2nd ed.). London: Edward Arnold.

Heath, S. B. (1983). *Ways with words.* Cambridge: Cambridge University Press.

Janks, H. (2010). *Literacy and power.* New York and London: Routledge.

McKinney, C. (2003). Developing critical literacy in a changing context. In S. Goodman, T. Lillis, J. Maybin, & N. Mercer (Eds.), *Language, literacy and education: A reader* (pp. 189–202). Stoke on Trent: Trentham books in association with the Open University.

The Metro(2007). Immigrants worth "4p to each of us". January 3.

Mellor, B., Hemming, J., & Leggett, J. (1984). *Changing stories.* London: the English Centre.

O'Brien, J. (1994). Critical literacy in early childhood classrooms. *Australian Journal of Language and Literacy, 17*(1), 36–44.

Paran, A. (2002). Critical thinking and reading in EFL: When do we start?. In *Challenge and creativity in teaching beginners*, proceedings of the 6th International Bilkent University School of English Language ELT Conference (pp. 156–167). Bilkent University School of English.

Scholes, R. (1985). *Textual power*. New Haven, CT: Yale University Press.

Soars, L., & Soars, J. (2009). *New headway intermediate student's book* (4th ed.). Oxford: Oxford University Press.

Street, B. (1984). *Literacy in theory and practice*. Cambridge: Cambridge University Press.

Wallace, C. (1992). *Reading*. Oxford: Oxford University Press.

Wallace, C. (2003). *Critical reading in language education*. Basingstoke: Palgrave Macmillan.

Wallace, C. (2008). Literacy and identity: A view from the bridge in two multilingual London schools. In D. Block (Ed.), Multilingual identities and language practices in a global city: Four London case studies: Special Issue of *Journal of Language, Identity and Education, 7*(1), 61–80.

Chapter 16

Controversy and Change in How We View L2 Writing in International Contexts

Christine Pearson Casanave

In this chapter I discuss five areas of controversy connected to some traditional ways of thinking about the teaching, learning, and assessment of writing. The perspectives are controversial in part because many second language educators cling to them as the "way things should be done" in spite of counter-evidence in the literature and in their own experience. The perspectives have often been taught in language teacher education programs, and have thus influenced how teachers think about L2 writing in international contexts. They include: the generic academic essay, the cognitive process writing movement, contrastive rhetoric, error correction, and particular ways of testing and assessing writing. I note that these five perspectives have paid little attention to the situated and local nature of writing in the past and hence have generated controversy. All five have, in one way or another, assumed a rather static, Western-influenced view of writing without considering a) that all writing is located in some kind of discourse community and emerges in relation to this environment; and b) that it does not make sense to look at L2 English writing practices through a monolingual "native speaker" or target language lens. I urge that writing in international settings be viewed ecologically (contextually), considering purposes, conventions, and relations within particular local discourse communities. Such a view fits well within the breadth, flexibility, and non-prescriptiveness of an EIL (English as an international language) approach. I provide no fixed answers but food for thought.

Introduction

In spite of recent interest (e.g., Manchón, 2009a), writing as a topic of inquiry and pedagogy has tended to play a minor role in L2 scholarship and classrooms throughout the world, where writing may be more closely aligned with translation and grammar study and with training for essay writing on examinations (Reichelt, 2009) or may simply not be taught at all.

But writing in English has taken on increasing importance as universities and workplaces throughout the world increasingly require graduate students and faculty to write and publish in English (Cargill, O'Connor, & Li, 2011; Lillis & Curry, 2010) and as global communication in business and politics increasingly takes place electronically in the medium of English (see McKay, this volume). In this sense, EFL is being removed from particular geographical sites, and increasingly being used across sites more as a lingua franca to accomplish particular activities (EIL).

Whatever we may think about the political injustice of the predominance of English in the academic and corporate worlds (see Canagarajah, 2002, for commentary on academic writing in a geopolitical context), we seem stuck with this reality. Attention to L2 writing in English is needed now more than ever, given the place of writing in international contexts, where writing has much to do with the specific writing demands within specialized and local discourse communities. These communities are not just rhetorical entities, but social and political ones (Casanave, 2003), involving relations among people, institutions, and purposes for writing.

Within the conceptualization of EIL that is explored in this book, the five perspectives I discuss in this chapter fit poorly because they are too ethnocentric, too monolingual, and too disassociated from the local, multilingual communities and contexts that most of the world's English learners are situated in. The controversies surrounding these perspectives have inspired changes in how we think about L2 writing. The EIL movement contributes to these changes, as does an ecological framework for L2 writing instruction, discussed in the conclusion. This framework is based on a widely held view that writing cannot be seen as a generic linguistic and rhetorical process based on a single standard of "correct" English, but that it is a social and political practice that inevitably takes place within a particular local context that is full of interested (in a political sense) social actors.

Controversial Perspectives on Writing in English

The five perspectives on teaching, learning, and assessing L2 writing that I discuss in this chapter include: (1) the "academic essay" as a genre that is supposedly transferable to other writing; (2) contrastive rhetoric, which presumed that a standard (read "American English") paragraph structure differs from paragraph and essay structures in other languages; (3) the cognitive process writing movement, which claimed to have identified differences in how novices and experts write; (4) error correction, which focuses on the common belief that students' writing will not improve without it being corrected; and (5) writing for assessment purposes via the one-shot essay for entrance, placement, and exit exams.

The Generic Essay

Traditionally in English dominant contexts, writing has been taught and researched as if it were its own academic genre, written for no particular discourse community beyond the ESL/EFL writing class or the L1 composition class. The fundamentals of the "academic essay" (stereotypically five paragraphs) certainly must be useful, we believe, because basic structures and skills transfer to other kinds of writing (Johns, 1988; Currie, 1999) and make it possible for students to enter the "academic discourse community" (Bizzell, 1982). We have all heard about, or taught, or are still teaching, the "academic essay" and its companion, the "research paper," with its argumentative or analytic purpose; its structure of thesis statement, positions, evidence, and conclusions; and its conventions for citing sources so that writers will not be accused of plagiarism (Pecorari, 2003). Writing textbooks typically prepare students to write this kind of generic academic essay or "research" paper.

However, the generic academic paper may be of little use outside the English or writing class except for purposes of placement and exit exams (see "Writing as an Assessment Tool" on p. 290, this chapter). Writing research increasingly has revealed that writing conventions are locally and contextually dependent on their use within different discourse and disciplinary communities (Hyland, 2009; Swales, 1988, 1990); that many genres are "hybrids"; and that writing mainly improves through practice and immersion in community-situated literacy activities rather than through instruction in, and correction of, the generic academic essay. And contrary to the beliefs of some writing teachers, it is also not clear whether features of and strategies for writing the generic academic essay will transfer to very different kinds of writing, even within the university context, particularly if students themselves do not see the connections (Leki, 2007).

But many L2 instructors have backgrounds only in applied linguistics or English literature. We must therefore ask how teachers of L2 writing can be expected to prepare students for writing practices within specialized disciplinary and discourse communities when the teachers themselves are not insiders to those communities. We must also ask whether there are general principles of English language writing that can be taught in a generic essay or paper, apart from foundational knowledge of grammar and vocabulary or certain basic skills of composing, or whether writing is best learned and taught in situ, as practiced within particular discourse communities. There is one thing we can be fairly sure of. Outside the L2 class, students throughout the world, in schools and workplaces, do not need to write the generic academic essay. The closest they may come to this kind of writing is the essay exam, now used worldwide in mass testing (e.g., TOEFL, TOEIC). From an EIL perspective, it makes sense to ask why we continue to teach this genre unless students need it for specific purposes.

Contrastive Rhetoric

As I described some years ago (Casanave, 2004), the contrastive rhetoric movement captured the attention of L2 writing instructors and applied linguists beginning with Robert Kaplan's article in *Language Learning* in 1966. It is not surprising that this article and those that followed and built on it were so compelling. Contrastive rhetoric, in a nutshell (but please see Kaplan's article for details), claimed that each culture has a rhetorical organization and set of thought patterns unique to it, and that these culturally specific organizations can be inferred from samples of (a) L2 students' writing in English (Kaplan) and (b) samples of L1 writing from different cultures (translated into English for purposes of analysis) (e.g., Hinds, 1983, 1987). The presumption was that L2 students write in English according to the rhetorical conventions of their home cultures, and that there is a negative transfer of L1 to L2 organization. Analysts supposedly can discover each culture's rhetorical traditions by analyzing sample texts, particularly in the students' L1s. This cross-cultural perspective is intuitively very compelling, and we do not need to look far to find evidence that fits this view.

The contrastive rhetoric project thus began with text analysis for pedagogical purposes. Kaplan, for his part, wanted to help his undergraduate students write English paragraphs that were linear, "logical," and straightforward. The pedagogy teaches students the "recipes" for English rhetorical organization, whether it be academic essays in the university, or other genres, such as business letters, empirical research, and so forth. All of this sounds deceptively easy to understand, to study, and to apply in the writing classroom. When Ulla Connor, a student of Kaplan's, published her 1996 book on contrastive rhetoric, many people welcomed it because it helped explain why L2 students' writing lacked the linearity, logic, and linguistically marked coherence of well-written English texts.

However, the contrastive rhetoric movement received a great deal of criticism, which accused it of representing rhetorical structures as static rather than dynamic (Matsuda, 1997), of ethnocentrism, of comparing apples and oranges, and of neglecting the hybrid and social-political nature of texts and text production (Kubota, 1997, 1998; Kubota & Lehner, 2004). In particular, we understand now that we cannot conclude anything about students' cultures or thinking abilities based on samples of their English language writing, or about the presumed uniqueness of each culture's rhetorical organization of writing (Casanave, 2004; Kubota, 1997). Many novice L1 writers also exhibit nonlinear and digressive rhetorical patterns, indicating a developmental stage. There are simply too many variables, too many local and situated factors such as level of expertise, purpose, and genre, and too many different discourse communities for us to be able to state any firm truths about the rhetorical organization of "English," "Japanese," or any other language.

Given its conflation of culture, thought patterns, and writing, contrastive rhetoric in its traditional form has outlived its usefulness. Connor (2004, 2011) has continued her interest in cross-cultural comparisons of various kinds of texts (genres) but is now calling her project "intercultural rhetoric" as a way to deflect the serious critiques of contrastive rhetoric. Still, assumptions linger in many people's minds about relatively stable forms of writing connected with particular languages and cultures rather than with local discourse communities. Such stereotypical views are even held by students themselves, if my students in Japan are at all representative. An EIL perspective, in contrast, will seek out evidence of diversity as well as stability of writing conventions and styles in particular contexts rather than presuming that languages and cultures have unique rhetorical patterns or that oversimplified American-English-based rhetorical structures and standard grammar should be taught throughout the world. (See further discussion in Casanave, 2004, Chapter 2.)

Process Writing

The cognitive process writing movement took the L1 writing community by storm in the early 1980s, in reaction to a historical focus on writing products—one-shot pieces of writing that were simply turned in and graded. It was influenced most profoundly by a model of the writing process proposed by Linda Flower and John R. Hayes (1981). This model helped writing scholars and teachers focus on how individuals write, not just on what they write, in particular, on what goes on in their minds as they compose. In the L2 field, Vivian Zamel soon became the TESOL field's charismatic cheerleader for looking at L2 writing through the writing process lens (1982, 1983). This movement later influenced ideas about how writing should be taught internationally.

Like the contrastive rhetoric movement, the writing process movement was supported both by research findings and by an intuitively compelling argument. It based its model of writing on distinctions between how expert and novice writers strategically approached a writing task as a problem to be solved. Expert and novice writers (L1 writers of English in US university laboratory settings) were observed as they composed from task prompts designed by the researchers, and who (in many cases) were taught to "think aloud" as they wrote. The think-aloud protocols, recorded by researchers, supposedly provided researchers with a record of what was going on in the writers' minds as they planned, solved problems, represented ideas, and revised. Not surprisingly, different cognitive processes of writing were discovered for experts and novices. Experts were found to write more recursively, plan more, attend to large ideas, let the process of writing itself lead them to discoveries, not be distracted by mechanical details until late in the writing process, and reread and revise often. They were also found to have better, and better organized, knowledge. Novices did not have well-organized knowledge, planned little, did not reread, worried about small details, and revised little.

During the peak of interest in the cognitive process writing movement, pedagogical principles and strategies were devised by L1 and L2 writing specialists in the US that asked novice writers not to worry about what the final product would look like, and in particular to disregard grammar errors during drafting stages. Students were asked instead to brainstorm before writing, write freely as a way to discover what they had to say, review what they had written, and write multiple drafts. The underlying assumptions were that expert writers write in similar ways, that novice writers should or could be taught to write like experts, and that the final product had for too many decades received way too much attention (Casanave, 2004).

But by the mid-1980s, some voices of protest began to appear that challenged some of these assumptions. Horowitz (1986) protested all the attention to process, stating that as a primary pedagogy it would not help students learn to write one of the most important genres in their school careers—the timed essay exam. (Such exams are ubiquitous worldwide and seem to be gaining in importance as high-stakes tests.) Reid (1984) then provided evidence that expert writers do not necessarily write in similar ways: Some brainstorm first and write freely, finding their focus and structure later (her husband), and some outline first, deciding on focus and structure before beginning to write, and revising little (Reid herself). I recall as well the exquisite descriptions by Annie Dillard (1989) of her own expert writing strategies—that of perfecting a sentence before going on to the next. My own writing strategies do not fit the general description of the expert writer that emerged from the process writing era either, other than my attention to revisions.

At the same time, good writers appear to read a lot, to revise a lot (especially if the writer is a brainstormer rather than an outliner), and to be able to recognize some problems that need fixing. They also know that setting writing aside for a time (sometimes a long time) and having a trusted but critical reader look at drafts help greatly. Finally, writers who know their topics thoroughly are more likely to write well. Topic knowledge, individual diversity, and local and situational constraints on writing tasks came to be seen as essential aspects of how we understand what it means to learn to write.

The problem that continues to plague "process writing," however, is that its features of pre-writing, drafting and recycling, revising, and polishing are presented in textbooks and course syllabuses in a way that Flower and Hayes (1981) did *not* intend: a more or less stage-oriented model of writing in which novice writers proceed through these steps together, as a class. Students do pre-writing exercises first; they then draft, and then revise perhaps two times, and then polish the final paper by attending to grammar and mechanical details. Students usually do what they are told, of course, but this stage model of writing is not what the nonlinear embedded process model of Flower and Hayes depicts. And apart from this model, which was based on the writing processes of L1 expert writers of American English, what is the teacher to do with the Annie Dillard-style student, who insists on perfecting every sentence as she goes? What if another student blends English and (say) Japanese throughout a piece of creative writing as she drafts, and then decides in the polishing stage she would like to keep some of the Japanese in the final copy? What if a student writer needs 10 revisions instead of two (my pattern as a writer)? Teachers have not yet found a way to incorporate an EIL perspective in their writing curriculum that would encourage the real diversity of writing processes that writers go through within equally diverse contexts and purposes for writing. At the very least, in the EIL process writing classroom, students would become acquainted with the many steps involved in writing, and would then work on their own to choose what to write and to discover how they best write, with individual guidance from teachers and classmates, using the L1 as needed.

Error Correction in Writing Instruction

The fourth perspective on writing instruction concerns the ongoing debate about the value of error correction in writing instruction, particularly with respect to grammar. For decades, writing teachers have assumed that one of their main jobs, in both L1 and L2 writing classes, was to take drafts of students' writing home every night, and mark, or correct, all the errors. The goal of correction in writing instruction is to help students eventually reach a target language standard, where "target language" tends to be defined as the language of an educated native speaker in an Inner-Circle country (the US, the UK, ...). This notion of target language is in itself a concept that fits poorly with an EIL approach to language acquisition and writing instruction, but is nevertheless deeply embedded in error correction activities.

The main discussion for many years was what kinds of correction worked best to help students learn eventually to correct their own writing, not whether to correct at all. Should errors simply be corrected by the teacher and the paper handed back to the students for their perusal? Should a coding system be used so that students would know what kinds of errors they had made and could then work to correct the errors themselves? Should, on the other hand, errors simply be underlined, leaving students to know the location of the error but nothing more, and then to correct on their own? Should revising a corrected draft be required?

Such questions were difficult but not controversial until John Truscott entered the scene claiming that there is little evidence that grammar correction helps students improve their writing (Truscott, 1996, 2007; Truscott & Hsu, 2008). He urged all of us to simply stop correcting students' grammar until research proves that it helps. What a shock this was to the millions of writing teachers who keep the red pen-and-pencil companies in business and who think that students will never learn to write without being corrected! What a shock this was to students whose teachers tell them that their grammar will not be corrected but that somehow they will improve their writing anyhow! Dana Ferris (1999) was the first to respond (there have been many others), arguing in favor of error correction, including grammar, and as I drafted this chapter, the feathers were still flying. Truscott (2009, 2010) was still dismissing his critics and making unhedged assertions that correction does not work.

The main argument is one worth thinking and reading about no matter what our position is. To summarize in an overly simple way, Truscott claims to have looked at a great deal of research on writing and revision, and has found little evidence that grammar correction helps students improve new pieces of writing. He rightly pointed out that it makes no sense to say that correction improves writing if all we are looking at is a revised draft of the same piece of writing. We need to know if L2 students have incorporated the corrections into new pieces of writing, i.e., learned from their mistakes. Otherwise, as Truscott has stated repeatedly, we are wasting our time (and a lot of it) correcting students' errors in any form. Improvement in writing, he and others have claimed, more likely comes in developmental stages, through practice, through reading, and through exposure to models (e.g., in the form of general instruction in English or of teachers' written comments on the content of students' writing).

The other side of the debate has three positions: first, students expect and want correction, so we should provide it. Otherwise, they may lose motivation to write, and motivation along with continued practice is essential to eventual improvement. Another argument is that correction does help, as shown in several studies, if done systematically, selectively, and consistently (Chandler, 2003; Ferris, 2002), particularly on small items, such as articles (Bitchener, 2008). A third argument is that we don't really know if correction helps because the research on correction has had design problems (Guénette, 2007). Truscott will have none of it. Whatever our position on this debate, Truscott demands that we use more than common sense and student expectations to decide whether to correct students' grammar. We need empirical evidence from studies that stand up to methodological scrutiny. Meanwhile, students need to be getting lots of writing practice, more than most of them get worldwide in their L2 classes.

Interestingly, if we give up our obsession with correction, students' drafts will contain not only more errors that we will *not* worry about, but also more examples of code-switching as writers search for words. If students are not obsessed with correctness, then L1 forms might usefully appear in drafts without writers or teachers worrying about them. From an EIL perspective, the only writing that needs to be polished according to standards of perfection in English-dominant contexts is writing that has high-stakes consequences if it is not "perfect": a job application essay for an English language company, an article for publication in an international journal, a business letter to an important English speaking client.

Writing as an Assessment Tool

Finally, writing has traditionally been used (and hence taught) worldwide as an assessment tool and as an instrument for language study, particularly in countries where there is no tradition of dedicated writing instruction. Practices in some classrooms, such as Japan, may be called "writing," but they often turn out to be grammar and translation exercises, and include preparation for high-stakes examinations. In my many years of teaching in Japan, most of my undergraduate students had never written even a paragraph in English, let alone an essay or a paper. They had only written or translated sentences.

The one area where writing as connected discourse is taught is essay exam training. This kind of writing instruction tends to follow models and recipes that have been used in exams and that follow more or less the generic essay structure. From a global perspective, Reichelt (2009) found that writing instruction in many parts of the world also focuses on building language proficiency rather than writing more broadly, and has instrumental purposes (for work, for use in international education), as well as exam-related purposes. In these cases, testing and assessment go hand in hand with writing instruction.

The reality in many parts of the world is that high-stakes essay exams cannot be avoided or dismissed. Entrance to schools and to companies may depend on them, as may graduation or promotion. The form and style of the essay exam may be found nowhere else but in these particular circumstances, and for this reason, writing teachers often resist teaching to it. This is very understandable resistance: I have never been able to teach essay-exam English, partly because I find the high-stakes exam supported too often by corporate profit-making interests (and therefore anti-educational), and partly because essay exam writing is usually not very interesting or inspiring either for writers or exam evaluators and teachers. But someone must help students learn to take such essay exams as long as this unfortunate requirement persists.

The controversies surrounding essay exams, particularly the one-shot high-stakes exam (Hayes, Hatch, & Silk, 2000) are profound, and the debates are emotional. Can such exams fairly represent students' writing abilities? Can they be evaluated fairly by multiple readers? Must raters be trained to read in the same way or does such training produce artificial readings? Can machines score such essays? I discuss many of these issues elsewhere (Casanave, 2004). Suffice it to say here that essay exams often require test-takers to use a generic Western-influenced structure and style and to write on topics that may not be relevant to them. Such essay tests are potentially biased against many L2 writers worldwide. I am not sure if home-grown essay exams (made by individual schools, departments, or companies; Huot, 1996) are equally biased, but the influence of TOEFL, TOEIC, and other standardized tests continues to grow in schools and workplaces worldwide. Although an EIL approach will encourage writing teachers to help students with whatever writing they must do within the purposes of their local contexts, it might also be able to work at resisting the increasing influence of the standardized essay exam, which serves purposes that have little to do with writing.

Changes in How L2 Writing Scholars Characterize the Practice of Writing: An Ecological Framework

The most important shift in how we view L2 writing has paralleled the shift in the social sciences in general and SLA (second language acquisition) in particular toward a view that is increasingly local, social, and political (the "social turn," Block, 2003). More than in the past, writing is discussed as a practice that goes beyond linguistics (how morphemes, words, sentences, syntax, and conventions of organization combine to make a text) in spite of lingering traditional realities (Casanave, 2009), and beyond SLA (how writing contributes to language acquisition; Harklau, 2002; Manchón, 2009b). We are moving toward a view that locates the practice of writing squarely within a socio-political context, full of local needs and social actors, all situated within different discourse communities (Li, 2006).

These social actors include particular writers with specific needs and purposes for writing, and particular readers, including those who will evaluate a student's writing in some way. This writing can include almost anything: a high-stakes essay exam, a course paper in a humanities or engineering class, a thesis or dissertation judged by a small committee, a paper for publication, a job application letter judged by a future employer, electronic communications judged as appropriate or not by recipients, who increasingly are not native speakers of English, and many other types.

This is not to say that we are no longer interested in the generic "academic essay," or contrastive/intercultural rhetoric, or writing processes, or error correction, or writing practice for exam purposes. Such interests and practices simply are not seen as ends in themselves, but as situated in an ecology of broader cognitive, social, and political contexts (Tudor, 2003; van Lier, 2002). "The context is central," van Lier reminded us, and it cannot be reduced or pushed aside (p. 144). If we teach a generic academic essay, we would ask why we are teaching this, for whose purposes (they may not necessarily be for the students' purposes), and in whose interests. If we use concepts from contrastive rhetoric to analyze two texts, we would ask why we are doing such text-specific analyses and what we will learn beyond the rather trivial comparison of surface differences. If we teach students about writing processes, we would look at the processes from far more complex and nuanced perspectives than the recipes for process writing in the past. We would try in particular to help students understand how their own writing processes may not fit what the experts have told us, how writing processes shift with task and topic knowledge, and how writers become more proficient with a great deal of practice. As well, most of us are unlikely to give up correcting students' writing, at least in some form, but we would ask why we are doing this, how our correcting practices might shift according to the kinds and purposes of writing students are doing, what students do with the corrections we make, and whether we see (not just believe) that our correcting helps students improve their writing over time. If we are obligated to test students by means of single writing samples, we will understand the inherent unfairness of this kind of test and the impossibility of evaluating students' actual writing proficiency this way.

In short, an ecological framework helps us understand why some of the earlier perspectives on the teaching, learning, and assessment of writing do not suit an EIL approach to English language education. Here are some principles, adapted from Kramsch (2002) and van Lier (2002, 2004), that writing instructors can use to think about their work. I hope it will be clear that the five controversial perspectives on L2 writing I discussed in this chapter, among others I did not discuss, need to be re-thought in more situated ways.

1 Writing practices, like language acquisition, are *embedded in social contexts*, i.e., environments that include actors, objects, physical spaces, temporal features, and personal and institutional histories and demands. An *ecological approach* is therefore not about learning recipes for writing, but *about identifying particular contexts and needs* within local, multilingual contexts.

2 As they learn to write, *students* interact with their local, multilingual environments, using both L1 and L2 (even L3) to negotiate their personal needs and dispositions with environmental factors so as to get what they need from their writing instruction and practices. They *form a relationship with their environments* that will help or hinder their progress. The five perspectives I discussed in this chapter do not address this relationship, but depict general, standardized, or target language norms.

3 Novice writers benefit only from *practices that they find meaningful and relevant* to their particular needs or desires, all of which will be situated within their own contexts and personal histories and mediated by multiple languages as needed.

4 Second language *writing development*, like language acquisition, *is not linear* or monolingually achieved. Rather, it is multilingual, organic, complex, unpredictable, and "emergent" (local phenomena interact with features of the environment to produce patterns of development; Kramsch, 2002, p. 17; Larsen-Freeman & Cameron, 2008). Therefore, stage and step-by-step models of instruction, though deemed necessary for instruction, do not reflect actual writing development.

5 An *ecological approach* to the study and practice of writing *is not reductive* (i.e., practices are not simplified and categorized for research purposes), *but expansive*. Detail and complexity are embraced, including the complexities of how L1 and L2 (L3...) interact. Although such a view complicates research and pedagogy, which thrive on simplicity, the ecological approach more closely connects with the real-life, locally situated writing needs of worldwide L2 English learners. These are inherently and necessarily complex.

6 An *ecological approach* to L2 writing *envisions L2 writers drawing on all relevant resources, including their L1s*. In a complex multilingual world, English-only requirements make little sense. Such English-only requirements eliminate the bulk of what is meaningful in the environments of multilingual writers.

In short, writing instruction in an ecological and EIL perspective needs to be "*experiential, contextualized, activity-based, and developmental*" (van Lier, 2002, p. 157).

Conclusion

One of the points of this chapter is that many traditional writing practices have made it difficult for instructors and policy makers to see beyond the (ethnocentric) practices themselves to the larger ecological context in which all educational practices are situated. In the past, we simply did not ask enough "why" questions. Why are we doing this activity? Why do students need it? Why must writing instruction follow Western-influenced L1 target language norms? or enough "who" questions. Who tells us to teach certain kinds of writing in certain ways? In whose interests are the writing activities done? Whose "target language" is taken as a model (and why)? We do not need to abandon anything in our teaching of writing that serves sensible purposes and that is understood in ecological (contextual) ways, including how all writing activities are done within and for particular local (often non-English or multilingual) communities. This purpose might include instruction in Western-influenced essay exams, if this is what students need to do to get into a graduate school of their choice, as well as practice in writing for publication for Inner-Circle venues (e.g., the US, the UK, Australia, Canada, New Zealand). But, as the EIL perspective argues, this kind of Western-influenced writing is only part of the story. I urge readers to look beyond these (powerful) stereotypes to deeper complexities within their own contexts.

Exploring the Ideas

1 Take one or more of the areas discussed in this chapter and discuss them in relation to your own experiences as a teacher and a learner and to your understanding of an EIL perspective. For example:
   a. What have been your experiences learning or teaching the generic academic essay?
   b. If you have ever compared two pieces of writing from different languages to look for rhetorical differences, why, and what did you find?
   c. What have been your experiences with and understanding of process writing, as a teacher or learner?
   d. What kinds of error correction have you given and received on writing? What were your assumptions and purposes, and your students' responses to this activity? How does your view fit, or not, within an EIL approach to L2 writing?
   e. What are your views of writing tests (e.g., essay exams) that seem to demand a narrowly defined "target language" norm? Have you ever taken such a test? If so, for what purposes?
2 In your experience, what are some examples of writing that you or your students have done that seem to have little to do with the

standard Western-influenced norms of writing? (These examples might come from outside a classroom context.) Discuss how they differ from what you see as typical Western-influenced writing.

3   From what you have read and discussed so far, what is your understanding of what an "ecological" and "EIL" approach to L2 writing might be? How might such an approach be carried out in the particular settings where you work or study?

Applying the Ideas

1   Locate several of the key readings cited in this chapter or elsewhere and consider how the ideas might or might not apply to your own teaching-learning context. Be specific about the details of your own context and about how the ideas might apply. Where feasible, try out some of these ideas.

2   Interview (formally or informally) instructors and/or students in your own teaching context about the kinds of writing they do. Ask them about the languages and strategies they use when they write, and the reasoning behind their choices.

3   If you have an interest in workplace writing, locate several people to ask about the kinds of writing they do at work, and the languages and strategies they use.

For either or both of these interview activities, what connections, if any, do you see between the ways writing is taught in your setting and the ways writing is used in subject matter classes and in workplaces?

4   Design a writing lesson (or whole course) for a teaching context that you know well that takes into account a contextualized EIL approach to writing instruction. Be sure to describe your context in detail, and to make clear your views on the use of L1 and L2 (L3…).

References

Bitchener, J. (2008). Evidence in support of written corrective feedback. *Journal of Second Language Writing, 17*(1), 102–118.

Bizzell, P. (1982). College composition: Initiation into the academic discourse community. *Curriculum Inquiry, 12*(2), 191–207.

Block, D. (2003). *The social turn in second language acquisition*. Washington, DC: Georgetown University Press.

Canagarajah, A. S. (2002). *A geopolitics of academic writing*. Pittsburgh, PA: University of Pittsburgh Press.

Cargill, M., O' Connor, P., & Li, Y. (2011). Educating Chinese scientists to write for international journals: Addressing the divide between science and technology education and English language teaching. *English for Specific Purposes*, doi:10.1016/ j.esp.2011.05.003

Casanave, C. P. (2003). Looking ahead to more sociopolitically-oriented case study research in L2 writing scholarship (But should it be called "post-process"?). *Journal of Second Language Writing, 12*(1), 85–102.

Casanave, C. P. (2004). *Controversies in second language writing: Dilemmas and decisions in research and instruction*. Ann Arbor, MI: University of Michigan Press.

Casanave, C. P. (2009). Training for writing or training for reality? Challenges facing writing teachers and students in language teacher education programs. In R. Manchón (Ed.), *Writing in foreign language contexts: Learning, teaching, and research* (pp. 256–277). Clevedon, UK: Multilingual Matters.

Chandler, J. (2003). The efficacy of various kinds of error feedback for improvement in the accuracy and fluency of L2 student writing. *Journal of Second Language Writing, 12*(3), 267–296.

Connor, U. (1996). *Contrastive rhetoric: Cross-cultural aspects of second-language writing*. New York: Cambridge University Press.

Connor, U. (2004). Intercultural rhetoric research: Beyond texts. *Journal of English for Academic Purposes, 3*(4), 291–304.

Connor, U. (2011). *Intercultural rhetoric in the writing classroom*. Ann Arbor, MI: University of Michigan Press.

Currie, P. (1999). Transferable skills: Promoting student research. *English for Specific Purposes, 18*(4), 329–345.

Dillard, A. (1989). *The writing life*. New York: Harper & Row.

Ferris, D. (1999). The case for grammar correction in L2 writing classes: A response to Truscott (1996). *Journal of Second Language Writing, 8*, 1–11.

Ferris, D. R. (2002). *Treatment of error in second language student writing*. Ann Arbor, MI: University of Michigan Press.

Flower, L., & Hayes, J. (1981). A cognitive process theory of writing. *College Composition and Communication, 32*(4), 365–387.

Guénette, D. (2007). Is feedback pedagogically correct? Research design issues in studies of feedback on writing. *Journal of Second Language Writing, 16*(1), 40–53.

Harklau, L. (2002). The role of writing in classroom second language acquisition. *Journal of Second Language Writing, 11*(4), 329–350.

Hayes, J. R., Hatch, J. A., & Silk, C. M. (2000). Does holistic assessment predict writing performance? Estimating the consistency of student performance on holistically scored writing assignments. *Written Communication, 17*(1), 3–26.

Hinds, J. (1983). Contrastive rhetoric: Japanese and English. *Text, 3*, 183–195.

Hinds, J. (1987). Reader versus writer responsibility: A new typology. In U. Connor, & R. Kaplan (Eds.), *Writing across languages: Analysis of L2 text* (pp. 141–152). Reading, MA: Addison-Wesley.

Horowitz, D. (1986). Process not product: Less than meets the eye. *TESOL Quarterly, 20*(1), 141–144.

Huot, B. (1996). Toward a new theory of writing assessment. *College Composition and Communication, 47*(4), 549–566.

Hyland, K. (2009). *Academic discourse*. London: Continuum.

Johns, A. M. (1988). The discourse community dilemma: Identifying transferable skills for the academic milieu. *English for Specific Purposes, 7*, 55–60.

Kaplan, R. B. (1966). Cultural thought patterns in intercultural communication. *Language Learning, 16*(1), 1–20.

Kramsch, C. (2002). "How can we tell the dancer from the dance?" In C. Kramsch (Ed.), *Language acquisition and language socialization: Ecological perspectives* (pp. 1–30). New York: Continuum.

Kubota, R. (1997). A reevaluation of the uniqueness of Japanese written discourse. *Written Communication, 14* (4), 460–480.

Kubota, R. (1998). An investigation of L1–L2 transfer in writing among Japanese university students: Implications for contrastive rhetoric. *Journal of Second Language Writing, 7*(1), 69–100.

Kubota, R., & Lehner, A. (2004). Toward critical contrastive rhetoric. *Journal of Second Language Writing, 13*(1), 7–27.

Larsen-Freeman, D., & Cameron, L. (2008). *Complex systems and applied linguistics*. Oxford: Oxford University Press.

Leki, I. (2007). *Undergraduates in a second language: Challenges and complexities of academic literacy development*. Mahwah, NJ: Lawrence Erlbaum Associates.

Li, Y. (2006). Negotiating knowledge contribution to multiple discourse communities: A doctoral student of computer science writing for publication. *Journal of Second Language Writing, 15*, 159–178.

Lillis, T., & Curry, M. J. (2010). *Academic writing in a global context: The politics and practices of publishing in English*. London: Routledge.

Manchón, R. (Ed.). (2009a). *Writing in foreign language contexts: Learning, teaching, and research*. Clevedon, UK: Multilingual Matters.

Manchón, R. (2009b). Introduction: Broadening the perspective of L2 writing scholarship: The contribution of research on foreign language writing. In R. Manchón (Ed.), *Writing in foreign language contexts: Learning, teaching, and research* (pp. 1–19). Clevedon, UK: Multilingual Matters.

Matsuda, P. K. (1997). Contrastive rhetoric in context: A dynamic model of L2 writing. *Journal of Second Language Writing, 6*(1), 45–60.

Pecorari, D. (2003). Good and original: Plagiarism and patchwriting in academic second language writing. *Journal of Second Language Writing, 12*(4), 317–345.

Reichelt, M. (2009). A critical evaluation of writing teaching programmes in different foreign language settings. In R. Manchón (Ed.), *Writing in foreign language contexts: Learning, teaching, and research* (pp. 183–206). Clevedon, UK: Multilingual Matters.

Reid, J. (1984). The radical outliner and the radical brainstormer. *TESOL Quarterly, 18*, 529–533.

Swales, J. (1988). Discourse communities, genres and English as an international language. *World Englishes, 7*(2), 211–220.

Swales, J. M. (1990). *Genre analysis: English in academic and research settings*. New York: Cambridge University Press.

Truscott, J. (1996). The case against grammar correction in L2 writing classes. *Language Learning, 46*(2), 327–369.

Truscott, J. (2007). The effect of error correction on learners' ability to write accurately. *Journal of Second Language Writing, 16*(4), 255–272.

Truscott, J. (2009). Dialogue: Arguments and appearances: A response to Chandler. *Journal of Second Language Writing, 18*(1), 59–60.

Truscott, J. (2010). Some thoughts on Anthony Bruton's critique of the correction debate. *System, 38*(2), 329–335.

Truscott, J., & Hsu, A. Y. (2008). Error correction, revision, and learning. *Journal of Second Language Writing, 17*(4), 292–305.

Tudor, I. (2003). Learning to live with complexity: An ecological perspective on language teaching. *System, 31*(1), 1–12.

van Lier, L. (2002). An ecological-semiotic perspective on language and linguistics. In C. Kramsch (Ed.), *Language acquisition and language socialization: Ecological perspectives* (pp. 140–164). New York: Continuum.

van Lier, L. (2004). *The ecology and semiotics of language learning: A sociocultural perspective*. Boston, MA: Kluwer Academic Publishers.

Zamel, V. (1982). Writing: The process of discovering meaning. *TESOL Quarterly, 16*(2), 195–209.

Zamel, V. (1983). The composing process of advanced ESL students: Six case studies. *TESOL Quarterly, 17*(2), 165–187.

Chapter 17

Literature in Language Teaching

Alan Maley

Introduction

Overview

In this chapter, I set out the justification for the inclusion of literature in English as an international language (EIL) contexts, examine the curricular settings, and discuss various interpretations of literature. I then examine possible approaches to the teaching of literature, making a case for "literature as appropriation" especially in EIL contexts. A powerful way of incorporating an EIL perspective is through text selection. Literature can also be incorporated into an EIL context through Extensive Reading, Performance, Creative Writing, and a variety of activities for getting inside the skin of a text. These are discussed and exemplified.

Background

Literature as part of the language teaching curriculum has weathered a number of storms over the past century. Initially regarded as the central feature, along with grammar, of language teaching in traditional approaches, it underwent rapid decline during the periods of Structural/Behavioral ascendancy, and the more recent pragmatic, use-focused Communicative regime. It is only relatively recently that it has regained a degree of recognition as one of the approaches competing for our pedagogical attention.

However, the case has to be made afresh for its relevance in the context of EIL. This is particularly the case given the current focus on speed, efficiency, accountability, performance objectives, and value for money in a global consumerist economy increasingly driven by digital technology. What conceivable use might literature have in such a context?

Why Literature?

Continuing Relevance of the Linguistic, Cultural and Personal-Growth Models?

It has been customary to propose three main models for the use of literature: the linguistic model, the cultural model, and the personal-growth model (Carter & McRae, 1996; Maley, 2001, p. 182; Duff & Maley, 2007, pp. 5–6). Do these models continue to have relevance?

Literary texts certainly continue to offer a rich and varied linguistic resource, and as such, provide the kind of input for phonological, lexical, syntactic, and discoursal acquisition regarded by many as essential for effective language learning, in contrast to the more restricted and narrow exposure offered by many pedagogically-driven texts. They are also an ideal resource for the development of language awareness: of language variation (historical, geographical, professional, sociological), of social appropriacy, of ideological bias, of illocutionary meaning, etc.

Particularly in the international context, where multi-cultural encounters are increasingly important, the cultural potential offered by literature is also undeniable. Literature cannot be used to "teach" culture but it can illuminate the multi-facetted contexts, practices, and beliefs our students may be expected to encounter in their professional and personal lives outside the classroom. In the words of Kramsch (1993, pp. 233–259), it can create "third places," from which students can critically examine both their own and other cultures.

And literary texts have lost none of their power to promote personal growth, through better understanding of human motivation and action. Students exposed to such texts are opened to better critical understanding of themselves and of others in a rapidly-changing and often confusing and paradoxical world.

The Place of Literature in Curricular Philosophies

Language education, like education in general, is not neutral as to ideology. It is intricately bound up with the curricular philosophies and beliefs which animate the system of teaching in question (whether state or institutional). Such ideological principles are commonly agreed to be: Humanist, Academic, Technological, and Reconstructionist/Social Reformist (Clark, 1987; Cook, 2010). Where does literature fit into these characterizations?

- *Academic.* Here the focus is on the transmission of knowledge of a particular academic discipline. Students are taught about the subject and are expected to learn what they are taught in order to preserve and pass on what is deemed valuable by the academic discourse community.

- *Humanist.* Here education is regarded as a way of helping students develop themselves fully as individuals. This emphasis on personal growth tends to favor methodologies which place responsibility for learning on the learners, and where interpersonal relationships, processes, and activities are of prime importance.
- *Technological.* Here education is regarded as serving practical purposes by equipping students with the skills and knowledge they need to perform their designated social and professional roles. Typically this will lead to the detailed specification of objectives in advance and to an emphasis on testing to ascertain whether they have been achieved.
- *Reconstructionist/Social Reformist.* Here education is regarded as the vehicle for bringing about desirable social change. This implies the inculcation of pre-determined beliefs and values, as well as the skills and knowledge regarded as necessary in a given society. It too is usually characterized by detailed objectives and assessment.

Most curricula will include elements from two or more of these philosophies, so we should not expect to find pure examples. However, it is probable that many curricula across the world lean towards a Technological or Reconstructionist model, while in more traditional societies, the Academic model is still favored. It is the Humanist model which most often finds itself left out in the cold. We should also realize that there may be, and often is, a mismatch between the declared curricular objectives and the way they are interpreted and activated in classrooms.

Superficially, it might seem that literature sits more comfortably with a Humanist or an Academic curricular philosophy. As we have seen above, literature is intrinsically more oriented towards the more personal, affective, and interactive aspects of learning which the Humanistic model embodies. However, there is no compelling reason for its exclusion from any model. Literature can act as a major resource for the inculcation of beliefs and values, and indeed of critical skills and world knowledge under a Reconstructionist model. It can also play a part within a Technological model by focusing more directly on the linguistic devices which literature deploys, and applying these to more instrumental uses.

However, given the strongly results-oriented, instrumentally-focused views now prevalent in many countries and institutions, the inclusion of literature, in whatever form, will continue to need persuasive advocacy and a sensitivity to local educational contexts.

Literature and How to Teach it

What is Literature?

How we teach literature is to a large degree contingent on our beliefs about the nature of literature itself. Among the more frequently-encountered beliefs are:

- that literature is a collection of texts regarded as the most significant within a language or cultural group. Such texts are sanctified by long familiarity and by academic authority. In English, this traditional canon would include works by Chaucer, Shakespeare, Dickens, etc. It rarely includes work by living authors. And it gathers about itself a cocoon of critical discussion, debate, and exegesis which often removes the original works from the center of attention (Calvino, 2009, pp. 3–9). This is Literature with a capital "L" and it still can and does form the basis of programs of study.
- that literature is made up of any text which needs to be read aesthetically rather than efferently (Kramsch, 1993, pp. 122–124)— or is open to representational, rather than referential interpretation (McRae, 1991). In this view of literature (what McRae calls "literature with a small 'l'"), the traditional canon is expanded to include a much wider variety of texts and a much less constrained approach to interpretation. It places the text at the center of attention and encourages a personal response to it (Rosenblatt, 1978).
- that literature is defined by a limited number of more or less rule-governed genres or text types. These normally include poetry with its many sub-genres, including songs; fiction, ranging from very short mini-sagas and flash fiction via short stories to very long novels, and including oral as well as written stories; drama, including comedy, tragedy, farce, absurdist plays, radio-drama, etc.; essays and letters; travel literature; biography and autobiography; history; philosophical and religious texts; journalism; speeches, etc. The focus is then on the ways in which such genres are constructed, how they function, and what value they may have for their communities of users.
- that literature comprises special uses of language peculiar to itself. The focus here is on the literary devices which are found in unusually high proportions in literary texts, though not confined to them. In such a definition, attention is drawn to the figurative/metaphorical aspects of literary texts and to the high degree of patterning found in them at all levels: phonological, lexical, syntactic, discoursal. Characteristically, approaches deriving from this definition would examine in detail the many literary tropes and devices: metaphor,

personification, repetition, parallelism, collocation, rhyme, alliteration, assonance, rhythm, intertextuality, visual layout, etc. and attempt to assign interpretations to them. This view of literature would suggest a more technically-oriented approach to the study of texts.

How Might Literature be Taught?

Traditionally, there have been two major approaches to the use of literature in language teaching programs.

- Literature as Study
  In one of them, the focus is on canonical texts as objects of study: set books, line-by-line analysis, and explication, etc. It essentially centers upon *teaching about* literature. Typically, this involves a good deal of transmission of received opinions about writers, their lives and times, their influences, critical views of their work, etc. The emphasis is on "telling" rather than on "discovery" and on memorizing content rather than on critical reflection and inquiry.
- Literature as Resource
  In the other approach, the texts tend to be drawn from a wider range, and are used either as samples of language use or as springboards into other language learning activities. In a sense, the literature is secondary to the language learning aims and objectives: it is a kind of vehicle for engaging with the language (Widdowson, 1997). This might be characterized as *teaching with* literature.

In the context of EIL both these approaches are open to criticism, however. The Literature as Study approach tends to focus on canonical texts drawn from Inner-Circle countries (Kachru, 1992). Such texts are often far removed from students' lived experience and may be culturally inaccessible. Even when more local texts are chosen, the transmission-dominated model of methodology usually remains unchanged, and this is inappropriate in an EIL context where there is a need for students to become active participants rather than passive recipients.

The Literature as Resource approach may also prove unsatisfactory. It may become nothing more than another way of introducing and practicing language as part of a pre-determined syllabus. The specifically literary value of texts may be overshadowed by the linguistic content and the methodological gymnastics played with it. This approach may be reduced to a box of tricks which students rapidly tire of.

This is not to deny that both these approaches may have valuable elements in them provided they are used appropriately. In a MA module I taught in Bangkok, for instance, within a Literature as Study framework I was able to combine a "set books" approach with the active participation of students in mini-projects based on the texts, which were drawn from one British, one African, and one Chinese author. In another module, using a Literature as Resource approach, I was able to transfer responsibility for the choice of texts and the activities based upon them to the students themselves. Both these instances offer pointers to a third possible approach, which I shall call Literature as Appropriation.

- Literature as Appropriation
  In this approach, the aim is to enable students to make literature their own, to appropriate it for their own learning purposes in ways relevant to themselves and to the context in which they move. Both the other approaches are to a greater or lesser degree external to the students, what I have termed elsewhere *literature from the outside in* (Maley, 2010). In the approach advocated here, I am suggesting ways of enabling students to get inside the skin of the texts—to apprehend them from the inside rather than simply to comprehend them from the outside—what I have termed *literature from the inside out*. We may characterize this approach as *learning through* literature, and it seems particularly appropriate in EIL contexts where a personalized and critical appreciation of English is crucial to students' development as independent users of the language. How might this be done? A number of possibilities suggest themselves: independent work on Extensive Reading and Listening (Maley, 2008, pp. 113–156); Performance of texts; Creation of texts by students themselves, both spoken and written; and a number of pedagogical techniques, including Project Work, where responsibility is passed largely to the students (Maley 2003, pp. 21–31). These types of work will be described in greater detail in the next section below.

Literature and EIL: From Principles to Practice

So far, I have attempted to justify the inclusion of literature in language programs, with particular attention to the changed situation with regard to EIL, and to characterize the curricular and methodological alternatives available when including literature in language programs. It is now time to suggest concrete ways to proceed. English teaching in the new reality of an EIL context cannot simply continue with business as usual. There are important differences in the current situation which affect the way we approach the use and teaching of literature. What are these new realities?

- As the demand for English as the language of opportunity continues to increase, there will be more students, many of whom will never have been exposed to literature before. This implies a democratic, inclusive rather than an elitist, exclusive teaching approach.
- As English itself spreads, both geographically and functionally, it will continue to change rapidly, and to become more varied. This diversity needs to be taken into consideration. An exclusive focus on "standard" English will no longer satisfy this reality.
- As English becomes a necessary condition for personal or professional success, it will no longer be a sufficient condition to be able to use it averagely well (Graddol, 2006). Increasingly the premium will be on those who can use it to a high degree of proficiency (Maley, 2009), and fuse it with "life skills" (Rogers, Taylor-Knowles, & Taylor-Knowles, 2008).
- As the opportunities for international exchanges become more frequent, there will be a corresponding need for social and cultural sensitivity. Social and emotional intelligence will become more important (Goleman 1996, 2006; Spendlove, 2008).
- As life in a consumerist world dominated by English becomes more demanding and more pressurized, the value of reflection and critical intelligence will be enhanced (Fisher, 2001; Honore, 2004; Naish, 2008; Postman, 1985; Postman & Weingartner, 1971; Unrau, 2008).
- As the demand for instant solutions and quick fixes in education becomes more insistent, so the value of a more deliberate mode of thinking will become more urgent (Claxton, 1997).
- As English becomes more international, so will the movement to more local independence become more pronounced. The tensions between English as a medium for global communication and English as a badge of local cultural identity will be intensified.

Within the context of literature, I believe that such pressures can to some extent be accommodated through the way we select the texts to which students will be exposed, and by the manner in which we utilize these texts. The following sections should therefore be read against the above list of realities to assess the value of a new orientation toward the value of including literature in our programs.

Principles and Issues in Text Selection

Essentially, we shall need to greatly expand both the range of texts which will form the basis of selection and the mechanisms used for making the selection. This will serve at least three purposes. It will better reflect the "balance of power" between Englishes in an EIL world. It will offer a window into the differing realities in that world. It can make access to literary texts less difficult by offering students content with which they are relatively familiar.

- *Extending the range of provenance of texts.*
  Since the second half of the 20th century there has been a spectacular explosion of literature in English written by those for whom English is not a first language (Skinner, 1998). Much of this literature emerged in the aftermath of the independence of former British colonial territories (King, 1987). Since then, there has been a steady growth of writing from the Indian Sub-continent, Singapore/Malaysia, the Philippines, West, East and southern Africa, and the Caribbean. Alongside this, writing from the Asian, African, Caribbean, and other diasporas—writing which deals with the experience of living in two cultures at once, has taken its place (Ali, 2003; Lahiri, 1999). And more recently still, writers have emerged from the Expanding-Circle countries: China, Iran, Nepal, Afghanistan, publishing their work directly in English. This abundance of new literatures, with their English tongue rooted in non-English soil, offers unparalleled opportunities to extend the boundaries of choice of texts for use in language teaching programs with an EIL orientation.
- *Extending the range of text-types for inclusion.*
  A second way of expanding the range of choice would be to include other genres, not usually regarded as literature (with a capital L). There is a large body of literature written primarily for children, for teenagers, and for fans of crime, mystery, romance, and science fiction. More radically, we should consider the inclusion of certain kinds of graded readers. A persuasive case has been made for the recognition of a new genre: Language Learner Literature (Day & Bamford, 1998). In the same way that we can identify other genres which target particular types of reader (children's fiction, teen fiction, popular romance, etc.) so, it is argued, the books written for a language learner audience also constitute a specific genre. This is particularly true of the latest generation of graded readers which, rather than simplifying existing texts, create original works within the linguistic limitations of their learner-readers. Some of these are classics of their kind, managing as they do to create highly compelling fiction within a limited vocabulary (Moses, 2004). Even simplified fiction would qualify for inclusion if well done and oriented to non-Inner Circle worlds (Bassett, 2008). There is also a strong case to be made for including literature written by

teachers and their students. I have referred in the case-study below to the poems and stories produced by just one small group of such writers in Asia (Maley, 2006; Maley & Mukundan, 2005–2009a, 2005–2009b).

- *Extending the number of stakeholders involved in text-selection.*
  Typically, texts are chosen by syllabus authorities, by textbook writers, and by directors of studies and teachers. However well-intentioned such choices may be, they are inevitably top-down: it is rare for those who will use these texts to be consulted about them in advance. One way of opening to the new realities of the EIL context is to empower students by making them party to decisions about text selection. Such choices would entail major shifts of power and practice. For example, offering students the simple choice between a class reader, which everyone would read at the same time, and a class library from which each student would select a book, implies massive change. Similarly, offering students small samples of books they might consider before requiring them to choose one title is another form of student enfranchisement. For more examples of extending power of choice to students, see Bamford and Day (2004).

- *Issues in text selection.*
  Clearly, the selection of texts is not unproblematic, whatever system is used. The following are among the most contentious:

1 Moral and cultural sensitivity will always pose problems for text selection. What is prized for its literary value often offends local sensitivities: moral, cultural, political. For instance, the stories of Frankie Sionil Jose (1984), the well-known Filipino writer, are of undoubted literary value. But they raise uncomfortable questions of sexual and economic exploitation which few educationists are willing to confront.

2 Many such texts are so local in their references that they are difficult for anyone outside the specific culture to access. This need not be a reason for rejecting them but it does create potential problems for the outside reader.

3 Many original, authentic texts from whatever source, are linguistically complex, and non-standard, which creates problems for the readers. Again, this is not a reason for outright rejection but it does need to be carefully considered.

4 Questions of quality also arise. The fact that a text has been written by a "non-native user" may make it interesting but is no guarantee of quality. Anyone, native or non-native, can write rubbish. Care needs to be exercised that texts are not chosen for reasons of political correctness alone.

Pedagogical Applications and Practices

Having made a selection of texts, what forms of activity might be most appropriate within the context of EIL? I suggested above (Literature as appropriation, p. 304, this chapter), that there were at least four main ways in which literature could be more effectively incorporated into such a context.

- Extensive Reading (and Listening)
- Performance
- Creative Writing and Speech
- Techniques for getting inside the skin of the text.

Extensive Reading

There has been a growing interest in the potential of Extensive Reading to promote language acquisition, especially of vocabulary and collocation (Day & Bamford, 1998; Goodman, 1996; Krashen, 2004; Maley, 2009; Smith, 2004).

For Extensive Reading to be effective, the following criteria have to be met:

1 Students read a lot and read often.
2 There is a wide variety of text types and topics to choose from.
3 The texts are not just interesting: they are engaging/compelling.
4 Students choose what to read.
5 Reading purposes focus on: pleasure, information, and general understanding.
6 Reading is its own reward.
7 There are no tests, no exercises, no questions, and no dictionaries.
8 Materials are within the language competence of the students.
9 Reading is individual, and silent.
10 Speed is faster, not deliberate and slow.
11 The teacher explains the goals and procedures clearly, then monitors and guides the students.
12 The teacher is a role model ... a reader, who participates along with the students.

The justification for introducing Extensive Reading programs is based partly on research evidence that such programs produce superior results (see Day & Bamford, 1998 and Krashen, 2004 for a summary of the research findings). It is also obvious that, given the limited hours of instruction in most programs, students will never be exposed to enough vocabulary, enough times, to acquire the necessary quantum in classrooms alone. Out of class learning is the only way, and one of the most convenient and proven ways of doing so is through massive independent reading, entailing repeated encounters with vocabulary in context.

In one sense, it is contradicting the tenets of Extensive Reading above to recommend activities. However, even such simple activities as mini-presentations of books read or poster presentations can help to both share and fix the texts in memory. For a more comprehensive set of ideas, see Bamford and Day (2004) and Waring (2000).

Extensive Reading does not only involve literary texts, of course, but they are among the most motivating genres. Moreover, although we cannot hope to "teach" the many varieties of English which our students will encounter in the EIL world, we can give a certain limited exposure to them through the medium of literary texts drawn from a variety of geographical sources.

In a similar way, exposure to extensive listening texts can reinforce and extend language acquisition. There is now a wide range of recorded fiction and poetry available in the form of talking books, DVDs, and film. One particularly rewarding and motivating type of listening is to hear and watch authors reading from their own work (see for example, Astley & Robertson-Pearce, 2008). In this way, they can begin to tune in to the many authentic voices and accents of living writers. In the absence of recordings, clear and sensitive reading aloud by the teacher can be almost equally inspiring (Maley, 2009).

Performance

One of the most effective ways of getting inside the skin of a text is to perform it. To do this well, the students have to have understood it and lived with it. There are also clear benefits in memorization (without tears), cooperation, self-esteem, and motivation.

Performance can take a variety of forms. It may consist simply of students performing short texts they have chosen. A more demanding and intensive type of performance is to ask students in groups of about six to prepare an orchestrated performance of a text. In doing so they will need to consider parameters of volume, pace, pitch, and rhythm, as well as which lines will be spoken by one or more speakers, etc. (Maley, 1999, 2000). This is related to work in "Readers' Theatre" by Shirley Brice-Heath (1983) and Courtney Cazden (1992) in the USA. The effects on retention and on motivation and self-esteem are remarkable.

An even more demanding example is the production of a full-length play. Peter Lutzker (2007) has investigated in depth the effects of such a production on his students in Germany, in terms of their linguistic and personal development, and reports strong evidence of growth in both areas. If the plays for performance are well chosen, they can also lead to a better understanding of social and personal issues in the real world. Lutzker chose *The Diary of Anne Frank,* which led to some really deep reflection on the part of his German students! Locally-written texts may be chosen but localized versions of classics, including Shakespeare, can also be connected to local realities (Kott, 1964).

Creative Writing

The act of writing creatively has a number of well-documented positive effects both on the learning of the language and on personal and social development (see the case study below). Taking the place of the writer—in fact, becoming a writer—helps students develop greater sensitivity to the ways the language functions, with particular benefits for vocabulary, collocation, rhythm, and syntactic variety. The game-like activity of writing creatively in the foreign language promotes willingness to take risks, to try out new things, and in the process helps develop awareness of the language, of the world, and of oneself. Even more importantly, perhaps, the act of creating original texts and "publishing" them (whether on a notice-board, a website, or as a leaflet), empowers the students, and enhances their self-esteem (Spendlove, 2008). They have in a sense *appropriated* the language—made it their own.

There are now many resources available to teachers wishing to try out creative writing with their students (Koch, 1990; Maley & Mukundan, 2011a, 2011b; Matthews, 1994; Spiro, 2004, 2006; Wright & Hill, 2009).

Techniques for Getting Inside the Skin of the Text

There are so many of these that it is not feasible to attempt a detailed catalogue. The following titles are a good starting point: McRae and Vethamani (1999), Maley (1993, 1995), Maley and Duff (1985), Maley and Moulding (1985), Lazar (1993), and Tomlinson (1986, 1998). Essentially, the activities offered in these books encourage students to engage personally with texts in interesting and challenging ways in order to uncover and discover them afresh. (See "Exploring the ideas" and "Applying the ideas" for some examples of such activities.)

Conclusion

I began this chapter by describing the continuing advantages of using literary texts, and how literature fits into different curricular frameworks. I went on to discuss four different views on what constitutes literature, as a preliminary to a discussion of three possible approaches to its use: teaching *about, with,* and *through* literature, expressing a preference

A Case Study: The Asia Teacher-Writers Group

This small project undertaken since 2003 is a practical example of literature within the EIL situation. A small, informal group of Asian teachers meets once a year in a different country to write original stories and poems in English. These are then published and made available for use as teaching input to classes in the Asia region. So far, the group has met in Bangkok, Thailand (2003), Melaka, Malaysia (2004), Fuzhou, China (2005), Hanoi, Vietnam (2006), Salatiga, Indonesia (2007), Kirtipur, Nepal (2008), Ho Chi Minh City, Vietnam (2009), Dhulikel, Nepal (2010), and Jember, Indonesia (March 2011). Participants to date have been drawn from twelve countries.

The group operates in the belief that NNS [Non-Native Speaker] teachers are not only capable of but are also uniquely well-placed to write literary materials for use by their own and other students in the Asia region. Because they share their students' background and contexts, they have an intuitive understanding of what will be culturally and topically relevant and attractive for them. What they so often lack is the confidence in their own ability to write interesting material. The group operates to dispel this misconception.

The following rationale underpins the activities of the group:

- A belief in the value of creative writing in English both for teachers and for students.
- A belief in the ability of teachers in the region to produce their own English teaching materials.
- A belief that these materials will provide useful input for promoting reading (and other activities) in English.
- A belief in the value for professional and personal development of forming a closely-knit, Asia-wide, mutually-supportive learning community of teacher/writers.

The objectives are:

- To produce poetry and stories appropriate in level and content for use by Asian students of English at secondary level.
- To publish and promote these as widely as possible, thus creating a wider awareness of the value of Creative Writing.
- To develop materials and activities for the teaching of creative writing with students too.
- To run creative writing conferences and workshops for the wider teaching community wherever possible.
- In this way, to boost the self-esteem and confidence of teachers of English in Asia.

For the publications of the group to date see Maley and Mukundan (2005–2009a and b) and Maley, Mukundan, and Rai (2009).

for the last of the three—*literature as appropriation*. Before discussing possible ways of rendering literature more relevant in a world of EIL, I listed the factors which characterize the new contexts in which English is being taught and used. I then argued that literature might serve a more obviously useful purpose in the EIL context if the way texts are chosen were to be extended, and by using four major types of activity: *Extensive Reading (and Listening), Performance, Creative Writing*, and *Techniques for Getting Inside the Skin of the Text*.

Throughout, I have had in mind the kinds of challenges students now face with respect to English, learning, and life. Among the most important of these are:

- the need to somehow survive the culture of speed and info-glut which threatens to overwhelm them. This implies the need to restore control over time and information, and to make available time for reflection, discrimination, and criticism.
- the almost exclusive focus on the short-term, utilitarian value of education, with scant attention given to the long-term values of aesthetic appreciation. This implies finding a place for texts and practices which do help develop aesthetic and affective appreciation (Jakobson, 1960).
- the all-too-frequent priority given to English at the expense of local languages and cultures. This implies the need to use English instead as a way of validating the local rather than submerging it, and restoring self-respect and self-esteem.
- the gap between the model of English offered in the classroom and the plurality of English uses outside it. This implies exposing students to many of the varieties they will encounter, even if these cannot be taught explicitly.

It is my contention that literature can achieve some success in meeting these four challenges. There are, of course, no easy options, and no sure-fire solutions. Given that literature will always be regarded by some at least as irrelevant, there will be a corresponding need to make a case for it in contrast to the more fashionable, the more "modern," the more technological, the more utilitarian approaches on offer. This entails constantly re-making the way literature is used to keep it fresh, interesting and thus relevant.

Exploring the Ideas

1   Should language teaching just be about teaching language? What other important factors are involved, according to the writer of this chapter?
2   A distinction has been made between Objectives (short-term, language-focused, measurable, etc.) and Aims (long-term, more broadly

educational, difficult to measure, etc.) (Widdowson, 1993). Draw up a list of the short-term objectives and the longer-term aims you would use for incorporating literature in your classroom.

3 How important is it for students to be exposed to non-standard varieties of English? How feasible is this? Is literature the best way of doing it?

4 *Literature as Appropriation* is advocated here. How feasible would this be in your own teaching context?

5 In the section "Literature and EIL: From principles to practice," seven "realities" are listed. Do you agree that these are valid? What other realities would you add?

6 How important are the four issues (p. 307, this chapter) raised by text selection? Rank the four criteria in order of importance for you and justify your ranking.

7 How would literature be implemented in response to the four challenges listed in the "Conclusion" (p. 310, this chapter)? Would you add any other challenges?

Applying the Ideas

Here are just four ideas for integrating literary texts into larger issues in EIL education:

1 Focus on language.
   Select a number of texts which touch on the issue of English language. For example:

   • John Agard's *Listen Mr Oxford Don*, which begins:

     Me not no Oxford don
     me a simple immigrant
     from Clapham Common.
     I didn't graduate
     I immigrate.

   • R. Parthasarathy's *Homecoming*, which begins "*My tongue in English chains…,*"
   • *Festival* by Kenneth Wee, which ends:

     We watch the organised festivities
     And are reminded of our culture, our roots
     And we think: "I'm proud to be Chinese,"
     In English.

- Guo Xiaolu's *A Concise Chinese-English Dictionary for Lovers*, pages 25–27, which begins,

> First week in language school, I speaking like this:
> Who is her name?

The students read the text extracts and discuss the attitudes towards English which each reveals. How might you use the excerpts above to teach your students about the way language is used in literature?

2 Focus on education.

Select a text or texts which compare and contrast different cultural views on what learning should be like. A good example is Timothy Mo's *Sour Sweet* where the little Hong Kong Chinese boy's English school (p. 229) is contrasted with his Saturday Chinese classes (p. 237).

Students again use the extracts as the starting point for a discussion of their own beliefs about learning. They should begin by listing how they think a language is best learned. Do they favor the approach in the English school or the Chinese Saturday school? They should justify their position.

3 Focus on a societal issue.

This might be family values, love and relationships, death and dying, social exploitation, etc.

A concrete example is the extended monologue by Aurangzeb on pages 184–185 of *Moth Smoke* by Mohsin Hamid, on corruption, which begins, *"Some say my dad's corrupt and I'm his money launderer. Well, it's true enough."* How important is corruption in the students' own society? What do they think should be done about it? Is corruption an issue that should be debated in literature?

4 Focus on choice.

Students will need one or more collections of short stories, preferably from Outer-Circle contexts. For example, Lee Sukim's *Kebaya Tales* or Jennifer Bassett's *Cries from the Heart*. Students are assigned one story each to read. They are then asked to argue in favor or against adopting their story for class reading. They should first draw up their criteria (e.g., language level, interest, relevance for them, cultural difficulties, etc.) then use these as the basis for their assessment.

An alternative is to ask them to skim the stories, looking for the one they would like to read first.

References

Agard, J. (n.d.) *Listen Mr Oxford Don*. Retrieved March 20, 2011, from http://images.hachette-livre.fr/media/contenuNumerique/036/3482565790. pdf

Ali, M. (2003). *Brick lane*. New York: Doubleday.

Astley, N., & Robertson-Pearce. P. (Eds.). (2008). *In person: 30 poets*. Bloodaxe Books (includes 2 DVDs).

Bamford, J., & Day, R. (Eds.). (2004). *Extensive reading activities for teaching language*. Cambridge: Cambridge University Press.

Bassett, J. (Ed.). (2008). *Stories from around the world series/Oxford Bookworms*. Oxford: Oxford University Press.

Bassett, J. (Ed.). (2009). *Cries from the heart: Stories from around the world*. Oxford: Oxford University Press.

Calvino, I. (2009). *Why read the Classics?* London: Penguin Classics.

Carter, R., & McRae, J. (1996). *Language, literature and the learner*. Harlow: Longman.

Cazden, C. (1992). Performing expository texts in the foreign language classroom. In C. Kramsch, & S. McConnell-Ginet (Eds.), *Text and context: Cross disciplinary perspectives on language study* (pp. 67–78). D.C Heath and Company.

Clark, J. (1987). *Curriculum renewal in school foreign language learning*. Oxford: Oxford University Press.

Claxton, G. (1997). *Hare brain: Tortoise mind*. London: Fourth Estate.

Cook, G. (2010). *Translation in language teaching: An argument for reassessment*. Oxford: Oxford University Press.

Day, R., & Bamford, J. (1998). *Extensive reading in the second language classroom*. Cambridge: Cambridge University Press.

Duff, A., & Maley, A. (2007). *Literature*. Oxford: Oxford University Press.

Fisher, A. (2001). *Critical thinking: An introduction*. Cambridge: Cambridge University Press.

Goleman, D. (1996). *Emotional intelligence*. London: Bloomsbury.

Goleman, D. (2006). *Social intelligence: The new science of human relationships*. London: Hutchinson.

Goodman, K. S. (1996). *On reading*. London: Heinemann.

Graddol, D. (2006). *English next*. London: British Council.

Guo, X. (2007). *A concise Chinese-English dictionary for lovers*. London: Vintage.

Hamid, M. (2000). *Moth smoke*. London: Granta Books.

Heath, S. B. (1983). *Ways with words: Language, life and work in communities and classrooms*. Cambridge: Cambridge University Press.

Honore, C. (2004). *In praise of slow*. London: Orion Books.

Jakobson, R. (1960). Closing statement: Linguistics and poetics. In T. Sebeok (Ed.), *Style in Language*. New York: Wiley.

Jose, F. S. (1984). *Platinum: Ten Filipino stories*. Manila: Solidaridad Publishing House.

Kachru, B. B. (Ed.). (1992). *The other tongue: English across cultures*. Urbana, IL: University of Illinois Press.

King, B. (1987). *Modern Indian poetry in English*. New Delhi: Oxford University Press.

Koch, K. (1990). *Rose, where did you get that red?* New York: Vintage.

Kott, J. (1964). *Shakespeare, our contemporary*. London: Methuen.

Kramsch, C. (1993). *Context and culture in language teaching*. Oxford: Oxford University Press.

Krashen, S. (2004). *The Power of reading: Insights from the research* (2nd ed.). Westport, CT: Libraries Unlimited.

Lahiri, J. (1999). *The interpreter of maladies*. New York: Houghton Mifflin.

Lazar, G. (1993). *Literature and language teaching*. Cambridge: Cambridge University Press.

Lee, S. K. (2010). *Kebaya tales*. Singapore: Marshall Cavendish.

Lutzker, P. (2007). *The art of foreign language teaching: Improvisation and drama in teacher development and language learning*. Tübingen and Basel: Francke Verlag.

Maley, A. (1993). *Short and sweet I*. London: Penguin.

Maley, A. (1995). *Short and sweet II*. London: Penguin.

Maley, A. (1999). Choral speaking. *English Teaching Professional, 12,* 9–11.

Maley, A. (2000). *The language teacher's voice*. Oxford: Heinemann.

Maley, A. (2001). Literature in the language classroom. In R. Carter & D. Nunan (Eds.), *The Cambridge guide to teaching English to speakers of other languages* (pp. 180–185). Cambridge: Cambridge University Press.

Maley, A. (2003). Inputs, processes and outcomes in materials development: Extending the range. In J. Mukundan (Ed.), *Readings in material development I* (pp. 21–31). Serdang: UPM Press.

Maley, A. (2006). Creative writers: Creative readers. In J. Mukundan (Ed.), *Creative writing in EFL classrooms II* (pp. 32–37). Petaling Jaya: Pearson Malaysia.

Maley, A. (2008). Extensive reading: Maid in waiting. In B. Tomlinson (Ed.), *English language learning materials: A critical review* (pp. 133–156). London and New York: Continuum Publishing.

Maley, A. (2009). *Advanced learners*. Oxford: Oxford University Press.

Maley, A. (2010, October). *Literature from the outside in and from the inside out*. Paper presented at the Asia TEFL Conference, Hanoi.

Maley, A., & Duff, A. (1985). *The inward ear*. Cambridge: Cambridge University Press.

Maley, A., & Moulding, S. (1985). *Poem into poem*. Cambridge: Cambridge University Press.

Maley, A., & Mukundan, J. (Eds.). (2005–9a). *Asian poems for young readers* (Vols. 1, 3, 5, 7, 9). Petaling Jaya: Pearson Malaysia.

Maley, A., & Mukundan, J. (Eds.). (2005–9b). *Asian short stories for young readers* (Vols. 2, 4, 6,8). Petaling Jaya: Pearson Malaysia.

Maley, A., & Mukundan, J. (2011a). *Writing poems: A resource book for teachers of English*. Petaling Jaya: Pearson Malaysia.

Maley, A., & Mukundan, J. (2011b). *Writing stories: A resource book for teachers of English*. Petaling Jaya: Pearson Malaysia.

Maley, A., Mukundan, J., & Rai, V. S. (Eds.). (2009). *Life in words and words in life*. Kathmandu: Bhundipuran Prakashan.

Matthews, P. (1994). *Sing me the creation*. Stroud: Hawthorne Press.

McRae, J. (1991). *Literature with a small 'l'*. London: Macmillan.

McRae, J., & Vethamani, E. M. (1999). *Now read on*. London: Routledge.

Mo, T. (1990). *Sour sweet*. London: Vintage.

Moses, A. (2004). *Jojo's story*. Cambridge: Cambridge University Press.

Naish, J. (2008). *Enough: Breaking free from the world of excess*. London: Hodder and Stoughton.

Parthasarathy, R. (1993) From *Homecoming*. In M. Paranjape (Ed.), *Indian poetry in English* (p. 171). Madras: Macmillan India.

Postman, N. (1985). *Amusing ourselves to death*. London: Penguin.

Postman, N. & Weingartner, C. (1971). *Teaching as a subversive activity*. Harmondsworth: Penguin.

Rogers, M., Taylor-Knowles, J., & Taylor-Knowles, S. (2008). *Open mind*. Macmillan.

Rosenblatt, L. M. (1978). *The reader, the text, the poem: The transactional theory of the literary work*. Carbondale, IL: Southern Illinois University Press.

Skinner, J. (1998). *The stepmother tongue*. New York: St. Martin's Press.

Smith, F. (2004). *Understanding reading* (4th ed.). Mahwah, NJ: Laurence Erlbaum Associates Inc.

Spendlove, D. (2008). *Emotional literacy*. London: Continuum.

Spiro, J. (2004). *Creative poetry writing*. Oxford: Oxford University Press.

Spiro, J. (2006). *Storybuilding*. Oxford: Oxford University Press.

Tomlinson, B. (1986). *Openings*. London: Penguin.

Tomlinson, B. (1998). Seeing what they mean: helping L2 readers to visualize. In B. Tomlinson (Ed.), *Materials development in language teaching* (pp. 265–278). Cambridge: Cambridge University Press.

Unrau, N. J. (2008). *Thoughtful teachers, thoughtful learners* (2nd ed.). Toronto: Pippin Publications.

Waring, R. (2000). *The 'why' and 'how' of using graded readers*. Japan: Oxford University Press. Retrieved from www.oupjapan.co.jp/teachers/tebiki/tebiki.shtml

Widdowson, H. G. (1997). *Practical stylistics*. Oxford: Oxford University Press.

Widdowson, H. G. (1993). *Learning purpose and language use*. Oxford: Oxford University Press.

Wright, A., & Hill, D. A. (2009). *Writing stories*. Innsbruck: Helbling.

Chapter 18

Language Learning Strategies

An EIL Perspective

Yongqi Gu

Introduction

Strategic learning refers to the learner's active, intentional engagement in the learning process by selectively attending to a learning problem, mobilizing available resources, deciding on the best available plan for action, carrying out the plan, monitoring the performance, and evaluating the results for future action. Strategic learning is triggered and defined by task demands, and is thus not a task-independent learner trait or capacity. Strategic learning is tied to a purpose. The purpose of strategic learning is to solve a learning problem, perform a novel task, accelerate the learning rate, or to achieve overall learning success.

Without the learner's active engagement in the learning process, second language acquisition is at best haphazard. Over the decades, we have seen applied linguists suggesting the right amount of comprehensible input, opportunities for output, corrective feedback, task-based presentation, and contextual scaffolding in the classroom. But after all these, the only thing teachers can do is to wait and hope that learners will notice the patterns or automatically activate their implicit learning mechanisms. While these might happen, the central thesis behind language learner strategies (LLS) research is that learners, and teachers, can play a much more active role in managing and controlling the learning process, and thereby maximizing the outcomes of learning.

So long as we reject a fundamentalist Stimulus-Response view and accept the role of agency in human learning, we need to study learners' active and proactive engagement in the learning process. So long as we agree that, in addition to the universal grammar we are born with, cognitive mechanisms play a role in second language acquisition as well, these cognitive dynamics will need to be uncovered. So long as we agree that, besides individual differences such as aptitude and motivation, learners' own learning decisions aimed at maximizing results make a difference in the learning process, strategic learning will need to be examined.

Research on LLS has caught the applied linguist's attention for more than three decades (Cohen & Macaro, 2007). Most of this research has either focused on the learners' general LLS, or their strategies in learning and using one particular aspect of language, e.g., the four skills or vocabulary. This chapter will begin by quickly summarizing the knowledge accumulated over the last 30 years, and then argue for a special agenda for the introduction of LLS in the teaching and learning of English as an international language (EIL). It is argued that teachers of EIL face challenges in empowering learners with strategic learning tools. The targets of EIL as reflected in classroom tasks of learning demand strategic refocusing different from traditional perspectives of LLS. A set of reflection questions and suggested activities on EIL learning strategies is provided at the end of the chapter.

Traditional Principles and Practices

LLS Research

Two major research approaches have been taken since Rubin (1975) and Stern (1975) started to focus on "the good language learner," an exploratory approach and an intervention approach. The first approach includes correlational studies in which the research question of whether learner strategies are correlated with learning results is answered, plus case studies that illustrate how high achievers differ from low achievers in the strategies they use. The second approach is basically concerned with the causal question of whether learning strategies effectively lead to improved learning results.

After thirty years of research on language learner strategies, many insights have been accumulated. The following four points summarize what we now know about strategies in learning a second/foreign language:

1 There is a quantitative, correlational pattern in general: the more strategies learners use, the better; and the more often they use strategies, the better the language performance.

2 However, the quantitative pattern is only at the surface level. The minute we look at specific cases in detail, we immediately realize that it is how a strategy is used, rather than whether it is used, that makes a difference.

3 Very often, it is not how many strategies one uses, but how a number of strategies are used together and how the learner orchestrates the use of these strategies that makes the real difference, and

4 The choice, use, and effectiveness of strategy use very much depend on who the learner is, what the task at hand demands, and what context the learner is in.

Despite recent critiques of the field (Dörnyei, 2005; Tseng, Dörnyei, & Schmitt, 2006),[1] a number of major contributions of LLS research are worth mentioning. First of all, a large repertoire of language learning strategies has been identified and classified. This is a tedious task that has to be done before any insights can emerge from the analysis. As a result of the laborious hard work of the 1980s and 1990s, various elicitation techniques have been explored; a few classification schemes have converged into the most popular tripartite of metacognitive, cognitive, and socio-affective strategies (O'Malley & Chamot, 1990). Second, LLS have been studied along major language learning tasks. For example, we have established an impressive body of research detailing the relationship between language learning outcomes and listening strategies (Vandergrift, 2003), reading strategies (Erler & Finkbeiner, 2007), writing strategies (Manchón, de Larios, & Murphy, 2007), and vocabulary strategies (Gu, 2003). Thirdly, LLS research started in ESL contexts and quickly spread to EFL environments. By now, LLS patterns of use have been documented from around the world (Oxford, 1996). Most of this research has focused on adult learners, although a number of major projects focusing on strategic language learning behaviors of young learners (e.g., Chamot & El-Dinary, 1999; Gu, Hu, & Zhang, 2005) have also become available. Lastly, strategy intervention has been found useful in boosting learning results. However, effects of LLS on learning have been found to be mediated by a host of person/task/context variables (Rubin, Chamot, Harris, & Anderson, 2007).

Research on LLS has reached a stage where we have found enough surface level patterns. We now need to deepen our understanding of the intricacies behind strategic learning mechanisms. In other words, we have explored enough of the "what" aspect of description, and will need to shift our attention to the "why" aspect of explanation, and the "how" aspect of application. To do that, we need to go deeper into the learner, the task, and the learning context respectively, and to explicate the dynamic chemistry of strategic learning when we put these together. Learning and teaching EIL not only poses new challenges to teachers and learners alike, but is also an angle that should provide deeper and newer insights into strategic language learning.

Strategy Instruction

The starting point and the ultimate aim of research on LLS are to help learners become better learners. It is therefore understandable that a wide range of methods have been explored to make use of research findings for language learning (Oxford, 2011). By far the most commonly seen is the integration of strategy training into the language classroom, known as strategy-based instruction (SBI) (e.g., Chamot, 2009). Other strategy instruction approaches include standalone "learning to learn" courses (e.g., Cohen & Weaver, 2005), learner guidebooks (e.g., Brown, 2001), and language textbooks such as the *Tapestry Series* that include built-in strategy training.

Probably due to the intentional nature of strategy use, scholars have come to the conclusion that explicit and direct (as opposed to indirect and camouflaged) instruction of LLS should be one of the best approaches to strategy instruction (Chamot, 2005). A number of models have been explored in integrating direct strategy instruction into the classroom. The Cognitive Academic Language Learning Approach (CALLA) developed by Chamot and her colleagues has been the most popularly received. In the CALLA model, strategy training sessions are built into language classes. Each training session includes objectives both for strategy training and for language learning. Five basic stages are involved in this model: preparation, presentation, practice, evaluation, and expansion. Strategies are first introduced and modeled by the teacher, before students are given tasks to practice using the taught strategies. Teachers and learners reflect along the way about the reasons for choosing and the effectiveness of using the strategy in question. Learners are finally encouraged to extend the use of the taught strategies to similar language learning and language use tasks. In this way, the responsibility for strategic decision making shifts gradually from the teacher to the learners as classroom instruction moves from stage to stage, resulting in full learner responsibility in strategy choice and use at the end of training. Similar models of strategy training have also shown encouraging results in helping students become more strategic in learning (e.g., Grenfell & Harris, 1999; Macaro, 2001). All these direct instruction models share four essential steps (1) awareness raising, (2) presentation and modeling, (3) multiple practice opportunities, and (4) evaluating the effectiveness of strategies and transferring them to new tasks (Rubin et al., 2007, p. 142).

Strategic Learning of EIL

English as an International Language

The British Empire and its colonization efforts brought English to the rest of the world. The first wave of English spread was thus associated with human migration. At the end of the Cold War, the United States emerged as the winning superpower. With the ubiquitous military, economic, political, cultural, ideological, religious, educational, scientific, and discursive power of the United States came the Coca-colonization of the world and the second wave in the spread of English, the linguistic vehicle that carries these sources of power (Phillipson, 2009). This second wave resulted in the spread of English not through physical migration, but through what McKay (2003) calls "large-scale bilingualism," i.e., millions of people around the world acquiring English as an additional language for various international or intranational purposes.

English has achieved a global lingua franca status (Seidlhofer, 2001), no matter whether we see it as a result of linguistic imperialism (Phillipson, 2007), or a conscious choice of the learners (Bisong, 1995), or simply because it happened in "the right place at the right time" (Crystal, 2003, p. 120). The sheer amount of people currently using English as an additional language for various purposes in different contexts and domains of use has meant that native speakers from what Kachru (1985) calls "Inner Circle countries" can no longer claim sole ownership of English. For example, English is often the working language of many international conferences. Japanese business executives fly around the world speaking English. Call up the customer relations of a company for after-sale service in New Zealand, and there is a high chance of speaking to someone working in India at the other end of the phone. English has become a bona fide international language. This has far reaching implications for the teaching and learning of English (McKay, 2002), and for strategic learning as well.

Foremost among these implications would be the broadened and diversified targets of learning. These targets range from our traditional constructs of linguistic competence to a whole array of communicative competence entailing not only EIL forms but also EIL meanings and functions. In other words, the native speaker's English is no longer seen as the ideal model for learning. In fact, for successful international communication with EIL as the lingua franca, native speakers of English need to develop awareness and competence of EIL as well. The first question following this argument would be: what are the core features of this international English that learners have to learn? In other words, if international intelligibility is one of these core features, then it can be argued that learners do not need to approximate a native norm or to master the "fine nuances of native speaker language use that are communicatively redundant or even counter-productive in lingua franca settings" (Seidlhofer, 2005, p. 340). To answer this question, there have been recent attempts in making these core features explicit (e.g., Acar, 2009; Jenkins, 2000).

In addition to an awareness of these features, it is suggested that learners should raise their awareness of the diversity of English and the relationship between language and identity (Jenkins, 2006). Today's EIL users often need to negotiate varieties and be multidialectal in both the receptive and productive use of the language. These language use tasks demand strategic learning and use of EIL that have not received enough attention. Teachers of EIL should help make these new targets clear to their students so that particular language features, uses, purposes, contexts, and learning needs can become part of the task analysis for strategic maneuvering.

Moreover, EIL targets of learning are not only an issue of linguistic forms and the awareness and use of these forms. In this age of "postmodern globalization" (Canagarajah, 2006), a proficient user of EIL is able to "shuttle between different varieties of English and different speech communities" (p. 233). In this sense, "strategies of negotiation, situated performance, communicative repertoire, and language awareness" (p. 229) have become core competences of EIL as well. Teachers and learners should be aware that the learning targets of EIL are pragmatically and culturally different from those of EFL/ESL, and that in addition to learning English and learning through English, communicative competence in EIL now means a pragmatic and sociolinguistic awareness of a wider behavior norm than our traditional understanding of appropriateness in communication. For instance, when an Asian EIL user shows his respect for the older age of his Western interlocutor, he may be using perfect English by any linguistic norm, but he violates the cultural norms of his interlocutor, especially when the Western person in question would prefer to be seen as young. Intercultural communication failures of this kind can result in very unpleasant consequences, which, I argue, is an apparent lack of EIL awareness and competence on both parties involved. On top of these, a final aim of learning EIL is to establish a critical voice for the learner and the learning community (Modiano, 2001; Pennycook, 1997) for communicating not just what they mean, but also who they are, and where they stand. With all the challenges for achieving all of the above and for creating harmonious and pleasant communication environments, EIL users, native and non-native speakers alike, need awareness raising and communication strategies that do not come naturally.

Besides the shift of learning targets, another major LLS implication of EIL is the context of language use and language learning. Often bilingual/ multilingual users of EIL use English for international communication, for higher education, for access to scientific development, for international business and trade, for traveling and entertainment, with or without the involvement of native speakers of English, in real or virtual worlds. With these differences in language use contexts comes the de-linking of English from specific cultural attachments. The domains, contexts, and associated purposes of EIL range from the very narrow, restricted, and formal to the very broad and multicultural. As a result, EIL "requires that researchers and educators thoroughly examine individual learner's specific uses of English within their particular speech community" (McKay, 2003, p. 7).

While I have not distinguished between EIL and English as a lingua franca (ELF), I use both terms synonymously here to refer to the broadened status of English, its diversified contexts of use, and the linguistic, pragmatic, and sociolinguistic demands that come with the increased domains and functions of EIL. I respect efforts in the codification of EIL so that learners who choose to learn EIL will have concrete goals, but I reject the minimalist notion that EIL is a reduced version of Standard English. On the contrary, EIL contexts place more demands on all users of English, native or non-native, to be more sensitive and receptive to linguistic variations such as accents, and to be more tolerant, understanding, and open-minded to each other's pragmatic and sociocultural traditions of language use. All these would mean that teaching methodologies and learning strategies for ESL/EFL may not be appropriate for EIL contexts.

Language Learning Strategies in EIL Contexts

Special learning targets and purposes of EIL mean that the tasks of learning need to be seen in a different light for each specific case. An awareness of this will prompt the use of learning strategies appropriate for such task demands. In the following section, I will anchor LLS in EIL settings into a person-task-context-strategies framework (Gu, 2003). I will argue that the new task and contextual demands will necessarily call for the learner's self-regulatory re-deployment of strategic learning behaviors, and for the development of this capacity with the teacher's help.

A Person-Task-Context-Strategies Framework

When people approach a challenging task, strategies are invoked to solve the problems and to complete the task. This problem-solving process is constrained by the learning context (e.g., ESL vs. EIL; formal vs. informal) where the problem is being tackled. Language learning involves such problem-solving tasks at different levels of complexity. The strategies a learner uses and the effectiveness of these strategies very much depend on learners themselves (e.g., attitudes, motivation, preferred style of learning, prior knowledge), the learning task at hand (e.g., type, complexity, difficulty, and generality), and the learning environment (e.g., the learning culture, the richness of input and output opportunities). Figure 18.1 shows in simple terms how learning strategies work in context.

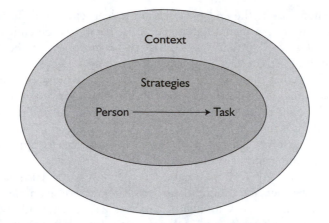

Figure 18.1 Person-Task-Context-Strategies: An Explanatory Model

Person. Learners are the agents of learning. They determine which variety of English they want to learn, and if and how strategies need to be employed in order to carry out the learning task. Learners also differ in the way they oversee and manage the learning process. Even at the very beginning stage, each learner brings to the language learning situation a wide range of individual differences that will influence the learning rate and the ultimate attainment. The most widely reported learner factors include age, sex, language aptitude, intelligence, prior knowledge, motivation and learning purpose, self-concept/image, personality, and cognitive and learning style. These person-dependent factors are relatively stable, and constitute the learner's preferred ways of dealing with learning tasks. Bruthiaux (2010) convincingly argued that in many input-poor environments of EFL, most learners will never have the opportunity of encountering English outside the classroom. For these learners, it is unrealistic to be talking about communicating with native speakers or other users of EIL. Their strategies for learning, therefore, will unlikely be related to a desire to use English for international communication.

Task. No strategies are needed if there is no task demand; and no strategic learning is needed if the task at hand can be done very easily. Perkins and Salomon's (1989) analogy of the relationship between hand and objects vividly summarizes the importance of tasks:

> Your hands alone are not enough; you need objects to grasp. Moreover, as you reach for an object, whether a pen or a ball, you shape your hand to assure a good grip. And you need to learn to handle different objects appropriately—you don't pick up a baby in the same way you pick up a basket of laundry.
>
> (p. 23)

A learning task is the end product in the learner's mind. It can be as broad as mastering a second language or as specific as remembering one meaning of a word. Broadly speaking, this conception of the learning task includes the materials being learned (such as the genre of a piece of reading) as well as the goal the learner is trying to achieve by using these materials (such as remembering, comprehending, or using language). It should be noted that this conception of "task" is in line with the traditional, broader understanding of task and is different from the more recent and narrower definition of "task" in "task-based" approaches to language teaching and learning.

Different types of task materials, task purposes, and tasks at various difficulty levels demand different learner strategies. For example, learning survival English as a new immigrant in New Zealand would entail very different learning strategies from learning academic English in order to complete postgraduate studies, which in turn is very different from learning English for international trade or business. It should be noted that EIL tasks do not mean that one local or international variety of English should take priority. If a learner is learning English in Singapore for the purpose of working in an outsourced international company, s/he would be best advised to focus on learning strategies for the development of knowledge of different varieties of English, and for the strategic competence to negotiate effective communication in different varieties of English.

Context. Learning context refers to the learning site or learning environment. The learning context can include the teachers, the peers, the classroom climate or ethos, the family support, the social, cultural tradition of learning, the curriculum, and the availability of input and output opportunities. Learning contexts constrain the ways learners approach learning tasks; they also shape learners' preferred styles and strategies of learning. For example, learning ESL in New Zealand demands strategic learning behaviors that are different from learning EIL in Vietnam. The sheer amount of language use opportunities for a variety of authentic communication makes the learning task dramatically different. Learners who are aware of and who exploit these differences deploy strategic learning efforts appropriate for each context. The situated and task/context-sensitive nature of LLS has been repeatedly shown to be a key ingredient of successful language learning (e.g., Gao, 2010; Gu, 2010; He, 2002).

Person, task, context, and strategies are interrelated and work together to form the chemistry of learning. Some strategies are more person-dependent, some are more task-dependent, and others are more context-dependent. If EIL tasks and learning contexts represent the major points of departure from traditional ELT, teachers and learners will need to re-adjust this four-way configuration of learning.

Introducing LLS for EIL

As I have been contending thus far, a major component of strategic learning involves the learner actively engaged in the analysis of the task at hand, of the self as a learner, and of the contextual support or constraints. Since the EIL perspective differs from traditional understanding of ELT mainly in terms of learning tasks, contexts, and purposes, it would be useful for the EIL teacher to help learners with task analysis. Without the teacher's help, many learners may not even realize that their targets of learning have changed.

Task analysis has long been regarded as a major component of strategic learning (Rubin, 2005; Wenden, 1995). It has also been shown that task analysis helps learners improve their learning outcomes (Rubin & McCoy, 2008). Table 18.1 shows Wenden's (1995) three-pronged approach to task analysis: task purpose, task classification, and task demands.

Table 18.1 Three Components of Task Knowledge (Adapted from Wenden, 1995, p. 185)

Task purpose: why should I do the task?	Learner needs
	• achievement
	• instrumental
	• integrative
	Task environment
	• learning-oriented
	• performance-oriented
Task classification: what kind of task is this?	Kinds of language learning tasks
	• medium (spoken versus written language)
	• setting (formal versus informal)
	• kind of skill (receptive versus productive)
	Kind of knowledge outcome
	• procedural
	• declarative
Task demands: how should I do the task?	Knowledge and skill required to do the task
	Knowledge of how to do the task
	• dividing the task
	• order
	• processing strategies

Task analysis can be done at various levels. The overall purpose for learning EIL, and the overall language needs for this purpose should be made clear first, followed by more concrete tasks for learning. For example, at the beginning of a semester, an EIL teacher can negotiate the target curriculum with his/her students by an awareness-raising session entitled "The English we need." Depending on the proficiency level of the students, the discussion and negotiation task can be done in either English or the students' native language. The students can be divided into groups to come up with answers to the following questions:

1 Task purpose: What do we learn English for?
2 Task classification: What aspects of English ability do we have to learn in order to reach our goals specified in our answers to question one?
3 Task demands: How best should we learn what we outline in question two?

In the case of a university where students are training to join the workforce for international commerce and trade in China, for example, students should be led to analyze the target language use domains and the need for English at work after they graduate. In this way, target language use scenarios and tasks will guide the kind of language learning tasks inside the classroom. Hopefully, the strategies and language thus learned will become useful beyond the classroom. To start the awareness raising, students and teachers can analyze the target group they will be using English with (e.g., native English speakers, non-native speaker employees in an international company, fellow Chinese speakers who work in the same company), the mode and genre of EIL they will be using (oral communication, written communication, business meetings and presentations, letters and reports, reading of technical documents, writing professional reports and articles), and target EIL contexts of use (e.g., international companies in China, Chinese companies abroad).

Teachers should next help their learners realize that, in addition to the linguistic core of EIL competencies, learners should also be increasing their language awareness (e.g., awareness of the intelligibility of linguistic features for in-group and out-group communication in multicultural business contexts), sociolinguistic sensitivity (of, for instance, pragmatic conventions and differences among Inner-Circle/Outer-Circle English speaking communities), and negotiation strategies (such as repair, rephrasing, clarification request, opening, closing, and changing a topic) especially during intercultural communication where English is used as a lingua franca. These constitute additional core competencies of an EIL user (Canagarajah, 2006) which will need to be highlighted in the EIL teaching/learning agenda.

Ultimately, ideal EIL users are not only linguistically versatile and sociolinguistically appropriate, they are open-minded international citizens who remain patriotic but not parochial and who celebrate differences and welcome diversity. They are critically aware of the biases and inequalities embedded in English as a dominant world language, and use EIL as an empowerment tool for identifying themselves as who they really are. They use EIL to negotiate harmonious business or professional relationships and create international win-win communities where mutual benefit, respect, and understanding are the common goal. Of course, it would be unrealistic to expect a lot from this awareness-raising session at the beginning of a semester. But I argue that if a teacher helps his/her class begin the critical awareness journey, EIL will have already planted the seed for a more understanding international community of the future.

Once students are guided to specify the nature of their target EIL learning tasks, they can start to consider how these task demands are best tackled through their strategic learning efforts. Learners should be encouraged to explore the best strategies to acquire the lingua franca core of business communication, and the learning strategies most appropriate for language awareness, sociolinguistic sensitivity, and communication negotiation. Moreover, learning strategies for critical awareness can also be explored.

This section has emphasized the importance of task analysis as an integral step in the strategic learning of EIL. An example is introduced using Wenden's (1995) framework of task analysis. This framework has been explored and expanded by Rubin and McCoy (2008) whose task analysis experiment in Mexico indicated that their students were not only able to improve task analysis skills following the experiment, but their exam scores also improved. The importance of task analysis and task interpretation has also been stressed by Butler and Cartier (2004), who showed that "students' knowledge about, conceptions of, and interpretations of tasks are foundational to performance" (p. 1729).

As of today, besides efforts on communication strategies (Nakatani & Goh, 2007) and some studies of strategic learning of speech acts (Cohen & Olshtain, 2011), LLS research has not extensively explored the various tasks of EIL learning discussed in this chapter. Nevertheless, teachers and learners of EIL do not have to wait for research studies to provide any conclusive evidence as to whether strategic learning of these EIL targets is helpful. In fact, I maintain that the best research of this kind should come from teachers doing action research inside the EIL classrooms.

Conclusion

This chapter introduces language learning strategies as an important line of scholarship informing the teaching and learning of EIL. After a general summary of thirty years of research on LLS, the EIL perspective is introduced. It is argued that seeing English as an international language changes the targets of learning, and necessitates the re-contextualization of language use and functions. The chapter next focuses on a task analysis of EIL with the contention that learners may not be aware of the changes EIL brings to the learning context. It is suggested that teachers of EIL need to train their learners with task analysis skills, so that the students' re-interpretation of task purpose, task structure, task component, and task demands as embedded in the changes that come with EIL will efficiently and effectively guide their self-regulatory endeavors in planning, monitoring, and evaluating their learning.

The premise of the contentions made in this chapter hinges on the conception of strategic learning as an important dimension of human agency. It is also assumed that strategic, self-regulatory learning will be effective only when the learner approaches the learning task at hand with context-appropriate task interpretations. Researchers, especially teacher researchers are encouraged to study how the perception of task and context changes in EIL influences the learner's strategic deployment and the effectiveness of such strategic efforts. Research should also provide teachers and learners with more reassuring empirical evidence that classroom-based LLS interventions indeed help the learning of EIL.

Exploring the Ideas

1 Seeing English as an international language has posed special challenges to not only teachers but also learners of English. What are the major challenges? What do these challenges mean for the learner's strategic learning of English?
2 As an English language teacher, to what extent is the EIL perspective relevant to your own teaching context? To what extent should your students' LLS be changed to accommodate EIL purposes and tasks?

Applying the Ideas

The following section contains two tasks teachers of EIL can consider in integrating LLS into EIL teaching and learning. Task 1 can be used as an in-class group sharing task among students. Task 2 is a more elaborate project integrating LLS into the teaching of EIL for students of international tourism. Both tasks are suitable for EIL learners of intermediate to advanced levels of English proficiency.

Task 1: EIL task analysis and LLS

In this chapter, there is an example of task analysis at a very general level. However, task analysis can be done at very specific levels as well. With a very specific EIL task in mind, e.g., presentation of a new business project to a potential foreign investor, discuss how the task purpose, task classification, and task demands influence the choice, use, and effectiveness of strategies.

Task 2: An international tourist project

The teacher starts by finding online an English class in, for example, an Asian country, and another one in a Latin American country. These classes are similar in age and English proficiency. All of these classes are not only interested in knowing more about traveling in each other's countries, but also keen to learn English for international tourism. The working language should be English.

SUB-TASK 1

Language use component: Students work as a whole class to decide which major tourist spots in their own country should be introduced to their foreign partners. They are then divided into groups with each group focusing on one spot. Group members will collect information about their tourist spot and jointly produce a tourist brochure.

Learning strategy component: Design strategy worksheets for students to work on periodically. These worksheets could resemble the following, although the task analysis should be much more detailed:

Task and subtasks	Strategies available	Strategy chosen	Strategy changes, if any	Strategy effectiveness
Task purpose				
Task classification				
Task demands				

SUB-TASK 2

Language use component: Use an Internet-based platform where both synchronous and asynchronous communication channels are available for students in all countries involved. Plan trips in each other's countries by asking each other questions, and serve as travel consultants for the foreign visitors.

Learning strategy component: For each sub-task, use the worksheet above to record strategy choice, use, and effectiveness. Include share and discussion times periodically when students come together and discuss the strategy demands of various tasks.

Note

1 The major criticism lies with the conceptual fuzziness of the term "learning strategies," which I believe is no less fuzzy than the proposed replacement term "self-regulation." Another criticism, that strategic learning should be seen as a trait, rather than behavioral patterns, ignores the task- and context-related nature of strategic learning.

References

Acar, A. (2009). On EIL competence. *Journal of English as an International Language, 5*, 11–26.

Bisong, J. (1995). Language choice and cultural imperialism: A Nigerian perspective. *ELT Journal, 49*(2), 122–132.

Brown, H. D. (2001). *Strategies for success: A practical guide to learning English*. Upper Saddle River, NJ: Pearson ESL.

Bruthiaux, P. (2010). World Englishes and the classroom: An EFL perspective. *TESOL Quarterly, 44*(2), 365–369.

Butler, D. L., & Cartier, S. C. (2004). Promoting effective task interpretation as an important work habit: A key to successful teaching and learning. *The Teachers College Record, 106*, 1729–1758.

Canagarajah, S. (2006). Changing communicative needs, revised assessment objectives: Testing English as an international language. *Language Assessment Quarterly, 3*(3), 229–242.

Chamot, A. U. (2005). Language learning strategy instruction: Current issues and research. *Annual Review of Applied Linguistics, 25*, 112–130.

Chamot, A. U. (2009). *The CALLA handbook: Implementing the cognitive academic language learning approach* (2nd ed.). White Plains, NY: Pearson Education.

Chamot, A. U., & El-Dinary, P. B. (1999). Children's learning strategies in language immersion classrooms. *The Modern Language Journal, 83*(3), 319–338.

Cohen, A. D., & Macaro, E. (Eds.). (2007). *Language learner strategies: 30 years of research and practice*. Oxford: Oxford University Press.

Cohen, A. D., & Olshtain, E. (2011). Strategies in producing oral speech acts. In A. D. Cohen (Ed.), *Strategies in learning and using a second language* (2nd ed., pp. 342–360). Harlow, UK: Pearson Education.

Cohen, A. D., & Weaver, S. J. (2005). *Styles and strategies-based instruction: A teacher's guide*. Center for Advanced Research on Language Acquisition, University of Minnesota.

Crystal, D. (2003). *English as a global language* (2nd ed.). Cambridge: Cambridge University Press.

Dörnyei, Z. (2005). *The psychology of the language learner: Individual differences in second language acquisition*. Mahwah, NJ: Lawrence Erlbaum.

Erler, L., & Finkbeiner, C. (2007). A review of reading strategies: Focus on the impact of first language. In A. D. Cohen & E. Macaro (Eds.), *Language learner strategies: 30 years of research and practice* (pp. 187–206). Oxford: Oxford University Press.

Gao, X. (2010). *Strategic language learning: The roles of agency and context*. Bristol, UK: Multilingual Matters.

Grenfell, M., & Harris, V. (1999). *Modern languages and learning strategies: In theory and practice*. London: Routledge.

Gu, Y. (2003). Vocabulary learning in a second language: Person, task, context and strategies. *TESL-EJ, 7*(2). Retrieved from http://www.tesl-ej.org/wordpress/issues/volume7/ej26/ej26a4/

Gu, Y. (2010). Learning strategies for vocabulary development. *Reflections on English Language Teaching, 9*(2), 105–118.

Gu, Y., Hu, G., & Zhang, L. J. (2005). Investigating language learner strategies among lower primary school pupils in Singapore. *Language and Education, 19*(4), 281–303.

He, A. E. (2002). Learning English in different linguistic and socio-cultural contexts. *Hong Kong Journal of Applied Linguistics, 7*(2), 107–121.

Jenkins, J. (2000). The phonology of English as an international language: New models, new norms, new goals. Oxford: Oxford University Press.

Jenkins, J. (2006). Current perspectives on teaching world Englishes and English as a lingua franca. *TESOL Quarterly, 40*(1), 157–181.

Kachru, B. B. (1985). Standards, codification and sociolinguistic realism: The English language in the Outer Circle. In R. Quirk & H. G. Widdowson (Eds.), *English in the world: Teaching and learning the language and literatures* (pp. 11–30). Cambridge: Cambridge University Press.

Macaro, E. (2001). *Learning strategies in foreign and second language classrooms*. London: Continuum.

Manchón, R. M., de Larios, J. R., & Murphy, L. (2007). A review of writing strategies: Focus on conceptualizations and impact of first language. In A. D. Cohen & E. Macaro (Eds.), *Language learner strategies: 30 years of research and practice* (pp. 229–250). Oxford: Oxford University Press.

McKay, S. L. (2002). *Teaching English as an international language: Rethinking goals and perspectives*. New York: Oxford University Press.

McKay, S. L. (2003). Toward an appropriate EIL pedagogy: re-examining common ELT assumptions. *International Journal of Applied Linguistics, 13*(1), 1–22.

Modiano, M. (2001). Linguistic imperialism, cultural integrity, and EIL. *ELT Journal, 55*(4), 339–347.

Nakatani, Y., & Goh, C. (2007). A review of oral communication strategies: Focus on interactionist and psycholinguistic perspectives. In A. D. Cohen & E. Macaro (Eds.), *Language learner strategies: 30 years of research and practice* (pp. 207–227). Oxford: Oxford University Press.

O'Malley, J. M., & Chamot, A. U. (1990). *Learning strategies in second language acquisition*. Cambridge: Cambridge University Press.

Oxford, R. L. (1996). *Language learning strategies around the world: Crosscultural perspectives*. Honolulu: University of Hawai'i Press.

Oxford, R. (2011). *Teaching and researching language learning strategies*. Harlow, Essex, UK: Pearson Longman.

Pennycook, A. (1997). Cultural alternatives and autonomy. In P. Benson & P. Voller (Eds.), *Autonomy and independence in language learning* (pp. 35–53). New York: Longman.

Perkins, D. N., & Salomon, G. (1989). Are cognitive skills context-bound? *Educational Researcher, 18*(1), 16–25.

Phillipson, R. (2007). Linguistic imperialism: A conspiracy, or a conspiracy of silence? *Language Policy, 6*(3–4), 377–383.

Phillipson, R. (2009). English in globalisation, a lingua franca or a lingua Frankensteinia? *TESOL Quarterly, 43*(2), 335–339.

Rubin, J. (1975). What the "good language learner" can teach us. *TESOL Quarterly, 9*(1), 41–51.

Rubin, J. (2005). The expert language learner: A review of good language learner studies and learner strategies. In K. Johnson (Ed.), *Expertise in second language learning and teaching* (pp. 37–63). Hampshire, UK: Palgrave Macmillan.

Rubin, J., Chamot, A. U., Harris, V., & Anderson, N. J. (2007). Intervening in the use of strategies. In A. D. Cohen & E. Macaro (Eds.), *Language learner strategies: 30 years of research and practice* (pp. 141–160). Oxford: Oxford University Press.

Rubin, J., & McCoy, P. (2008). Tasks and good language learners. In C. Griffiths (Ed.), *Lessons from good language learners* (pp. 294–305). Cambridge: Cambridge University Press.

Seidlhofer, B. (2001). Closing a conceptual gap: The case for a description of English as a lingua franca. *International Journal of Applied Linguistics, 11*(2), 133–158.

Seidlhofer, B. (2005). English as a lingua franca. *ELT Journal, 59*(4), 339–341.

Stern, H. H. (1975). What can we learn from the good language learner? *Canadian Modern Language Review, 31*, 304–318.

Tseng, W.-T., Dörnyei, Z., & Schmitt, N. (2006). A new approach to assessing strategic learning: The case of self-regulation in vocabulary acquisition. *Applied Linguistics, 27*(1), 78–102.

Vandergrift, L. (2003). Orchestrating strategy use: Toward a model of the skilled second language listener. *Language Learning, 53*(3), 463–496.

Wenden, A. L. (1995). Learner training in context: A knowledge-based approach. *System, 23*(2), 183–194.

Part IV

Forging Ahead

Chapter 19

English as an International Language

A Time For Change

Sandra Lee McKay

Taken together the chapters in this book point to the need for an entirely new perspective on what it means to teach English today. Not only do they make a significant argument for the need for change, but they also suggest innovative ways forward in EIL practice. The chapter begins by summarizing some of the changes called for in the book and then describes some new ways forward.

The Need for Change

The changes called for in the book have developed from the continued spread of English, accompanied by a growth in the number of bilingual speakers of English, the expanding forces of globalization, and breakthroughs in technology. Kumaravadivelu is perhaps the most passionate in his call for change, arguing for what he calls a "radical reconceptualization" of the field of EIL pedagogy. As he puts it,

> in order for our profession to meet the challenges of globalism in a deeply meaningful way, what is required is no less than an epistemic break from its dependency on the current West-oriented, Center-based knowledge systems that carry an indelible colonial coloration.

Terming the needed change an *epistemic break*, he maintains that only by breaking with the traditional dependency on Western approaches and the privileging of the native speaker can we proceed to make the changes needed in EIL teaching methods, the teaching of culture, and instructional materials.

Nelson and Kern echo Kumaravadivelu's call for change but see the need for change developing from new ways of exchanging meaning in "an era of globalized, digitally mediated communication." Central to their call for change is an emphasis not just on the linguistic elements involved in communication, but more importantly on all of the other resources available in a digitalized world. As they put it, if people in different places and social circumstances can now "meet" and communicate in ways heretofore unseen, applying different experiential frames and knowledge sets to their interpretations of these new multimodal texts, how do we anticipate the requirements for successful, productive interchange and also prepare our students to understand and meet these requirements? These questions have yet to be satisfactorily answered, but we suggest that the most fruitful perspectives will be those that do not regard language as the default access point from which to derive meaning, but rather look at how people combine linguistic elements with other resources (e.g., images, spatial arrangement, sounds, color, typeface, animation, and video) when they interpret texts.

Ware, Warschauer, and Liaw also view a need for change as arising from new modes of communication in "which digital media become essential tools of global interaction and global literacy." Like Kumaravadivelu they recognize a need to reduce the traditional emphasis on Western culture but argue for a blending of the local culture with global overtones: "an international community need not be grounded in Western, English-speaking countries, nor would it necessarily prioritize local cultures; rather, it should provide space for multiple converging and contested voices in English from around the world to interact."

The need to allow for both local and global concerns in a new world of communication is also recognized by Leung and Street. Calling for an ethnographic perspective on approaches to literacy, the authors maintain that "an ethnographic perspective does intrinsically take into account the dynamic links between 'local' and 'global'." Like many authors in the book, they reject a blind support of native-speaker norms, arguing instead for a balance between local and global standards.

They maintain that teachers and researchers of the English language in different world locations should question the extent to which language norms and pragmatic conventions drawn from particular native-speaker varieties should be seen as benchmarks for communicative competence. They believe it is not a question of the wholesale rejection of everything to do with metropolitan language varieties; rather it is a case of sensitively observing and examining how English as a set of linguistic resources has been taken hold of in local contexts, and how it is used to serve particular communication needs that may involve interlocutors from diverse ethnic and language backgrounds.

Alsagoff also recognizes the diverse contexts in which EIL is used today. However, her call for change develops from a new understanding of language itself, a view in which language is seen not simply as a set of rules and patterns that one acquires but rather as a way of making meaning within various social and discourse groups. Her chapter focuses specifically on recent findings in research on identity and language learning. She argues persuasively that "research on identity in language learning highlights the transformative and discursive nature of language learning, in which issues are explored and re-articulated through concepts such as identity, agency, investment, and communities of practice." She maintains that examining sociocultural identity in the teaching and learning of EIL is central because of the highly diverse learning contexts and profiles of EIL learners.

Hu's chapter focuses specifically on needed changes in assessment procedures. He argues that while established practices of assessment have in many ways been productive in enhancing the psychometric qualities of an English proficiency test, such an approach has not acknowledged

> the fundamental changes that have been taking place in the sociolinguistic realities of EIL, and the profound implications these changes have for such crucial notions as the construct of English proficiency, the authenticity of target English use, and the impact of native-speaker normed English tests at the societal and individual levels.

To remedy this situation he sets forth five macro principles for test design that are "grounded in a sound understanding of the postmodern conditions of EIL that can guide an informed redefinition of the test construct for a fair, relevant, and valid assessment of EIL proficiency."

Implementing Change

Clearly, the call for change in our concept of what it means to teach an international language in a globalized and digital world echoes throughout the volume. Fortunately, there are also many suggestions as to how these changes can be implemented in very practical ways in developing curricula and materials, promoting oral and literacy skills, encouraging learner autonomy, and promoting teacher development. We turn now to a consideration of some of these ways forward.

Developing Curricula and Materials in an EIL Framework

Like many of the authors in the book, Brown argues for the need to disentangle EIL pedagogy from its traditional dependency on a native-speaker framework. Arguing for a break from this tradition, Brown maintains that for too long curriculum developers:

have assumed (a) that students need to learn the English of native speakers (NSs), (b) that educated NSs of English should serve as the model and standard, (c) that *big* C American or British culture should be taught, and (d) that communicative language teaching is the most productive way to teach English.

In its place, Brown suggests that EIL curriculum developers make various changes such as

- Including successful bilinguals as English language and pedagogic models
- Providing students with awareness of linguistic and cultural differences in the various contexts in which English is learned and used, and furnishing them with strategies for handling such differences
- Using "global appropriacy and local appropriation" (Alptekin, 2002, p. 63) to help learners be "both global and local speakers of English" who can function both at home in their national culture as well as internationally (Kramsch & Sullivan, 1996, p. 211)
- Respecting the local culture of learning and promoting a sense of ownership and confidence in the local varieties of English
- Including models of Outer-Circle and Expanding-Circle users of English so students realize that English does not belong exclusively to the Inner Circle.

Taken together such suggestions promote a respect for both local and global concerns, methods and culture.

Matsuda too rejects a dependency on native-speaker models in the design of materials. Based on her analysis of Japanese 7th grade textbooks, she is able to document the manner in which many textbooks on the market today promote the view that the use of English takes place primarily between native speakers and L2 speakers with native speakers doing most of the talking. As she puts it,

> materials published specifically for classroom use ... tend to be based on and reinforce a common assumption in the field of ELT that English is the language of the Inner Circle, particularly that of the US and the UK, and the reason for learning English is to interact with native English speakers, which often is equated with those from the UK and the US.

She argues that EIL materials designers today need to develop materials that promote "awareness of and sensitivity toward differences—in forms, uses, and users—and learn to respect (or at least tolerate) those differences."

Promoting Oral Skill and Lexical Development

Given that EIL is used extensively in cross-cultural exchanges, House argues that the teaching of EIL oral skills needs to address the potential for misunderstandings that can occur in EIL interactions. In order to accomplish this goal, House suggests that the teachers of oral skills help students to become mini-ethnographers, studying real exchanges, and analyzing the possible causes of misunderstanding. Her very specific strategy would involve the following.

> it seems necessary first and foremost to heighten learners' awareness of the nature of the spoken language in general and the nature of ELF in particular and to use an interactional approach where individual learners are exposed to interactions in ELF, taught to become experts in the use of ELF in interaction and become aware of their own and others' interactional behavior. In this context it is important to provide ELF learners and users with an appropriate meta-language with which to describe interactional moves and strategies. For this a brief introduction to interaction and intercultural pragmatics is essential.

In her approach, then, learners become aware of basic pragmatic tenets and use this framework to analyze real exchanges as a way of heightening their own intercultural competency.

Oral exchanges in EIL attest to the widespread innovation that is occurring in the lexicon of English. As English spreads, it is embedded in many new bilingual contexts where speakers of English use the language alongside one or more languages. What this suggests for Bokhorst-Heng is that first, the primacy of native-speaker norms needs to be challenged: "what lexical innovation signals in EIL is the dismantling of the simplistic notion of the imperial and hegemonic spread of ENGLISH as some kind of monolithic entity." It further challenges the notion that all speakers of English wish to achieve native-like competency: "because bilingual speakers of English frequently have different purposes in using English than do monolingual speakers, it is unwarranted to assume that bilingual speakers necessarily want or need to attain native-like competence." In order to help learners become aware of the diversity of English use today, Bokhorst-Heng advocates the lexical approach outlined in her chapter since such an approach demonstrates the lexical nature of language and the plurality of use.

Bokhorst-Heng's focus on the diversity of English use today and the centrality of lexical items is echoed by Flowerdew in his chapter. He addresses head on the controversial issue of what standards to promote in an EIL classroom. He maintains that the best approach would be to help all speakers of English become aware of two varieties of English—that which gives the speaker a local identity and that which connects the speaker to a more globalized and written standard. As he says,

> Given the distinctiveness of some of these emerging varieties, it can be argued that, for international communication, speakers of these varieties still need to acquire (at least certain features of) an Inner-Circle variety.... At the same time, EIL users from the Inner-Circle countries, if they interact with Outer-Circle speakers of English, may need to develop familiarity with one or more of these emerging varieties.

He argues that this awareness can be achieved if learners are exposed to various corpora, those that illustrate local standards and those that exemplify a widely accepted written standard.

Standards and Literacy

The controversial issue of what is meant by Standard English in an EIL context is central to Gupta's chapter. Unlike some other authors in the collection, Gupta argues strongly for the need to provide all English users with access to a standard of English that is taught in the schools and exemplified in most written texts of English. She argues that

> If we compare the written Standard English of writers from around the world, we can see that there is general agreement about most of the grammar of Standard English. And the areas of disagreement vary more from one individual to another than they do from one region to another. There are some features of Standard English grammar that all users should be able to learn to identify. At the heart of Standard English are features of grammar that are clearly defined and easy to identify, which characterize Standard English and about which there is no disagreement. I refer to these features as being "criterial" of Standard English.

For Gupta, while conceding that various varieties of English have a place in education and should be respected, ultimately she maintains that "Standard English has wide currency and prestige and a student who was denied access to it would be being cheated." Gupta's stance highlights the fact that the choice of what standard(s) to promote in an EIL classroom is a controversial one, one in which local and global concerns need to be balanced, particularly as they relate to English use in local contexts.

The need to balance the local and global is a central theme of Wallace's chapter on critical reading. She questions what the role of reading should be within an EIL pedagogy tailored for the demands of the 21st century. She maintains that because English is one of the major languages of the world and a central repository of knowledge, it is essential that users of English learn to read critically so that they are aware of how power can frame what is said or not said and how it is said. She argues that

> because critical reading aims to challenge conventional choices of texts for teaching and ways of reading which privilege the center-based native speaker, it has particular resonance for the teaching of English internationally, where both texts and readers are coming from a range of different perspectives and with different needs, knowledge, and cultural assumptions.

Wallace's concern with the relationship between power and written discourse is shared by Casanave who questions the traditional emphasis on Inner-Circle writing conventions and its adherence to the teaching of the academic essay. For Casanave, it is time for EIL literacy instruction to recognize the social turn that is informing much of social sciences. She argues that literacy instruction must be modified for the local context.

> The most important shift in how we view L2 writing has paralleled the shift in the social sciences in general and SLA (second language acquisition) in particular toward a view that is increasingly local, social, and political (the "social turn," Block, 2003). More than in the past, writing is discussed as a practice that goes beyond linguistics (how morphemes, words, sentences, syntax, and conventions of organization combine to make a text) in spite of lingering traditional realities (Casanave, 2009) and beyond SLA (how writing contributes to language acquisition; Harklau, 2002; Manchón, 2009b). We are moving toward a view that locates the practice of writing squarely within a socio-political context, full of local needs and social actors, all situated within different discourse communities (Li, 2006).

Learner Autonomy

Along with a call to contextualize and localize the teaching of EIL, several authors raise the need to encourage learner autonomy since users of English today have highly individualized needs and wants in their use of English. Maley suggests that the use of literature in EIL classrooms can be one important way to provide users of English with a choice in what they read and respond to. He terms this approach one of *literature as appropriation* and describes it in the following manner:

> In this approach, the aim is to enable students to make literature their own, to appropriate it for their own learning purposes in ways relevant to themselves and to the context in which they move ... In the approach advocated here, I am suggesting ways of enabling students to get inside the skin of the texts—to apprehend them from the inside rather than simply to comprehend them from the outside—what I have termed *literature from the inside out*. We may characterize this approach as *learning through* literature, and it seems particularly appropriate in EIL contexts where a personalized and critical appreciation of English is crucial to students' development as independent users of the language.

In order to implement such an approach to literature, Maley argues for greater variety in the selection of literary texts included in the curriculum. He contends that expanding the range of texts will serve three important purposes:

> It will better reflect the "balance of power" between Englishes in an EIL world. It will offer a window into the differing realities in that world. It can make access to literary texts less difficult by offering students content with which they are relatively familiar.

Another call for greater user autonomy in EIL pedagogy is made by Gu. Like many authors in the book, Gu argues persuasively against relying on native-speaker needs and preferences in language learner strategy pedagogy. Rather he maintains that learners need to carefully assess their own learning goals and to select learning tasks that will allow them to do this. As he puts it, all students, either in English or their L1, need to address the following questions:

1 Task purpose: What do we learn English for?
2 Task classification: What aspects of English ability do we have to learn in order to reach our goals specified in our answers to question one?
3 Task demands: How best should we learn what we outline in question two?

While Gu emphasizes the importance of learner autonomy in setting learning goals, he also believes that EIL users need to increase their general language awareness:

Teachers should next help their learners realize that, in addition to the linguistic core of EIL competencies, learners should also be increasing their language awareness (e.g., awareness of the intelligibility of linguistic features for in-group and out-group communication in multicultural business contexts), sociolinguistic sensitivity (of, for instance, pragmatic conventions and differences among Inner-Circle/Outer-Circle English speaking communities), and negotiation strategies (such as repair, rephrasing, clarification request, opening, closing, and changing a topic) especially during intercultural communication where English is used as a lingua franca. These constitute additional core competencies of an EIL user (Canagarajah, 2006) which will need to be highlighted in the EIL teaching/learning agenda.

The Way Forward: Common Themes and Principles

Taken together the authors of this volume make a strong case for the need to radically change the way English has traditionally been taught, leading to an EIL pedagogy that is sensitive to the local teaching context and to achieving a balance between local and global concerns. Key to the way forward is a recognition by curriculum and materials designers and by teachers that the traditional focus on native-speaker norms and native-speaker cultural tendencies is no longer tenable in a globalized digital world in which EIL belongs to all who claim ownership of it.

Along with a break from a native-speaker bias in English pedagogy is a need to acknowledge the plurality of present-day English use and usage. While there is no doubt that the standard of English promoted in written discourse and supported by those in positions of prestige still wields power, it is equally true that there is a growing plurality in English use based on local conditions and needs. These local standards are just as important as written standard English because of their ability to promote a sense of English ownership and community.

Another theme that runs through the chapters is the need to promote critical language awareness among all users of English, both L1 and L2 speakers, so that all EIL users are aware of notions such as language innovation, varying linguistic and pragmatic norms, negotiation strategies, and social sensitivity in language use. Informed by this awareness, several authors highlight the need for users of English to define their own individual English language needs and to design a path to meet those needs.

It is clear that central to transforming the teaching of English in the coming decades is a need for teachers to inform themselves of the many changes that are occurring both in the use of English and the mode of present-day communication. Given that knowledge, local teachers need to be at the forefront of designing a pedagogy that is localized and socially sensitive to the diversity and richness of the English used today in an increasingly globalized and complex world. It is our hope that this book has raised teachers' awareness of the need for such change.

References

Alptekin, C. (2002). Towards intercultural communicative competence in ELT. *ELT Journal, 56*(1), 57–64.

Block, D. (2003). *The social turn in second language acquisition.* Washington, DC: Georgetown University Press.

Canagarajah, S. (2006). Changing communicative needs, revised assessment objectives: Testing English as an international language. *Language Assessment Quarterly, 3*(3), 229–242.

Casanave, C. P. (2009). Training for writing or training for reality? Challenges facing writing teachers and students in language teacher education programs. In R.Manchón (Ed.). *Writing in foreign language contexts: Learning, teaching, and research* (pp. 256–277). Clevedon, UK: Multilingual Matters.

Harklau, L. (2002). The role of writing in classroom second language acquisition. *Journal of Second Language Writing, 11*(4), 329–350.

Kramsch, C., & Sullivan, P. (1996). Appropriate pedagogy. *ELT Journal, 50*(3), 199–212.

Li, Y. (2006). Negotiating knowledge contribution to multiple discourse communities: A doctoral student of computer science writing for publication. *Journal of Second Language Writing, 15*, 159–178.

Manchón, R. (2009b). Introduction: Broadening the perspective of L2 writing scholarship: The contribution of research on foreign language writing. In R. Manchón (Ed.), *Writing in foreign language contexts: Learning, teaching, and research* (pp. 1–19). Clevedon, UK: Multilingual Matters.

Contributors

Lubna Alsagoff is Associate Professor and Head of English Language and Literature at the National Institute of Education, Nanyang Technological University, Singapore. Dr. Alsagoff balances her work at the University as a researcher and administrator with her responsibilities at the Ministry of Education where she consults and advises on various areas regarding teacher development and the teaching of English language in Singapore. Dr. Alsagoff's main research interests include investigating the effect of globalization on identity, language, and culture; developing a sociocultural grammar of Singapore English; and exploring teacher identity and development.

Wendy D. Bokhorst-Heng is Assistant Professor of Education at Crandall University, Canada, and has formerly taught internationally in Singapore (National Institute for Education), USA (American University), and China (British Council). Her research interests include language ideology and policy, multilingualism/bilingualism, literacy and multiliteracies, and multicultural education. She has co-authored a book, *International English in its Sociolinguistic Contexts: Toward a Socially Sensitive EIL Pedagogy* with Sandra McKay; an edited volume, *Redesigning Pedagogy: Reflections on Theory and Praxis*; and articles appearing in *Multilingua, World Englishes, Journal of Current Issues in Language Planning*, and is a contributor to Blommaert's edited volume, *Language Ideological Debates*.

James Dean ("JD") Brown is Professor and Chair in the Department of Second Language Studies at the University of Hawai'i at Manoa. He has lectured and taught courses in places ranging from Brazil to Yugoslavia, and has published numerous articles and books on language testing, curriculum design, program evaluation, research methods, and connected speech.

Christine Pearson Casanave taught at a Japanese university for many years and then part time at Temple University's Japan campus. She has published and edited books and articles on second language writing, and currently assists Temple University graduate students with their doctoral dissertation projects.

John Flowerdew's research and teaching is in the field of Applied Linguistics, focusing on discourse studies and on language learning. He has authored or edited eleven books and special editions of journals, including *Academic Listening: Research Perspectives* (1994); *The Final Years of British Hong Kong: The Discourse of Colonial Withdrawal* (1998); *English for Academic Purposes: Research Perspectives* (with M. Peacock) (2001); *Academic Discourse* (2002); *Second Language Listening: Theory and Practice* (with L. Miller) (2005); *Advances in Discourse Studies* (with V. K. Bhatia and R. Jones) (Routledge, 2008); and *Lexical Cohesion and Corpus Linguistics* (with M. Mahlberg) (2009). In addition, he has published over seventy-five book chapters and internationally refereed journal articles. He serves on the editorial boards of a range of international journals and book series and is regularly invited to give plenary talks at conferences internationally.

Yongqi Gu is a Senior Lecturer at Victoria University of Wellington, New Zealand. He is also an adjunct research fellow at the National Research Centre for Foreign Language Education in China. Dr. Gu's main research interests include learner strategies, vocabulary acquisition, and language assessment.

Anthea Fraser Gupta has researched and taught the linguistics of English in three continents. She was a university teacher in Singapore for twenty-one years, in Leeds for fifteen, and currently lives in Australia. Her publications include *The Steptongue: Children's English in Singapore* and many papers on aspects of English as a world language. Another book, *One World English*, will be published in 2012.

Juliane House is Professor Emerita of Applied Linguistics at Hamburg University. Her research interests are contrastive pragmatics, discourse analysis, translation theory, intercultural communication, English as a lingua franca, and second language learning and teaching. She has published widely in all these areas. Her most recent book publications are *Translation* (2009) and *Convergence and Divergence in Language Contact Situations* (2009, ed. with K. Braunmueller).

Guangwei Hu is an Associate Professor at the National Institute of Education, Nanyang Technological University, Singapore. Dr. Hu's main research interests include academic literacy, bilingual education, language policy, language teacher education, psycholinguistics, and second language writing. He has published in many international journals, including *Instructional Science; Journal of Multilingual and Multicultural Development; Journal of Pragmatics; Language, Culture and Curriculum; Language Learning; Language Policy; Review of Educational Research; Research in the Teaching of English; Studies in Second Language Acquisition; Teachers College Record;* and *TESOL Quarterly*. His newest co-authored book is *Strategy-Based Instruction: Focusing on Reading and Writing Strategies* (2011).

Richard Kern is Associate Professor of French and Director of the Berkeley Language Center at the University of California at Berkeley. His research interests include language acquisition, literacy, and relationships between language and technology. His book *Literacy and Language Teaching* (2000) deals with reading and writing in a foreign language. He is currently working on a book entitled *Language, Technology, and Literacy: Communication by Design*, and recently co-edited a volume on interaction in videoconferencing: *Décrire la conversation en ligne* (2011).

B. Kumaravadivelu is Professor of Applied Linguistics and TESOL at San José State University, California. He is the author of *Beyond Methods: Macrostrategies for Language Teaching* (2003), *Understanding Language Teaching: From Method to Postmethod* (Routledge, 2006), *Cultural Globalization and Language Education* (2008), and *Language Teacher Education for a Global Society* (Routledge, 2011).

Constant Leung is Professor of Educational Linguistics in the Department of Education and Professional Studies at King's College London University. He also serves as Deputy Head of Department. His research interests include additional/second language curriculum, language assessment, language education in ethnically and linguistically diverse societies, language policy, and teacher professional development. He is Associate Editor for *Language Assessment Quarterly* and Editor of Research Issues for *TESOL Quarterly*.

Meei-Ling Liaw is professor of the Department of English at National Taichung University. Her research focuses on using computer technology to facilitate EFL teaching and learning, intercultural learning, and teacher education. Her publications have appeared in professional journals including *System*, *Foreign Language Annals*, *Computer-Assisted Language Learning*, *ReCALL*, and *Language Learning and Technology*. She has been serving on the editorial board of *Language Learning and Technology* since 2008.

Alan Maley has been involved with EFL/ESL for over fifty years. He worked for the British Council in Yugoslavia, Ghana, Italy, France, PR China, and India. After five years as Director-General of the Bell Educational Trust in Cambridge, he was Senior Fellow at NUS. He has published over forty books and numerous articles. He is now in active retirement mode.

Aya Matsuda is Assistant Professor of English at Arizona State University, where she teaches courses in applied linguistics. Her primary research focus has been the global spread of English, its use as an international language, and its implications for pedagogy. Her work has appeared in the leading journals, including *World Englishes*, *TESOL Quarterly*, and *Written Communication*, as well as a number of edited collections.

Sandra Lee McKay is a Professor Emerita at San Francisco State University. Her main areas of interest are sociolinguistics, globalization, and the spread of English, particularly as these areas relate to second language learning and teaching. For most of her career she has been involved in second language teacher education, both in the United States and abroad. She has received four Fulbright grants, as well as many academic specialists awards and distinguished lecturer invitations. Her books include *Sociolinguistics and Language Education* (edited with Nancy Hornberger, 2010, Multlingual Matters), *International English in its Sociolinguistic Contexts: Towards a Socially Sensitive Pedagogy* (with Wendy Bokhorst-Heng, Routledge, 2008), and *Teaching English as an International Language: Rethinking Goals and Approaches* (2002, Winner of the Ben Warren International Book Award for outstanding teacher education materials).

Mark Evan Nelson is Lecturer in English Language and Literacy at Deakin University, Australia. Mark has also worked as a teacher of both art and English in Japan and the US and as a teacher-trainer in Singapore. His research is concerned with understanding the semiotic, sociocultural, and pedagogical implications of multimodal textual communication, and his notable publications include "Locating the Semiotic Power of Multimodality" (with Dr. Glynda Hull, in *Written Communication*) and "Mode, Meaning and Synaesthesia in Multimedia L2 Writing" (in *Language Learning & Technology*).

Willy A. Renandya is a language teacher educator with extensive teaching experience in Asia. Dr. Renandya currently teaches applied linguistics courses at the National Institute of Education, Nanyang Technological University, Singapore, where he also serves as Head of the Teachers' Language Development Centre. He has published articles and books on various topics, including an edited book entitled *Methodology in Language Teaching: An Anthology of Current Practice* with Jack C. Richards (2002, 2008). His latest publication "Teacher, the Tape is too Fast—Extensive Listening in ELT" (co-authored with Thomas S. C. Farrell) appeared in the *ELT Journal* (2011).

Brian V. Street is Emeritus Professor of Language in Education at King's College, London University and Visiting Professor of Education in the Graduate School of Education, University of Pennsylvania. He has a commitment to linking ethnographic-style research on the cultural dimension of language and literacy with contemporary practice in education and in development. Over the past twenty-five years he has undertaken anthropological field research and been consultant to projects in these fields in countries of both the North and South (e.g., Nepal, S. Africa, India, the USA, the UK). He has published eighteen books and 120 scholarly papers.

Catherine Wallace is Professor of Education in the Faculty of Children and Learning at the Institute of Education, University of London. She has published widely in the field of early literacy and the teaching of reading to learners of English as a second or foreign language. Her major current research and teaching interests are in the fields of critical literacy, literacy and identity, and classroom interaction in multilingual settings.

Paige Ware is an Associate Professor of Education at Southern Methodist University. She earned her doctoral degree in Education, Language, Literacy, and Culture at the University of California at Berkeley in 2003. Her research focuses on the use of multimedia technologies for fostering language and literacy growth among adolescents, as well as on the use of Internet-based communication for promoting intercultural awareness through international and domestic online language and culture partnerships. Her research has been funded by the International Research Foundation for English Language Education (TIRF), by the

Ford scholars program at SMU, and by the National Academy of Education through a Spencer postdoctoral fellowship. In addition to her research and teaching, she is also the principal investigator of a Department of Education Office of English Language Acquisition (OELA) professional development grant that supports secondary school educators in obtaining their ESL supplemental certification.

Mark Warschauer is Professor of Education and Informatics at the University of California, Irvine and Director of the university's Ph.D. in Education program. He has previously taught or conducted research in Russia, the Czech Republic, Egypt, and Japan. He is the founding editor of *Language Learning & Technology* journal. His most recent book is *Learning in the Cloud: How (and Why) to Transform Schools with Digital Media* (2011).

Index